CORPORATIONS AND SOCIETY

CORPORATIONS AND SOCIETY

The Social Anthropology of Collective Action

M.G. Smith

Professor of Anthropology,
University College London

Aldine Publishing Company

Copyright © 1974 by M.G. Smith

Published 1975 by
Aldine Publishing Company
529 South Wabash Avenue
Chicago, Illinois 60605

First published 1974 by
Gerald Duckworth & Company Limited
London, ENGLAND

ISBN 0-202-01132-1 clothbound edition

Library of Congress Catalog Number 74-84079

Contents

Preface   7

1. On Segmentary Lineage Systems   13
2. Anthropological Studies of Politics   71
3. A Structural Approach to Comparative Politics   91
4. The Sociological Framework of Law   107
5. Pre-Industrial Stratification Systems   133
6. A Structural Approach to the Study of Political Change   165
7. Institutional and Political Conditions of Pluralism   205
8. The Comparative Study of Complex Societies   241
9. Race and Stratification in the Caribbean   271

Bibliography   347
Index   367

Preface

The republication of his essays in a single volume always requires some justification by the author, whether or not they are supplemented, as these are, by unpublished pieces. My primary justification for the present volume is that it brings together a number of scattered essays which separately illustrate, develop and apply a common conceptual framework for the study of social life. I hope that by publishing them together I may demonstrate the range, sensitivity and analytic power of that framework in ways that the separate essays never could. Moreover, as this conceptual framework is ideologically neutral, free of questionable assumptions about the nature of society and social relations, and has an obvious, immediate applicability to all concrete forms of social organization, I hope that it may prove of value for comparative and intensive studies of empirical situations and processes in human societies.

It seems to me that social anthropology and sociology currently need some new conceptual framework free of unverifiable postulates on which to base comparative or monographic studies of societies and their major components. For several generations social scientists have sought such a framework in the idea of society as a functional system having such institutionally or analytically differentiated sections as government, economy, religion or education as subsystems, each operationally and normatively integrated in itself and with the others.[1] However, although this conception of societies as normatively and functionally integrated systems of action has inspired major advances in social theory and research, it is so heavily laden with questionable assumptions that it can neither supply a neutral analytic framework nor an objective set of research procedures for the comparative or intensive analysis of societies or their components, synchronically or over time. Too many generalizations that remain problematic and others at variance with fact must be accepted *a priori*, and too many social phenomena of equal prevalence and significance must be ignored or devalued in order that we may describe societies or their institutional sectors as functional

1. Montesquieu (1949); Durkheim (1938, 1947); G. and M. Wilson (1948); Radcliffe-Brown (1952c, 1957); Malinowski (1944); Parsons and Shils (1951b); Parsons (1952); M. Levy (1952); Lévi-Strauss (1953).

systems in terms of this theory. Moreover, despite many modifications to these old ideas, modern systems theory has neither entirely repudiated their dubious foundations nor their objectives and predicates.[2] At the very least, then, our traditional ideas of societies as normatively and functionally integrated systems of action need to be supplemented and perhaps replaced by concepts that suspend such assumptions and allow us to study social units, their components and relations, directly as concrete empirical structures. The various shortcomings of our traditional theory and models indicate that we should neither conceive societies as 'systems', nor postulate their functional integration, structural consistency, normative consensus, equilibrium, closure or homogeneity, as general features. Such postulates constrain us to document the ways in which empirical collectivities illustrate the theory, often by casuistry or data manipulation. For an objective, analytic framework, free of such presuppositions, the notion of corporations that informs these essays may thus provide social science with a basis superior to the familiar system-model. At least this alternative seems worthy of exposition and trial.

Assembled here for joint publication are nine essays written over a period of eighteen years that illustrate the slow and hesitant development of the idea that, as the major perduring frameworks of social action, and the most inclusive regulative units of social organization, corporations constitute and demarcate societies by discontinuities in their composition and articulation. It will be obvious from a cursory reading of these essays that the analytic and processual implications of the various kinds of corporations, their bases, requisites, properties and entailments, are only stated and illustrated but not systematically developed here. It should be equally obvious that this conceptual framework, however appropriate for macro-sociological analysis and comparison, neither pretends to treat issues of genuine significance to social science for which the micro-sociological models of role, dyads, interaction and network are particularly apt, nor does it dispense with the need for analysis of those cognitive structures of assumption, classification and symbolism that so pervasively and variably inform the routine activities of individuals and social aggregates. Indeed, the macrosociological framework of corporation theory assumes and requires these and other types of analysis as essential complements in any comprehensive study of human situations or societies. For these reasons, no claim is made, however obliquely, that these essays expound a total theory of social structures and processes, though I do hope that they may provide a general framework for such theories, and that they do illustrate scope and utility application to such topics as law, pluralism, 'race relations', stratification, political

2. For examples see Buckley (1967); Easton (1965); Barth (1966).

organization and change, all patent features of macro-structure in societies.

To indicate the range of materials to which we can usefully apply the ideas of corporation theory, I have included three unpublished essays: 'Race and Stratification in the Caribbean', 'A Structural Approach to the Study of Political Change', and 'The Comparative Study of Complex Societies'. In different ways, these essays illustrate the capacity of corporation theory to order and integrate diverse bodies of synchronic and diachronic data within a single analytic framework. It may also be worth mention that the approach outlined in the essay on political change will be tested and developed or modified as appropriate, in a series of detailed monographs on the political histories of Daura, Katsina, Maradi, Kano and Sokoto, five Muslim states of the Central Sudan, which is now under way.

Thus one general justification for re-issuing the earlier essays with these three unpublished ones is that together they illustrate the development, analytic power and applicability of the conceptions of corporations that inform them all. Since corporations provide the major institutional frameworks and agencies of collective regulation, it is neither surprising that their theoretical significance was initially grasped by scholars trained or interested in the law, such as H.S. Maine, Otto von Gierke, J.P. Davis and Max Weber, nor that several essays in this volume should discuss social phenomena of a political kind.[3] However, other papers on kinship, stratification, pluralism, race relations and social evolution demonstrate that law and political organization do not exhaust the relevance of corporations for the study of social organization. Moreover, as indicated above, studies of collective behaviour and micro-sociological analyses of roles, networks, interpersonal relations and interaction are readily assimilated within corporate frameworks, since these furnish the contexts that determine their form, content, distribution, implications and meaning. While attempts to crystallize such a synthesis must await the future, their roots and directions are clearly implicit in the papers presented below.

Of these essays, the first, 'On Segmentary Lineage Systems', written in 1954, used the ideas of Maine and Weber on corporations as the basis for a theory of government that could relativize current conceptions of the political features of segmentary lineage systems as the characteristic form of an acephalous society. However, between 1954 and 1963, when the second paper in this collection, 'A Structural Approach to Comparative Politics' (Chapter 3) was written, I had found it necessary to elaborate the ideas of Maine and Weber on corporations in order to develop a comprehensive and discriminating framework for the structural analysis and comparison

3. Maine (1905); J.P. Davis (1961); Gierke (1900, 1960), particularly both introductions; Weber (1947, 1954).

of traditional and modern polities. That essay, presented by David Easton's invitation at the 1963 meeting of the American Political Science Association, sketches the framework that underlies all others in this book. Thus, when invited by Professor Malcolm Parsons to participate in a series of guest lectures on political science at the State University of Florida, Tallahassee, in 1964, I tried to review the recent development and shortcomings of anthropological studies of politics in the light of corporation theory, in order to identify, and at least provisionally, to clarify some unresolved issues (Chapter 2). Later that year I also explored the relations between corporations and law in a paper contributed to a seminar of the African Studies Centre of the University of California, Los Angeles, on the development and adaptations of African law during and after colonialism (Chapter 4). In like fashion I employed these ideas to sort the fragmentary and rather bewildering materials on pre-industrial stratification systems for a conference convened at San Francisco by Professors Neil J. Smelser and S.M. Lipset early in 1964 (Chapter 5). In the following year I employed corporation theory to review the forms, foundations and conditions of plural societies at another seminar of the African Studies Centre at UCLA which Professor Leo Kuper initiated and organized (Chapter 7). Following that essay I contributed two others to the seminar on various aspects of pluralism, after which it seemed useful to test the capacity of corporation theory to provide a framework for the analysis of political change. Having by then prepared detailed preliminary accounts of the political histories of the five Hausa-Fulani emirates listed above, I wrote the essay on political change printed here for my graduate seminar in the Department of Anthropology at UCLA in 1967 (Chapter 6). Then, in response to the social-psychological interpretation of Caribbean race relations advanced by H. Hoetink,[4] I tried to analyse the conditions and development of the racial aspects of social stratification in West Indian societies, in order to clarify their corporate bases, forms and characteristics (Chapter 9). Unavoidably, this review of the forms and development of Caribbean racial stratification required the combination of historical and contemporary materials within a single comparative scheme, and thus showed whether the complementary conceptions of corporation and modes of incorporation could provide an appropriate framework for the integration of synchronic and diachronic analyses. Finally, as an alternative to the system-based approach to the study of social evolution put forward by Emile Durkheim, to illustrate the relevance of corporation theory for sociologists concerned with the study of complex societies, and to apply the corporation framework to a new

---

4. Hoetink (1967). For a review of this work, see M.G. Smith (1968). For a comprehensive account of Caribbean social stratification and race relations see Lowenthal (1972).

set of problems, I employed it in my Presidential Address on this topic to Section N of the British Association for the Advancement of Science at its Leicester meeting in September 1972 (Chapter 8). Thus the nine essays assembled here illustrate, in an order that casually approximates their preparation, the chronological development and successive applications of this conceptual scheme to the comparative analysis of such institutional frameworks of social order as lineage systems, stratification, government, law, race relations and pluralism. The capacity of these concepts to order and illuminate other ranges of social phenomena, including ideological and economic structures, interpersonal relations and collective or mass behaviour, is not seriously in doubt; nor need one hesitate to employ corporation theory to integrate and co-ordinate historical and synchronic materials on one or more societies within a single analytic framework.

Thus while there is inevitably some repetition of the central conceptions in these essays, they illustrate the progressive development and extension of the framework, both as regards its logical foundations and its empirical application. While Chapter 3 elaborates the conceptions of Weber and Maine introduced on pp. 43-5 of Chapter 1, Section 4 of Chapter 6, Section 3 of Chapter 7, and Section 4 of Chapter 8 repeat and elaborate these concepts before applying them to new problems and data. Likewise, the concluding essay develops and applies those ideas of the modes of incorporation which first appear in Chapter 6. After considerable hesitation I have decided to let these repetitions stand, while recommending those readers who have grasped these ideas and their implications to skip the passages just listed. However the central criteria and varieties of corporations and incorporation are sufficiently unfamiliar that many readers will probably find the various restatements of these ideas helpful before they are applied to new problems and ranges of data. Moreover, the theoretical emphases and elements in the essays assembled here supplement one another in several respects that parallel their applications to diverse ranges of social phenomena. Until the series of monographs on the developments of the Hausa-Fulani emirates listed above is finished, further attempts to systematize and extend the framework of corporation theory can only appear in the context of occasional papers. Accordingly, since I hope that this framework may be of interest to social scientists, it seems preferable to issue this selection now, with all its redundancies and imperfections, rather than delay further the effective dissemination of these ideas. In preparing these essays for republication I have confined myself to minor stylistic changes, and made no attempt to update them.

I wish to thank the following for permission to republish:
The editors of *Man* and the Royal Anthropological Institute for

Chapter 1, 'On Segmentary Lineage Systems', first published in the *Journal of the Royal Anthropological Institute* 86 (1956), part 2, pp. 39-80;

Professor Malcolm S. Parsons and Messrs. Rand McNally for Chapter 2, 'Anthropological Studies of Politics', first published in Malcolm S. Parsons (ed.), *Perspectives in the Study of Politics*, 1968, Rand McNally & Co., pp. 102-23;

Professor David Easton and Messrs. Prentice-Hall for Chapter 3, 'A Structural Approach to Comparative Politics', first published in David Easton (ed.), *Varieties of Political Theory*, 1966, Prentice-Hall, pp. 113-28;

Professors Leo and Hilda Kuper and the University of California Press for Chapter 4, 'The Sociological Framework of Law', first published in Hilda and Leo Kuper (eds.), *African Law: Development and Adaptation*, 1965, University of California Press, pp. 24-48 and 245-7;

Professors Neil J. Smelser and Seymour Martin Lipset and the Aldine Publishing Company for Chapter 5, 'Pre-Industrial Stratification Systems', first published in Neil J. Smelser and Seymour Martin Lipset (eds.), *Social Structure and Mobility in Economic Development*, 1966, Aldine Publishing Company, pp. 141-76;

Professor Leo Kuper and the University of California Press for Chapter 7, 'Institutional and Political Conditions of Pluralism', first published in Leo Kuper and M.G. Smith (eds.), *Pluralism in Africa*, 1969, University of California Press, pp. 27-65;

The British Association for the Advancement of Science for 'The Comparative Study of Complex Societies', delivered as the Presidential Address to Section N of the British Association at its annual meeting held in Leicester between 4 and 9 September 1972.

For detailed criticism of an earlier draft of Chapter 9, 'Race and Stratification in the Caribbean', I wish to express my appreciation to Professor Sally F. Moore, University of Southern California, Professor Leo Kuper, UCLA, and Professor David Lowenthal, University College, London.

1.

On Segmentary Lineage Systems

The value of a new point of view in science is shown by the research which it stimulates, as well as the material which it brings into ordered relations. In these terms, there can be little doubt that the concept of segmentary lineage systems has proved to be valuable both in fieldwork and analysis, and has been associated with many of the most important developments in recent social anthropology. It is therefore worth while to re-examine its bases, both theoretical and methodological; and this is the task of the present essay. We shall attempt this task, after giving a brief outline of the concept of a lineage system, by considering segmentary lineage systems from three points of view: as political systems; dynamically, as systems developing in a particular way, and sharing certain formal characters; and thirdly, as distinct categories of kinship system.

1.

A lineage is a group of persons differentiated genealogically from others in terms of unilineal descent. Within the lineage, descent also provides the basis for differentiation of lineage members in terms of generation remove from a common ancestor, as well as of half-siblingship. Descent is the socially defined relationship which obtains between a son and a daughter on the one hand, and their father or mother on the other. This does not always connote biological parenthood, since, for example, an adopted son will trace descent from the person who adopted him.

Lineages are groups of persons claiming genealogical relations unilineally; they may or may not be localized, and may or may not be exogamous units. The type of descent used in unilineal systems may be either through females or males; and in certain societies, both types of unilineal descent obtain concurrently to provide two sets of lineages to which all persons belong, their matrilineages, membership of which is traced through the mother, and their patrilineages, membership of which is derived from the father. The Yakö are an instance of such a society.[1]

Unilineal descent of itself does not, however, imply the necessary

1. Forde (1939a, 1950b).

existence of lineages.[2] Unilineal descent is a necessary foundation for
the development of lineage groups, but it is not the efficient cause.
Lineage groups are conceived of as segmentary in structure and
corporate in function. Where unilineal descent obtains without
groups of this character, there are no lineages in the sense of this
theory. Lineages are thus corporate groups of a segmentary character
defined in terms of unilineal descent. The internal differentiation of
a lineage is expressed in genealogical terms, and functional differences characterize the levels of this differentiation. This differentiation is held to proceed by segmentary processes, and to produce
segmentary forms. Within the total unit interests vary in range and
type according to genealogical distances. Stable sub-units of the
system are defined as segments of the lineage, and are characterized
by dual differentiation in terms of interests and descent. These
segments, within limits, operate as internally autonomous groups. It
is recognized that the type and degree of internal autonomy of these
segments at any level of lineage organization varies widely among
different societies, and that this variability reflects the influence of
other factors on lineage structure. The nature of this variability and
of the factors associated with it is less clearly understood than many
other features of lineage structure.[3]

There is a well-known order of segmentation in lineages, from
maximal levels, through major and minor orders, to the minimal
level, in descending scale. As a scheme of reference and a form of
group organization, this order is pervasively relativistic. Thus, the
minor lineage is a major segment in relation to the minimal lineage.
Definition of genealogical segments therefore depends on the apical
point of reference. One difference noted between lineage structures
in different societies centres on the relative fixity of these points of
reference. Among the Gusii, the ultimate reference is to the tribal
ancestor, and lineage differentiation proceeds from there.[4] Yakö
patrilineages reduce their generation depth to keep a constant span,
while expanding by reproduction.[5] Tiv genealogies are reorganized to
fit the contemporary situation of the segments they are formulated
to incorporate and differentiate.[6]

Among the Tallensi, the apical ancestors of maximal lineages are
fixed, and thus all subordinate orders of their segmentation have a
constant character. Thus Fortes says:

A maximal lineage is fixed with reference to its founding ancestor . . . Every
maximal lineage is continually expanding and proliferating through the fission of
its minor segments . . . It has a fixed centre and a fixed locus, we might say. In
theory it always remains the same lineage, and new maximal lineages cannot

2. Evans-Pritchard (1940*b*).
3. Fortes (1953).
4. P. Mayer (1949).
5. Forde (1950*b*).
6. L. Bohannan (1952).

arise through the splitting up of an existing maximal lineage . . . In any maximal lineage, therefore, the fission of minor segments does not alter the equilibrium of the major segments at any given time. Changes in minimal lineages, in fact, cannot alter the equilibrium of any segment greater than the minimal. This is reflected in the naming of lineages and their segments . . . The names of segments greater than the minimal may be regarded as fixed once for all. [7]

The self-contradictory tendency of such a system can be defined in terms of segmentation within and below the minimal lineage. Given the fixity of lineage morphology, and the interdependence of this formal organization on segmentary process, how can the minimal lineage retain its fixity of character and position in the order of segmentation, when continually itself giving rise by fission to further segments of the same order?

Lineage structure has two distinct but closely related aspects, the hierarchic and the contrapuntal. The hierarchic aspect is obvious in the genealogical pyramid that signposts the structure. Thus Evans-Pritchard writes of the Nandi-speaking peoples:

They had not a lineage structure, but a different form of segmentation. We can use the word 'sub-clans', a word often used in the literature, to describe these clan segments lacking a genealogical structure. There is possibly a correlation between the absence of political function and the absence of genealogical structure in the clan system. [8]

The contrapuntal aspect of lineage structure is equally clear in that collateral segments at every level of the system other than the most inclusive are defined by co-ordinate relationships. In Fortes' view, this is so 'since a lineage necessarily divides into segments of equal order'. [9] In 'segmentary societies' this co-ordinate status of collateral units also extends theoretically to the maximal lineages or clans, since there is no single directing authority superordinate to these social groupings. But here we are faced with the problem of ranked lineages or segments of lineages. If segmentary lineages are defined in terms of the presence of segments of equal order, lineages or segments of the same genealogical order which are differentiated in terms of seniority or rank cannot be regarded as of segmentary character, since there is inequality in their contraposition. None the less, such contraposition, together with its accompanying segmentation, occurs, in so far as there is an actual competition for power among segments or lineages of unequal status. This competition may develop whether lineages and their segments are ranked hierarchically or not; for example, when a junior lineage segment challenges the

7. Fortes (1945), p. 33.
8. Evans-Pritchard (1940*b*), pp. 265-6. This article by Evans-Pritchard is especially interesting, in that it comes very close to recognizing the need for explicit formulations concerning the relations of segmentary, political and administrative processes to one another on the one hand, and to lineage structure on the other. See pp. 264-7 especially.
9. Fortes (1945) p. 33.

authority of a senior lineage segment, and attempts to act as though it were of equivalent status. Such competition is always latent, and certainly implicit where fission occurs. The essential point to note is that although the co-ordinate status of lineages or segments is defined in terms of contrapuntal equivalence, these relations have a dynamic as well as a formal aspect. In segmentary lineage systems such as those of the Tallensi, the formal aspect of the structure is expressed genealogically. In systems like those of the Zulu, Nsaw, and Bemba, the formal aspect also involves differentiation by rank, and appears to differentiate them from segmentary lineages.[10] But dynamic contraposition occurs in both types of system, and involves segmentation through competition between the units concerned. Hence decisions about the classification of lineages as segmentary or other depend as well on the criteria adopted for the definition of segmentation itself, as on the implications of rank-ordering or collateral lines for formal contraposition or equivalence. We shall have to refer to the implications of this distinction between formal and dynamic segmentation or contraposition at many points of the following discussion.

The emergence and growth of segmentary lineages is generally handled in terms of family structure and complementary filiation,[11] that is, differentiation between half-siblings within a lineage by reference to the parent through whom lineage membership is not traced. Evans-Pritchard in his first book on the Nuer placed great weight on lineage definition in terms of segmentary territorial organization.[12] Finding among the Nandi-speaking group of peoples that the lineage system did not provide a principle for the organization of political activities on territorial lines, he therefore concluded that they lack segmentary lineage organization.[13] Lineage localization is of special interest, therefore, where associated with the discharge of important political functions by lineage units. A dichotomy of political systems was formulated partly on this basis. Societies lacking centralized paramount authorities, but internally organized on a lineage basis, formed one category; those having centralized authority the other. The first category of segmentary societies was said to lack government, to consist in ordered anarchy;[14] the other category was characterized by government. Since lineage principles provided a substitute for governmental organization, they were distinguished from the forms of kinship principles which do not discharge these political functions. Finally, since lineage development follows the pattern laid down in family organization by the principle of complementary filiation, segmen-

10. Gluckman (1940); Kaberry (1952); Richards (1950).
11. Radcliffe-Brown (1941); Fortes (1949, 1953); Southall (1952).
12. Evans-Pritchard (1940a).
13. Evans-Pritchard (1940b).
14. Fortes and Evans-Pritchard (1940a).

tation occurs as an independent internal process of lineage growth, and fission, fusion, accretion and assimilation tend to develop likewise.

Fortes' 1953 paper gives an excellent summary of recent studies of lineage organization and the theory of lineage segmentation, with which the preceding résumé does not attempt to compete. Our interest here lies mainly in directing attention to certain of the key concepts of the theory as a system of definitions, and to the nature of their relations with one another. Such specialized conceptions of kinship, lineage, corporate group, government, political system, social structure, descent, segmentation, and territorial organization are clearly units in a system of interconnected definitions. This character of the terminological system of lineage theory has hitherto received insufficient attention. Yet it forms the essential starting-point for any critical examination of the nature and utility of this theory, in the same way that analysis of the assumptions of logic as a system of postulates forms the essential first step in the revision of its canons. We must ask, then, what is the order and type of interrelation of these concepts? What concepts are central to this system, and which are the peripheral ones? If we can determine the logical relationships holding within the units of this conceptual system, and their priority, we are in a good position to begin an examination of the theory as a whole. Unless this is done, it is difficult to assess the theory and field-studies of segmentary lineage systems appropriately, since the type of terminological system which forms the structure of such work is not directly open to the test of comparative materials in the way that less complex terminological systems and more limited theories usually are. The fact that the Yakö and Tullishi may practise double unilineal descent and that the former of these societies has a political system in which wards and other associations play an important part, as well as lineages, does not prove or disprove the theory of segmentary lineage systems. Such comparative materials cannot directly disprove the theory, simply because the latter consists in a specialized use of certain words, and a type of conceptual system not directly open to controversion by comparative materials. It follows that comparative materials will only carry their full weight after a critical analysis has been made of the theory as a system of interrelated definitions, and when the crucial assumptions and relations of its key concepts have been clearly understood. Because this is so, evaluation of segmentary theory depends initially on theoretical terminological criticism, with comparative materials playing a subsidiary role, rather than the other way about. This procedure will be followed here, and we shall begin with an attempt to discover the decisive order of logical priority among the key concepts.

Broadly speaking, there is agreement among writers employing this theory that the distinction between lineage and kinship reflects the political primacy of the first principle. This political character of lineage organization is also linked with the corporate character of lineage groups, a feature normally lacking in kinship associations. It is also found under conditions where centralized administration is absent or weak, and normally in these conditions lineages are local groupings discharging political functions within their areas. This provides a subdivision of the population into territorial segments, and the correlation of these territorial segments with the genealogical segments of the lineage units directs attention to the segmentary organization of such societies, with its dual but closely related aspects and reference to localization and descent. Concepts such as fission, fusion, accretion, assimilation, intercalary lineages[15] and the like, are simply specialized derivatives of this concept of segmentary organization. Similarly, Evans-Pritchard's definition of social structure in terms of inter-group relations is, as he has observed, not directly crucial for the theory of segmentary societies and lineages, although this conception of structure reflects the basic assumptions of this theory in a most revealing manner.

In contrast to these dependent conceptions, there is the critical implication that segmentary lineage systems only obtain in acephalous societies; that is to say, the segmentary processes which define some unilineal descent groups as lineages, and others differently, must be coextensive with the social structure if lineage segmentation is to reach its full development. This is the type of basic assumption which defeats the direct application of comparative material as tests of the theory, unless these follow on a critical examination of the concepts of segmentation and political system which are central to it. We can therefore say that the fundamental concepts of segmentary theory centre about the definition of a system of political relations, and on the basis of this, differentiate lineages from other kinship groupings in terms of segmentary principles and structures which reflect and discharge political functions. This regressive procedure can be carried no further, and it therefore seems that the foundation of segmentary theory consists in a combination of two basic concepts, segmentation as a structure and process on the one hand, and political organization on the other. Where these conceptions are combined with unilineal descent groupings, segmentary lineages exist; otherwise they do not.[16] The specialized conceptions and terminology of segmentary theory follow from these principal ideas.

It is noteworthy that the two basic notions of this theory belong to different categories of analysis. The concept of political relations is a substantive concept. The concept of segmentation is a formal concept. We shall have therefore to consider the substance of political relations at some length, and assess the adequacy of the conception of these relations which informs segmentary theory. In

15. Fortes (1945).
16. Evans-Pritchard (1940b); Bernardi (1952).

contrast, the formal character of segmentation requires little discussion at this stage. This concept is drawn from biological studies, where it describes the processes of simultaneous cellular subdivision and multiplication. In lineage theory it also describes the contrary process of aggregation by combination of separate cells, whether these be lineage or territorial segments. Segmentary processes are those which are associated with a structure composed of segments or divisions; and a segment is a division of a larger unit. A social system is said to have a segmentary form when the principle of subdivision or segmentation is pervasive and basic to its social structure. These are morphological concepts of an abstract character, and are only of interest in association with particular substantive categories, as for example the cells of biology, or the political relations of lineage theory. But here we must note that this general abstract character of segmentation as a process of subdivision by progressive extension has been redefined and limited in lineage theory, by the supplementary character of contraposition. Thus segments in lineage theory are defined by contraposition, and of course the process of contraposition is defined by the presence of balanced segments.[17] Contraposition reflects the implicitly political substance of the segmentary processes, and involves units of co-ordinate status. Thus multiplication of collateral lines of a lineage does not of itself necessarily involve segmentation, in so far as the contraposition which characterizes lineage segmentation does not obtain between these units. This view of the matter is apparently not shared by Fortes,[18] who sees the internal segmentation of a lineage proceeding 'with an almost mechanical precision', in the manner of the multiplication of biological cells, although aware of the Tiv procedures to redefine segments when appropriate.[19] We are not concerned to show differences of view between students of segmentary theory, except where these differences themselves reflect ambiguities of the theory, or are critical for its evaluation. But here we must note that the differences between Evans-Pritchard's early formulation and that of Fortes are associated with differing conceptions of the development of segmentary lineage structures, Evans-Pritchard giving primacy to localization and territorial administrative functions, whereas Fortes seems inclined to attribute most importance to family processes, population growth, and complementary filiation. Some of the factors involved in this developmental process will require attention later on.

2.

The crucial nature of the definition of political relations for

17. Evans-Pritchard (1940a).
18. Fortes (1953).
19. L. Bohannan (1952).

segmentary theory will be more evident from a brief glance at the literature. We shall also find some uncertainty about the definition of political action, but shall not be able to elaborate on all these variations.

Evans-Pritchard concludes his first book on the Nuer with this question: 'Can we speak of political behaviour as a distinct type of social behaviour?' He finds that 'between local groups there are relations of a structural order that can be called political', but that it is not useful to say 'that a man is acting politically or otherwise'.[20] Here, territorial organization, political relations, and social structure defined in terms of group segmentation form an interdependent conceptual system:

Faced with the initial difficulty of defining what is political, we decided to regard the relations between territorial groups as such ... These tendencies in, or principles of, political structure control actual behaviour between persons through values ... By political values we mean the common feeling and acknowledgement of members of local communities that they are an exclusive group distinct from, and opposed to, other communities of the same order, and that they ought to act together in certain circumstances and to observe certain conventions among themselves.[21]

In our view the territorial system of the Nuer is always the dominant variable in its relation to the other social systems.[22]

However, as Radcliffe-Brown observed:

The system of local aggregation and segregation as such has nothing specifically political about it; it is the basis of all social life.[23]

Radcliffe-Brown proposed another definition of political relations:

The political organization of a society is that aspect of the total organization which is concerned with the control and regulation of the use of physical force.[24]

It is worth while pausing a moment over these two definitions. Evans-Pritchard was looking for 'a distinct type of social behaviour' which could be called political. He found it 'on the more abstract plane of structural relations between groups'.[25] Radcliffe-Brown's first distinguishing point is that political relations are an aspect of social relations, not a special mode of behaviour. It follows from this view that political relations or organization occur within groups as well as between them; and that Evans-Pritchard's definition of structural relations and political system in terms of one another is

20. Evans-Pritchard (1940a), pp. 264-5.
21. ibid., p. 263.
22. ibid., p. 265.
23. Radcliffe-Brown (1940), p. xiv.
24. ibid., p. xxiii.
25. Evans-Pritchard (1940a), p. 264.

mistaken, and rules out a large body of relevant data from the study of political organization.

The second difference between Radcliffe-Brown and Evans-Pritchard in their definitions of political behaviour consists in difference of emphasis on the specific character of this behaviour. Radcliffe-Brown defines it in terms of control and regulation of force, and develops this to distinguish law and feud or war. Evans-Pritchard finds it to consist primarily in the definition of local groups by contradistinction, as can be seen from the quotation given above; and this of course simply means that a system of political relations is defined in terms of its segmentary form. Likewise, segmentation is defined in terms of political content. These differences are worth bearing in mind during the following discussion of political systems and theory in the composite volume of *African Political Systems.*

In their joint typological Introduction to this volume, Fortes and Evans-Pritchard follow Radcliffe-Brown's definition of political organization in terms of 'the organized exercise of coercive authority through the use, or the possibility of use, of physical force'.[26] This leads naturally to differentiations of political systems in terms of the presence or absence of centralized 'coercive authority', with which are linked regulated vengeance, feud, war, law-courts, armies, offices and the like:

It will be noted that the political systems described in this book fall into two main categories. One group, which we refer to as Group A, consists of those societies which have centralized authority, administrative machinery, and judicial institutions — in short, a government — and in which cleavages of wealth, privilege, and status correspond to the distribution of power and authority . . . The other group, which we refer to as Group B, consists of those societies which lack centralized authority, administrative machinery, and constituted judicial institutions — in short, which lack government — and in which there are no sharp divisions of rank, status and wealth.[27] . . . Those who consider that a state should be defined by the presence of government institutions will regard the first group as primitive states, and the second group as stateless societies.[28]

Thus in this passage, government is a component of a political system, instead of the political system, as is more usual, being a component of government; and secondly, political systems are distinguished according to the presence or absence of governments within them. The definition of government implicit in this distinction equates it with administrative structures of a bureaucratic type. Where formal governmental institutions are lacking, therefore, it is necessary to examine the social structure to see how these essential governmental functions are discharged:

26. Radcliffe-Brown (1940), p. xiv.
27. Fortes and Evans-Pritchard (1940b), p. 5.
28. ibid., p. 5.

The kind of information related and the kind of problems discussed in a description of each society (of the volume) have largely depended on the category to which it belongs. Those who have studied societies of Group A are mainly concerned to describe governmental organization. They therefore give an account of the status of kings and classes, the roles of administrative officials of one kind or another, the privileges of rank, the differences in wealth and power, the regulation of tax and tribute, the territorial divisions of the state and their relation to its central authority, the rights of subjects and the obligations of rulers, and the checks on authority. Those who studied societies of Group B had no such matters to discuss and were therefore forced to consider what, in the absence of explicit forms of government, could be held to constitute the political structure of a people.[29] . . . This problem was simplest among the Nuer, who have very distinct territorial divisions. The difficulty was greater for the Logoli and Tallensi, who have no clear spatially-defined political units.[30]

This is the dilemma about the limits of a political community which Radcliffe-Brown raises in the Preface: 'in some societies such a political community is indeterminate';[31] and this really means that functional analyses alone are appropriate in determining these community limits, and that structural study cannot yield further refinements in the classification of 'stateless societies' beyond that distinguishing those with definite political communities and those with indefinite units. This really means the abandonment of the comparative study of structures in favour of a series of 'functional' descriptions, and since, as is clear from the quotation already given, 'the kind of information related and the kind of problems discussed' reflects the dichotomy between states and stateless societies, the contrasts of these descriptions are predetermined by the method of study, as well as by any inherent qualities of the data.

This misuse of the comparative method itself has been predetermined by the definition which equates political system and government, and both with the centralized control of force. The difficulty is thus created of understanding how, if this is so, the Logoli, Tallensi, and Nuer can be credited with political institutions at all:

A particular right or duty or political sentiment occurs as an item of behaviour of an individual or a small section of an African society and is enforceable by secular sanctions brought to bear on these individuals by small sections. But in a politically organized community a particular right, duty or sentiment exists only as an element in a whole body of common, reciprocal and mutually balancing rights, duties and sentiments, the body of moral and legal norms.[32]

Thus the politically organized community is defined as the area within which there is an equilibrium in the operation of these moral and legal norms; but the expectation that descriptive cultural

29. ibid., pp. 5-6.
30. ibid., p. 6.
31. Radcliffe-Brown (1940), pp. xviii-xix.
32. Fortes and Evans-Pritchard (1940a), p. 20.

summaries will be presented as substitutes for the analysis of the political systems of the eight societies discussed in that volume is not uniformly fulfilled, since 'the kind of information related and the kind of problems discussed' vary according to the classification of the system concerned. This methodology is unsatisfactory; in this it reflects an inadequate theory, and follows an inadequate typology. All three deficiencies are inseparably linked with the inadequate definition of political organization, behaviour, and community, the uncertainty about the relation between political organization and government, the mistaken choice of centralized force as a criterion for classification of political systems, and the failure to define and analyse administrative process explicitly. A false problem has been created by an inadequate understanding of political action, and this leads to a false dichotomy. Finally it issues in a false, because inconstant, method of substantiating that dichotomy; and, more importantly, extends beyond the formal study of political systems to misguide and misinterpret segmentary theory and analyses. The manner in which this extension occurs is most clearly expressed in the following passage, discussing the typology of political systems:

One of the outstanding differences between the two groups [of societies] is the part played by the lineage system in political structure. We must here distinguish between the set of relationships linking the individual to other persons and to particular social units through the transient, bilateral family, which we call the kinship system, and the segmentary system of permanent, unilineal descent groups, which we call the lineage system. Only the latter establishes corporate units with political functions. In both groups of societies kinship and domestic ties have an important role in the lives of individuals, but their relation to the political system is of a secondary order. In the societies of Group A it is the administrative organization, in societies of Group B it is the segmentary lineage system, which primarily regulates political relations between territorial segments.[33] ... [In these segmentary societies] the lineage structure is the framework of the political system, there being a precise co-ordination between the two, so that they are consistent with each other, though each remains distinct and autonomous in its own sphere.[34]

This conception of political relations has such fundamental value for the understanding of segmentary theory, and is itself of such a complex character, that extended quotations have been necessary to give an adequate view of it, and to indicate its relation to the development of segmentary theory. Criticism, to be effective, must focus on the definition of political relations, and show whether and how this is inadequate or imprecise. Indications that it may be unsatisfactory are provided by the studies of Brown and Bernardi which show that the typology of political systems proposed by Fortes and Evans-Pritchard in 1940 is inadequate and in need of revision. Yet, as suggested above, the conceptions of government and

33. ibid., p. 6.
34. ibid., p. 7.

political organization which inform their classification do not permit of much further refinement of the categories developed about them. Of itself, this would strongly suggest that the conceptions informing these categories are of doubtful value, and may need revision. This view is strengthened by an examination of the relations between government, political system, and administration, as set out in segmentary theory. At one time, government is equated with political system,[35] at another time it is equated with administrative structure, and regarded as a component of political systems.[36] At one time political relations are defined as inter-group relations,[37] at another in terms of coercive force,[38] at yet another in terms of community values;[39] in one version of the theory, territorially distinct sections provide the basis of segmentary political organization; in another, we are told that similar organization obtains among the Logoli and the Tallensi, 'who have no clear spatially-defined units'.[40] And the problem of the limits of political communities is never resolved, since the two criteria of political action used in its examination are contradictory, namely force, which would operate through feud, war, and the like, and moral or legal norms, sacralized by ritual, to sustain an equilibrium.[41]

As Forde pointed out in 1939, the concept of government includes a good deal more than the political system of a society, and forms the logical as well as the empirical category for analysis of this type.[42] The perplexity which results when the concept of political system is applied variously to this wider area of action has been illustrated by the quotations we have given above. The kind of information given in the volume under discussion about centralized societies consists mainly in a description of the administrative systems of such societies; whereas the information given about segmentary societies divides equally between administrative and political aspects. Unless these two aspects of the inclusive process of government are distinguished analytically, and their interrelations determined, it is difficult not to confuse the analysis of either or both forms of organization, as for instance has been done in segmentary theory.

Government is the process by which the public affairs of a people or any social group are directed and managed. The definition of the 'public' and of the type of 'affairs' which fall within the scope of this political administration is a matter for empirical investigation; but the two terms are interdependent and mutually definitive, as for

35. ibid., p. 6.
36. ibid., p. 5.
37. Evans-Pritchard (1940*a*).
38. ibid., p. xxiii.
39. ibid., pp. 20-1.
40. ibid., p. 6.
41. See Fortes and Evans-Pritchard (1940*a*), pp. 22-3.
42. Forde (1939*b*, 1950*a*).

instance in the distinctions between local and national governments, which besides having references to different, though overlapping publics, also have reference to different though overlapping sets of affairs. Thus the indeterminacy of 'political units' from one point of view consists in the variability of the 'affairs' and 'public' concerned, political units being defined by reference to government.

From another point of view, indeterminacy in the boundary of political units reflects lack of consensus about the type of activities over which authority is to be exercised, or the type of authority to be exercised over these activities. Where the latter basis of indeterminacy occurs, it indicates a condition of dynamic change, during or through which new types of political groupings may emerge. Where indeterminacy appears with respect to the type of activities over which authority is to be exercised, then such lack of consensus itself indicates the boundaries of the governmental units, and defines their interrelations. At any point in time, the boundaries of the political system can be clearly defined in terms of certain actions which have political implications, that is, actions associated with competition in terms of power. Over a period of time, the boundaries of such a system may shift in response to a variety of factors, but although it is clearly impracticable for reasons of space to deal here with the dynamics of this type of structural change, it may be mentioned that the analysis of such change is highly rewarding in terms of the concept of government under discussion.[43] The point to note is surely that indeterminacy of the political unit only presents a serious difficulty for analysis when political action is itself defined in terms of such units, and is not explicitly distinguished from its administrative counterpart within the common process of government. There can be little problem of indeterminacy if such a conceptual frame is adopted, and if administrative and political process are defined initially by their interrelation within the common process of government, rather than in terms of units or social groups. This point is especially important, since, as we shall see, the same structure or unit may discharge both political and administrative functions. Hence the definition of either of these functions in terms of such structures tends to obscure the other, and to inhibit their explicit differentiation. This seems to have been Evans-Pritchard's initial problem among the Nuer.

Government is a process; 'a government' is a structure. All societies anywhere must have governmental processes of some sort. Thus since these processes eventuate through structures of some kind, and have their own internal structure through the relations of their parts and phases, all societies must have governmental structures. The principal difference on this point is between societies in which the governmental processes are explicitly allocated to particu-

43. M.G. Smith (1960a).

lar social forms on the one hand, and those in which they are discharged through other institutions. In the first of these two types of governmental forms, there is an explicit structure, itself defined in terms of more or less clearly and exclusively defined governmental functions. In the second, the governmental structure is implicit in other institutions and processes, and governmental functions are therefore not rigorously distinguished from other forms of process, but tend to ramify throughout them. The first type of government, that with an explicit structure, is generally distinguished from the second in terms of the dichotomy of states and stateless societies. In our view, both are forms of government equally, and the differences between them are ultimately reducible to degrees in the differentiation of political and administrative functions in terms of units and forms specialized to discharge them. We shall return to this problem later, after certain essential concepts and relations have been clarified.

Government is an inclusive concept, and the analytically distinct components or aspects of the process are two interdependent systems of action, the political and the administrative. These categories of action are analytically distinct, although they frequently occur together. Examination of the type and extent of their combination is of great value in the comparative study of governmental systems and processes.

A political system is simply a system of political action. The limits of that system will vary with the issue involved and may include most of mankind, as in the last war. Normally, however, the regularity and form of the issues and relations involved tend to define a system as more or less isolated and distinct from other systems on its borders. Thus we can speak of the political system of a Hausa-Fulani State, though in fact this is a sub-system of the Fulani Empire.

The nature of *political action* defines the nature of political units. Action is political when it seeks to influence the decision of policy. The content of policy decisions varies according to the culture and the social unit within which they are formulated, but the process of policy decision always occurs within the context of competitive action by individuals and groups to determine the decision. The units involved in this competition to influence and control policy decisions are the political units of the systems involved, whether they be lineages, lineage segments, official cadres, political parties, religious groups, firms, or individuals. Policy decisions define a programme of action, implicitly or otherwise. The execution and organization of this programme is an administrative process. At any level, programmes decided by superior levels of the political structure are regarded as policy by the subordinate units. That this is so indicates that the total political system of a society is coextensive with its boundary, since policy-making processes characterize all levels of grouping within it, though of course the range of policy varies as a function of relative power, and subordinate units of a system may find that adjustment to or reinterpretation of programmes implicit in the decisions of higher levels constitute the questions of policy which they have to decide.

Policy determination proceeds by and gives expression to competition in terms of power and influence. Political action is therefore that aspect or form of social action which seeks to influence decisions of policy by competition in power. That is to say, political action is always and inherently segmentary, expressed through the contraposition of competing groups or persons. This inseparability of political action from segmentary organization is the basis for the combination of these two concepts which lies at the foundation of the theory of segmentary lineage systems, as we have seen. Segmentary lineage organization simply expresses the political character of the units in which it obtains, as systems or sub-systems, within and about which competition to determine or influence policy decisions takes place on various issues. The relativistic reference characteristic of such systems simply indicates the variability of the issues which form the content of policy decisions, and the association of different types of issue with different levels of social grouping. From this it follows that political relations obtain within groups or lineage segments as well as between them. This point was made differently by Radcliffe-Brown. As will shortly be shown, the same principle of segmentary contraposition orders political relations in any type of state, and necessarily, since competition to determine policy decisions proceeds by relative power and influence, and can have no other form.

In contrast with political action, *administrative action* consists in the authorized processes of organization and management of the affairs of a given unit, whatever its range and character. Thus administrative action is defined in terms of authority; and this authority derives from rules, conventions, traditional procedures, laws, variable from one society to the next in their precise definition, content and extent, but never absent. In terms of these rules, relations of superordinate and subordinate within the administrative structure, as well as on its margins, are laid down. Authorized action, where of a novel kind, derives its authority from the policy decisions made on behalf of the unit to which such action applies, and these policy decisions reflect and follow on political action. Thus, the conduct of war is mainly a matter of administration, though during the course of conflict issues of policy may develop more or less frequently, according to circumstance. In contrast, the declaration of war is never an administrative matter, nor can it ever become so, since this is a policy decision involving contraposed groups, and as such is only capable of expression by political action.

As political action is defined by power competition, and is

inherently segmentary, so administrative action is defined by authority, and is inherently hierarchic. Whereas the form of political systems is segmentary, and only displays hierarchic patterns to the extent that the political structures are directly involved in administration, the form of an administrative system only displays segmentary patterns to the extent that the administration itself constitutes a political system. This most important point applies alike to totalitarian structures,[44] and to segmentary lineage systems. It holds equally for administrations in democracies and feudal states. It exposes the basic fallacy of the view that an all-dominating bureaucracy is a more rational or superior organ of government than a controlled bureaucracy insulated against the direct operation of political action. For, to the extent that the administrative structure decides policy, it becomes thereby a political system, and its hierarchic devolution of authority and functions is transformed into a segmentary contraposition of components, which, if it is not to lead to administrative breakdown, requires the elimination of the unsuccessful party in the conflict about policy from the single coextensive field of political and administrative action. In Russia this elimination may involve liquidation; in segmentary societies, it proceeds by lineage redefinition, notably in the form of fission.

A comparative science of government consists in the study of political and administrative systems and of their interrelations in different societies. The typology implicit in this study distinguishes different categories of political system, different categories of administrative system, and different types of relation holding between these two systems. The examination of such data will show whether or not functional relations obtain between these diverse aspects of government, and if they do, in what they consist. Such hypotheses will guide theory and stimulate research, and will have the merit of precise verifiability. Well-founded hypotheses based on this analysis of governmental process can then be applied to the wider problem of the general relations holding between governmental systems of various types and the total social structures of which they are part. To begin with social structures and proceed to define government on this basis is faulty procedure. It may well involve the definitions of social structure and government as interchangeable terms. It defeats the purpose of a comparative science by defining the field in insufficiently clear terms, and at an insufficiently general level of abstraction.

Economic action is defined by reference to certain values which are diacritical for economic science. Religious action is defined also by reference to certain values, such as faith. So too with governmental processes, which in their administrative aspect embody and express the value of authority, and in their political aspect the value

44. Deutscher (1953).

of power. Just as kinship, religion and economy cannot be adequately defined in terms of particular procedures or forms of grouping, so too with government. Even though initially there may be marked increases in the complexity of the analyses made of government when these analyses are founded upon abstractions with an appropriate level of generality, there is little doubt that only by means of such studies can a comparative science of government be established.

We have defined government in terms of the dual values of power and authority. Authority is the right to order certain actions, power is the ability to secure their performance. Authority is an allocated and defined right. Power is a condition with varying degrees of latency, legitimacy, and legality. Frequently there is an overlap between these two values, as in the office of the Prime Minister, which combines high authority with great power. This overlap or association of the two principles varies widely from one position in a system to another, or as between systems, but the principles always remain analytically distinguishable. The action of an administrative official outside the scope of his allotted authority is action *ultra vires*, and is subject to punishment by superior authority. Political action is not subject to this *ultra vires* limitation, though unsuccessful deviations from the norms of competition invite reprisal. Administrative action is further defined by positive injunctions detailing the execution of certain tasks, the majority of which are normally routine. The content of political action is not definable in this manner, nor are the majority of issues entailing policy decision normally recurrent routine problems of the type handled by administrative action. Since policy decisions are made on a basis of power competition, they normally represent the preferences of the successful competitor; and since the unsuccessful competing party cannot bind the successful opponent in a competition by power, the content of political decision and action cannot be defined in advance by injunctions, although negative rules are valuable to protect the unsuccessful competitors, and thereby to preserve the system of competition as such. Power which is inherently segmentary and conditional, latent as well as manifest, is relativistic in nature and expression, and cannot be centralized. The 'centralization' of power proceeds by its transformation into authority, with a specific administrative hierarchy of its own. In contrast, authority is always by definition to some extent centralized, since it consists in an allocated right, and this is true even in such small groups as the family. Logically also, authority cannot take a segmentary form, since that involves parity of power. The mode and scale of the centralization of authority permits the comparison of administrative systems. Thus the dichotomy of centralized and segmentary systems is doubly misleading. It compares administrative systems of one type with political systems of another; it also ignores the analytically critical distinctions of authority and power, and attempts to base the study of government on inappropriate abstractions, such as group relations, or control of force.

Both power and authority may be associated with force or its control; but normally, as we should expect, this association differentiates the two governmental principles within any society. The significant point about the authorized control of force which characterizes a centralized administrative system is critically that it consists in *an allocated right* to use and control force in such a manner as to ensure the continuity of the system, and not simply the concentration of force itself. It is due to this monopoly of the right to control force within the territory by the administrative head and his staff that unauthorized concentrations of force by political units come to be classified as rebellions, riots, sedition, and the like. Rebellions, successful or otherwise, indicate the empirical significance of this distinction. The successful rebel group faces the problem of having to legitimize its use of force, the failures are punished for the illegitimacy of their acts; but both the successful and the unsuccessful groups which mobilize force to rebel do not thereby reduce the degree of centralization of the administrative system one whit. Instead they express a new pattern of political action, a competition for power by force, which is always inherently latent in political systems. Force and its control are therefore an illusory ground for differentiation of political and administrative systems, or types of these systems, such as is involved in the dichotomy of centralized and segmentary systems. Force is force, whether constitutional, that is, authorized and administrative, or unconstitutional, that is, unauthorized and political; and coercion is wider than force.

Governmental action always and everywhere involves both political and administrative action. Even simple bands such as those of the Andamanese conform to this pattern. Internally they are units of a primarily administrative character. Externally, they are linked to one another by political relations, the content of which reflects their hunting and gathering economy, as well as marriage and ritual organization. Naturally, as could be expected, the definition of administrative and political issues is not marked in Andamanese society; but there is none the less a fair degree of differentiation of these principles in relation to the context of the bands themselves. Internally, bands are conceived of as administrative groups, even though competition to determine decisions sometimes occurs within them. Externally, they are conceived of as political groups, even though the competition between bands may be latent rather than actual; and in the context of ritual action some administrative action involving two or more bands may occur.

Political and administrative action may be distinguished and entrusted to different structures, or to the same structure in different situations; and there is indeed a great range of degree and type in their empirical combinations and differentiations. This range defines the continuum of governmental structures which permits and requires a continuous typology on the basis of detailed comparative studies of particular systems, as the first stage of a truly comparative science of government. The typological discontinuity of centralized and segmentary systems which has been developed on the basis of inadequate formulations about the nature and limits of the systems under study actively inhibits such comparative analysis of structure and process. Variability in the types and degrees of differentiation and combination of specifically administrative and specifically political systems of action, and thus of the units involved, simply reflects the generality and adaptability of the structural principles which inform the processes of government, and thereby the taxonomic unity of the different forms as a single series.

A fuller exposition of this concept of government cannot be given here. We must now turn to consider segmentary lineages in terms of administrative and political action as defined above, and see whether these conceptions contribute more fully to our understanding of segmentary societies than do the special definitions of politics and lineage organization in terms of which these lineage studies have been made.

Segmentary lineage systems in their administrative arrangements exhibit a hierarchic authority structure. This is very clearly recognized by Fortes, Brown and others,[4][5] but the implications of this fact have been obscured by the syncretism inherent in the definition of political action, whether in terms of force or group relations, with which all these writers operate. It is none the less clear that in 'decentralized political systems' of the segmentary lineage type, lineages of any order are separably units of internal administration and common concern with problems of management of defined affairs. The control of sub-units of the lineage, and hence the equilibrium of the structure, is thus a function of its administrative character, and a prominent focus of its system of administrative action. At the same time, relations between co-ordinate lineages of whatever order are inherently segmentary in character, and are either latently, as in marriage, ritual, inheritance and succession, or manifestly, as in feud, political. This means that the external relations of a lineage are primarily political relations, while its manifold internal relations are primarily administrative. None the less, relations between lineages may involve administrative action, either on specific issues or as a recurrent form, for instance in the context of ritual or marriage. Similarly, political relations obtain within lineages as well as between them, and this holds true down to the lowest level of lineage organization, in so far as competition develops over decisions involving policy.

45. Fortes (1953), p. 52; P. Brown (1951).

Put another way, this simply means that in a lineage system, relations between superordinate and subordinate lineages are normally administrative and based on authority, whereas relations between co-ordinate units are normally political and express relative power. Since the dimensions of lineage organization embrace superordination and co-ordination together, and since it is in these dual terms that the position of any segment of the structure is defined, this simply means that each segment is latently or actually involved in simultaneous contraposition and subordination with reference to at least two other segments. Thus the administrative and political actions which inform lineage systems normally and normatively have different foci; but where at any time units do not conform to this structured relation of the two governmental principles, then those which have been normatively defined in terms of separate political entities come to form a common system of administrative action; and units which have been normatively defined as single administrative systems develop political opposition and come to form separate systems of this type. Hence the phenomena of genealogical revision, segmentation, fission, fusion, accretion, amalgamation, and the like, by means of which the canons of lineage descent and behaviour are reinterpreted, revised, or redistributed to accord more closely with the realities of their political and administrative functions.[46]

Since the internal structure of a lineage at any level presents a series of co-ordinate sub-units, and since, as co-ordinates, these sub-units are characterized by interrelations expressed in power rather than authority, the maintenance of such a structure requires a patterned devolution of authority which runs parallel to and is integrated with the descending hierarchy of co-ordinate segments. Thus, not only are lineages, or any segments of them, administrative units in certain contexts and political units in others, but the political and administrative aspects of the system are directly interdependent, and the scope and nature of authority is directly defined for and within any lineage by the political structure which forms its context, and vice versa. A moment's reflection will serve to show how this particular mode of interrelating administrative and political action, and embodying them in a single structure as appropriate at alternate levels, defines the form, function, and processes of lineage development, segmentation, fission, and fusion. The variety of processes by which the constitution of lineages develops and changes simply reflects the dynamic conditions of these structures, inherent in their dual political and administrative natures. At any moment lineage equilibrium consists in a balanced distribution of these functions within and between all levels and segments of the system. Changes in this balance, that is, in the distribution of

---

46. Fortes (1945); L. Bohannan (1952); P. Mayer (1949); Southall (1952).

political and administrative functions, are expressed as changes in lineage equilibrium directly; and these may involve changes in the lineage structure. This occurs at the lowest level of the lineage system as well as at the most inclusive level; and for this reason, it is unacceptable to limit political relations to interrelations of major groups alone, as Evans-Pritchard has done.[47]

It is, furthermore, easy to show on the data from these types of society that beyond the internal administrative systems of the lineage units there are agencies of a predominantly administrative character, which operate to reduce the latent dangers of conflict between maximal lineages for the stability of the society as a whole, and that, from an analytic point of view, these agencies resemble rudimentary offices. Thus the Tallensi statuses of *tendaana* and chief; the *omuseni, omulasi, ovwali,* dream-prophet, rain-maker, and war-leader of the Bantu Kavirondo; and the leopard-skin chief and prophet among the Nuer, are all agencies of this type.[48] By means of these institutionalized positions, administrative action limiting the range and type of political conflict among the major political units of the societies concerned was effected. Notably also, rules and conventions governed the action of these extra-lineage agencies, and limited the expression of opposition between lineages, as well as within them. Once the inherent fallacies of defining government solely in terms of political action, and political action in terms of force, are clearly recognized, differences in the range, precise definition, and degree of authority characteristic of these supra-lineage agencies found in segmentary societies on the one hand, and offices typical of states on the other, are seen to be obviously differences of degree rather than kind. Thus a continuum obtains, linking the Nuer, Tallensi, Kavirondo, and other 'segmentary' societies, with the Ibo, Yakö, Nandi, Ashanti, Sotho, and Zulu and extending to Britain and modern nations, in which government embraces segmentary principles of a non-lineage kind to greater or less degree, and includes administrative forms characterized by explicit systems of hierarchic offices.

The segmentary lineage system is thus definable as a particular combination of administrative and political action within and between structures defined formally in terms of unilineal descent. It cannot therefore be considered adequately in terms of political action only, and for that reason is neither a separate category of political system nor a reflection of a separate political principle at all. Lineages become segmentary and hierarchic in form and character through this cross-cutting combination of political and administrative action within their genealogical and territorial structure; and similarly, societies which interrelate their administrative and political systems in this particular way show a similar pattern of organization. Here we must recall those societies, such as Nsaw, Zulu, or Bemba,

47. Evans-Pritchard (1940*a*), pp. 263-5.
48. Fortes and Evans-Pritchard (1940*b*).

within which unilineal groups or their segments are differentiated in terms of seniority and rank, and these differentiae reflect their governmental significance. In such systems, there may well be segmentation within the lineages despite these positional differences. But the particular allocation, interdependence, and integration of administrative and political functions characteristic of segmentary lineages which lack rank differentiation is modified to some degree by the factor of rank itself. Although we cannot discuss these types of structure in detail in this place, they are of critical significance. Within such systems of ranked lineages, the administrative and political significance of different lineages or segments will vary with the position of the unit in the governmental system at any moment. Under such circumstances, also, tendencies emerge favouring the specialization of units in political or administrative function. This specialization may eventuate in disbalances in the combination of these functions, and the new combination may define a form different from the type of segmentary lineage structure obtaining in societies lacking rank organization. Thus in a sense we can speak of balances in the governmental functions which define segmentary lineages; and it follows that where disbalances of governmental function occur, they may have a formal expression distinguishing the unilineal descent groups in which they obtain from the strict segmentary model. Yet such rank-structured unilineal descent groups may continue to display segmentary form in some degree, or at some level of organization, and often such segments provide the constituent units for segmentary processes. The Hausa-Fulani dynasties of Zaria discussed below are unilineal groups of this type.

The essentials of our argument can be stated briefly: all societies manage their public affairs by a process known as government; this varies a great deal in form and content, but always involves two modes of action and their interrelation; one mode of action is administrative, has a hierarchic form, and expresses authority; the other mode is political action, which has a segmentary form and embodies relations of power. The maintenance of any given administrative system depends on its being supported by effective force and political power. The exercise of political power depends on the provision of an administrative system whereby authority to execute political decisions is allocated. Thus all societies have political and administrative organization, and hence *both* hierarchic and segmentary structures. The important differentiae in social structures looked at as governmental organizations are the degree of overlap or of disassociation of these administrative and political systems on the one hand, and the character and constitution of the units involved in such structures, on the other. Since all political organization involves segmentation, and since political organization is only one aspect of the process of government, a distinction cannot be drawn between societies which are organized on segmentary principles, that is, lineage societies, and those which are not. What is crucial in any particular case is the nature of the segments. In some societies these may be lineages, in others localities, in others age-sets or regiments, in others cult-groups or associations, in others official orders, and so on. Moreover, political segments may be of different kinds in the same society at different levels, or in different situations; at one level lineages, at another age-sets may provide the units of political organization and action.

Since political action has a segmentary form and process, unilineal groups which are political units have a segmentary structure, down to the lowest level of their political organization. Where unilineal groups do not form the units of political competition, they lack such segmentary structure, except in a genealogical diagram. This is one half of the story. The other half reflects the administrative aspect of governmental process. Since administration has a hierarchic form and process, unilineal groups which are administrative units have a hierarchic structure up to their highest level of administrative organization. Where unilineal groups do not form the units of administrative organization, they lack such hierarchic structure, except in a genealogical diagram. Segmentary lineage structures, in the current sense of this term, represent the coincidence and interrelation of these administrative and political principles of action and organization in units recruited on a basis of unilineal descent. The segments of such lineages at any level have a common nature. This common nature consists in their dual character as political and administrative units, and it is this which defines their boundaries. To the extent that a discordance obtains between these diverse governmental functions which together provide the basis for lineage development and define its structure, the lineage structure reflects this by deviation from the norms characteristic of segmentary lineages having coincident political and administrative functions in acephalous societies. Thus seniority of a collateral branch involves departures from the standard lineage paradigm to reflect inequality of the lineage divisions in terms of a 'segmentation' which does not involve parity or contraposition, but attempts the extension of hierarchic principles of superordination to apply to collateral branches ordered in rank. Similarly, centralized authority structures which reduce the political functions of lineages, correspondingly increase their relative administrative significance and entail corresponding departures from the simple segmentary model.[49] The structure of segmentary lineage systems therefore represents more correctly and adequately a particular balance in the combination, interrelation, and distribution of political and administrative functions and processes, by virtue of which the segments are defined, than it does any of the apparent bases of group organization, whether this be

49. Kaberry (1952); Herskovits (1938), vol. i.

unilineal descent, locality, or their combination. The sophisticated Tiv, who understand this relation very well, attempt to preserve their form of government by revising relations between lineage segments to correspond with the current balance and form of the combination, as far as they might, and are prepared to do considerable violence to the strict principles of unilineal descent and genealogical seniority to this end.[50]

The impression of greater internal complexity which lineage segments give when compared, for instance, with other types of political unit such as age-sets or political parties, simply reflects the wider range of governmental functions which are recurrently discharged as administrative and political functions by lineage segments in segmentary societies. Thus age-sets may or may not be the dominant political units, but even if they are, and also simultaneously discharge corresponding administrative functions, age-sets cannot rival lineages in the complexity and order of their dual hierarchic and segmentary organization, since organizational complexity simply expresses the great range of administrative and political functions involved, and their combination at all lineage levels, in societies where government is by lineage.

The contrast with political parties is even clearer. Parties mobilize segments in competition for control of the state by election or revolution. But the administrative unity of the state is entrusted to a special staff insulated against direct interference by the competing parties. The administrative functions of party organizations are therefore limited to the execution of policy decisions focused on the mobilization and maintenance of support. For this reason, a revolutionary party requires a more elaborate and active party administration than others. But this is only so because the revolutionary party seeks to organize its supporters into a segment which will operate as a solidary unit in a competition which will involve force. This means an extension of party administration beyond the norms typical of non-revolutionary parties into the processes of daily life of the supporters. Even so, a good many of these social processes remain outside the administrative scope of the revolutionary party, and to that extent, the identification of the members with the party remains occasional and incomplete. In lineage structures, however, there is very little of importance in the individual's life which does not fall within the frame of lineage administrative or political action, from marriage to inheritance and succession, from group membership and obligations to ritual, access to resources, residence, and kinship. The integration of multiple functions within the dual frame of political and administrative organization forms the basis for a corresponding continuity in the identification of persons with any type of group. Where, as in

50. L. Bohannan (1952).

political parties of the non-revolutionary type, this occurs mainly at a psychological level for a limited occasion, as during election campaigns, the segments mobilized dissolve as they pass through the election booths. Where, as in revolutionary parties, multi-functional organization has greater range and continuity, the party segment has correspondingly greater solidarity. These considerations apply equally to age-sets, cult-groups, community units, associations, official cadres, and lineages. The content and form taken by the concurrent political and administrative principles of action determine the internal structure and solidarity of the units which they define.

3.

Study of the processes of lineage formation and development is not an exercise in the quest for origins, but proceeds in a comparative and theoretical framework. We have to answer such questions as the following: What structural principles are basic to lineage development? Under what conditions do these principles obtain without giving rise to lineages of segmentary character? To what extent are they consistent with and exemplified in segmentary lineage organization? In other words, what are the variables associated with the emergence, articulation, and change of segmentary lineage systems, and what are their relative weights?

Thanks to Radcliffe-Brown[51] there is no doubt about the kinship principles which are essential to the development of unilineal descent groups. But they do not provide a sufficient basis for the development of segmentary lineages, even where such recognition of unilineal descent obtains. On the one hand, the emergence of segmentary lineages may be inhibited when principles of unilineal descent are linked in certain ways with certain other principles of social organization, or with one another in systems of double descent.[52] On the other hand, simple recognition of unilineal descent may not serve as the basis for lineage development.[53] We have therefore to consider the types of conditions which are associated with the emergence of unilineal descent groups, and especially with the segmentary forms of such units. Clearly, the essential kinship principles on which these structures develop do not account for their development; they make lineage units possible, but they do not imply or determine them. Clearly also, the definition of segmentary lineage structure will significantly influence the study of its developmental processes and context.

We have already seen that segmentation is sometimes defined explicitly in terms of contraposition, sometimes without this, simply

51. Radcliffe-Brown (1941, 1950).
52. Richards (1950); Forde (1950a, 1950b); Evans-Pritchard (1940b); Bernardi (1952).
53. Fortes (1953), p. 25; M.G. Smith (1954a), pp. 21-2.

in terms of multiplication by subdivision. Also, it has been noted that different views have been advanced concerning the primacy of locality and descent in the corporate definition and character of lineage groups. There is also some uncertainty in theory about the relation of external and internal factors in the segmentary differentiation of lineage structures. Fortes' 1953 paper shows this very well. Fortes begins, as we have done, by noting that segmentary lineages and the principle of unilineal descent are not one and the same; and goes on to indicate the importance which extra-lineage factors exercise over the degree of lineage incorporation, that is, their definition and development as corporate groups:

> The more centralized the political system the greater the tendency seems to be for the corporate strength of descent groups to be reduced, or for such corporate groups to be non-existent. Legal and political status are conferred by allegiance to the state not by descent, though rank and property may still be vested in descent lines. The Nupe, the Zulu, the Hausa, and other state organizations exemplify this in different ways. There is, in these societies, a clearer structural differentiation between the field of domestic relations based on kinship and descent and the field of political relations, than in segmentary societies.[54]

This is clear enough, although it would require some qualification to stand. But gradually the boot goes over to the other foot:

> The dynamic character of lineage structure can be seen most easily in the balance that is reached between its external relations and its internal structure . . . Fission and accretion are processes inherent in lineage structure . . . An African lineage is never, according to our present knowledge, internally undifferentiated. It is always segmented and is in process of continuous further segmentation at any given time. Among some of the peoples I have mentioned (e.g. the Tallensi and probably the Ibo) the internal segmentation of a lineage is quite rigorous and the process of further segmentation has an almost mechanical precision. The general rule is that every segment is in form a replica of every other segment, and of the whole lineage. But the segments are, as a rule, hierarchically organized by fixed steps of greater and greater inclusiveness, each step being defined by genealogical reference. It is perhaps hardly necessary to mention again that when we talk of lineage structure we are really concerned, from a particular analytical angle, with the organization of jural, economic, and ritual activities. The point here is that lineage organization corresponds to gradation in the institutional norms and activities in which the total lineage organization is actualized.[55]

> Lineage segmentation follows a model laid down in the parental family. It is indeed generally thought of as the perpetuation through the rule of the jural unity of the descent line and of the sibling group, of the social relations that constitute the parental family. So we find a lineage segment conceptualized as a sibling group in symmetrical relationship with segments of like order.[56]

> Thus lineage segmentation as a process in time links the lineage with the parental family; for it is through the family that the lineage (and therefore the

54. Fortes (1953), p. 26.
55. ibid., p. 31.
56. ibid., p. 32.

society) is replenished by successive generations; and it is on the basis of the ties and cleavages between husband and wife, between polygynous wives, between siblings, and between generations that growth and segmentation take place in the lineage . . . Complementary filiation appears to be the principal mechanism by which segmentation in the lineage is brought about.[57]

This dual account of the matter is not satisfactory as it stands. The definition of segmentary lineage structure and segmentation itself is highly ambiguous and obscure. Fortes emphasizes the corporate character of segmentary lineages, instancing Ashanti; and then goes on to refer to the Ashanti lineages in discussing state organization.[58] But in his account of the Ashanti kinship system it does not appear that their lineages fulfil the definition of segmentary organization, though he describes them in these terms:

The lineage has a segmentary structure, each segment being defined in relation to other segments of a like order by reference to common and differentiating ancestresses. This allows of both accretion to and differentiation within lineages . . . Though the lineage is segmentary in form it is dominated by the rule of inclusive unity. There is no hierarchy of jural status or religious authority corresponding to the hierarchy of segments. The corporate unit recognized for political, legal, and ritual purposes is generally the most inclusive lineage of a particular clan in the community . . . Ashanti are reluctant to admit to outsiders that lineage kinship is a matter of degree. They insist on the identification with one another of all lineage kin. But in personal matters and in the relations of lineage members among themselves, degrees of matrilineal connection are closely observed.[59]

It seems from this that Fortes uses the term segmentation in some contexts to mean organizational differentiation, and in others to mean genealogical distinction. Also that segmentary lineages may or may not have internal hierarchic structure of segments. And since this is so, that lineage segmentation is not to be accounted for on the ground of familial structure and complementary filiation. It is also clear that these familial processes, occurring as they do in all polygynous societies, are an insufficient basis for lineage segmentation and development, since they are not associated with lineages everywhere (e.g. Hausa, Lozi, Plateau Tonga, etc.), nor does familial process everywhere determine the development of segmentary lineage structures where it occurs among groups practising unilineal descent (e.g. Kipsigis, Nandi, Yakö, etc.).

If our interpretation of Fortes is correct, his difficulty stems from dualism in the definition of lineage segmentation and segments, first, with reference to their organizational aspects, and secondly, their derivation in genealogical terms. It is of course essential in understanding the nature of either of these aspects of lineage segmentation and their relation, that both should be clearly

57. ibid., p. 33.
58. ibid., pp. 25-6.
59. Fortes (1950).

distinguished in analysis. Segments which are simply defined by genealogical reference are purely heuristic, and of a different character from those embodied and defined organizationally. In the latter case, continuity of the units presupposes both contraposition with similar units, and recurrent common activities. This in turn involves administrative and political differentiation from collateral segments within the segment thus defined. Fortes seems at one time to have this in mind, at another to assume the primacy of genealogical differentiation in familial terms as the basis of segmentary development. But differentiation and segmentation are not identical. Differentiation by sex does not imply segmentation, which essentially consists in definition of units by contraposition with like units. The genealogical differentiation of father and son does not imply their contraposition. Failure to emphasize this distinction clearly leads Fortes away from his initial attention to the relations holding between lineages and their wider social contexts, with which he begins, to the conclusion that lineage segmentation develops internally as an autonomous process or consequence of lineage growth, and that these developments are channelled by family norms. This is also the position of Mayer and Southall.[60]

Yet when Fortes faces the question of the range and depth of genealogical charters which are implicit in segmentation, his answer places primary emphasis on the external context rather than on those internal factors which are held to activate segmentation:

> We can as yet only guess at the conditions that lie behind these limits of genealogical depth in the lineage structure. These genealogies obviously do not represent a true record of all the ancestors of a group . . . In structural terms the answer seems to lie in the spread or span of internal segmentation of the lineage, and this apparently has inherent limits. As I interpret the evidence we have, these limits are set by the condition of stability in the social structure, which it is one of the chief functions of lineage systems to maintain. The segmentary spread found in a given lineage system is that which makes for the maximum stability; and in a stable social system it is kept at a particular spread by continual internal adjustments which are conceptualized by clipping, patching, and telescoping genealogies to fit. Just what the optimum spread of lineage segmentation in a particular society tends to be depends presumably on extra-lineage factors of political and economic organization of the kind referred to by Forde (1947).[61]

Thus Fortes' several accounts of the development of segmentary lineage structures are not consistent. Their shifting emphases reflect some uncertainty about the nature of their genealogical models.

Locality as well as descent has played a prominent part in the development of lineage theory. This is especially clear in Evans-Pritchard's study of the Nuer political system:

---

60. P. Mayer (1949), p. 21; Southall (1952), p. 39.
61. Fortes (1953), pp. 31-2.

The processes of lineage segmentation and political segmentation are to some extent co-ordinate.[62]

Nuer lineages are not corporate localized communities, though they are frequently associated with territorial units, and those members of a lineage who live in an area associated with it see themselves as a residential group, and the value or concept of lineage thus functions through the political system. Every Nuer village is associated with a lineage, and, though the members of it often constitute only a small proportion of the village population, the village community is identified with them in such a way that we may speak of it as an aggregate of persons clustered around an agnatic nucleus ... A Nuer rarely talks about his lineage as distinct from his community ... I have watched a Nuer who knew precisely what I wanted, trying on my behalf to discover from a stranger the name of his lineage. He often found great difficulty in making the man understand the information required of him, for Nuer think generally in terms of local divisions and of the relations between them, and an attempt to discover lineage affiliations apart from their community relations, and outside a ceremonial context, generally leads to misunderstanding in the opening stages of an inquiry.[63]

Even their lineages have no corporate life.[64]

In our view the territorial system of the Nuer is always the dominant variable in its relations to the other social systems. Among the Nuer, relationships are generally expressed in kinship terms, and these terms have great emotional content, but living together counts more than kinship, and as we have seen, community ties are always in one way or another, turned into, or assimilated to kinship ties, and the lineage system is twisted into the form of the territorial system within its functions.[65]

Fortes sees lineage organization and development differently:

A compact nucleus may be enough to act as a local centre for a group that is widely dispersed. I think it would be agreed that lineage and locality are independently variable, and how they interact depends on other factors in the social structure. As I interpret the evidence, local ties are of secondary significance, *pace* Kroeber, for local ties do not appear to give rise to structural bonds in and of themselves. There must be common political or economic or kinship or ritual interests for structural bonds to emerge. Again spatial dispersion does not immediately put an end to lineage ties, or to the ramifying ties found in cognatic systems like that of the Lozi ... The dynamic pattern of lineage organization contains within itself the springs of disintegration, at the corporate level in the rule of segmentation, at the individual level in the rule of complementary filiation.[66]

These different interpretations lay bare the root of lineage theory, and reveal its weakness. Both Fortes and Evans-Pritchard are well aware of the close but variable relations linking lineage and locality; and both as field-workers studied societies sharply differentiated in these respects. The semi-nomadic Nuer have scattered small communities, and their ecological cycle naturally emphasizes the local

62. Evans-Pritchard (1940*a*), p. 199.
63. ibid., p. 203.
64. ibid., p. 264.
65. ibid., p. 65.
66. Fortes (1953), p. 36.

group at the expense of competing loyalties. Among the sedentary Tallensi, settlement patterns are denser, community boundaries less clearly marked, and local aggregates contain members of distinct adjacent lineages.

But the differences of interpretation have a wider reference than these two field situations. They reflect different conceptions of segmentary processes themselves, and thus, by extension, of segmentary lineages. Evans-Pritchard's view treats the lineage as a political conception, a territorial unit, members of which conceive themselves to be a distinct unit in a system of such units, and express their identity in terms of the lineage system, which has a spatial aspect reflecting or associated with the territorial pattern. In Fortes' view the lineage is a primary, and not a derived or secondary political conception, and its growth or change occurs largely through internal processes. It will be clear that this position of Fortes differs a good deal from his other view that 'spread of lineage segmentation . . . depends . . . on extra-lineage factors'.[67]

The difference in conception of segmentary process which lies at the base of these different assessments of descent and locality factors in lineage development is important. Evans-Pritchard writes of segmentation in terms of contradistinction and contraposition, organizationally, and emphasizes the active corporate life of the communities, in contrast to the lack of corporate life of lineages. Fortes argues from the postulate of lineage perpetuity to its real corporate character, and thus to its internal differentiation by pressure of internal forces, cleavages, and the like. Whereas Evans-Pritchard's position implicitly recognizes the ideological nature of lineage as compared with territorial segmentation or unity, Fortes' view seems to attribute priority to the lineage in the development of the political system:

In societies of this type the lineage is not only a corporate unit in the legal and jural sense, but is also the primary political association. Thus the individual has no legal or political status except as a member of a lineage; or to put it in another way, all legal and political relations in the society take place in the context of the lineage system.[68]

The complexity of the problems under discussion has required these extensive quotations, and has been illustrated by them. If we are to provide a more satisfying interpretation of lineage form and formation than those offered by Fortes and Evans-Pritchard, it will have to reconcile their apparent differences, and be based on principles capable of an almost indefinite extension to all forms of political organization, those without lineages as well as those with them. The only possible basis for such an interpretation is a general theory of government, such as we have partially set out above. Thus

67. ibid., p. 32.
68. ibid., p. 26.

we have to show that lineages are one of a number of types of governmental institution, and that the form and development of lineages reflect the conditions of their context and operation.

The division of 'political systems' into segmentary and centralized types which is closely linked with the development of segmentary theory has unfortunately obscured the typological and functional continuity of lineages and other governmental institutions, with the result that lineages have been taken as institutions *sui generis*, and the tendency has developed to define political organization in segmentary societies in terms of lineage organization, instead of the other way about. Ascription of corporate character to lineage units has helped towards this interpretation; but this corporate character is itself in need of examination. In 1940 Evans-Pritchard pointed out that 'Nuer lineages have no corporate life',[69] and he contrasts this condition with the corporate life of Nuer communities, although at the same time recognizing the conceptually corporate character of lineages for the Nuer. Fortes also defines lineages in terms of their corporate organization: 'the most important character of unilineal descent groups in Africa brought into focus by recent field research is their corporation organization',[70] and he stresses the external unity of the corporate group — 'one person' — and its presumed perpetuity as the essential corporate characteristics. This emphasis differs from that of Evans-Pritchard in emphasizing the conceptual character of corporateness as distinguished from its organizational embodiment in action. Fortes seems inclined to interpret actual organization of social activities in terms of the ideals and postulates of lineage structure and corporateness. Evans-Pritchard's distinction between the type of corporateness of local and lineage units among the Nuer implies a recognition of distinctions between the ideological and organizational aspects of social units, and as such, between corporateness evidenced by group action, and corporateness postulated as such. This distinction is basic to the different interpretations of lineage formation which appear in their writings.

Maine (1905) and Weber (1905) are our two guides about corporate units. Maine distinguishes 'corporations aggregate' — *groups with a collective social personality* — and 'corporations sole' — *offices enjoying rights and benefits successively held by duly selected persons;*[71] and he stresses perpetuity, collective unity of the group corporations, and universal succession — *that is the rights and duties of all members present and future in them.* Weber emphasizes the 'closure of the group, its exclusiveness, and its authority structure'. ' "Corporate action" is either the action of the administrative staff, which by virtue of its governing or representative authority is oriented to carrying out the terms of the order, or it is

69. Evans-Pritchard (1940a), p. 264.
70. Fortes (1953), p. 25.
71. Maine (1905), p. 155.

the action of·the members as directed by the administrative staff.'[72] Weber's discussion of offices as 'administrative organs' shows clearly that they are instances of corporations sole,[73] and, like Evans-Pritchard, he defines 'political action as such, the actual *corporate* action of political groups'.[74] The question of the limits of corporate groups arises when Weber goes on to define the modern state in terms which include the 'organized corporate activity of the administrative staff',[75] units of which, as offices, clearly have an independent corporate status of their own. This problem is essentially the same as that arising in the analysis of lineages as corporate groups. Does the corporate group character of lineages extend equally to all levels of the lineage structure? And if so, in what sense can the total lineage be classified as a corporate unit? Or does the total lineage alone have corporate status, in which case what is the position of the included segments? This is apparently a problem of the difference between external and internal aspects of a corporate unit, and we have seen that Fortes' interpretation of lineage formation reflects this relation.

The notion of corporateness is clearly complex and variable, as Radcliffe-Brown has pointed out.[76] It includes group unity, authority, exclusiveness, co-ordinated or common action, continuity, and internal organization. These features are shared by corporations aggregate and corporations sole in greater or less extent. Lineages and offices are both members of the inclusive category of corporate units; hence their differences as well as their similarities are of critical value in the comparative analysis of political and administrative systems, and also in the assessment of segmentary theory. Both offices and lineages share the characteristics of determinateness, exclusiveness, perpetuity by presumption, codes of conduct, control and regulation of defined spheres of behaviour, sanction systems, and membership in hierarchic serial organizations. This last characteristic of offices, their·hierarchic serial organization, is clearly important. Viewed externally an office exists within the framework of such a series. Internally, the office exercises its functions through a hierarchically organized staff within which political competition frequently obtains on a variety of grounds, as for succession, promotion, increased rewards, the appropriation of increased power, and the like. This internal aspect of office, and in particular its expression in a hierarchic staff, led Weber to define office in terms of 'administrative organs',[77] and thereby to obscure the inter-relations between political and administrative action on the one hand, and between corporate groups and offices on the other.

72. Weber (1947), p. 133.
73. ibid., pp. 302-3.
74. ibid., p. 143. His italics.
75. ibid., p. 143.
76. Radcliffe-Brown (1950), p. 41.
77. Weber (1947), p. 303.

Moreover the internal segmentation of an official staff is often paralleled by segmentary organization within the series of offices themselves; and this higher level of segmentary relations may simultaneously express a variety of principles as will be shown.

Lineages are recruited on the principle of unilineal descent, lineage leaders normally being chosen on the basis of seniority, whereas offices, or unit-corporations, are normally filled by processes involving some degree or type of selection. There is, however, a simple logical connection between these obvious differences. As a corporation sole, an office can never have two or more incumbents simultaneously, and even in its committee form is conceptualized as an indivisible unit. Conversely, the lineage, being conceptualized as a group, can never contain less than two persons of the determinant sex. But despite their manifest differences, conceptualizations of the two types of corporation tend to converge. A corporate group is conceptualized as 'a person', a unity; the corporation sole is clearly a unity, even when elements of the idea of a group enter into its conception. The different modes of succession to lineage headship and offices reflect these conditions. Here the great historical and developmental importance of linkages between particular offices and descent lines on the basis of hereditary title or eligibility must be borne in mind. This mechanism of hereditary office bridges the apparent gap between acephalous lineage-structured societies and centralized states to a greater degree than is currently recognized. Flexibility in succession rules for offices of this or any other kind is also paralleled to some degree by flexibilities in succession to lineage headship, within as well as between societies, despite the critical significance of uniform succession procedures for lineage systems. Whether it is governed by traditional rules, personal favour, technical standards, or group consensus, succession to lineage headship and office is a process of appointment marked by installation, frequently of a ritual kind, and varies according to the cultural context.

Similarly, the fact that rules which serve to prescribe and limit the action of lineage-heads or office-holders of various types show a wide variety, both in substance and form, must not be allowed to obscure their similar modes of applicability in both cases. Procedures, spheres of operation, the content of goals, the types and sanctions of authority, these will naturally vary as a reflex of different cultural contexts. But both lineage members and persons subordinate to particular offices recognize and define the responsibilities of their superior as the subordinate's rights, and the various sanctions which the superior controls are strictly defined and governed in their application by tradition, precedent, conventions, and rules. Thus, performance of the role of leadership in ways culturally defined as illegitimate, either by extending the claims of office, or by reducing and dishonouring its obligations, produce complaint, defection, political action to remove the office or its incumbent, and possibly secession or rebellion among the administered group, in a manner parallel to the fission and differentiation of lineage segments as functional units. In official systems where this type of secession has obtained, such as the Fulani Empire in Northern Nigeria during the last century, it involved some decentralization, and an increase in the number of offices which parallels the increase in the number of lineages or lineage segments that arise in segmentary societies in similar circumstances. Where secession is not possible, but these disturbing conditions obtain, political action, whether in a society with or without lineage segments, proceeds openly by rebellion, or covertly by attempts to reduce the authority of the unpopular office or corporate unit, in favour of new administrative structures more under the control of the dissidents. Ibo, Yakö, Ashanti and many other societies reveal these processes.

If lineages in a system composed of such units are comparable with offices of state in their corporate nature, administrative and political capacities, then the lineage-leader's role, in so far as it personalizes the lineage, and is defined and sanctioned by tradition, is also comparable with that of the office-holder who represents the administrative group. In the same way that all subordinate officials are responsible to superiors, so too is any segment of a lineage below the most inclusive level, and in clearly defined ways. Moreover, although the lineage-head's responsibilities to and dependence on the group of which he is head normally exceeds that of the official in its range of obligations, the real dependence of the lineage-head, even in such cases, is on the support of his segment and his peers, the lineage elders, among whom are his equals and successors, in the same way that the official is dependent rather on his peers and superiors in office, than on people of clearly subordinate status.

If we accept the similarity of lineage and office as forms of corporation discharging governmental functions, then we are implicitly recognizing a single continuum of governmental forms as defined by abstract general categories of governmental action. These abstract categories are administrative and political action, the values they express are values of authority and power. The corporate character of lineage and office is similar, in reflection of their similar functions; but lineage and office differ also, and they differ as a reflex of their different functions. The similarity of function shared by lineage and office is the political and administrative task of government and organization. Their difference consists in the way in which these different aspects of governmental action are combined in the two forms of corporation. As shown above, lineage structures are defined in terms of dualistic or coterminous administrative and political references. Offices do sometimes combine political and administrative capacity, but they vary widely in the modes and degrees of combination, and are quite frequently specialized to discharge these functions separately. That is to say, whereas lineage structures can only develop in segmentary fashion to the extent that administrative and political functions are tied together to particular points in a graded series of segments and statuses, office permits the differentiation of these functions variously within a system of government, as well as over time. This involves or permits increased adaptability, resilience, efficiency, centralization, scope, and differentiation of function in governmental structures which are organized on the bases of corporate office. At the extremes of such developments, a purely bureaucratic official structure may emerge, specialized and defined by administrative tasks, while the political system of competition has a separate existence and identity. Under such circumstances, the administrative structure has functionally as well as formally a purely hierarchic operation, while segmentary patterns obtain only in the political system. But to the extent that the differentiation of political and administrative functions of offices does not obtain, then segmentary organization as well as hierarchic arrangement characterizes the structure; and does so in different areas precisely in accordance with the measure of differentiation of political or administrative functions.

To illustrate this point, we may summarize the transformation and development of government in the 'centralized' state of Zaria or Zazzau over a period of 150 years, since 1800. Before their conquest by the Fulani, the Hausa of Zaria had a government which contained official orders of various kinds, under a king. Some of these official orders were specialized as purely administrative orders. These included the order of chamber officials, a eunuch staff entrusted with communications, control of the treasury, and the like; the order of religious officials, to whom was also entrusted the task of selecting the kings; and the slaves, who were entrusted with military tasks, and also with supply duties. There were also two orders which combined administrative and political functions. These orders were hierarchically arranged, as the senior and junior public orders, and their common administrative task was territorial administration. They were divided otherwise in various ways. One segment was in charge of military administration and war; another in charge of civil administration, police, prisons, tax, road repairs, markets and the like. Promotional ladders and status differences underlined this segmentation by function, and each division of these public orders included both senior and junior officials, under a head of higher rank. There was also a purely political order, the household officials, who lacked territorial functions but controlled the royal council, and could veto proposals of the other orders, including of course appointments. This household group was also segmented internally, by civil and military interests, as well as by its internal promotional series. They were on the other hand contraposed with the public orders, and in this contraposition emerge as a corporate group under their head, the chief of the household officials. The role of the king in such a system was limited by the constitution, that is, by the actual structure of government. He could take no independent action on any matter extending beyond his household, unless there was a deadlock between the household and public orders. Otherwise his role was that of co-ordination. Succession to the chieftainship was removed from his control, and was also placed beyond reach of any of the orders involved in the political system, that is, the process of deciding policy in council. The succession was placed in the hands of the religious order, whose political functions were exhausted in the selection of the candidate. This was an essential condition if the constitution was to be maintained. Whereas in this government, the administrative orders have a simple hierarchic structure, and are not contraposed one with the other, or with any of the other orders, those involved in the political system of action show segmentary organization in ratio to their involvements. Promotional careers, corporate rank-orders, functional specialization, status differences, and constitutional differentiation in the policy-making councils, as well as in remuneration and reward, provided some of the main bases for a variety of alignments between these political competitors.

After the Fulani conquest of Zaria in 1804, this system gradually changed, and was replaced *pari passu* by one based on autocratic administration under the king, who was drawn from one of four competing patrilineal dynasties. The hierarchy of officials under the king was drawn from his kinsmen, clients, and trusted slaves, and was thus stratified in terms of status and correlated promotional prospects; but they were not internally segmented, since the administration was monolithic. In contrast, the competition of dynasties for supreme office, and thus for control of the administrative structure, had an inherently segmentary form and process. These dynasties and their clients, each of which was maintained economically by its property rights over estates and slaves, were the constitutive units of the field of political action, and acted as corporate groups in that competition. Exclusion of rivals and their supporters from office was an obligation which the condition of government itself imposed on each king at succession. There was thus a marked differentiation of political and administrative action, and this was paralleled by structural differentiation of the two fields.

Since the British Occupation of Northern Nigeria in 1900, a further system has gradually developed, as the political context of the state was redefined, and as the initially hierarchic relation between the British and Native Administrations gradually changed into the contraposition of co-ordinate units. Together with this redefinition of context, there has occurred the virtual elimination of three of the former dynasties by serial appointments to the throne from the fourth. This has involved the dissolution of the former political system, and its replacement by a new political order, in which segmentary relations hold primarily between the British

Administration and the Native Authority under its head, the king, who derives support mainly from the Native Judiciary. This new political prominence of the Judiciary has accordingly been matched by the development of a new field of political relations within that structure, and by an internal segmentation based on the competition of two or three lineages for the control of appointments within it.[78]

These data show that political relations and segmentation are synonymous, and that corporate group character emerges in the context of segmentary political relations. Group incorporation proceeds and is defined segmentarily, and the processes are interdependent. The corporate character of a segmentary lineage is thus its administrative structure viewed as a unit in a system of political relations. The corporate character lapses, together with the segmentary structure, by the removal of the political conditions which define it. This has already occurred for one of the four dynasties of Zaria which has been unsuccessful in competition for the throne over so long a period that it has lost royal status, and thereby corporate character, and internal or external segmentary definition. In Zaria, dynasties are unilineal groups with a segmentary character. Lineage principles and structures are defined by and associated with rank and office, and where this association breaks down or lapses, lineage segmentation or continuity ceases. In other words, political and administrative functions tied to unilineal descent principles in a variety of ways, define lineages variously as political and administrative units within different schemes of relations, and of different forms. The principle of unilineal descent on which the lineage is ideologically based, and in terms of which it is defined as a perpetual or corporate group, is simply an abstract category of kinship relation which can be invested with these variable political and administrative significances and used as a guiding principle for the organization of political and administrative relations. Where offices discharge this governmental role, then the differentiation of political and administrative functions utilizes another appropriate ideology, such as democracy, or the division of powers, and so on. Where an identification of administrative and political functions pervades a system of offices, a religious ideology emphasizing elite status frequently acts as its charter. This was the case in Imperial Rome and in medieval European states, as well as Hausa and Fulani Zaria. The relations of these political ideologies or charters to government on the one hand, and to the organization of society on the other are very complex; but there is no difficulty in comprehending the redefinitions and reinterpretations of the ideological principle to accord with governmental necessities or realities.

In the case of lineage systems, redefinition of the ideology of unilineal descent and lineage occurs in terms of accretion, amalgamation, segmentation within the lineage, and fission, as well as by

78. M.G. Smith (1960a).

the conceptualization of local groups in lineage terms. The lineage principle which forms the ideological basis of governmental organization permits many deviations from genealogical descent as well as correspondences with it, without thereby being in any way invalidated, or its dominance challenged. This is matched by the persistence of the concept of kingship in states which combine this principle of organization with recurrent rebellion and wars of succession.[79] The lineage is an ideological conception of governmental character in some societies, just as the nation, the class, or the party is among ourselves. In lineage systems the principle of unilineal descent is redefined, reinterpreted, followed, or deviated from as the conditions of governmental organization make necessary or convenient. The lineage principle of itself does not entail organization in terms of lineage corporations, just as the democratic principle of itself does not entail democratic states, while the dictatorial principle is one thing, and dictatorship is another. The problem of lineage development, its form and formation, is therefore a problem of the governmental significance of lineage structures in any society. The segmentary aspect of lineage organization reflects its political aspect, and persists to the extent that it corresponds to the boundaries between corporate and durable administrative units. The segmentation, which expresses political action and assumes it, is inadequate as a definition of lineage structure, since the administrative character of the unit is at least equally essential to its definition. The segmentation characteristic of a lineage system is not therefore an inherent aspect of the genealogical principles of lineage constitution, but reflects the variable combination and relation of administrative and political functions, and their association with units of varying scope and range, within the inclusive governmental structure of the society.

The process of segmentation and the definition of segments with regard both to lineages and other groupings are equally matters of degree; and the same applies to the complementary processes of aggregation and incorporation. This is most clear in political coalitions among ourselves, and in accretion, fusion, amalgamation, and the like in segmentary societies. The governmental aspects of these processes are always the same, namely, administrative and political action. The internal segmentation of a lineage is thus not so much a matter of genealogical distance or community, though normally it is expressed in these terms, since that is the dogma and idiom of governmental organization, as it is on the more abstract categories of political and administrative relations, which are subsumed within this idiom and dogma, but are common to all societies. The grave weakness of lineage theory and study hitherto has been to mistake the ideology for actuality, and not to look behind it for the more general and abstract categories of action, in

79. Gluckman (1954).

terms of which it is to be explained and its constitution determined. Lineage theory has fallen short of its task by regarding the lineage principle as constitutive of lineage units, and the lineages as constitutive of societies in which they occur, when in fact both are only intelligible as expressions of more general and abstract principles of political and administrative action, and owe their constitution to these.

The question which arises from this discussion is, why then do some societies organize their governments along lineage lines, while others do not? This is easily answered in terms of the differentiation of the administrative and political functions of government, to which attention has already been drawn. All governmental institutions must have a corporate character ideologically, and this stress on the corporateness of any unit varies directly in relation to its significance for the total structure; but only those systems which approximate the concept of the corporation sole permit of a systematic differentiation of administrative and political functions. The corporate group always involves the dual discharge of these functions, and their combination is extensive to the extent that the group incorporation is coextensive with the activities of group members. Associations can be compared with lineages in this respect. The lineage is a self-perpetuating unit. In theory the association is not. The lineage is joined involuntarily, the association normally is not. The lineage encompasses and defines the goals and forms of a far larger portion of the individual member's action than the association normally does. And so on. For this reason, the lineage is a corporate group with a functional and structural manifold normally far more comprehensive than that of the association, and also of the office. This multifunctional character of lineage units simply expresses their definitive dualism as political and administrative units. The functional manifold which constitutes lineage action, itself expresses the intrinsic association of political and administrative action and processes in their constitution. The ideological principle of unilineal descent provides a particular type of basis for group organization which has the following values for political and administrative organization. It associates the two functions in terms of a continuous hierarchic arrangement of structural levels, while facilitating their differentiation in particular contexts. It utilizes an element of the pervasive kinship idiom for this mode of organization. It orders and integrates relations between units distinguished by administrative and political functions in terms of marriage, ritual, and locality, and permits these relations to be incorporated in the ideology of descent. It admits of a variable division of rights, interests, and responsibilities between kinsfolk, corresponding with the governmental structure through the society. It assumes invariance and uniformity in the constitution and relations of the differentiated units, while permitting their internal differentiation, cohesion, or development according to circumstance, and rationalizing these departures as consistent with its ideology. It predicates equality of status within the system for constituent units of the same level, but also permits a hierarchic organization, and a conceptual level which defines the limits of community. It is thus clear that consolidation of administrative and political functions with the norm of unilineal descent provides a wide basis for the organization and co-ordination of government functions in society; and that where these functions are not differentiated in terms of particular structures, the advantages of their combination with descent groups are great, especially with respect to continuity of the governmental system.

The notion of centralized administration involves a completed hierarchy of offices, that is to say, an organization of corporations sole or aggregate which, whatever the allocations of power and authority between them, has a pyramidal continuity from base to head. If we call such a structure a completed hierarchy, then a society of segmentary lineages can be described as an uncompleted hierarchy, even when, like the Gusii and the Tiv, they recognize a common mythical ancestor. The question why some societies organize their governments on lineage lines, and others as states, therefore reduces to the relation between systematic differentiation of political and administrative functions among the governmental agencies, the allocation of these functions among group or unit corporations, and the completeness, or incompleteness of governmental hierarchies. Put thus, the answer is clear. For a governmental hierarchy to be complete, it assumes some differentiation of political and administrative functions, which is only possible through the development of corporations sole. In answer to the question why some societies completely lack this concept of corporation sole, we can only point out that to the best of our knowledge, this is not the case. Materials on simple groups, such as the Bushmen or Andamanese, do not permit opinion, but certainly segmentary lineage societies do not completely lack the notion of corporations sole. What they do lack is the explicit formulation of these concepts, and explicitly governmental organization of this type. But this itself is no matter for surprise, since if these societies contained these concepts and structures in any developed or explicit form, they would cease thereby to be classifiable as segmentary societies in terms of lineage theory. This is, for instance, apparently the case with societies such as the Zulu, Bemba, Yoruba, and others, which associate organization in terms of office and rank with defined lineages. But if we glance at the Tallensi material, the position of Mosuor *biis*, and its definition in terms of chieftainship, is surely significant. Among the Nuer, apart from such agencies as the leopard-skin chief, the association of aristocratic lineages with territorial sections has a parallel interest; while the multiplicity of *ad hoc* agencies to be found among the Logoli and Vugusu indicate yet another line of development. In all these cases the concept of the corporation sole is implicit within the framework of inter-lineage relations. Among the Tallensi this concept finds partial expression in the chieftainship; but, as implied above, one office does not make a centralized administration, any more than one swallow makes a summer. Tallensi lack a completed hierarchy of explicitly governmental character, although having, in a rudimentary form, the concepts essential for its formulation. Nuer meet the problem of essential administrative unity within a territorial area differently, by the conception of particular lineages as dominant in special areas, that is, by allocation of supervisory functions of a rudimentary kind to such dominant lineages. Among the Bantu Kavirondo, the fragmentation of functions among a variety of extra-lineage agencies has weakened the emergence of clearly defined corporations sole at the outset. None the less, all three societies provide evidence of different kinds which indicates a type of differentiation of political and administrative functions in terms of special units such as is basic to and implicit in the emergence of corporations sole.

These societies also illustrate the character of the forces which inhibit further development of this concept. Among these forces are the values of lineage organization itself. Among the Nuer, for instance, the territorial administrative role of the dominant lineage is clearly analogous to that of an office; but here it is discharged by and conceived in terms of a lineage, which is itself defined in terms of this function. Among the Tallensi, despite the presence of a paramount and other chiefs, the hierarchic series of offices develops no explicit governmental significance, simply because of the opposition between the two principles of corporate administration, those of the corporate group and corporation sole, which are involved. Thus the *tendaana*, a ritual official, represents lineage solidarity *vis-à-vis* the chief. The polarity in the relations of *tendaana* and chief symbolize and express the basic dynamic cleavage of Tallensi society, the opposition between governmental forms based on corporate lineage groups on the one hand, or on a series of corporations sole such as chieftainship on the other. Here again, as Fortes' data have shown with such detail and sensitivity, the development of the emergent principle of the corporation sole is inhibited by the principle of group corporateness which it must displace or redefine, if a completed hierarchy is to develop. Its explicit development proceeds by a specialization of function through units which clearly involves radical alteration in the nature of lineage relations and structure on the one hand, and some loss of lineage autonomy on the other. Hence it cannot normally win acceptance except under conditions which threaten the lineages with more unpleasant alternatives. Such conditions would conceivably obtain during or after war, famine, or serious epidemics; but for their effect to be favourable to the extension of corporations sole within such a society, they would probably have to be associated with serious loss of support for the local religion, which underpins and sacralizes the governmental structure. Christianity and modern conditions will probably effect this in due course.

Our point here is only that some departure from the pure model of government by corporate lineage groups occurs even in segmentary lineage societies; and this movement is in the direction of differentiation of governmental functions, and their association with agencies of different types, whether associations, age-sets, or offices. These features of structural and functional differentiation, however rudimentary, are essential to the societies within which they obtain. That is to say, a society characterized by a government organized at all levels solely in terms of co-ordinate group corporations is no more practicable than one organized similarly in terms of corporations sole. Empirical governments vary in their combination of these two principles, and the explicitness of their formulation. This variation is itself dependent on the variable differentiation of governmental functions and structures which characterizes each society. In conditions such as those of the Nuer, Tallensi, and Bantu Kavirondo, the concept of a completed hierarchy of corporations sole which is essential to the structure of any centralized administration or government, only receives expression by implication, and in an inexplicit and rudimentary fashion. But these developments reflect the necessities for some level or type of functional specialization and differentiation, if the unity of a system of co-ordinate lineages characterized by high degrees of internal autonomy is to be maintained. On the other hand, such developments must themselves be consistent with the structure of the total system. Failure of such societies to make this differentiation of governmental functions more explicit, or to organize them in a single hierarchy, reflects the resilience, functional complexity, and central role of lineage organization itself; but even this low level of differentiation none the less involves inexplicit conceptions of differentiated governmental systems organized in terms of completed hierarchies, and thus of corporations sole.

These two aspects of centralized governmental systems, the completed hierarchy of corporations sole and the differentiation of governmental units in terms of their political and administrative reference, are mutually essential. The one cannot obtain in any degree without implicitly or otherwise connoting the other. Granted this, it is of interest to see how societies which combine the notion of corporations sole and aggregate fare in the classification of political systems to which segmentary theory gives rise. Brown has recently discussed this variable association in some detail for West Africa.[80] She notes a variety of types of association of lineage units with other forms of corporation, explicitly or inexplicitly govern-

80. Brown (1951).

mental in function, such as characterize and differentiate the Yoruba, Yakö, Ashanti, Ibo, Dahomey and Nupe. In terms of the dichotomy of centralized and segmentary systems, the types of governmental system defined by Brown are, as she shows, not simply classifiable in either of the two opposed categories. In terms of our theory and distinctions, however, such a classification as Brown puts forward indicates the continuity of governmental systems, and illustrates the analytic bases of this continuity. These analytic bases consist in the variable associations of corporations sole and aggregate in governmental systems on the one hand, and the variability in differentiation of governmental functions and their allocation among these units on the other. Segmentary theory simply avoids this continuity of governmental systems by a specialized definition of government which equates it with explicitly centralized administration on the one hand, and by an opposed definition of segmentary systems which obscures the tendencies towards such differentiation of governmental functions and the development of corporations sole, which are inherent in lineage societies, on the other. In terms of such a dichotomy, the numerous societies such as Akan chiefdoms in which government by corporation sole of a hereditary character involves the participation of lineage units, themselves having corporate status, are simply dismissed as instances of centralized administration of various types. Yet hereditary lineage-defined systems of offices and functions differ from these more completely segmentary lineage governments simply in being more explicitly organized with regard to their functional specialization, on the one hand, and to the hierarchy with which this differentiation is associated, on the other.

This simply means that the old problem of 'states' and 'stateless societies' is largely spurious. It derives from a specialized set of definitions, which in fact serve to create and perpetuate the problem, while obscuring the continuities between the two categories. In a real sense, therefore, the distinction between states and stateless societies reduces to variability in combination and degree of explicitness in hierarchic organization, differentiation of governmental units in terms of political and administrative functions, and the variable distribution of these functions among corporations aggregate or sole, organized with varying degrees of explicitness. Detailed comparative analysis of state systems defined in terms of hereditary offices tied to lineages, or of lineages characterized by rank organization and differentiation, is thus essential to the theory and typology of governmental and lineage systems alike; and exclusion of these comparative data on the basis of specialized definitions of segmentary lineages and segmentary societies simply involves exclusion of the principal type of evidence which illustrates the fallacious nature of the dichotomy between segmentary and centralized systems, the inadequacy of the definitions of political action and lineage on which it is based, and the type of factors which govern lineage form and formation.

Everything that we have said above about the interdependence between functional specialization of governmental units, the character of governmental hierarchies, and the variable relations of corporations sole and aggregate, simply indicates that the approximation to pure models of segmentary societies occurs in exactly inverse ratio with the approximation to completed governmental hierarchies of corporations sole, as these in turn are and must be characterized by high degrees of functional differentiation.

It should now be clear that discussion of such problems as those posed by the difference between states and stateless societies is unlikely to be profitable until relations between the concepts essential to this discussion have first been clarified. The problem posed, being apparently one of social dynamics and corporate development, is more fruitfully considered in relation to lineage formation than as a taxonomic exercise. We have seen that lineage forms and formations reflect their governmental contexts, processes and functions. In these terms, for example, Hausa-Fulani dynasties approximate the pure model of segmentary lineage structure no more and no less than their governmental roles and contexts warrant. Similarly, the governmental systems of Nandi-speaking peoples differ from one another and from the segmentary model as well as the centralized types of government, simply by their particular constitution as systems, the units of which are functionally differentiated in various ways and are structurally differentiated as corporations of various types. Under such circumstances unilineal descent groups will show corresponding differences from the pure form of segmentary lineage structure, as is indeed the case.[81]

There are two points of central importance here. First, the dichotomy between segmentary societies and centralized systems is misleading, and primarily definitional. Secondly, analyses of lineage systems which accept this dichotomy as valid exclude the types of comparative material essential for adequate understanding of lineage form and formation. To take the first point, the dichotomy between segmentary and centralized systems is often expressed in terms of stateless societies and states. This is misleading, because there are many forms of stateless society, such as those of Yakö, Ibo, and Nandi-speaking peoples, which yet do not conform to the definition of segmentary society current in lineage theory, primarily because governmental functions are not exhaustively associated with corporate lineages in these non-segmentary forms of stateless society. Thus, in terms of the definition of segmentary society, all other governmental forms constitute a single residual category. That is to say, the dichotomy is purely definitional. Given a different definition of segmentary society, or of particular types of governmental systems, the contraposed categories would have different boundaries.

81. Evans-Pritchard (1940*b*).

Our second point is that in terms of such a definition of segmentary systems, the analysis of lineage form and formation cannot be other than inadequate. This is so, since for an adequate analysis of these matters, comparative data are clearly essential. Now the type of definition which rules out consideration of rank-stratified lineage groups (e.g. Akan), descent groups such as those of the Hausa, Bemba, and Yoruba defined in relation to particular offices, and other forms of unilineal system, consists in a rigorous exclusion of all material which illustrates variability in the approximation to segmentary lineage structure as a function of variability in governmental context. At the same time, analysis of lineage systems defined as segmentary proceeds by underestimating the degrees, forms, and significances of governmental differentiation occurring within such societies in forms not directly reducible to lineage dogma. We have illustrated this by considering the Nuer, Tallensi, and Bantu Kavirondo, each of which differs significantly from the other in a way which reflects these differing extra-lineage governmental institutions. If all relevant data are excluded by definition from the frame of reference adopted for the study of lineage form and formation, then lineages can be explained only in terms of themselves.

We can now return to consider the views of Evans-Pritchard and Fortes. They have attempted to 'explain' lineage organization partly in terms of locality, partly in terms of the principles of unilineal descent and affiliation. In our view this is inadequate. It consists in explaining the myth by itself. We must look deeper, behind the myth to the abstract conditions it expresses, conceptualizes, and reflects. The concept of unilineal descent and the concept of segmentary lineage are distinct things; the former does not directly entail the latter. It provides a basis for its emergence, provided that certain other conditions obtain. The most important of these conditions is the association of lineages with governmental functions, linked in a particular way. This involves lineage incorporation, segmentation, and the like. The descent dogma which forms the myth or charter of the units discharging these functions can be understood only with reference to the functions which the units are constituted to discharge; and these can be understood only in the context of the society as a governmental structure and process of a particular type, a type only differentiated from others by virtue of its particular combination of political and administrative functions with units constituted in a particular way. The correspondence of social relations to the ideology, and the deviations from the ideology, are both of equal importance in revealing the conditions which limit and determine the development of lineage units in such societies. But they cannot be fully appreciated if they continue to be assessed in terms of lineage ideology alone, or its components, such as locality or descent. They must be analysed with reference to those abstract categories of political and administrative process and organization in terms of which lineage definition obtains, as instances indicating the type of functional conditions at work in lineage development, and their impact on the ideology of relations and accord with it. It is this ideological nature of descent, and its relations to the political and social structure of the wider unit, which is the task of analysis, and these cannot be determined without recourse to an abstract and general theoretical frame of government, such as we have attempted to set out.

4.

Evans-Pritchard in his first book on the Nuer laid down the distinction between lineage and kinship clearly:

We thus formally distinguish between the lineage system, which is a system of agnatic groups, and the kinship system, which is a system of categories of relationship to any individual; and we speak of these relationships as a man's paternal kin and his maternal kin, and together as his kindred. Political and lineage groups are not identical, but they have a certain correspondence, and often bear the same name.[82]

This is the view of Fortes also;[83] but not that of Radcliffe-Brown:

In many societies the kinship system also includes a different kind of structure by which the whole society is divided into a number of separate groups, each consisting of a body of persons who are, or regard themselves as being, a unilineal body of kindred. Such kinship groups are moieties, clans and lineages.[84]

It is worth while examining the context of this differentiation of lineage and kinship before proceeding to discuss the validity or utility of the distinction.

Let us follow Evans-Pritchard:

Structural relations are relations between groups which form a system.[85] ... In this sense a tribal segment, a lineage and an age-set are groups, but a man's kindred are not a group. The social structure of a people is a system of separate but interrelated structures ... The complementary tendencies of fission and fusion, which we have called the segmentary principle, is a very evident characteristic of Nuer political structure.[86] ... We have defined structure by what amounts to the presence of group segmentation.[87]

We have here a circular system of definitions. It runs somewhat as follows. 'Political relations are segmentary group relations. Segmentary groups are political groups. Kinship groups which are segmentary groups are political groups because they are members of a

82. Evans-Pritchard (1940*a*), p. 194.
83. Fortes (1949), pp. 12 ff.
84. Radcliffe-Brown (1950), p. 39.
85. Evans-Pritchard (1940*a*), p. 264.
86. ibid., p. 263.
87. ibid., p. 265. See also pp. 136-8.

segmentary system.' And so on. Thus politics is defined by group segmentation, and groups by political segmentation, segmentation by political groups. Where kinship principles are involved in group organization they are differentiated terminologically to reflect their political status. Thus, lineages are political groups based on kinship. They are political because they segment. They are groups because they are political. They segment because they are groups. In this way the analysis is in no danger of going beyond the repetition of a system of definitions, even though the interdependence of lineage and territorial systems, and the relative lack of any such interdependence between the age-set and the two other Nuer systems, points up one series of problems not dealt with in these terms, while the variable association of Nuer communities with lineages, and the composition of communities, which are themselves annually dissolved and reformed by migration, points up another.

Now it is clear that the concept of a kinship system includes the notion of unilineal descent potentially, and that where unilineal descent is traced, it marks off a subdivision of the kinship system. The real difference does not consist in the fact that kinship is cognatic or bilateral, whereas lineages presume unilineal descent; but that lineages are political units, defined as corporate groups in a system of such groups. Lineages are defined in these terms by the process of segmentation itself, that is, by political contraposition, actively or latently. But as Fortes points out, 'it is when we consider the lineage from within that kinship becomes decisive'. Yet it is just in its internal organization that lineage segmentation is most elaborate, and most directly observable. What does this mean, except that segmentation as a condition is continuous with lineage span and organization, and thus that the postulated contrasts between lineage and kinship is self-contradictory? There are political relations within a lineage, and within all of its segments as well as beyond its frontiers, and there is thus a relativity about lineage corporateness, as there is about corporations sole, illustrations of which have already been given from the State of Zaria. There is this relativity, not merely because corporateness is an ideological concept, and governmental units are endowed with it by virtue of and in proportion to their governmental roles, but also because political action is *an aspect* of action, not a special type of behaviour such as playing hockey. Political action occurs, therefore, as well within groups as between them, and for this reason the corporate postulate of lineage unity is modified by the internal segmentary differentiation of groups which are themselves constituted as corporations, and which have similar internal divisions. Here the ideological theorem of lineage unity and corporateness will clearly defeat any analysis which does not proceed on the basis of a general theory of government and the two processes of administrative and political action, which together, and in certain relations, define lineage units. The mistaken conceptualization of political behaviour as a special type of behaviour, to which we have initially directed attention, has led to an arbitrary division of social life into planes of group relations, which are defined in segmentary terms as political, and others which lack such qualities. This is clearly not in accord with fact, and as such is inadequate analysis. If it is inadequate analysis, then it implies an inadequate conceptualization of governmental processes, since this is diacritical for the distinction of lineage and kinship. This is indeed the case.

Two questions arise at this stage: What is the alternative to this distinction? What are the advantages to be gained from abandoning it in lineage studies? Both questions are closely related, as are their answers.

The alternative to this distinction between kinship and lineage is simply to regard the principles as forming one common system of kinship. Both are clearly of the same abstract order, being kinship relations. But the difference is important. Lineage is governmental and ideological kinship. It is simultaneously a kinship concept and a myth of political and administrative organization. This is shown by its definition in terms of the dual governmental functions of administration and political organization, in the combination of segmentary and hierarchic character, and in its relativistic corporate form. Analysis must seek to distinguish the strict principle of unilineal descent from its governmental connotations; then proceed to examine the ways in which this principle is associated with the discharge of these governmental functions; and the deviations from dogma which express adaptations to these governmental conditions. We cannot attempt to explain lineage realities in terms of lineage dogma, or lineage dogma in terms of those principles of unilineal descent which Radcliffe-Brown has so clearly set out, and these unilineal principles in terms of differences from kinship. We must look outward from the kinship system, and in lineage studies attempt to relate the data to a general theory of governmental organization and process, within which the lineage dogma, form, and deviation will appear reducible to a balance of particular functions within a group constituted in terms of a particular ideological principle.

The advantages of such an approach to the problem are many, not the least of them being the abandonment of a circular terminology, and an unfortunate because misleading combination of dichotomies, between kinship and lineage on one hand, centralized and segmentary political systems on the other, corporate and non-corporate groups, structural and non-structural relations. These distinctions obscure the problem they were devised to analyse. Let us consider one very simple and obvious aspect of lineage-kinship continuity, namely that of marriage. Exogamous lineages are associated with one another through marriage; but the marriage ties do not extend to all persons in the lineages concerned. They have decreasing content as range expands from the persons actually linked. This is the norm in many systems of marriage. But in such systems as that of the Kagoro of Northern Nigeria, who practise a form known as secondary marriage, meticulous observance of inter-clan marriage arrangements is essential, and the *kwai* or maximal lineages are differentiated from one another in terms of this system of marriage relations. Where a unit practises a single set of common marriage relations, it forms a *kwai*, irrespective of kinship in terms of unilineal descent, or compactness within the community. Where an agnatic descent group contains segments which are differentiated from one another by practising different sets of marriage relations, they form different *kwai*, even though the dogma of agnatic kinship persists in ritual solidarity, exogamy, and in the sense of corporate community between the differentiated segments. Size does not matter. There is one *kwai* consisting of nine souls, differentiated from its former lineage of 225 by difference with regard to one single marriage relation. There are in the same village two major segments of a *kwai* which differentiate sharply between themselves. These two latter segments practise identical marriage relations, however, and do not receive public recognition as separate units. There are on the other hand numerous cases in which the dogma of agnatic relation is clearly contradicted by facts, and several *kwai* contain unrelated lineages of equal status using this dogma to define their relations. None of the Kagoro suspected that the principle of identical and unique marriage relations was basic to the constitution of their *kwai*, though all were aware of the part that these relations play in subdividing *kwai*, when segments come to have different relations.[88]

What can we gather from this? First, that among the Kagoro, marriage is a political relation obtaining between groups, and serving to define them. Secondly, that the dogma of agnatic descent on which the Kagoro have explicitly founded their clans and lineages is an insufficient and inadequate basis for the analysis of Kagoro lineages, which are in fact constituted around the principle of inter-group marriage relations. Thirdly, that the governmental functions which these lineages discharge, and which are parallel to those of better known acephalous societies, include the organization and main-tenance of stable patterns of inter-lineage marriage relations. Fourthly, we cannot proceed directly from the descent dogma in this case to its analysis in terms of abstract categories of governmental action, except by first examining the marriage system which mediates between them. Fifthly, any lineage segmentation and fission involves other units of the system, and only occurs with their concurrence or participation. It does not develop as an internal function of lineage growth, but is inherently a function of the total system of units. Sixthly, the distinction between kinship and lineage is inappropriate to the analysis of marriage relations which are simultaneously inter-lineage relations of a political character, and

88. M.G. Smith (1953a), pp. 311-12; (1952) (unpublished), pp. 71-92.

kinship relations. The division of the lineage system from the system of kinship and marriage, therefore, inhibits an adequate analysis of the former by removing some of the most significant data bearing on the subject of lineage constitution and function. If marriage is a group relation, it is also an individual relation. It links the kinship and lineage system, and rules out the possibility of their separate consideration.

This is one grave weakness of Fortes' magnificent study of Tallensi society. In the analysis of the lineage system, he continually refers to definitions of clans and lineages in terms of marriage relations, prohibitions, and the like; but he never attempts a frontal analysis of these relations as a system interdependent with the lineage system. Later in the study of 'the second part of an analysis of the social structure' of the Tallensi, that is, his book on kinship, he mentions in a footnote that the Tallensi seem to practise 'experimental marriages' on a considerable scale, giving some figures.[89] There is no formal procedure of divorce among the Tallensi,[90] but there does appear to be something similar to the Kagoro secondary marriage; and among the 'critical norms of clanship', most of which are defined in terms of marriage, we find that 'it is a serious breach of solidarity for one member of the sub-clans to abduct the wife of a member of any other'.[91] It seems likely that the complexity of Fortes' account of Tallensi clanship is due in some part at least to an exclusion of the marriage system from the field of direct analysis. It would certainly be a perilous undertaking to analyse the Kagoro system of clans and lineages without an initial study of their marriage system. Yet such a study of marriage and lineage would be at variance with the division between kinship and lineage, 'the bony framework which shapes their body politic',[92] which is methodologically basic to segmentary studies, and which, as just instanced, leads to an inversion of relations between the governmental organization and the lineages in which it is embodied, and which it defines. Yet Leach has also shown that such a study of marriage and lineage is essential to the analysis of lineage systems of the Kachin type.[93]

Some of the differences noted above between the views of Fortes and Evans-Pritchard about lineage development seem to reflect different interpretations of the relationship of kinship and lineage, a problem which is implicit in this dichotomy of principles. Fortes apparently by the sub-title of his second book links the two planes in terms of a single concept of structure. Evans-Pritchard, however, reserves 'structure' for relations between corporate groups. Fortes' recognition of the structural nature of kinship relations therefore indicates that for him, corporateness is not a definitive character of

89. Fortes (1949), p. 85.
90. ibid., p. 85.
91. Fortes (1945), pp. 41-2.
92. ibid., p. 30.
93. Leach (1952).

structure. This leaves him free to explain and analyse corporate kin groups in terms of 'domestic relations':

Fission in the lineage follows the pattern of cellular segmentation in the joint family; and fission in the joint family, as we shall see, follows the lines of cleavage in the effective minimal lineage.[94]

In Evans-Pritchard's view,

it is the interaction of the lineage principle with the values of the kinship system which makes any neighbourhood or residential group structurally significant. Through the fusion of all elements into the dominant lineage within each local community, when the community functions as a political unit, the lineage system becomes the organizing principle of the political structure of the wider society which contains it . . . The whole society can be regarded as a network of strands of relationship which regulates relations between persons throughout Nuerland, or can be viewed as a set of relations between local groups in which these strands are ordered by the lineage system into corporate collectivities on the basis of territorial distribution.[95]

There seem to be three possible procedures. Evans-Pritchard's seems to preclude treatment of lineage and kinship in a single continuous frame of analysis, and does so on grounds which forbid the reduction of the former to the latter. Fortes does not seem to share Evans-Pritchard's unhappy equation of structure and corporate groups, but follows him in differentiating lineage analysis from kinship analysis, thereby increasing the difficulties of the former. On the other hand, he seems prepared to reduce certain aspects of lineage to kinship terms, and relies heavily on the family in his theory of lineage development. The third procedure, which is suggested here, consists in the simultaneous study of kinship, marriage, and lineage, and the study of these systems of norms in relation to the total context. This is especially important in the handling of lineage dogma, since this dogma of lineage organization only occurs where it discharges important functions extrinsic to the strict unilineal principles of kinship. Instead of assuming the reality of the myth, and then having to rationalize departures from it, as Fortes and Evans-Pritchard have had to do,[96] it is far more rewarding to relate the dogma, and deviations therefrom, to the context in which it is found. This context includes the kinship and marriage systems on the one hand, and the governmental processes on the other. Since lineage is a kinship principle invested with governmental functions, it necessarily has these two aspects, and their interrelation is critical to the understanding of lineage form and development. The limitations of the lineage principle as a means of organizing government are to some extent given by its kinship

94. Fortes (1949), p. 12.
95. Evans-Pritchard (1951), pp. 177-8.
96. Fortes (1945), pp. 30-8; (1949), pp. 4-11; Evans-Pritchard (1940), pp. 192-211; (1951), pp. 1-28, 175-80.

components and inseparability from the kinship system, in the same way that the great value of lineage principles for the organization of governmental process derives from the kinship content and form of those principles.

An interesting type of problem may be mentioned at this point, since it illustrates the difference between the lineage principle and segmentary lineages, and makes clear that if segmentary processes are taken to define lineage organization and to distinguish it from kinship, then we shall not only have to speak of lineage and kinship, but of more and less lineage, in terms of more and less segmentary organization and political-administrative significance, and conversely of more or less kinship. This is clearly out of the question, and would hardly make for fruitful comparative analysis.

Our problem consists in the taxonomic position of descent lines associated with official ranks on a basis of succession, in terms of this dichotomy of lineage and kinship. Such descent lines are normally traced unilineally, though under certain circumstances cognatic connections are sometimes given precedence for purposes of succession, as when rank differences of a certain order are held to override the unilineal principle. This may be the future position of the British monarchy. In other systems of hereditary title, however, the unilineal principle always prevails over cognation, whatever the differences of rank between the claimants. Where such systems obtain, polygyny is usually practised, and numerous progeny of eligible candidates are assured.

The Hausa-Fulani kingdom of Zaria provides an instance of this type of organization. Under the Fulani, the kingdom of Zaria contained four distinct and competing unilineal dynasties, and was supervised by the Sultan of Sokoto, who took care to limit the rivalry of these units for the throne by rotating kingship among them, and defining succession in terms of the following principles: (1) Only males whose fathers had previously been kings were eligible for the succession. (2) Of this group, only those who had held certain prominent territorial offices themselves were eligible. (3) As far as possible, two consecutive kings should not belong to the same dynasty.

Rank thus qualified patrilineal descent in a number of highly important ways. At the same time, patrilineal descent qualified rank allocation. The dynasties operated as maximal lineages in competition for the throne, and, at a lesser level, aristocratic Fulani lineages repeated this pattern in their competition for subordinate offices. Within these different lineages, royal and aristocratic, segmentation proceeded along the lines of complementary filiation to some extent, but the inheritance was divided equally among all males who were heirs of the father. Differentiation, however, principally reflected, and developed through, rank. 'Segmentary' processes were naturally most advanced and explicit among the dynasties, in view of

the rules governing the royal succession, and the extensive appointments of kinsmen to office which all kings made. Rank modifies the
pattern of lineage segmentation which we have been discussing in
several important ways. Dynastic segments are defined reciprocally in
terms of descent from ancestors of equal rank within the same
generation. Living descendants of former kings two or three generations removed, whose immediate male ancestors have not held the
throne, are marginal to the lineage organization, and may often be
forgotten in genealogies, when territorial rank is also lacking in their
recent ancestry. At any moment, the effective royal line of a dynasty
consists of those descendants of its former kings whose competition
for the throne is simultaneously sanctioned by descent and present
rank. Lineage 'segmentation' reflects the political competition of
these potential kings, as well as their solidarity *vis-à-vis* rival
dynasties. Most importantly, lineage membership, and hence lineage
relationship, varies formally and functionally in relation to the
political significance of the members concerned. The distances
between marginal and effective membership are not to be measured
in genealogical span, but in terms of political competitiveness, rank,
and the like. Lineage membership has a variable significance for the
members, and this is expressed in the distribution of authority and
control of resources, as well as in the spread of kinship obligations
and status.

The titled descendants of a recent king constitute the effective
royal segment of the dynasty; those members whose immediate
ancestors did not occupy the throne are at best nominal royals, and
are marginal to the dynastic competition. Political or effective
royalty involves effective competition for the throne. Nominal
royalty is a birth-status, lacking present or future political significance in this respect. But the nominal nature of royalty is itself
variable according to genealogical and political ties and administrative positions. There are thus wide concrete differences of status
as well as rank between members of any dynasty. Assuming
continued failure of the members of a descent-line (*zuri'a*) to secure
important office over two or three generations, lineage membership
and social recognition as royals lapses for that group. Despite this, it
must be noted that the dynasties are conceptualized as corporate
units, perpetual and solidary structures, about which political
relations are articulated. But the modifications of the unilineal
descent principle which adjust it to the principle of competition for
rank, and to the prevailing governmental organization of Zaria, have
profound developmental implications for the system of royal lineages
itself. One dynasty of the last century, the Suleibawa, has now lost
dynastic status and corporate lineage character, consequent on its
continued failure to acquire the throne, and the death of those
members eligible to succeed by virtue of direct descent from a
previous king. Something remarkably similar is happening at the

present time in Zaria, as the British Administration makes successive appointments to the kingship from only one of the remaining dynasties, and those members of the others whose fathers were kings gradually die off, leaving no eligible successors. Thus descent-lines as well as their individual segments or members may lose status, and since political status defines their structure, such a loss involves the dissolution of the lineage principle for the group concerned, at the same time as the loss of political function. This has already occurred for the Suleibawa of Zaria, and for several sections of formerly important aristocratic lineages.

There is another aspect of these dynastic lines which deserves attention. As mentioned above, rank differentiates the segments of the dynasties in terms of seniority and juniority, and this is expressed in the differential distribution of authority, resources, and status among the segments. Thus these differentiated units are not all co-ordinate, even though they may occupy parallel genealogical positions. Regular subdivision of inheritance further fragments them as administrative units; and marks or emphasizes the differentiation in terms of rank. Thus the internal structure of these dynastic groups departs from the norms of segmentary lineage systems in expression of this administrative and political difference between the dynasties and segmentary lineages. Within a dynasty, the divisions are administratively as well as politically distinct, and their interrelation is organized in terms of rank difference, and competition with other dynasties. In this competition they emerge as conceptually corporate units. Internally, such differentiation departs from the segmentary patterns of co-ordinate segments, since the dual administrative and political functions of these segments vary widely in reference to the political context of dynastic organization.

How does one cope with such structures in terms of the current lineage-kinship polarity of segmentary theory? Are they specifically kinship or lineage groups? If lineages, are they equally so at different periods of their history, or different points of their span, or in different situations? Since they are constituted as political units in terms of rank, and their administrative components and functions are decentralized by inheritance, what is their strict status in the classification of unilineal descent groups as segmentary or non-segmentary? As structural units, tied to and defined in terms of office, are these descent-lines classifiable in terms of corporate groups, or as systems of interpersonal relations? Is it useful to distinguish the external and internal systems of their relations for purposes of analysis, or does not this procedure defeat the analysis itself?

It is clear that the dichotomies introduced in segmentary theory as part of a circular terminology are ill-based and of doubtful taxonomic utility. It is a prime mistake to conceive of political relations purely as inter-group relations, and to exclude the political aspect of intra-group relations from analysis. This involves a combination of fallacies of reification. The political aspect of organization is reified, and groups as an organizational aspect of population aggregates are reified. But political relations are simply those aspects of social relations expressing competition in power and influence. This competition occurs as well within as between groups. For this reason, the notion of group corporateness is clearly an ideological datum. The corporateness varies according to the definition of the group. We have seen how universal this postulate of corporateness is, where units discharge governmental functions. This is so, since the presumption of continuity is essential to the conduct or stability of government, and this presumption involves the myth of unity and perpetuity for units of whatever character and constitution that discharge and combine these governmental functions. But the ideology of corporateness is a datum for analysis, and not its theoretical frame. To accept the postulate of corporateness which, as we have shown, is an inherent postulate of governmental ideology of all kinds, is to open the door to serious methodological and analytic errors. In lineage theory it leads to the 'principle of contradiction' which Evans-Pritchard candidly notes as basic to his analysis.[97] But really there is no contradiction at all. There is an ideological postulate of corporateness, and this is inherently relativistic in its application to the actual plane of social groupings, which it conceptualizes as structures of governmental type. It is only when the myth is taken for actuality, and its functional and analytic character or its relation to the wider context and necessities of the governmental system is obscured, that it is possible to hypostatize lineage groups as corporate units, and misapprehend the variability of group unity, and of corporateness as a condition of grouping.

Attention to the mythical nature of descent dogmas, and their function in the governmental system, invites examination of other governmental systems not utilizing these principles of organization. This can only lead to further understanding of the more abstract conditions of governmental systems by directing attention to the parallelism of office and lineage, the interdependence of administrative and political action in government, the relativism of corporateness, and the essential dependence of government on a system of myths about organization, of which the postulate of corporateness is an intrinsic and essential element. In this way, the dichotomy erected between centralized and segmentary systems naturally dissolves into a wider, more abstract analysis of governmental systems of all kinds, within some general frame of theory such as we have attempted to outline here. The grave weakness of lineage theory has been its lack of such general concepts and theories of government, and this has led to unhappy attempts to analyse myths within segmentary societies, in terms of their own postulates,

97. Evans-Pritchard (1940*a*), pp. 265-6.

without simultaneously examining their functional values for such governmental systems; and this has encouraged attempts to illustrate the actualization of these myths in social patterns, even where the latter clearly depart from the myth which rationalizes them, as in accretions, kinship composition of communities conceptualized as lineages, dispersion of segments, relativism of corporations, and the like. It would be easy to show that the governmental functions which define groups variously, and unilineal groups differently also, according to their distribution and identification with such units, by their absence also define other kinship structures which lack such governmental functions, in terms of range, span, and character. Thus Hausa, who lack interest in political office on a hereditary basis, lack organization in terms of unilineal descent, though recognizing the primacy of agnatic kinship in succession, inheritance, and localization. When descent-groups are marginal governmentally, their organization reflects this condition, as well as the emphasis on their corporateness and its character. Where, however, they are constitutive governmental units, their primacy and conceptual elaborations follow equally. The meaning and nature of group membership in descent units under these variable conditions will vary correspondingly, and so too will the content, status, actualization, and notion of descent.

It is this ideological nature of descent, and its relations with the political and administrative structure of the wider unit, which is the task of analysis, and we have already indicated certain approaches to this set of problems. It is clearly methodologically inadequate to accept at face value these myths of descent, or of any other bases of group and administrative incorporation, without further inquiry into their constitutive functions. In lineage systems the principle of descent is itself utilized in terms of political and administrative functions, and owes its prominence to these. It is thus an ideological basis for a particular form of political and administrative organization. Its analysis must therefore consist in reducing it to these organizational functions on the one hand, and distinguishing the strict principles of unilineal descent on the other. The appropriate method of such analysis consists initially in the study of marriage, kinship, and lineage as a total system, and then proceeds to consider the specific political and administrative constructions and the implications of these principles in relation to their contexts, and to other principles and forms of political administration. It is only too obvious that descent specifies individual relations as well as group relations, and that the individual's membership in his primary groups is defined in terms of kinship categories and interpersonal relations. The problem is not whether there is a formal difference between kinship and lineage of the order requiring their separate analysis, since this is simply a terminological issue, distinguishing lineage from kinship by defining the latter as non-lineage kinship, which leads to a repetition of social myths about lineage derivation, corporateness, and the like. The real problem consists in the classification and comparative analysis of types of relation holding between particular sets of governmental process and system on the one hand, and the mythology or actualization of corporate units on the other, whether these units are lineages, titled orders, associations, age-sets, or locality units. The antithesis is not between kinship and lineage, but between those systems of government which predicate corporate units based on descent of certain types, and those which have different predicates, all equally ideological, and all equally instrumental in organizing the relations between the political and administrative systems of governmental process.

5.

There are two different approaches to the theory of segmentary lineage systems: the ethnographic and the theoretical. For the reasons given in our introductory summary of this theory, we have decided to keep the direct reference to ethnographic materials to a minimum, and to attempt the examination of segmentary theory, primarily in theoretical terms. We have selected this theoretical approach because it appeared the more useful in the light of the complex and specialized nature of segmentary theory and terminology.

Kinship studies entered a new phase with the emergence of segmentary theory, and to some extent the deficiencies of the theory inevitably reflect the suddenness and size of the advance it marks. Evans-Pritchard summed up the position quite accurately in the concluding paragraph of his first book on the Nuer:

We have attempted in this book a short excursion into sociological theory, but we can only make a theoretical analysis up to a certain point, beyond which we perceive vaguely how further analysis might be made . . . It is necessary for further advance to denote relations, defined in terms of social situations, and relations between these relations. The task of exploring new country is particularly difficult in the discipline of politics, where so little work has been done, and so little is known. We feel like an explorer in the desert whose supplies have run short.[98]

This essay is an attempt to carry on with Evans-Pritchard's task by an examination of the theory and branch of studies which he developed, to discover 'relations between relations'.

As Leach observes, 'if a kinship scheme be considered without reference to its political, demographic, or economic implications it is inevitably thought of as a logically closed system. If it is not closed it cannot work.'[99] But if it is closed, it is irreducible, and only analysable formally, as a system. This has been the great weakness of

98. ibid., p. 266.
99. Leach (1952), p. 45.

lineage theory, just as it was of kinship studies, before lineage theory opened the doors to their political and other implications by systematic study. For if lineage theory conceives of lineage and political relations identically in specialized conditions, and restricts its analysis to these, then it has only a closed system to study, and the problems of closure, limits, development, and change, which faced earlier studies of kinship by the terminological method, alone remain to indicate the inadequacy of the analysis, and to suggest further lines of development by the extension of these lineage studies to their widest field of reference.

These considerations have been expressed in segmentary theory in terms of the problem of lineage form and formation, certain aspects of which have been discussed above. We suggested there that the reduction of the lineage conditionally to locality or familial groupings was an inadequate answer to the problems raised; and indeed, that the problems would have little significance if the frame of reference within which the study of lineage systems is made was extended through a general theory of governmental processes and forms. We have attempted to outline one possible approach to this problem. It may very well prove inadequate; but even so, the general point remains. Lineages, like kinship systems, cannot be explained in terms of themselves. Their examination and analysis is only fruitful in a wider frame of reference with comparative implications, and proceeding by the comparative method. We have suggested that one important aspect of this examination must be the study of the variations of myths and ideologies which correspond to similarities or differences in the organization of governmental systems and processes, as these in turn show variability in the interrelation of political and administrative functions, units and systems. Perhaps this line of investigation may lead to the type of comparative work which proceeds by the study of co-variations, and may yield a continuous typology of governmental systems, in which kinship and lineage may find a fuller analysis, and those 'relations between relations' which Evans-Pritchard suggests that we seek, may be traced.

2.

Anthropological Studies of Politics

My purpose here is briefly to review anthropological studies of government and politics, to identify the main interests of anthropologists in this field, to say something about their methods and conceptual schemes, and to indicate some problems and findings of these inquiries. For this exposition it is convenient to adopt a historical approach. In conclusion I shall illustrate the current position by discussing two examples.

1.

Anthropology emerged in the eighteenth century as an empirical reaction to deductive social and political philosophy. From the beginning, its relations with politics were thus very close. The forerunners were such men as Vico, Turgot, Montesquieu and David Hume, who were dissatisfied with the speculative methods to which social philosophy was then wedded. For more than a century, jurists and political philosophers had based their theories of law and government on such fictions as the state of nature and the social contract; their methods of argument being speculative, their theories differed with the creator's conception of these fictive states; and thus the same postulates might support philosophies which favoured absolutism, oligarchy or plebiscitarian democracy. However these philosophers might disagree in their conclusions, they all regarded society and the state of nature as polar opposites. Society they identified with order, government and law, while the state of nature was identified by the absence of these conditions, and thus of any durable forms of human association above the level of the family. The realities to which this philosophical contrast referred were the observable differences between centralized political systems and the acephalous or stateless communities which were then the subject of reports by missionaries, traders and explorers. To Vico, Montesquieu, Turgot and Hume, these philosophical fictions were inadequate substitutes for the information on simpler peoples which was then becoming available, and which seemed likely to provide a more reliable guide to the condition of man in the state of nature than the speculations of rival philosophical schools. Although some of these exotic societies lacked discernible institutions of government and law, they were evidently durable and self-regulating. Following Montesquieu, Adam Ferguson, John Millar, Lord Kames and others made systematic studies of this ethnographic literature and of the historical records of early Eurasiatic peoples, to isolate such general regularities as an inductive analysis of these data would permit.

In his *Spirit of the Laws*, Montesquieu had tried to formulate universal relations which hold between legal systems and their social and ecological environments. In this inquiry, he employed materials from simple societies with rudimentary political institutions as well as from those which were more organized. In his exposition Montesquieu tried to demonstrate the interdependence of such social institutions as law, religion, economy, with one another and with their ecological framework. Using historical materials, Vico identified a series of phases through which he thought all dynamic societies would necessarily pass, and he also tried to show how legal institutions were moulded by the history of their social context. The Scottish anthropologists sought to combine the approaches of Vico and Montesquieu. In examining the range and variety of human society, they also tried to delimit stages of its development, and to discover how the various parts of society interacted with each other to generate this development. Much of their interest focused on the differences between the societies with centralized political institutions and those acephalous communities which philosophers regarded as forms in a state of nature.

By the end of the eighteenth century, this phase of anthropology had reached its close. Competing theories of social development and causation were in the air. The new discipline had clearly separated from philosophy, its parent, and though retaining an interest in certain problems which were common to both, it employed different methods and data to yield theories of quite different types. For some early anthropologists, intellectual and moral forces determined the rate and course of social development; for others, technological and economic factors were more concrete and pervasive; for some, innate racial capacities regulated cultural development and differentiation.

Thus from the start, anthropology has been identified with the study of human variety and its development; and in government and politics, it was especially concerned with the study of those simpler peoples whose modes of life and organization corresponded most closely to the philosophical conceptions of the state of nature. By studies which range from these most rudimentary societies to include the most complex modern or historical states, anthropologists still seek to isolate the generic features and conditions of social life, to identify its principal forms and varieties, to demonstrate the course of its development. In addition, following the example of Montesquieu, we seek to trace the relations which hold between various aspects of social life, and to determine the influence which differences of habitat, population size, density, or technology exercise in similar or different types of social and cultural organization.

Given these interests, it would seem an essential first task for anthropologists to determine the variety of social and cultural types. However, during the eighteenth and nineteenth centuries there was no tradition of anthropological field study, and the scholars of those days carried out their investigations at home, with the field reports available to them. In constructing their social typologies, they first emphasized differences in modes of livelihood and political organization, and then employed these taxonomies to facilitate theories of social development and evolution. We are still indebted to the evolutionary anthropologists of the late nineteenth century for the gross classifications and developmental schema that we casually employ. Of these evolutionary theorists, Sir Henry Maine and Lewis H. Morgan are of special interest to us here.[1]

Maine was a historical jurist who opposed the doctrines of natural law, and argued that even in simple societies which lacked courts and formal administration, primitive man still knew government and law. To support this thesis, Maine employed the legal concepts of corporations aggregate and sole. He argued that in some societies, corporate groups based on kinship and having jural capacities were the dominant social forms. In societies with chiefs and a centralized administration, corporations sole or offices tended to become prominent. Maine went on to distinguish two great classes of society, one of which was static and archaic, while the other was progressive and modern. To Maine, these two types of societies differed most sharply in the principles which regulated social relations within them. In the static, archaic society, conditions of status prescribed the form and content of social relations; and among these prescriptions, the membership obligations of the corporate kinship groups in which the populations were organized were especially important. By contrast, in modern progressive societies, under the protection of supervisory corporations sole, individuals are free from such restrictions and may regulate their relations at will by contracts based on mutual interest. For ancient Rome, Maine went on to show how the prescriptions of corporate kin groups were replaced by contractual relations, as the lineage lost its jural autonomy to new judicial and executive offices through which the public affairs of the citizens were regulated. In his view, the earliest social groups were familial units headed by patriarchs whose joint decisions also regulated community affairs. Maine offered no formal definitions of government or law, but sought to demonstrate their substance in primitive conditions. He made no effort to identify any single factor as the determinant of social development, and also confined his inquiries to the early patriarchal societies of Indo-European speaking peoples. He there-

1. Maine (1905); Morgan (1875); see Gierke (1960).

fore presented a theory of historical evolution limited to a particular case.

The American anthropologist Lewis Morgan advanced a global theory based on his field work and studies of kinship terminologies. He began by distinguishing two 'plans of government', a 'gentile' plan based on unilineal descent, and a 'political' one based on territorial organization and the transmission of property. In addition, he held that the primordial human aggregates were organized purely on the basis of sex and age, without any clear distinctions of kinship or residence. At this primeval level of social development, both government and 'political' organization are absent, in Morgan's view. Their technology being rudimentary in the extreme, for subsistence these populations followed nomadic routines of hunting and gathering. According to Morgan, their promiscuous mating habits were reflected in kinship terminologies of the Hawaiian type. With the passage of generations, relations of kinship were recognized and descent was traced initially through women. On this basis matrilineal descent groups emerged as durable social units. These matrilineages regulated their interrelations by rules of exogamy, post-marital residence, adoption, feud, burial rites and the like; and it is this type of organization, which is characteristic of segmentary lineage societies lacking central institutions, that Morgan identifies as 'gentile' government. For such aggregates, he reserves the term *societas*, in contradistinction to *civitas*, which he translates as the state, and identifies with 'political' organization. Only when the unit of public organization is a territorial group — village, deme, or ward — does Morgan concede the presence of political organization.

Besides the original promiscuous aggregate from which the matrilineal descent groups emerged, Morgan postulates further changes in kinship institutions which give rise to property-holding patrilineages. These, being localized, are easily absorbed in territorial aggregates, thereby giving rise to the state. Thus Morgan redefined Maine's stateless societies based on kinship and status as pre-political aggregates by developing special notions of government and politics. As the determinant of this evolutionary process, Morgan points to technology and property, the development of which he regards as prerequisite for monogamy and for the localization of kinship groups. Thus he constructed a universal scheme of social evolution based on a hypothetical succession of types of social organization, each of which represented a distinct combination of social, economic and technical traits. Since this evolutionary theory rested on his kinship analysis, the immediate effect of Morgan's work was to concentrate attention on the study of kinship and marriage, at the expense of government and politics. In the furore of kinship controversy, Morgan's scheme of political evolution virtually lapsed from notice, though Engels incorporated it wholesale into the Marxist doctrine. Recently, this aspect of Morgan's work has been the subject of a critical discussion by Isaac Schapera in the light of materials on native societies in South Africa.[2]

Morgan was not the only global evolutionist whose theory required an account of the origin of the state. Herbert Spencer also shared this problem. Spencer identified processes of social growth with the serial compounding of social aggregates. By these means, units would increase in scale and internal complexity as the Spencerian doctrine of evolution required. First, two small autonomous societies would be brought under the rule of a single chief; then this simply compound society would be absorbed into a larger, more heterogeneous unit, generally through conquest; and so the process would continue, until large-scale units with identifiable administrative organization emerged. Thus for Spencer the state originates in the context of conquest and consolidation, and is essential to further evolutionary growth. These views were adopted by Ludwig Gumplowicz and Franz Oppenheimer, who also held that the state originated in conquest, though they made little attempt to define the state except by centralized domination of a territory. This theory was later the subject of a critical study by Robert Lowie, who also took the notion of the state for granted. Lowie argued that 'states' may have emerged from men's societies, such as the Crow Indian military societies, age grades, and the like, without any conquests.[3]

Few of these early theorists had any experience of field research. They generally relied on reports of uneven quality and coverage by travellers and others. Since these accounts were usually incomplete, the scholars concerned to analyse them were unable to see how these societies really worked, and the data encouraged them to speculate about historical connections and evolution. In reaction against such historical researches based on imperfect materials, some anthropologists decided to study contemporary societies as going concerns at first hand. To this new tradition of field work, Bronislaw Malinowski made the greatest contribution. He showed how rewarding it was for the anthropologist to live among the people he was studying, to conduct his researches in the native language, and to participate as fully as possible in the daily life of the people. The materials which Malinowski gathered by these methods in the Trobriand Islands of Melanesia also served to dispel a large number of earlier speculations.[4] In addition, Malinowski and Radcliffe-Brown, who had studied the Andaman Islanders in 1906, between them trained a number of students in these methods, and encouraged them to study the contemporary life of simpler peoples. With some additions and changes of emphasis, these field methods are still a basic resource of social anthropology today. Their reliability is

2. Schapera (1956).
3. Lowie (1926); Apthorpe (1959).
4. Malinowski (1959).

evident from the abundance of significant studies they have yielded.

An important feature of this anthropological approach to field work is its emphasis on the interconnection of social and cultural facts. Whether we use conceptual frameworks based on culture or society, the anthropologist regards the whole round of the people's life as a system of interdependent phases and parts. With this orientation, he is obliged to investigate all the recurrent features of social life, to determine their interrelation and relative autonomy. In this way an investigation of the political organization of a simple society presumes a thorough knowledge of the social ecology, the economy, the people's historical traditions, their values, beliefs and modes of thought, their kinship and local organization, marriage arrangements, forms of property and other social institutions. Though the anthropologist distinguishes these various facets of social life as economic, kinship, ritual, political and ecological systems by reference to such criteria as the mode of livelihood, maintenance of social order, or relations with the unseen, his basic assumption that these various sub-systems together constitute a viable, self-perpetuating form of social life enjoins careful investigation of their interconnections and mutual influences. Yet, although he assumes some interdependence among these elements, the anthropologist can hardly know in advance what form or intensity these relations may take; thus the primary significance of his assumption that the society does form a system of some sort is that it requires him to investigate the elements of social life in a systematic manner.

For this investigation, the social anthropologist employs a number of organizing concepts. Having identified the principal types of social group, he seeks to analyse their inner organizations as structures of status and role. The various positions which constitute these group structures are defined by rights, privileges and obligations, through which they are related to each other to constitute the group. These relations are maintained or changed by a variety of mechanisms, including sanctions and the exercise of power, which the anthropologist seeks to identify and analyse. Such groups are generally identified with particular functions and resources by charters which legitimate their organization and endow their structure and operations with authority. These charters also set the framework of relations between groups of similar and differing type.

Often the anthropologist will find that a single type of grouping discharges many institutional functions which the society requires; for different activities such a group may also be subdivided into smaller units, as Bushman bands are composed of separate households. In such multifunctional groupings, the structure of social relations contains a number of built-in mechanisms for order and control. If two kinsmen are obliged to co-operate in economic and ritual activities, their differences in one sphere tend to be offset by their mutual dependence in another. Sometimes, however, these multiplex relations generate such tensions that their maintenance becomes difficult, and they break down. The anthropologist is interested in these many-stranded relations, to determine the ways in which their various elements support or obstruct one another, and the types of situation in which conflicts develop or dissolve. In this way, he seeks to identify the dynamic conditions which underlie the social order, and to document the forms and principles of social differentiation within as well as between groups.

In studying political organization among simpler peoples with a limited social differentiation, the anthropologist has to make careful distinctions between the political order and other forms and phases of social order. Although these distinctions may only be analytic, they are none the less important. In some societies, political and jural relations are submerged in activities which have quite different bases and purposes; for example, bonds of kinship may regulate relations of property, marriage, collective responsibility, compensation and the like. In this case, the institutions of kinship may embrace the political order and extend beyond it; and the greater the role of kinship, the more the social order depends upon it for its form, span and scope. In similar fashion, ritual beliefs and organization embody a certain order, which may be highly relevant to the analysis of political organization. Such conditions require us to proceed with caution when we distinguish the specifically political aspects of social organization, and I shall try to say something about this later.

By comparative analysis, the anthropologist seeks to clarify his concepts, to develop hypotheses, and to formulate models of social structure and process which may then be tested in field researches of other societies. He seeks also to develop generalizations about social processes which later study may refine and extend. Though traditionally concerned with simple societies, the anthropologist seeks a theory which may apply to all; and for several years, anthropologists have engaged in field studies of complex industrial systems.

In 1940, the first generation of social anthropologists schooled in these methods and orientations by Malinowski and Radcliffe-Brown collaborated in a joint volume (on *African Political Systems*) which marked the start of modern comparative studies of politics and government in anthropology.[5] In reviewing their data on these African polities, Meyer Fortes and Evans-Pritchard, who edited this volume, observed that

three types of political systems can be distinguished. Firstly, there are those very small societies . . . in which even the largest political unit embraces a group of people, all of whom are united to one another by ties of kinship, so that political relations are coterminous with kinship relations, and the political structure and kinship organization are completely fused. Secondly, there are societies in which a lineage structure is the framework of the political system, there being a precise

5. Fortes and Evans-Pritchard (1940*b*); see also Fortes (1945, 1949).

co-ordination between the two, so that they are consistent with each other, though each remains distinct and autonomous in its own sphere. Thirdly, there are societies in which an administrative organization is the framework of the political structure. The numerical and territorial range of a political system would vary according to the type to which it belongs.[6]

In several respects this recent typology reproduces those of Morgan and Durkheim; and its developmental implications are also clear. But there is an important difference in the use to which these models are put. Fortes and Evans-Pritchard have shown us how to investigate the 'stateless' societies, to determine their properties and organization.

The volume just cited assembled field reports of very high quality on the political organization of eight African societies. Five of these societies were territorial chiefdoms, while the remainder lacked chiefs or central agencies of any sort. Within either category there were important variations; but the differences between the categories were overriding. *African Political Systems* was followed by substantial monographs in which the institutional mechanisms on which these acephalous polysegmentary societies depended for social order and cohesion were carefully documented and analysed. In consequence, we now know much more about the conditions which underlie these uncentralized societies than was the case in 1940; and this knowledge may be applicable to the analysis of other multi-centric political systems, such as the network of international relations, the political alignments of international firms, or cleavages within and between the ranks of labour and capital. As this area is theoretically significant I shall discuss some features of acephalous organization later.

One weakness in the analysis of Fortes and Evans-Pritchard was the typology on which their argument hung. This was inadequate even for the data then available. In establishing their trichotomy of African polities, these writers ignored certain African forms of acephalous organization, such as the age-set systems of the Nilo-Hamites and the village societies of Eastern Nigeria. They also ignored numerous cases in which segmentary lineage and state organizations were combined, as for example among the Ashanti, the Bemba or the Yoruba. In the simplest societies, they also tended to over-emphasize kinship at the expense of locality and other ties.

A series of timely papers by Paula Brown, Bernardi, Daryll Forde, and by Evans-Pritchard himself sought to modify and refine this typology.[7] So did a number of monographs. In 1954 John Barnes described the simultaneous processes of fission and expansion in Ngoni conquest states, through which residential segments hived off from the parent body at fairly regular intervals, in response to

6. Fortes and Evans-Pritchard (1940b), pp. 6, 7.
7. Evans-Pritchard (1940a, 1940b, 1948); Bernardi (1952); P. Brown (1951); Forde (1939b, 1950a, 1961, 1962).

internal strains and external opportunities. Here the segmentary units were centralized communities rather than lineages.[8] Two years later Aidan Southall identified the segmentary state as an intermediate political form in which chiefs having identical powers and drawn from a common lineage administered personal domains, though in a loose association which emphasized hierarchical allegiance.[9] Among the Busoga of Uganda, Lloyd Fallers observed three distinctive modes of political authority: clientage, lineage, and Western bureaucratic patterns; and analysed their interrelation.[10] On his observations, he argued that relations of lineage and clientage tended to conflict with one another, and that both these types of alignment were inconsistent with the requisites of bureaucratic organization. He advanced the hypothesis that 'existence in a society of corporate lineages with institutions of the state type makes for strain and instability',[11] and concluded that 'societies with hierarchical centralized political systems incorporate the Western type of civil service structure with less strain and instability than do societies having other types of political system, e.g., segmentary ones'.[12] These generalizations hark back to the typological contrasts drawn by Fortes and Evans-Pritchard but also to Max Weber's theory of authority systems. Being significant and clearly stated, they have been the subject of comparative studies by Audrey Richards, Raymond Apthorpe, and others.[13]

Among the Kachins of Highland Burma, Edmund Leach analysed political instability in terms of conflicting principles and ideologies of rank and chieftaincy on the one hand, and lineage solidarity and egalitarianism on the other.[14] In a number of incisive essays, Max Gluckman has also concentrated on the conditions and functions of conflict in political systems of differing type; and he has argued that under certain conditions, such oppositions may foster political integration by increasing participation.[15]

2.

It will be clear from this summary that the anthropological approach to political studies has been primarily empirical. Such theories as it embraces hardly merit the name. The most inclusive are simply unverifiable evolutionary speculations. To date, anthropologists have made little attempt to clarify their conceptions of the issues under study. Perhaps this has not seemed necessary, because

8. Barnes (1954).
9. Southall (1956).
10. Fallers (1956).
11. ibid., p. 17.
12. ibid., p. 242.
13. Richards (1960); Apthorpe (1959).
14. Leach (1954).
15. Gluckman (1955, 1963).

we have been working with such gross differences as those between centralized and uncentralized societies. Yet even here, our terms reveal some imprecision of thought; we tend to regard acephalous, uncentralized and stateless societies as identical, and to contrast these as a single category with centralized societies or states. Yet it seems clear that many acephalous societies are at least partially centralized; and if eleventh-century France or the Holy Roman Empire of the sixteenth century are representative states, we should not lightly assume that all states are centralized. The simplicity and convenience of this dichotomy has enabled us to ignore the problem of defining centralization.

A similar tendency is evident in anthropological discussions of political organization. This term has many connotations, not all of which are identical. Yet, instead of analysing these notions to clarify their own ideas, anthropologists generally seek to identify political organization by one or two concrete criteria, which seem sufficiently general to apply to all types of society. As we have seen, it is an anthropological credo inherited from the eighteenth century that all societies have political organization, but when anthropologists reserve this term for the societal level, they fail to consider the political organization of units within the society. They differ also in the criteria by which they define the political organization.

Thus Radcliffe-Brown, in his Preface to the book edited by Fortes and Evans-Pritchard, defines political organization as

that aspect of the total organization which is concerned with the control and regulation of the use of physical force . . . A political system . . . involves a set of relations between territorial groups . . . In dealing with political systems, therefore, we are dealing with law on the one hand and with war on the other. But there are certain institutions such as regulated vengeance, which come between the two . . . In seeking to define the political structure in a simple society, we have to look for a territorial community which is united by the rule of law . . . But . . . in some societies such a political community is indeterminate.[16]

However, these notions are circular at base. Radcliffe-Brown's two criteria, 'the organized exercise of coercive authority', and 'the political community' merely serve to define one another. Where there is no machinery for 'the maintenance or establishment of social order within a territorial community by the organized exercise of authority', we should therefore conclude that there is neither a political community nor political organization. But since he regards political organization as a universal feature of social life, Radcliffe-Brown tactfully sets this difficulty aside.

Reacting against this definition of the political community in terms of force, Professor Schapera goes to the other extreme. In his view, political organization is 'that aspect of the total organization which is concerned with the establishment and maintenance of

16. Radcliffe-Brown (1940), pp. xiv-xxiii.

internal co-operation and external independence'. This definition presents us with the problem of delimiting the various mechanisms involved in the 'establishment and maintenance of internal co-operation', since this may take many forms, not all of which are equally relevant to the analysis of political structure. However, on this subject Schapera says that 'we have to study in fact the whole system of the communal leadership, and all the functions (as well as the powers) of the leaders; and in this context such activities as the organization of religious ceremonies or collective hunts or the concentration and redistribution of wealth are as relevant as the administration of justice'.[17] Thus Schapera correctly requires that we undertake a detailed field study of the relations between political and other social institutions; but in place of political analysis, he seems to recommend an ethnographic inventory of all practices that foster internal co-operation, from toilet training to mortuary rites, on the assumption that they are all equally relevant. Thus, starting with the conception of government as one aspect of the social organiz-ation, he assimilates almost all the rest to it. None the less, by confining his emphasis to co-operation, he seems to exclude the study of internal conflicts, instability and structural change, though these are likely to be central to the political process.

However, on either of these definitions, we should have to conclude that many acephalous societies lack political organization, in so far as they contain a number of relatively discrete communities, within or between which there is neither established co-operation, nor procedures for the regulation of force. Acephalous societies having these features include for example the Murngin, Bwamba and the Vugusu. Lucy Mair, in her recent book, also discusses this point in some detail for the Nuer.[18]

Despite their apparent differences, these two definitions really rest on the same criterion; both identify political organization with the rule of law, and neither specifies clearly what this involves. Although they are closely related, it seems preferable to separate the polity and law initially, so that we may examine each on its own terms. I shall try to show how they are related later.

In specifying concrete criteria of political organization, these definitions arbitrarily limit political organization to the level of the society at the same time that they restrict its scope. But since many forms of political organization are concerned neither with the maintenance of co-operation nor with the regulation of force, we still need a definition which is simultaneously applicable to all societies, and to all levels of social organization. On general grounds it seems likely that such a definition should not be too specific. It should not seek to predetermine the objects of political action.

17. Schapera (1956), p. 218.
18. Mair (1962), pp. 46-7, 104.

3.

The common element in such terms as political organization, political action, political system, political unit or process, is the term political. If we ask, to what does this refer, what is its subject matter, only one answer is possible: namely, public affairs, whatever these may be. A political organization is thus the organization which regulates these public affairs. Just how the public is defined and what are its affairs, we can determine empirically. But comparative studies show that publics have certain features. They are enduring units, presumed to be perpetual. They have clear identities, boundaries, and membership; an exclusive body of interests and affairs; and the autonomy, organization and procedures necessary to manage these. Thus, publics differ from categories and other aggregates in their internal organization, their continuity, their positive modes of action, and their self-regulating capacities. Such units are always corporate groups.

In an acephalous society based on localized lineages, each quite distinct and autonomous, the affairs of any one lineage will only concern members of other lineages in specific cases. Thus, while many public affairs of each lineage are purely internal, others involve its relations to units of similar type. Societies organized on such a basis derive their order from the fact that in inter-lineage relations, each collectivity is treated as a single indivisible unit. From this derives the principle of the collective responsibility of lineage members for one another, and from this the tendencies towards feud, collective compensation, ritual pollution and purification of an offender's lineage, collective tenure of a given site, collective interests in the daughters and wives of the lineage, in its cult, etc. Because these lineage corporations are durable and identical in character, the distribution of rights and obligations between them is symmetrical and predictable; and the social structure based on these units has continuity over time as well as uniformity in space. The individual, as Maine observed, is subjected to their corporate regulation; but in return, he derives all his jural and political status from membership in one of these units.

In such a case, the various publics which together constitute the society each represent a distinct unit of internal order; and the total aggregate, being uncentralized, depends for its unity on the replication of identical corporate forms, each characterized by the same properties, requisites and modes of external relation. In this sense, one may correctly describe an acephalous society as exhibiting a common law, even though this notion becomes ambiguous if the constituent lineages engage in feud and hostile relations. However, if we postpone this problem of law for a while, and define government as the regulation of public affairs, then, despite its decentralized character, there is little difficulty in showing that the acephalous society exhibits government, even though it does not exhibit societal co-operation or societal regulation of force.

Let us look a little closer at our model. The lineage group is often defined by a genealogical tradition which lays down its main sub-divisions in terms of ancestry and descent. Each lineage may thus contain a number of segments, and these may be subdivided likewise on similar lines. These segments are defined as separate publics for different issues, and all segments of the same order administer a similar set of affairs for their members. While the affairs reserved to minor segments of a lineage are generally familial, and mainly involve domestic rights, external affairs of the total lineage mobilize its entire membership directly or indirectly, especially if any modi-fication in its relations with other lineages is involved. The distribution of land, the siting of houses, allocation of inheritance rights in widows, farms or crops, domestic order and subsistence — these functions are usually reserved to the segments of lower order. The lineage is also linked through its parts to other lineages in the society by ties of marriage, by the non-lineal kinship of its members, by local contiguity, by ritual alliance, and by traditions of common descent and origin. In some societies, lineages are grouped in phratries or moieties, and subjected to common rules of exogamy; in other societies lineages may be linked by patterns of marriage alliance. Among the Tallensi of Northern Ghana, who were studied by Meyer Fortes, each inclusive lineage is also associated with two sets of other lineages for ritual purposes; for the earth cult it participates in one congregation, for the cult of the external *boyar* it belongs to another. While each of these congregations represents a distinct public, the lineages which constitute it are also distinct publics themselves; and, by virtue of these dispersed ties of ritual alliance, each lineage belongs to a series of societal networks which may provide assistance when needed, or mediators as disputes arise.

A rather different type of organization is found among the Yakö of the Cross River area in South-eastern Nigeria, where every individual belongs to two different lineages. By virtue of descent from his father, he belongs to his father's patrilineage and lives with them in their part of the village. But through his mother he is also a member of her matrilineage, and they will inherit all his movable goods and will demand redress if he suffers injury. He may not marry either his matrilineal or patrilineal kin.

As a youth, the Yakö is initiated into an age-set in his ward of the village and is subject to the discipline which this exercises, independently and on behalf of the senior men of the ward. As he matures and marries he becomes eligible to join one of a number of corporate associations within the ward which exercise jural and ritual powers of various sorts. The ward leaders are senior members of the various patrilineages and matrilineages settled within it. These men form a group known as the *Yakamban*, which advises the ward head, who represents the senior lineage in the unit, and with him they regulate ward affairs. Most members of the *Yakamban* also belong to a number of other associations, which recruit their membership from the various wards of the village. Each of these village associations has its own distinct membership and functions; and some members of each association will also be found in the senior village association, the *Yabot*, which is the highest ritual and executive body of the village.

The various Yakö villages are each quite independent of one another; but all have this mode of organization. Thus, although Yakö society is stateless or acephalous, it is clear that within their villages, which include populations of more than 13,000, they have achieved a fair degree of centralization. The Yakö polity consists of several types of corporate groups, lineages, age-sets, associations of various sorts at the ward and village level, and also the village and its wards, each of which forms a distinct public regulating certain affairs for its members. These Yakö publics each include one or more officials who act as executive agents of the group, and who also represent it in other units. Thus, while Tallensi derive cohesion from the ritual congregations in which lineages are incorporated as units, Yakö rely on the overlapping representation and membership of their lineage males in a hierarchic series of functionally differentiated associations for such societal co-ordination as they achieve.

4.

With these examples, we can explore certain issues of political theory which are of special interest to anthropologists. These issues include centralization, the nature of political units, and law.

I have argued that it is inadequate to define political organization by such specific criteria as the control of force or maintenance of co-operation; instead I have suggested that we should regard action to regulate public affairs as political. Such regulation either involves the formation of new policy, or implements institutionalized procedures. If we ask what are the usual contents of these procedures and policies, to what do they usually refer, we can derive some general answers from the notion of the public given above. Since public affairs are the subject-matter of politics, the properties of the public, their maintenance or modification, will be the normal objects of political activity. These affairs include the maintenance or modification of the unit's autonomy, of its internal procedures or organization, of its corpus of common affairs, and its identity, boundaries, membership and continuity. With reference to these conditions, the public acts as a unit to regulate its internal organization and its external relations. This is equally true whether we are dealing with municipalities, trade unions, professional associations, universities and other modern corporations, or with the lineages, secret societies, age-sets, or village communities of simpler societies. And because this is so, we must recognize that all units at any level of social organization which have the features of the public outlined above will also have political properties and organization, however rudimentary or insignificant these may seem to an outsider. This is so because all social units assumed to be perpetual and identified by distinct autonomies within given spheres which have the organization necessary to manage these affairs, are units with a public character and capacity. As such they are central to the political alignments of the populations inside and around them.

Of necessity these corporate units are based on particular principles, such as ties of descent, seniority, locality, property, ritual, or occupation, and they are thus defined by rules and traditions which delimit their spheres and modes of action and also establish their organization. By reference to these rules and charters the corporation enjoys sufficient authority and autonomy for the management of its affairs. Its internal organization consists in the distribution of this authority, and relations between its subdivisions represent a balance of obligations and rights. Thus one 'important principle by which publics are organized to regulate their common affairs is that of authority, which being rule-bound is not really autonomous. The other regulatory capacity is power. Power is the capacity for effective action, beyond the requirements of rules or in the face of opposition. Within any corporation, whether this is a lineage, a village, an association or a municipal government, internal and external issues repeatedly arise to which the corpus of agreed rules and precedents are not fully applicable. In these situations, divergent opinions and interests set up cleavages within the plurality over the appropriate course of action. Such conflicts express the exercise of power and are generally resolved by this means. Likewise, competitions for office or movements to introduce new rules or to modify old procedures and organization, or actions to maintain or change the unit's network of external relations — these are occasions on which public affairs are generally regulated through contests of power. It is therefore useful to distinguish two different modes of regulatory action. We may regard as administration those actions which express authority — that is, public regulatory actions pre-scribed and bound by rules; and as political, all actions which employ power to pursue courses and goals beyond or against what the rules enjoin. Any public will simultaneously exhibit these political and administrative modes of action, because its framework of rules is at once the source of authority and the subject of change. Thus any public is a unit of political administration; and this means that its form and regulation depend on the interplay of power relations and an authority structure.

Though publics have governmental qualities and organization, this does not mean that they are all sovereign bodies. It is merely necessary that each public should have a distinct body of exclusive common affairs which it regulates autonomously by procedures that involve simultaneous exercise of authority and power.

In Tallensi society the lineages are governmental units of this sort. Each is identified with a particular locality, certain farmlands, property rights, including rights in its members' persons and rights in certain ritual objects and procedures. Each lineage embodies an authority structure by which its various segments are related, and their separate spheres of action are distinguished; each forms a unit within which cleavages of interest and opinion on internal or external issues mobilize opposing parties, which then compete to regulate these common affairs within the framework of the lineage. In segmentary lineages the opposing parties are typically drawn from different segments of the lineage. If the intensity of the political dissension exceeds the carrying capacity of the common authority structure, the lineage may split into two or more distinct and independent units. Until this occurs, its authority structure will contain the recurrent political cleavages within the lineage. Within as well as between states, the same processes can be observed.

While each Tallensi lineage is a governmental unit, relations between lineages which participate jointly in any common wider public are purely political, that is to say, they are not subject to an inclusive authority structure. Where several lineages are settled close together, the local community is often recognized as an inclusive public within which the peaceful settlement of disputes is required and sacralized by ritual. But at the same time, each lineage within it maintains a number of external ties and alliances through which it participates in a number of differing publics with other lineages settled in other localities. In each of these lineage alliances, the participating lineages acquire new rights and new obligations. The new obligations impose some restrictions on the external autonomy of the member lineages, while the new rights provide them with compensating advantages. Such arrangements are not unlike current relations between states in the European Common Market. However, we cannot regard these interlocking networks of lineage alliances as modes of centralization, even though they constitute the political system, as for instance among the Tallensi, primarily because they lack any corresponding authority structure; each lineage remains the centre of its own network, and is in principle free to alter its alliances. The social structure accordingly represents an interlocking series of sets of lateral ties rather than a pyramid.

Among the Yakö, on the other hand, there is an evident hierarchy with regulatory powers. The different levels of this hierarchy differ in the range of the aggregates they span. As we move from the lineage level to that of the ward and the village, we are also moving through a progressive series of functionally differentiated corporations, each of which rests on quite distinct bases and exercises a distinct jurisdiction. The most important regulatory associations at the ward and village level forcibly recruit their members from the various lineage groups. They reserve to themselves the right to reject lineage nominees for membership in favour of those they prefer. Clearly, such action by external bodies interferes with lineage autonomy; but the autonomies thus removed from the lineages are transferred to the associations, in which these lineages jointly exercise new regulatory powers through their representatives; so that the resulting co-ordination of inter-lineage relations is proportionate to the reductions in lineage autonomy.

The Yakö hierarchy of associations and offices is imperfect and incomplete; but, being flexible and highly inclusive, it provides for the adequate representation of lineages and ward associations on the various village societies and councils, so that the affairs of the entire village community are handled smoothly and predictably. In contrast, despite their community restraints and external alliances, Tallensi lineages are rather autarchic. For the most part these external ties impose no positive obligations on the lineages they serve to link. Their content is mainly negative. They prohibit violence, adultery, and other common causes of dispute between the ritual partners. They also provide a machinery for mediation when any of the linked lineages has a dispute with some outsider. However, among Yakö the senior associations can impose positive obligations on lineages because they represent the wider community. Moreover, the most senior associations at the village level indirectly impose positive obligations on lower-ranking village and ward associations on similar grounds.

Thus, by comparing Yakö and Tallensi political organization, we can see how the scope and degree of centralization corresponds with the autonomy vested in one or several linked agencies to co-ordinate the affairs of a given aggregate by imposing positive obligations which simultaneously restrict the autonomy of the corporations that constitute it. The new public is accordingly defined by the span of the co-ordinating agency and by the scope of common affairs which are the subject of its positive regulation. Such autonomy as this agency exercises, it initially enjoys at the expense of other corporate forms. At the minimum, it seems prerequisite for centralization that some agency should have the power to forbid the various units subordinate to it to establish independent alliances or hostilities with foreign bodies. This is the structural precondition for the maintenance of internal peace.

Our Yakö and Tallensi examples may also help us to understand the relations between government and law. Anthropologists have been traditionally torn between two apparently exclusive conceptions of law: that which identifies it with 'social control through the systematic application of the force of a politically organized society'[19] and that which defines law as binding obligations sanctioned by individual reciprocity, mutual dependence, and publicity.[20] Neither of these views adequately represents the essential facts. For example, among the Tallensi, marriages, inheritance and land tenure are normal events regulated by definite rules, the infringement of which gives rise to definite reactions. This is also the case among the Yakö, although the content and sanctions of these rules differ in detail. Both these societies have clear ideas of the difference between legal and illegal practice in these fields. Children born out of wedlock belong to their mother's lineage while those born in wedlock belong to their father's. It is evident that among Yakö and Tallensi, marriage, inheritance, land tenure, and property relations are regulated by bodies of law which although unwritten and unsanctioned by central authorities, are none the less observed and enforced by the political units of these societies. For their formulation and maintenance, such laws depend neither on individual relations and interests, nor on a central organ, but on the jurisdiction of the lineages, to which these affairs directly relate.

When they are localized and exogamous, lineages are simultaneously concerned with the regulation of marriage, inheritance, land and with the persons and property of the members, which constitute the common lineage estate. Being structurally and functionally homologous, each lineage has an identical interest in these respects. Accordingly, all observe and enforce a common body of rules based on their common requirements; and when these rules are infringed, each lineage exercises pressure on the offenders within or outside it to make reparation and restore the rule. Thus in these primitive societies, the rules and procedures of law are corollaries of the corporate organization. Indeed, it is by reference to these jural rights that the autonomy, organization, procedures, affairs, identities and memberships of these various corporations are defined. The authority which these corporations exercise simply expresses the legal validity of their organization.

With royal centralization in Europe during the sixteenth and seventeenth centuries, theories of natural law and the social contract were employed to discredit the legal autonomy and historical priority of these older corporations, so that all should be subordinated to the state. This subordination is now so complete that we find it difficult to see how corporations could provide the framework for substantive and procedural law; but the myth of the state of nature, with its war of all against all, merely asserts the jurists' claim that law could not exist in decentralized societies; it does not substantiate this.

19. Radcliffe-Brown (1952c).
20. Malinowski (1959), p. 55.

5.

In conclusion, it would seem that the anthropological contribution to the study of government is modest, though promising. While we have a reasonable idea of the course of political evolution and a serviceable typology of political organization, both schemes require critical analysis and refinement. Likewise, although we now know how the various types of acephalous society maintain their social order, we need also to re-examine these data critically, and at the same time to re-examine our concepts of political organization and of the significant theoretical issues in political anthropology. On the positive side, we now have a reliable method of field investigation which has already yielded much useful data, and which underlies our main achievements over the past thirty years.

3.

A Structural Approach to Comparative Politics

Comparative politics seeks to discover regularities and variations of political organization by comparative analysis of historical and contemporary systems. Having isolated these regularities and variations, it seeks to determine the factors which underlie them, in order to discover the properties and conditions of polities of varying types. It then seeks to reduce these observations to a series of interconnected propositions applicable to all these systems in both static and changing conditions. Hopefully, one can then inquire how these governmental processes relate to the wider milieus of which they are part.

It would seem that this comparative inquiry may be pursued in various ways that all share the same basic strategy, but differ in emphases and starting-points. Their common strategy is to abstract one aspect of political reality and develop it as a frame of reference. With this variable held constant, inquiries can seek to determine the limits within which other dimensions vary; as the value of the primary variable is changed, the forms and values of the others, separately or together, can also be investigated. Ideally, we should seek to deduce relevant hypotheses from a general body of theory, and then to check and refine them by inductive analyses of historical and ethnographic data. Actual procedures vary.

Initially, we might expect any one of four approaches to be useful in the comparative study of political systems. These four approaches use respectively the dimensions of process, content, function, and form as the bases for their conceptual frameworks. In fact, comparative studies based on process and content face insuperable obstacles due to the enormous variability of political systems. In centralized polities, the institutional processes of government are elaborately differentiated, discrete, and easy to identify. They are often the subject, as well as the source, of a more or less complex and precise body of rules which may require specialists to interpret them. In simpler societies, the corresponding processes are rarely differentiated and discrete. They normally occur within the context of institutional activities with multiple functions, and are often difficult to abstract and segregate for analysis as self-contained processual systems. Before this is possible, we need independent criteria to distinguish the governmental and non-governmental dimensions of these institutional forms.

The substantive approach rests on the category of content. By the content of a governmental system, I mean its specific substantive concerns and resources, whether material, human, or symbolic. As a rule, the more differentiated and complex the governmental processes are, the greater the range and complexity of content. This follows because the content and processes of government vary together. Since both these frameworks are interdependent and derivative, both presuppose independent criteria for identifying government.

The functional approach avoids these limitations. It defines government functionally as all those activities which influence 'the way in which authoritative decisions are formulated and executed for a society'.[1] From this starting-point, various refined conceptual schemes can be developed. As requisites or implications of these decisional processes, David Easton identifies five modes of action as necessary elements of all political systems: legislation, administration, adjudication, the development of demands, and the development of support and solidarity. They may be grouped as input and output requisites of governmental systems. According to Almond, the universally necessary inputs are political socialization and recruitment, interest articulation, interest aggregation, and political communication. As outputs, he states that rule making, rule application, and rule adjudication are all universal.[2] Neither of these categorical schemes specifies foreign relations and defence, which are two very general governmental concerns; nor is it easy to see how these schemes could accommodate political processes in non-societal units.

Such deductive models suffer from certain inexplicit assumptions without which the initial exclusive stress on political functions might be impossible. But despite their universal claims, it remains to be shown that Bushmen, Pygmies, or Eskimos have governments which are functionally homologous with those of the United States and the Soviet Union. Legislation, rule adjudication, and interest articulation are categories appropriate to the discussion of complex, modern polities rather than simple, primitive ones. But the problem which faces the student of comparative politics is to develop a conceptual framework useful and applicable to all. To impute the features and conditions of modern polities to the less differentiated primitive systems is virtually to abandon the central problem of comparative politics.

The functional approach, as usually presented, suffers from a further defect: it assumes a rather special ensemble of structural conditions. When 'authoritative decisions are formulated and executed for a society', this unit must be territorially delimited and politically centralized. The mode of centralization should also endow government with 'more-or-less legitimate physical compulsion'.[3] In

1. Easton (1957), p. 384.
2. Almond (1961).
3. ibid., p. 7.

short, the reality to which the model refers is the modern nation-state.

By such criteria, ethnography shows that the boundaries of many societies are fluctuating and obscure, and that the authoritative status of decisions made in and for them are even more so. Clearly bounded societies with centralized authority systems are perhaps a small minority of the polities with which we have to deal. A structural approach free of these functional presumptions may thus be useful, but only if it can accommodate the full range of political systems and elucidate the principles which underlie their variety. In this essay, I shall only indicate the broad outlines of this approach. I hope to present it more fully in the future.

Government is the regulation of public affairs. This regulation is a set of processes which defines government functionally, and which also identifies its content as the affairs which are regulated, and the resources used to regulate them. It does not seem useful or necessary to begin a comparative study of governmental systems by deductive theories which predicate their minimum universal content, requisites, or features. The critical element in government is its public character. Without a public, there can be neither public affairs nor processes to regulate them. Moreover, while all governments presuppose publics, all publics have governments for the management of their affairs. The nature of these publics is therefore the first object of study.

Publics vary in scale, composition, and character, and it is reasonable to suppose that their common affairs and regulatory arrangements will vary correspondingly. The first task of a structural approach to comparative politics is thus to identify the properties of a public and to indicate the principal varieties and bases of publics.

As I use the term, *public* does not include mobs, crowds, casual assemblies, or mass-communication audiences. It does not refer to such categories as resident aliens, the ill, aged, or unwed, or to those social segments which lack common affairs and organized procedures to regulate them — for example, slaves, some clans, and unenfranchised strata such as the medieval serfs or the *harijans* of India. Such categories are part of one or more publics; they are not separate publics of their own. For example, in an Indian village, a medieval manor, or a slave plantation, members of the disprivileged categories constitute a public only if they form an enduring group having certain common affairs and the organization and autonomy necessary to regulate them; but the existence of such local publics is not in itself sufficient for the strata from which their memberships are drawn to have the status of publics. For this to be the case, these local publics must be organized into a single group coextensive with the stratum. With such organization, we shall expect to find a set of common affairs and procedures to regulate them. The organization is itself an important common affair and a system of institutional procedures.

By a *public*, then, I mean an enduring, presumably perpetual group with determinate boundaries and membership, having an internal organization and a unitary set of external relations, an exclusive body of common affairs, and autonomy and procedures adequate to regulate them.

It will be evident that a public can neither come into being nor maintain its existence without some set of procedures by which it regulates its internal and external affairs. These procedures together form the governmental process of the public. Mobs, crowds, and audiences are not publics, because they lack presumptive continuity, internal organization, common affairs, procedures, and autonomy. For this reason, they also lack the determinate boundaries and membership which are essential for a durable group. While the categories mentioned above are fixed and durable, they also lack the internal organization and procedures which constitute a group.

When groups are constituted so that their continuity, identity, autonomy, organization, and exclusive affairs are not disturbed by the entrance or exit of their individual members, they have the character of a public. The city of Santa Monica shares these properties with the United States, the Roman Catholic Church, Bushman bands, the dominant caste of an Indian village, the Mende *Poro*, an African lineage, a Nahuatl or Slavonic village community, Galla and Kikuyu age-sets, societies among the Crow and Hidatsa Indians, universities, medieval guilds, chartered companies, regiments, and such 'voluntary' associations as the Yoruba *Ogboni*, the Yakö *Ikpungkara*, and the American Medical Association. The units just listed are all publics and all are corporate groups; the governmental process inherent in publics is a feature of all corporate groups.

Corporate groups — Maine's 'corporations aggregate' — are one species of 'perfect' or fully-fledged corporation, the other being the 'corporation sole' exemplified by such offices as the American Presidency, the British Crown, the Papacy, governorships, chieftaincies, and university chancellorships. Corporations sole and corporate groups share the following characteristics, all of which are necessary for 'perfect' or full corporate status: identity, presumed perpetuity, closure and membership, autonomy within a given sphere, exclusive common affairs, set procedures, and organization. The first four of these qualities are formal and primarily external in their reference; they define the unit in relation to its context. The last four conditions are processual and functional, and primarily internal in their reference.

The main differences between corporations sole and corporate groups are structural, though developmental differences are also important. Corporate groups are pluralities to which an unchanging unity is ascribed; viewed externally, each forms '*one person*', as

Fortes characterized the Ashanti matrilineages.[4] This external indivisibility of the corporate group is not merely a jural postulate. It inevitably presumes and involves governmental processes within the group.

In contrast with a corporate group, an office is a unique status having only one incumbent at any given time. None the less, successive holders of a common office are often conceived of and addressed as a group. The present incumbent is merely one link in a chain of indefinite extent, the temporary custodian of all the properties, powers, and privileges which constitute the office. As such, incumbents may legitimately seek to aggrandize their offices at the expense of similar units or of the publics to which these offices relate; but they are not personally authorized to alienate or reduce the rights and powers of the status temporarily entrusted to them. The distinction between the capital of an enterprise and the personalty of its owners is similar to the distinction between the office and its incumbent. It is this distinction that enables us to distinguish offices from other personal statuses most easily.

It is very possible that in social evolution the corporate group preceded the corporation sole. However, once authority is adequately centralized, offices tend to become dominant; and then we often find that offices are instituted in advance of the publics they will regulate or represent, as, for example, when autocrats order the establishment of new towns, settlements, or colonies under officials designated to set up and administer them. There are many instances in which corporate groups and offices emerge and develop in harmony and congruence, and both may often lapse at once as, for example, when a given public is conquered and assimilated.

These developmental relations are merely one aspect of the very variable but fundamental relation between offices and corporate groups. Despite Weber, there are a wide range of corporate groups which lack stable leaders, much less official heads. Others may have senior members whose authority is at best advisory and representative; yet others have a definite council or an official head, or both. In many cases, we have to deal with a public constituted by a number of co-ordinate corporate groups of similar type. The senior members of these groups may form a collegial body to administer the common affairs of the public, with variable powers. Ibo and Indian village communities illustrate this well. In such contexts, where superordinate offices emerge, they often have a primarily sacred symbolic quality, as do the divine kingships of the Ngonde and Shilluk, but lack effective secular control. Between this extreme and an absolute despotism, there are a number of differing arrangements which only a comparative structural analysis may reduce to a single general order.

Different writers stress different features of corporate organi-

4. Fortes (1950).

zation, and sometimes employ these to 'explain' these social forms. Weber, who recognizes the central role of corporate groups in political systems, fails to distinguish them adequately from offices (or 'administrative organs', as he calls them).[5] For Weber, corporate groups are defined by co-ordinated action under leaders who exercise *de facto* powers of command over them. The inadequacy of this view is patent when Barth employs it as the basis for denying to lineages and certain other units the corporate status they normally have, while reserving the term *corporate* for factions of a heterogeneous and contingent character.[6] Maine, on the other hand, stresses the perpetuity of the corporation and its inalienable bundle of rights and obligations, the estate with which it is indentified.[7] For Gierke,[8] Durkheim,[9] and Davis,[10] corporate groups are identified by their common will, collective conscience, and group personality. For Goody, only named groups holding material property in common are corporate.[11]

These definitions all suffer from overemphasis on some elements, and corresponding inattention to others. The common action characteristic of corporate groups rarely embraces the application of violence which both Weber and Barth seem to stress. Mass violence often proceeds independently of corporate groups. Corporate action is typically action to regulate corporate affairs — that is, to exercise and protect corporate rights, to enforce corporate obligations, and to allocate corporate responsibilities and privileges. When a group holds a common estate, this tenure and its exercise inevitably involves corporate action, as does any ritual in which the members or representatives of the group engage as a unit. Even the maintenance of the group's identity and closure entails modes of corporate action, the complexity and implications of which vary with the situation. It is thus quite fallacious to identify corporate action solely with co-ordinated physical movements. A chorus is not a corporate group.

The presumed perpetuity, boundedness, determinate membership, and identity of a corporation, all more or less clearly entail one another, as do its requisite features of autonomy, organization, procedure, and common affairs. It is largely because of this interdependence and circularity among their elements that corporations die so hard; but by the same token, none of these elements alone can constitute or maintain a corporation.

An office persists as a unit even if it is not occupied, providing that the corpus of rights, responsibilities, and powers which constitute it still persists. To modify or eliminate the office, it is

5. Weber (1947), pp. 133-7, 302-5.
6. Barth (1959).
7. Maine (1905), p. 155.
8. Gierke (1960).
9. Durkheim (1947).
10. J.P. Davis (1961), p. 34.
11. Goody (1961), pp. 5, 22-3.

necessary to modify or eliminate its content. Among !Kung bushmen, bands persist as corporate groups even when they have no members or heads;[12] these bands are units holding an inalienable estate of water holes, *veldkos* areas, etc., and constitute the fixed points of !Kung geography and society. The Bushman's world being constituted by corporate bands, the reconstitution of these bands is unavoidable, whenever their dissolution makes this necessary.

As units which are each defined by an exclusive *universitas juris*, corporations provide the frameworks of law and authoritative regulation for the societies that they constitute. The corporate estate includes rights in the persons of its members as well as in material or incorporeal goods. In simpler societies, the bulk of substantive law consists in these systems of corporate right and obligation, and includes the conditions and correlates of membership in corporate groups of differing type. In such societies, adjectival law consists in the usual modes of corporate procedure. To a much greater extent than is commonly realized, this is also the case with modern societies.

The persistence, internal autonomy, and structural uniformity of the corporations which constitute the society ensure corresponding uniformity in its jural rules and their regular application over space and time. As modal units of social process and structure, corporations provide the framework in which the jural aspects of social relations are defined and enforced.

Tribunals are merely functionally specific corporations charged with handling issues of certain kinds. Neither tribunals nor 'the systematic application of the force of politically organized society'[13] are necessary or sufficient for the establishment of law. The law of a primitive society consists in its traditional procedures and modes of corporate action, and is implicit in the traditional rights, obligations, and conditions of corporate membership. In such societies, units which hold the same type of corporate estate are structurally homologous, and are generally articulated in such a way that each depends on the tacit recognition or active support of its fellows to maintain and enjoy its estate. Thus, in these simpler systems, social order consists in the regulation of relations between the constitutive corporations as well as within them.

In societies which lack central political organs, societal boundaries coincide with the maximum range of an identical corporate constitution, on the articulation of which the social order depends. Though the component corporations are all discrete, they are also interdependent. But they may be linked together in a number of different ways, with consequent differences in their social systems. In some cases, functionally distinct corporations may be classified together in purely formal categories, such as moieties, clans, or

12. L. Marshall (1960).
13. Pound (1913), p. 4.

castes. The Kagoro of Northern Nigeria illustrate this.[14] In other cases, corporations which are formally and functionally distinct may form a wider public having certain common interests and affairs. The LoDagaba of Northern Ghana and Upper Volta are an example.[15] In still other cases, corporations are linked individually to one another in a complex series of alliances and associations, with overlapping margins in such a way that they all are related, directly or indirectly, in the same network. Fortes has given us a very detailed analysis of such a system among the Tallensi.[16] However they are articulated in societies which lack central institutions, it is the extensive replication of these corporate forms which defines the unit as a separate system. Institutional uniformities, which include similarities of organization, ideology, and procedure, are quite sufficient to give these acephalous societies systemic unity, even where, as among the Kachins of Burma, competing institutional forms divide the allegiance of their members.[17]

To say that corporations provide the frameworks of primitive law, and that the tribunals of modern societies are also corporate forms, is simply to say that corporations are the central agencies for the regulation of public affairs, being themselves each a separate public or organ, administering certain affairs, and together constituting wider publics or associations of publics for others. By the same token, they are the sources or frameworks of disorder. In some acephalous societies, disorder seems more or less perennial, and consists mainly in strife within and between corporations. Centralization, despite its merits, does not really exclude disorder. In concentrating authority, it simultaneously concentrates the vulnerability of the system. Accordingly, in centralized societies, serious conflicts revolve around the central regulative structures, as, for instance, in secessionist or revolutionary struggles, dynastic or religious wars, and 'rituals of rebellion'.[18] Such conflicts with or for central power normally affect the entire social body. In acephalous societies, on the other hand, conflicts over the regime may proceed in one region without implicating the others.[19] In both the centralized and decentralized systems, the sources and objects of conflict are generally corporate. Careful study of Barth's account of the Swat Pathans shows that this is true for them also, although the aggregates directly contraposed are factions and blocs.[20]

Societal differences in the scale, type, and degree of order and co-ordination, or in the frequency, occasions, and forms of social

14. M.G. Smith (1960*b*).
15. Goody (1957).
16. Fortes (1945).
17. Leach (1954).
18. Gluckman (1954); Introduction to Gluckman (1963).
19. Leach (1954).
20. Barth (1959).

conflict are important data and problems for political science. To analyse them adequately, one must use a comparative structural approach. Briefly, recent work suggests that the quality and modes of order in any social system reflect its corporate constitution — that is, the variety of corporate types which constitute it, their distinctive bases and properties, and the way in which they are related to one another. The variability of political systems which derives from this condition is far more complex and interesting than the traditional dichotomy of centralized and non-centralized systems would suggest. I have already indicated some important typological differences within the category of acephalous societies; equally significant differences within the centralized category are familiar to all. This traditional dichotomy assumes that centralization has a relatively clear meaning, from which a single, inclusive scale may be directly derived. This assumption subsumes a range of problems which require careful study; but in any event, centralization is merely one aspect of political organization, and not necessarily the most revealing.

Given variability in the relations between corporations sole and corporate groups, and in their bases and forms, it seems more useful to distinguish systems according to their structural simplicity or complexity, by reference to the variety of corporate units of differing forms, bases, and functions which they contain, and the principles which serve to articulate them. Patently, such differences in composition imply differences in the relational networks in which these corporations articulate. Such differences in structural composition simultaneously describe the variety of political forms and processes, and explain differences in the scale, order, and co-ordination of polities. This is so because corporate organization provides the framework, content, and procedures for the regulation of public affairs. For this reason, the analysis of corporate structure should be the first task in the case study of a political system and in comparative work.

For many political scientists, the concept of sovereignty is essential as the foundation of governmental order and autonomy. In my view, this notion is best dispensed with. It is a hindrance rather than a help to analysis, an unhappy solution of a very real problem which has been poorly formulated. In a system of sovereign states, no state is sovereign. As etymology shows, the idea of sovereignty derives from the historically antecedent condition of personal dominion such as kingship, and simply generalizes the essential features of this form as an ideology appropriate to legitimate and guide other forms of centralization. The real problem with which the notion of sovereignty deals is the relation between autonomy and co-ordination. As the fundamental myth of the modern nation-state, the concept is undoubtedly important in the study of these states; its historical or analytical usefulness is otherwise very doubtful. It seems best to formulate the problems of simultaneous co-ordination and autonomy in neutral terms.

As units administering exclusive common affairs, corporations presuppose well-defined spheres and levels of autonomy, which are generally no more nor less than the affairs of these units require for their adequate regulation. Where a corporation fully subsumes all the juridical rights of its members so that their corporate identification is exclusive and life-long, the tendencies towards autarchy are generally greatest, the stress on internal autonomy most pronounced, and relations between corporations most brittle. This seems to be the case with certain types of segmentary lineage systems, such as the Tallensi. Yet even in these conditions, and perhaps to cope with them, we usually find institutional bonds of various types such as ritual co-operation, local community, intermarriage, clanship, and kinship which serve to bind the autarchic individual units into a series of wider publics, or a set of dyadic or triadic associations, the members of which belong to several such publics simultaneously. Weber's classification of corporate groups as heteronomous or autonomous, heterocephalous or autocephalous, touches only those aspects of this problem in which he was directly interested.[21] We need also to analyse and compare differing levels, types, and degrees of autonomy and dependence in differing social spheres and situations. From comparative studies of these problems, we may hope to derive precise hypotheses about the conditions and limits of corporate autonomy and articulation in systems of differing composition and span. These hypotheses should also illuminate the conditions and limits of social disorder.

Besides the 'perfect' or fully-fledged corporations, offices and corporate groups, there are 'imperfect' quasi-corporations which must also be studied explicitly. The two main forms here are the corporate category and the commission. A corporate category is a clearly bounded, identifiable, and permanent aggregate which differs from the corporate group in lacking exclusive common affairs, autonomy, procedures adequate for their regulation, and the internal organization which constitutes the group. Viewed externally, acephalous societies may be regarded as corporate categories in their geographical contexts, since each lacks a single inclusive frame of organization. But they are categories of a rather special type, since, as we have seen, their institutional uniformity provides an effective basis for functional unity.

In medieval Europe, serfs formed a corporate category even though on particular manors they may have formed corporate groups. Among the Turkana[22] and Karimojong[23] of East Africa, age-sets are corporate categories since they lack internal organization,

21. Weber (1947), pp. 135-6.
22. P.H. Gulliver (1958).
23. Neville Dyson-Hudson to author, 1963.

exclusive affairs, distinctive procedures, and autonomy. Among the nearby Kipsigi[24] and Nandi[25] clans are categorical units. These clans have names and identifying symbols, a determinate membership recruited by agnatic descent, certain ritual and social prohibitions of which exogamy is most important, and continuity over time; but they lack internal organization, common affairs, procedures and autonomy to regulate them. Though they provide a set of categories into which all members of these societies are distributed, they never function as social groups. Not far to the south, in Ruanda, the subject Hutu caste formed a corporate category not so long ago.[26] This 'caste' had a fixed membership, closure, easy identification, and formed a permanent structural unit in the Tutsi state. Hutu were excluded from the political process, as a category and almost to a man. They lacked any inclusive internal organization, exclusive affairs, autonomy, or procedures to regulate them. Under their Tutsi masters, they held the status of serfs; but when universal suffrage was recently introduced, Hutu enrolled in political parties such as the Parmehutu Aprosoma which succeeded in throwing off the Tutsi yoke and expelling the monarchy.[27] In order to become corporate groups, corporate categories need to develop an effective representative organization, such for instance as may now be emerging among American Negroes. In the American case, this corporate category is seeking to organize itself in order to remove the disprivileges which define it as a category. Some corporate categories are thus merely formal units lacking common functions; others are defined by common disabilities and burdens, though lacking common affairs. Under Islam, the *dhimmi* formed such a category; in India, so do the individual castes. The disabilities and prohibitions which define categories are not always directly political; they include exogamy and ritual taboos.

Commissions differ from offices along lines which recall the differences between corporate categories and corporate groups. Like categories, commissions fall into two main classes: one class includes *ad hoc* and normally discontinuous capacities of a vaguely defined character, having diffuse or specific objects. The other class includes continuing series of indefinite number, the units of which are all defined in such general terms as to appear structurally and functionally equivalent and interchangeable. Familiar examples of the latter class are military commissions, magistracies, professorships, and priesthoods; but the sheiks and *sa'ids* of Islam belong here also. Examples of the first class, in which the powers exercised are unique but discontinuous and ill-defined, include parliamentary commissions of inquiry or other *ad hoc* commissions, and plenipotentiaries

24. Peristiany (1939).
25. Huntingford (1953).
26. Maquet (1960).
27. D'Hertefelt (1960*b*).

commissioned to negotiate special arrangements. In some societies, such as the Eskimo, Bushman, and Nuer, individuals having certain gifts may exercise informal commissions which derive support and authority from public opinion. The Nuer 'bull', prophet and leopard-skin priests are examples.[28] Among the Eskimos, the shaman and the fearless hunter-warrior have similar positions.[29] The persistence of these commissions, despite turnover of personnel and their discontinuous action, is perhaps the best evidence of their importance in these social systems. For their immediate publics, such commissions personalize social values of high relevance and provide agencies for *ad hoc* regulation and guidance of action. In these humble forms, we may perceive the seeds of modern bureaucracy.

Commissions are especially important as regulatory agencies in social movements under charismatic leaders, and during periods of popular unrest. The charismatic leadership is itself merely the supreme directing commission. As occasion requires, the charismatic leader creates new commissions by delegating authority and power to chosen individuals for special tasks. The careers of Gandhi, Muhammad, Hitler, and Shehu Usumanu dan Fodio in Hausaland illustrate this pattern well. So does the organization and development of the various Melanesian 'cargo cults'.[30] But if the commission is to be institutionalized as a unit of permanent administration, its arbitrary character must be replaced by set rules, procedures, and spheres of action; this institutionalization converts the commission into an office in the same way that its organization converts the corporate category into a corporate group. Moreover, in the processes by which corporate categories organize themselves as groups, charismatic leadership and its attached commissions are the critical agencies. The current movement for civil rights among American Negroes illustrates this neatly.

Any given public may include offices, commissions, corporate categories, and corporate groups of differing bases and type. In studying governmental systems, we must therefore begin by identifying publics and analysing their internal constitution as well as their external relationships in these terms. It is entirely a matter of convenience whether we choose to begin with the smallest units and work outwards to the limits of their relational systems, or to proceed in the opposite direction. Given equal thoroughness, the results should be the same in both cases. Any governmental unit is corporate, and any public may include, wholly or in part, a number of such corporations. These units and their interrelations together define the internal order and constitution of the public and its network of external relations. Both in the analysis of particular systems and in comparative work, we should therefore begin by

28. Evans-Pritchard (1940*a*).
29. Birket-Smith (1960); Stefansson (1962).
30. Worsley (1957).

determining the corporate composition of the public under study, by distinguishing its corporate groups, offices, commissions, and categories, and by defining their several properties and features.

As already mentioned, we may find, in some acephalous societies, a series of linked publics with intercalary corporations and overlapping margins. We may also find that a single corporate form, such as the Mende Poro or the Roman Catholic Church, cuts across a number of quite distinct and mutually independent publics. An alternative mode of integration depends on the simultaneous membership of individuals in several distinct corporations of differing constitution, interest and kind. Thus, an adult Yakö[31] simultaneously belongs to a patrilineage, a matrilineage, an age-set in his ward, the ward (which is a distinct corporate group), one or more functionally specific corporate associations at the ward or village level, and the village, which is the widest public. Such patterns of overlapping and dispersed membership may characterize both individuals and corporations equally. The corporations will then participate in several discrete publics, each with its exclusive affairs, autonomy, membership, and procedures, just as the individual participates in several corporations. It is this dispersed, multiple membership which is basic to societal unity, whether or not government is centralized. Even though the inclusive public with a centralized authority system is a corporate group, and a culturally distinct population without this remains a corporate category, functionally both aggregates derive their underlying unities from the same mechanism of cross-cutting memberships, loyalties, and cleavages.

In the structural study of a given political system, we must therefore define its corporate constitution, determine the principles on which these corporate forms are based, and see how they articulate with one another. In comparative study, we seek to determine what differences or uniformities of political process, content, and function correspond with observable differences or uniformities of corporate composition and articulation. For this purpose, we must isolate the structural principles on which the various types of corporations are based in order to determine their requisites and implications, and to assess their congruence or discongruence.

To indicate my meaning, it is sufficient to list the various principles on which corporate groups and categories may be based. These include sex, age, locality, ethnicity, descent, common property interests, ritual and belief, occupation, and 'voluntary' association for diffuse or specific pursuits. Ethnographic data show that we shall rarely find corporate groups which are based exclusively on one of these principles. As a rule, their foundations combine two, three, or more principles, with corresponding complexity and stability in their

31. Forde (1964); Little (1951).

organization. Thus, lineages are recruited and defined by descent, common property interests, and generally co-residence. Besides equivalence in age, age-sets presume sameness of sex and, for effective incorporation, local co-residence. Guilds typically stressed occupation and locality; but they were also united by property interests in common market facilities. In India, caste is incorporated on the principles of descent, ritual, and occupation.

Clearly, differing combinations of these basic structural principles will give rise to corporations of differing type, complexity, and capacity; and these differences will also affect the content, functions, forms, and contextual relations of the units which incorporate them. It follows that differing combinations of these differing corporate forms underlie the observable differences of order and process in political organization. This is the broad hypothesis to which the comparative structural study of political systems leads. It is eminently suited to verification or disproof. By the same token, uniformities in corporate composition and organization between, as well as within, societies should entail virtual identities of political process, content, and form. When, to the various possible forms of corporate group differentiated by the combination of structural principles on which they are based and by the relations to their corporate contexts which these entail, we add the other alternatives of office, commission, and category, themselves variable with respect to the principles which constitute them, we simultaneously itemize the principal elements which give rise to the variety of political forms, and the principles and methods by which we can reasonably hope to reduce them to a single general order. Since corporations are essential regulatory units of variable character, their different combinations encompass the entire range of variability of political systems on the functional, processual, and substantive, as well as on the structural levels.

Within this structural framework, we may also examine the nature of the regulatory process, its constituents, modes, and objectives. The basic elements of regulation are authority and power. Though always interdependent and often combined, they should not be confused. As a regulatory capacity, authority is legitimated and identified by the rules, traditions, and precedents which embody it and which govern its exercise and objects. Power is also regulatory, but is neither fully prescribed nor governed by norms and rules. Whereas authority presumes and expresses normative consensus, power is most evident in conflict and contraposition where dissensus obtains. In systems of public regulation, these conditions of consent and dissent inevitably concur, although they vary in their forms, objects, and proportions. Such systems accordingly depend on the simultaneous exercise and interrelation of the power and authority with which they are identified.

Structural analysis enables us to identify the various contexts in which these values and capacities appear, the forms they may take, the objectives they may pursue, and their typical relations with one another within as well as between corporate units. In a structurally homogeneous system based on replication of a single corporate form, the mode of corporate organization will canalize the authority structure and the issues of conflict. It will simultaneously determine the forms of congruence or incongruence between the separate corporate groups. In a structurally heterogeneous system having a variety of corporate forms, we shall also have to look for congruence or incongruence among corporations of differing types, and for interdependence or competition at the various structural levels. Any corporate group embodies a set of structures and procedures which enjoy authority. By definition, all corporations sole are such units. Within, around, and between corporations we shall expect to find recurrent disagreements over alternative courses of action, the interpretation and application of relevant rules, the allocation of positions, privileges and obligations, etc. These issues recurrently develop within the framework of corporate interests, and are settled by direct or indirect exercise of authority and power.

Few serious students now attempt to reduce political systems to the modality of power alone; but many, under Weber's influence, seek to analyse governments solely in terms of authority. Both alternatives are misleading. Our analysis simultaneously stresses the difference and the interdependence of authority and power. The greater the structural simplicity of a given system, that is, its dependence on replication of a single corporate form, such as the Bushman band or Tallensi lineage, the greater its decentralization and the narrower the range in which authority and power may apply. The greater the heterogeneity of corporate types in a given system, the greater the number of levels on which authority and power are simultaneously requisite and manifest, and the more critical their congruence for the integration of the system as a whole.

4.

The Sociological Framework of Law

My main objective in this essay is to show the relevance of a comparative history of the growth of legal systems and theory to the sociological analysis of jural institutions and legal development, with special reference to Africa.

1.

Law in Africa is only in part African law. It includes also certain elements of European law — Roman-Dutch, Portuguese, Belgian, French, or British — together with their local development in the African context. Further, there is a substantial body of Muslim law, often claiming greater local antiquity than European codes.

Under various accepted definitions of law, indigenous African societies may be said to have lacked law, or at best to have had an exiguous and erratic public law. On such views, before the Muslims or the Europeans overran tribal Africa, its peoples knew only custom instead of law. Sociologists and anthropologists have debated these notions at length, as features of a general difference between 'primitive' and 'modern' law, but as yet have reached no significant conclusions. As a rule, all parties to this debate have assumed that European legal theory and framework provide the appropriate standard, and arguments have accordingly centred on the presence of comparable or substitute patterns or their functional equivalents among primitive peoples. It seems possible, however, that the differences between European and Muslim law in sources, content, procedure, development, and political framework are quite enough to suggest the inadequacy, in a cross-cultural framework, of those European axioms that identify law with centralized administration and its apparatus of tribunals, registries, legislatures or police.

An independent African state has to select the legal framework it will use. To date, the evidence suggests that Europeanized Africans, the political elite in most new African states, may prefer to retain the basic framework of European law inherited from the previous regime, with such modifications, especially in constitutional spheres, as seem immediately appropriate. Likewise, African Muslims prefer to retain traditional Islamic law, with modifications in the penal code and in personal and commercial law appropriate to modern circumstances. Tribesmen, lacking alternatives, continue to observe or modify their tribal laws as the political superstructure permits. One issue that no new African government can indefinitely avoid is the integration of these tribal traditions in the law of the state. Before independence, this problem preoccupied the colonial regimes; and before the establishment of European rule the problem of tribal jurisdiction confronted all Muslim and non-Muslim conquerors who subjugated culturally alien groups. Today, when new elites proclaim the African personality and the African heritage, it is well to recall that African tribal tradition, law, and custom are clearly among the most authentic and fundamental expressions of this heritage. It would be ironic if these new ideologies functioned to legitimate further displacement of tribal law and custom by state rules based on alien models.

There are many sociological frameworks of law. The sociologist examines law in the broad context of social relationships. Thus, for Durkheim, law is the prototype of social fact: the sociological framework in which law arises, develops, and operates is society itself. But law is also a rather special type of social fact because it is regulatory in distinctive ways and spheres. In this sense the sociological framework of law consists in the institutional machinery through which its regulation is manifest. In another sense, we may identify the sociological framework with the milieus of thought in which systems and theories of law develop. As these systems of thought directly influence the operation of law in societies, this framework may be the most fundamental of all.

Until recently, the African continent was almost entirely partitioned into colonies. Thus the most important general experience shared by Africans was the colonial situation. Adriano Moreira has defined this situation rather neatly:

There is a colonial situation whenever one and the same territory is inhabited by ethnical groups of different civilization, the political power being usually exercised entirely by one group under the sign of superiority, and of the restraining influence of its own particular civilization.[1]

After 1945 and mainly in Africa, there was a

sudden awakening of racial groups which had no political power, the emergence of an elite struggling for political supremacy, and, in consequence of all problems of citizenship, of representation, of the communities on an equitable basis, of the right of the people to self-determination.[2]

Moreira identifies this situation as one of social and cultural pluralism. The basic character of colonial pluralities is worth attention:

1. Moreira (1957), p. 496.
2. ibid., p. 498.

By virtue of their cultural and social constitutions, plural societies are only units in a political sense. Each is a political unit simply because it has a single government . . . Democratic governmental forms appropriate to plural societies are usually federal. Autocratic governmental forms reserve the ultimate political functions for one or other of the constituent cultural sections, even where other sections are separated territorially, for instance on reservations, and are allowed some internal autonomy. But some uniformity of laws and government is essential, if the society is to remain a political unit at all. Excluding government and law, the institutional differences which indicate plurality relate to marriage, family, education, property, religion, economic institutions, language and folklore.[3]

In this sense these African states, colonies, and protectorates were all plural societies, and their colonial character directly confronts us with the basic significance of the sociological framework of law.

Such pluralisms generally arise through the domination of one culturally distinctive collectivity by another, and, as Moreira says, in this condition the dominant group is subject only 'to the restraining influence of its own particular civilization', especially its own laws, customs, and morals. The effective limits of political power may determine the boundaries of dominance thus established; they cannot directly account for the form, administrative or legal, which this dominance takes. Whereas in homogeneous societies it is society that constitutes law, in plural societies, such as those of Africa, there is evidence that law may serve to constitute society. Thus law both derives from and may establish society.

In the first instance the social milieu is typically homogeneous, ethnically and culturally, and the basis of society is primarily consensual; in this situation law may express organic institutional relations. In plural societies, on the other hand, the social milieu is heterogeneous in cultural and ethnic constitution and coercive in base, and the law that seeks to constitute it and serves to regulate it is essentially sectional. In the culturally·homogeneous society, the state – that is, the central political institutions – is, like law, a derivative, expressive, and secondary structure. In the evolution of plural units the state pre-exists society, and provides the legal framework within which the new society may or may not emerge. This distinction between society and polity, or, as it is often phrased, between society and the state, combined with the basic differences in structure and function of governmental institutions in these two differing types of society, indicates yet another range of problems that lurk in the general concept of law.

While law is a social fact in homogeneous units, as Durkheim holds, in colonial pluralism it is clearly in some sense pre-societal. In the homogeneous society the state claims legitimacy as the derivative authorized regulatory institution. In the plural society, whether protectorate, colony, or racially exclusive union, the state seeks to

3. M.G. Smith (1957).

constitute a new society within a legal framework which it legitimates independently. Given the profound differences in legal, political, and communal structure between these two social contexts, it would be surprising if they did not also exhibit comparable differences in legal form, substance, and mode of operation, even where the rulers hold to a doctrine of the state which Dicey and others have summarized as the rule of law. For an example, Sir Ernest Barker's statement of this widely accepted doctrine serves well:

> The purpose of the state is . . . a specific purpose of law. Other purposes, so far as they concern or affect this purpose, must necessarily be squared with it . . . but the adjustment is not a matter of discretion, and it is not absolute: it is controlled by the purpose of the state . . . In a word, we see and accept the sovereignty of law — both the law of the constitution which expresses the fundamental purpose on which the state is based, and the ordinary law of the courts, duly made in accordance with the constitution which expresses that purpose in detail.[4]

These are the final self-restraining influences to which Moreira refers.

The significance of the doctrine of the rule of law is no more deniable than its ethnocentrism, which imposes on sociologists the important task of formulating culture-free definitions of law and government which may have comparable significance. But we shall advance nowhere if we adopt the current formulas of European political and legal philosophy without a careful comparative study of their histories. Manifestly, also, the culturally neutral analyses of developments in African law and politics may contribute much to such understanding.

2.

The history of law and government in Islam presents a vivid contrast to European developments, and may accordingly show how inadequate for comparative study are conceptions of law and the state drawn solely from Europe. Attention to Islamic law is also relevant here, for Islam has been one of the major sources of external influence on Africa. Formally and otherwise, European colonial powers in Africa have made various special provisions to accommodate their Muslim populations.

Islamic law developed by paths and mechanisms almost exactly the reverse of those by which European law developed. Until Muhammad's time, the Arabs had lived in tribal communities with temporary confederations, following an unwritten, variable body of custom in which agnation, the jural autonomy of lineages, *lex talionis*, and jural subordination of women were the principal elements.[5] As Allah's Prophet and Messenger, Muhammad simul-

4. Barker (1960), p. lxxxvii.
5. Robertson Smith (1885).

taneously proselytized, organized the Muslim community, and delivered Allah's pronouncements in the Holy Koran. On his death, this book became the unquestioned basis of Islam, regarded both as a faith and as a system of law, divinely ordained to regulate and protect the Faithful. The serious incompleteness in Koranic rules, however, soon became evident through the rapid expansion of Islamic territory by conquest in obedience to the Prophet's command of *jihad* (holy war). Muhammad's death also raised certain central problems of succession, of continuity and co-ordination in Islam, which had important legal and political as well as religious implications.

To rationalize their procedures of adaptation in accordance with the requirements of the Faith, Muslim doctors compiled the Sunna, or traditions of the Prophet and his Companions, and used these as a source of guidance to supplement and interpret the Koran. A number of other principles were also employed to amplify and develop a substantial code of laws from the slim body of given rules. These include exegesis, opinion (*ra'y*), analogy (*qiyās*), and consensus (*ijmā'*) as elements of *fiqh*, or the finding of judgment. Of these, *ra'y* was the first to develop; a tradition of the Caliph Omar II (717-20) authorized its use by a *qādī* where the texts gave no guidance.[6] Analogy, which rests on the interpretation of Sunna or Koranic rules to identify the reason or purpose (*illa*) of particular passages so that it may then be validly extended to other circumstances, sought to limit the scope for independent opinions, to exclude arbitrary judgments, *Fiqh* originally meant finding (the basis) of judgment by knowledge of the Koran and the Sunna, or by analogy. Later, in consequence of the development of formal law, it came to mean knowledge of the practical rules of religion.

Ijmā' was a further important source of law legitimated by the Sunna: 'The Prophet said, "My community will never agree in an error" '. By inference this saying came to mean that the agreement of the community could supplement revealed law by further rules. Opinions would inevitably differ, as the Prophet, according to tradition, had anticipated: 'The Prophet said: "Difference of opinion is a gift of Allah" '. These two sayings of the Prophet 'were destined to explain the variety of legal schools and also the origin of *ijmā'* '.[7]

Opinions initially varied about the membership and the location of the community whose consensus was relevant as a further source of law, and also about the legal status of minority views. Eventually, the *'ulamā'*, or body of devout and learned Muslims, was identified as the relevant group. On this basis jurists and doctors sought to develop a law consistent with Koranic directions and adequate for daily use.

6. R. Levy (1957), p. 165. For a fundamental study of the part these elements played in the growth of Muslim law, see Schacht (1950).

7. Lammens (1926), p. 104. See also von Grunebaum (1953), pp. 149-52; Schacht (1950), pp. 82-97. I should like to stress that the nature and role of *ijmā'* in Muslim law are matters on which specialists may differ.

General agreement obtained about the need to restrict the scope for arbitrary opinions (*ra'y*) by means of precise legal rules. As each successive school of law emerged, the scope for *ra'y* decreased. Opinions differed among the founders of these schools about the admissibility of analogy as a source of law, and about other details of substance. The founders of the four orthodox rites or legal schools — Abu Hanifa, Malik b. Anas, Ash-Shaf'i and Ahmad b. Hanbal — all owed their authority and legitimacy to the doctrine of *ijtihad*, by which the right of the most learned to initiate new interpretations of Sunna or Koranic texts, independent of previous exegesis or traditional glosses, was admitted. The doctrine of *ihtilaf*, or divergence of opinion, itself served to legitimate the division of Islam among the followers of these four jurists.

This sketch of early Islamic legal development focuses on sources of law internal to the law itself. Along with the Sunna and the Koran, from which their legitimacy derives, opinion, analogy, interpretation, *ihtilaf*, and *ijmā'* are the principles that constitute the law (*shar'*, *sharī'a*). Two other sources of law, political and customary practice, remained outside this logical framework. Islamic expansion did not await the development of legal codes; neither were the political problems of succession and administrative continuity which followed Muhammad's death resolved by earlier directives from Allah. *Ad hoc* adaptations to these new situations which were simultaneously consistent with Islam and appropriate to the circumstances were the best the Faithful could do. Later generations in unforeseen circumstances likewise sought the most advantageous accommodations consistent with their Faith and its obligations. The alternatives open to believers in these conditions were strictly limited. If Islam was to prevail politically and socially, as the Prophet had enjoined, it was necessary for Muslims to allocate substantial discretionary powers to their ruler the caliph, his official, or the local chief in his capacity as *imām* or head of their community. From this developed the doctrine of *siyāsa*, which empowered rulers to exercise discretion corresponding to their responsibilities for the maintenance and spread of Islam. In theory, the ruler should be a *mujtahid*, which means that in the absence of qualified legal advice he must be capable of finding the appropriate solution in keeping with accepted principles and precedents. In effect, the *siyāsa*, or political jurisdiction, guided by reasons of state, could supersede, supplement, or, on occasion, abrogate the *sharī'a* with a legitimacy that varied with the *'ulamā'*'s consensus or the force of circumstances.[8] As the Koran enjoins obedience to the ruler,[9] however, this discretionary power could also claim the ultimate legitimacy of Koranic sanction, even when it directly contradicted the *sharī'a*.

This basic ambiguity in the relation of *sharī'a* and *siyāsa*, code and

8. R. Levy (1957), pp. 259-61.
9. Koran 4:62 (cited in von Grunebaum (1953), p. 157).

discretion, has always exercised a profound influence on legal administration in Islam. Even under the early caliphates, 'the *qāḍī's* jurisdiction was handed over to the executive arm of the government to be decided by the vizier, or the governor, who presided over the so-called *mazālim* [lit., wrongs] court',[10] which exercised a jurisdiction in some ways similar to the French *droit administratif*. Gustave von Grunebaum holds that 'this innovation . . . fatally wounds the idea of uniform administration of divinely ordained justice among the Muslims'.[11]

A religious obligation which no Muslim ruler should disregard requires that he establish or maintain a *qāḍī* court to administer the *shar'*. In the Western Sudan, one of the grounds on which Fulani Muslims justified their *jihad* of 1804-10 was the absence of such courts in the Muslim Hausa states they overran.[12] But the functional significance of these *qāḍī* courts varies with their number, distribution, and independence of the executive *siyāsa*. No rule of religion clearly regulates the distribution of such courts in terms of area or population. One *qāḍī* court seems both essential and formally sufficient for qualification as a Muslim state, but it may have little work if the court of the *nazr al-mazālim* is very active.

One implication of this situation is the recognition of non-Muslim practice or custom (*'urf, 'ada*) as valid in regulating social relations. Another implication is that deviant practices which arise may also be recognized among Muslims as valid tradition (*'urf*). For example, in Northern Nigeria it is now accepted as local custom that issues involving claims in land should be reserved for the ruler's courts or handled by executive officials.[13] This executive jurisdiction over suits involving land persisted after the Fulani *jihad* which expressly sought to enforce Islamic observance.

The simple absence of an effective administration of the *sharī'a* through *qāḍī* courts, itself in part a correlate of the *siyāsa* power to create and maintain or quietly to ignore such courts, suffices to perpetuate adherence to old customs and to promote the recognition of new ones as further indirect sources of law. Levy points out that this position was held even during the Prophet's lifetime: 'The Koran declares that no Muslim under penalty of everlasting torment in Hell may slay another who is innocent of offence. Yet to this day the exaction of blood-revenge remains an important part of tribal life.' Further:

Where family life is concerned, in marriage, divorce and the distribution of inheritance, the provisions of the *shar'* would appear to be very widely neglected . . . There have not been lacking attempts to regard *'urf* as one of the roots of the *fiqh*, but excepting the works of the early Sunni *mujtahids*, the

10. von Grunebaum (1953), pp. 163-4.
11. ibid., p. 164.
12. Hiskett (1960).
13. Cole (1948), pp. 32-41, 65, 69, 74-82.

customary laws have generally gone unrecorded by the legists. Yet they have not gone unrecognized, for by some *faqihs* they were preferred to laws derived by means of *qiyās*, and where local influences have been strong, custom has frequently been held to be decisive.[14]

Thus, although various customs have been integrated in the law by special devices, the total body of custom as such has not been integrated, perhaps because such integration would formally abrogate the *sharī'a* in many areas. The integration of specific customs is more readily achieved because Muslim law is a deontology, a series of moral injunctions, rather than a logically systematized body of law, although the Mālikite elaboration of the sacred law comes perhaps closest to a system owing to its concentration on the *furu*, that is, the substantive regulation of detail. From the earliest times, elements from *'urf* entered the *sharī'a* through *ijmā'* and judicial decision.

In its own theory, then, Islam is a theocracy, based on and regulated by a divinely revealed law, the *sharī'a*, which is developed by *fiqh* on the foundations of the Sunna and the Koran. In practice, the *sharī'a* has various sources and an application that varies inversely with the range of *siyāsa* and *'urf*. Under these conditions Muslims stress the diacritical significance of certain symbolic, formal acts, such as Ramadan, pilgrimage, or the daily prayers, by which adherence to Islam is expressed. The *sharī'a* as an ideal system of law is dependent for its realization on secular pragmatic considerations, as well as on historic political precedents. Thus Muslim law as applied represents a system based on revelation, rules of interpretation, precedent, and consensus, as well as on custom and reasons of state expediency. The basic religious premise and goal set certain limits to the variability this mixture of elements might otherwise exhibit. The Sunnite world formally subdivides among the followers of the.four orthodox legal schools, West Africa being mainly of Mālikite persuasion. In practice, legal recognition of *'urf* considerably increases the variety of substantive laws, whereas *siyāsa* introduces comparable variations in procedure. Political fragmentation of the Muslims further enhances this diversity. The overriding religious obligation of rulers to maintain and expand Islam serves to legitimate expedient deviations. In consequence, local differences in political and legal administration are quite as impressive as Muslim continuities. Moreover, much of the operative law, both *'urf* and *siyāsa*, remains unwritten, applied by Muslim courts but forming no part of *sharī'a*. The theory of Islam as a theocratic civilization, regulated by God's revealed law, accordingly remains unaffected by these contrary, secular developments.

3.

Legal theory and institutions in Europe developed on lines sharply

14. R. Levy (1957), pp. 243, 244, 248.

different from those in Islam. From Rome to the present, European law has had a secular base and orientation even where formal structure or theory was absent. As we shall see, such qualities are not easily integrated with the requirements of theocracy.

Greece did not produce a theory of law before Zeno, mainly, it seems, because of the character of the *polis*. Cities varied widely in their political constitutions, but in the typical city the assembly of notables which decided policy also decided important legal issues, and no clear distinction between the two was consistently maintained. In effect, Greek thinkers directed their attention to the requisites of the desirable *polis*, that is, to social and political philosophy, rather than to the theory or analysis of law. In such conditions, legislation and jurisprudence are equally inhibited. Moral, political, and religious issues tend to invest the judgment of critical cases of law.[15] None the less, the seeds of a future theory of law are to be found in Aristotle's casual references to natural law as both general and inherent in human nature, in contrast with particular positive rules.[16] With the decline of Hellas, Stoics developed the notion of natural law both as empirical truth and as normative ideal.

Rome lacked speculative philosophers, and produced little literature of a theoretical sort. Instead, from an early separation of judicial and political functions, the Romans gradually developed a refined and inclusive system of secular law, backed by a technical jurisprudence directed towards the clarification of precedents, legal conceptions, and the like. The nearest approaches to a formal theory of law in these Roman writings centre on discussions of natural law and of the imperium or sovereign power. As Roman jurists and praetors developed the *jus gentium* to supplement the ancient civil law, they identified the idea of natural law with this emerging law of nations and used it to rationalize innovations of procedure and substantive law. Such jurisconsults as Gaius, however, undertook no formal discussion of the notion of natural law. In their *responsa* (as in the *responsa* of the rabbis and the *fatāwī* of the Muslim legists) they simply gave their opinions on specific issues of law put to them, initially by praetors, and later by the emperors, citing appropriate precedents, distinctions, rules, and reasons for their conclusions. The results were valuable manuals of a rational, technical kind suitable for practising lawyers, but devoid of general theoretical content. In due course codification followed, to eliminate conflicting *responsa* and reduce the corpus to an authoritative order. It was at this point that the nature of imperium, the source of authority for this finished code, emerged as a theoretical problem. Under the republic, the nature and the locus of imperium had, perhaps deliberately, remained obscure, the relative powers of senate, *populus*, and tribunes varying within certain ill-defined limits which constitutional

15. Weber (1960), pp. 168-72.
16. Aristotle, *Ethics* 1134*b*, 18-21; *Rhetoric* 1373*b*, 4.

history, unwritten traditions, and the political situation sanctioned. Under the principate and the early emperors these ambiguities persisted, though in a differing form. Justinian, in the preface to his *Institutes*, first sought to define and rationalize the imperium, and did so on logically inconsistent grounds, claiming the sovereign power simultaneously as the ruler appointed by God, and also in accordance with secular constitutional practice. In his code, then, the source of law is imperium or sovereignty, but the source and the legitimacy of this sovereign power remain obscure.

A formal theory of law in Europe derives from the competitions of church and state during and after the twelfth century. In outline this struggle had long been foreshadowed. Even before Justinian based his claims to imperium on divine appointment as well as on secular practice, in the politically insecure West, Augustine had stated the superior claims of church to state and the incompatibility between the laws of human society and those of the City of God. With the rise of the Holy Roman Empire and the political dominance of the Western church under and after Gregory VII, relations between church and state, and between divine and secular law, became problematic. Implementation of Augustine's ideals seemed quite possible for the popes. Feudal Europe was at this time a patchwork of loosely connected jurisdictions. The Holy Roman Empire itself was an *ad hoc* assemblage of scattered principalities, often held by the same individual under quite different titles, and typically distinguished by differences of law and jurisdiction. Of contemporary systems, canon law was superior in its rational structure, and appeared likely to develop the only universally applicable law. In between estate-stratified feudal jurisdictions, during these centuries, the law merchant gradually emerged as an applicable autonomous code based on elements of old Roman law, supplemented or modified as conditions required. In Britain there was the further peculiarity of an evolving royal law, relatively centralized, and superior to that of the courts baron and leet in range and scope as well as in structure.[17]

Papal dominance produced its own crop of problems, initially in papal control of political appointments, but also in the relations between canon and secular law. Aquinas, for instance, sought to harmonize the notions of Aristotle and Augustine with the realities of the early thirteenth century. He proposed a classification of law into four species: divine law, most nearly represented by ecclesiastical law; positive law, enforced in the courts of princes whose authority derived principally from God; the *lex aeterna*, or divine purpose immanent in all creatures; and natural law, identified with man's rational faculty as applied to the understanding of divine rules and purposes. St. Thomas supplemented this hierarchy of law with injunctions requiring Christians to fulfil the obligations of their

17. Hanbury (1944), chs. 2-4.

social status, and appealed to the feudal nobility to practice *noblesse oblige*.[18] Thus Aquinas ultimately sanctioned the heterogeneity of feudal jurisdictions while seeking to subordinate them to the higher, divinely sanctioned jurisdiction of the church.

This papal theory of law was challenged sharply by Marsilius and Dante, who drew on the studies of Roman law carried out at Bologna. Marsilius bluntly denied the legitimacy of papal claims to the religious leadership of Christendom, recommended a democratic collegial system of government for both church and state, and advanced a utilitarian theory of reason and natural law. Dante preferred a secular autocracy to that of the church, and harked back to Byzantium and the Antonines.[19] This competition between secular and theocratic ideologies and interests accordingly focused attention on the problem of the nature and functions of law, especially since both theses drew their inspiration from common sources, the Roman codices and late classical doctrine of natural law. Both these schools of opinion were also disturbed at the legal chaos of late feudalism, and sought to replace it by a uniform and universally applicable system, in one instance with secular base and rational orientation, in the other with a theocratic order. In this period the Holy Roman emperors began to refer legal cases to jurists trained in civilian (Roman) law in order to promote some uniformity of legal administration within their diverse territories.[20] Other monarchs followed suit. In consequence, the Roman civil code came to serve both as a reservoir from which positive law could be borrowed and adapted for current application, and as the model from which systems of natural law could be developed. The civilians whose technical knowledge facilitated this process rationalized their activities by doctrines of natural law which inevitably drew their attention to problems of jurisdiction and its sources, and thus to the theory of society, government, and law. Their position as juris-consults of the monarch further encouraged these thinkers to formulate their problems on secular lines, favourable to the rulers' claims.

It was in this context that the theories of social contract were developed to provide a logical basis for the secular theories of state and law necessary to legitimate a structure of centralized administration.[21] Grotius and Hobbes are admirable examples of these dual concerns, the development of a social philosophy appropriate to centralized administration and of a rational universally applicable code. To institute this rational legal structure, political centralization and the elimination of feudal jurisdictions were both prerequisite. The competing theories of natural law and social contract which

18. Thomas Aquinas, cited in Bierstedt (1959), pp. 52-7.
19. Bierstedt (1959), pp. 60-76.
20. Rheinstein (1954), pp. 274-5; Barker (1960), pp. xxxix-xlii.
21. Barker (1960, 1947).

advanced solutions to these questions were thus no less significant for men of the sixteenth to the eighteenth centuries than theories of democracy or communism may be for us today. The first direct political expressions of this movement took place during the Thirty Years' War, after which secularization and centralization proceeded apace, and absolute monarchies replaced feudalism in most of Europe, their ideologies and legal systems alike being shaped by doctrines of natural law and social contract. As Weber has shown, Britain escaped the legal reforms linked with this development, owing partly to an earlier centralization and partly to the presence of a well-entrenched professional group with vested interests in the maintenance of common law.[22]

A pivotal element in these theories of natural law and social contract is imperium or sovereignty. As legal unity and uniform administration presume an imperium, these two doctrines reinforced each other and also supported centralization. In Rome, legal unity and centralization had obtained without any formal theory of imperium. In the modern Europe emerging from theocracy and feudalism, an explicit theory was indispensable, as well to legitimate absolutism as to determine the most suitable form of political reorganization. Theorists differed. Grotius, though advocating the sovereign power of the monarch, derived such power from the people, with consequent ambiguities about the final locus of imperium.[23] Althusius advocated a federal type of structure based on the historical priority of lesser corporations to the state they composed. This federalist view denied an unrestricted absolute sovereignty to the ruler, whose role and powers were thus defined as in essence representative.[24] The practical difficulty with this thesis is that it implied the preservation of the historical feudatories as modal units of political and legal administration, thereby obstructing the desired growth of central power. Hobbes, seeking to cut this Gordian knot, in his theory derived social unity entirely from the prior overriding power of a central absolute ruler. In this view the imperium and the system of law were virtually identified, and the legal validity of any corporations not explicitly created by or based upon concessions by the state was denied.[25] With the triumph of these ideas, the essentials of the modern theory of the law and the state were complete.

Later reactions against monocratic centralization took the form of a doctrine of natural rights, itself clearly derivative from earlier natural law. In Britain, Locke employed this notion to advocate the sovereignty of Parliament. In America these 'inalienable rights of man' helped to dissolve the British connection; in France they helped

22. Rheinstein (1954), p. 275.
23. Gierke (1960), pp. 45-7, 77-9.
24. ibid., pp. 70-6.
25. Hobbes, *Leviathan* (1651), chs. 13-15, 17-30. See also Peters (1956), pp. 190-239.

to overthrow the monarchy. In neither revolution do we find successful movements towards decentralization. In both instances arguments centre upon the locus and the exercise of imperium, but its indispensability for law and the state remains unquestioned. These three notions — sovereignty, law, and the state — once related in this way, may thereafter have seemed to lawyers and political philosophers alike almost inseparable. Each presumes and expresses the others.

4.

These historical developments furnish the essential background for evaluating the modern European theory of law. After movements for the introduction of civil law in Britain and Blackstone's defence of custom and common law, British legal reformers such as Bentham and Austin were driven to examine the relations of custom and law, questions of significance to continental jurists only where custom competed with civil law. Thus the search for a general theory of law developed in Britain and America, in countries committed to common law as well as to a central imperium. The apparent logical indispensability of the central imperium for the existence of law to these theorists is striking, given the history and composition of Anglo-Saxon common law.

Thus Austin defined law in clearly Hobbesian terms as the commands of a sovereign which his subjects must obey. This Austinian emphasis on sovereignty and centralization persists despite other modifications in the writings of Salmond, Holmes, Pound and Cardozo. It represents the received tradition and theory of law in Europe and the Anglo-Saxon world, one that sociologists and anthropologists have borrowed and applied or debated without adequate scrutiny of its historical basis.

For Salmond, 'all law, however made, is recognized by the Courts, and no rules are recognized by the Courts which are not rules of law'.[26] For Holmes, law is simply 'the prophecies of what the Courts will do in fact'.[27] For Cardozo, law is 'a principle or rule of conduct so established as to justify a prediction with reasonable certainty that it will be enforced by the Courts if its authority is challenged'.[28] In place of Austin's sovereign, these views identify law solely by reference to courts, without considering legislation or other processes by which courts are constituted and maintained, but denying the possibility of law where courts are absent. Notably all these definitions share Austin's preoccupation with a centralized imperium, although, unlike Austin, later writers presume the imperium without direct mention. Like Austin also, these later definitions

26. Salmond (1947), p. 60.
27. Wendell Holmes (1897), cited in Allen (1961), p. 42.
28. Cardozo (1924), p. 52.

focus on substantive rules, the form of legal procedure and machinery of administration being assumed as essential for the existence of law.

Long ago, Sir Henry Maine, defending common law against advocates of codification, the derivative of natural-law theory, questioned the relevance of imperium for the existence and recognition of law: 'It is certain that in the infancy of mankind, no sort of legislature, nor even a distinct author of law, was contemplated or conceived of.' In such states of social development, says Maine, 'law has scarcely reached the footing of custom: it is rather a habit'.[29] In Allen's words, however,

to call these legal rules is something of an anachronism, for in many cases they are equally rules of religion and morality, which, at this early stage, have not become distinguished from law; but they are 'legal' in the sense which is nowadays attached to that term, inasmuch as they are binding and obligatory rules of conduct (not merely of faith and conviction), and that the breach of them is a breach of positive duty. Austin denies them the force of law until they have been expressly recognized by the sovereign.[30]

Holmes, Cardozo, and Salmond agree that these rules are legal only when courts exist to enforce them.

Anthropologists and sociologists have tended to adopt one or other of these two opposing views, without adequate attention to their place in the historical development of European legal and political theory. Malinowski aligned himself on the side of Maine, while Radcliffe-Brown adopted Roscoe Pound's definition of law as 'social control through the systematic application of the force of politically organized society',[31] and on this basis concluded that many primitive societies lacked law because they lacked 'political organization'. In his classification of sanctions, only those 'imposed by a constituted authority, military, political, or ecclesiastical', rank as legal.[32] Here, also following Pound, Radcliffe-Brown assumes a particular type of machinery and procedure as a precondition of law. In both writers the underlying assumption is that of the modern state, defined by MacIver, for instance, as 'an association which, acting through law as promulgated by a government endowed to this end with coercive power, maintains within a territorially demarcated community the universal external conditions of social order'.[33]

The retreat from Austin's position that we have observed in the views of Cardozo and Holmes is continued by Pound. Whereas Cardozo, Holmes, and Salmond replace Austin's ruler by the courts, Pound replaces the courts by the 'systematic application of force', a

29. Maine (1905), p. 6.
30. Allen (1961), pp. 66-7.
31. Radcliffe-Brown (1952c), quoting Pound (1913, 1959). See also E.A. Hoebel (1962).
32. Radcliffe-Brown (1952a), in Radcliffe-Brown (1952d), p. 208.
33. MacIver (1926), p. 22.

criterion that led Radcliffe-Brown to wonder whether feud is law or war, while denying that obligatory compensation or indemnification was legal.

The opposed view is presented in its most extreme form by Sidney Hartland, who asserts that the law of savage societies consists in the totality of tribal custom.[34] 'The core of legislation is a series of taboos . . . an atmosphere of terror is sufficient to prevent a breach of custom . . . the savage is . . . bound in the chains of an immemorial tradition . . . These fetters are accepted by him as a matter of course; he never seeks to break forth.'[35] In this way, Maine's 'legal habits' are made to include all tribal culture, but since in this view primitive man is the willing automatic slave of tradition, there can be neither lawlessness nor law.

It is clear that the problem that confronts writers with both these differing views is in essence the problem that social contract theorists sought to resolve: what is the logical relation of the state, society, and their components to one another? And what are the minimum reciprocal relations of law and polity? I have already suggested how the doctrine of the necessary priority of sovereignty came to seem historically indispensable in modern Europe for the movement from theocracy and feudalism towards a secular centralized state. If my interpretation is correct, then we should expect that these rather special historical circumstances and interests would produce equally special theories of law, society, and the state. In so far as sociologists and anthropologists have adopted this special frame of theory, it furnishes the decisive element in the sociological framework of law, for it guides their hypotheses, research, and analysis on lines consistent with its own axioms and equations.

For a neutral comparative sociology, these European developments and definitions have no superior claim to furnish general categories or guidance over comparable developments in other cultures, such as Islam. In fact, the inadequacy of a framework preoccupied with the problem of political centralization and indivisible sovereignty or its opposite is readily apparent from the history of Islam. This civilization owed its religious and political impetus and the territorial basis of its establishment to central sovereign direction. It persisted despite dispersal of sovereignty as a unit with a common basic law. This law itself has positive validity, even though it incorporates unwritten customs, both ancient and modern, and applies in courts authorized by religion, in strictly executive courts, or informally and by various means. I am therefore suggesting, first, that the traditional preoccupation of Western sociologists with legal uniformity and centralized administration — 'the systematic application of the force of politically organized society' — is intelligible only in terms of criteria drawn from Western political and legal

34. Hartland (1924), p. 138.
35. ibid., pp. 8, 214.

development; and, secondly, that these criteria are inadequate as a basis or sociological framework for the comparative study of law. Indeed, some inadequacies of this special viewpoint are well known. International law obtains even without 'machinery for enforcement', and perhaps precisely because societies are politically organized. In Celtic Ireland, Brehon law flourished without courts, without central authority, and without any enforcement machinery, even after conversion of the Irish to Christianity had removed its original ritual sanctions.[36] In Sweden, the law delivered by *lagmen* likewise took effect without direct sanctions.[37] In Anglo-Saxon law as well as in Islamic law, where custom enjoys legal status with judicial precedent and legislation, further difficulties arise.[38]

The adherence of many British sociologists to a theory of law which is essentially derived from Hobbes and Grotius presents a problem of some interest, especially because it seems that pre-occupation with the problems of law, its nature and place in society, has been confined mainly to scholars who live under common law systems rather than codes, and also because in essence the theory they espouse is at odds with common law. Durkheim's role in promoting this viewpoint may be decisive. He restated Maine's evolutionary movement from societies based on kinship and regulated by customary status to those based on territory and regulated by legal contract in terms of a movement from extreme decentralization and mechanical solidarity towards centralization and organic solidarity. According to Durkheim, only a repressive public law, such as Radcliffe-Brown claimed among Kikuyu and Akamba, obtains in the earlier phase, whereas the latter exhibits restitutive private law administered by tribunals.[39] The crucial criterion of law advanced by Durkheim and Radcliffe-Brown is thus the repressive sanction backed by collective force. A moment's thought will show that this sanction might as easily characterize lawlessness.

Durkheim's difficulty may have been cultural. As a Frenchman, he lived in a climate of thought structured by doctrines of natural rights and natural law and by the Code Napoléon, the crowning triumph of the movement for legal rationalism, and the prototype of other modern codes. He could not therefore recognize the independent jural significance of corporations, other than those created or formally acknowledged by an evident state; in consequence, he could not initially discern their evolutionary and structural significance as units of jural regulation. Later Durkheim was to change his view, and to advocate the establishment of occupational corporations, intermediary between individual and state, on historical and functional grounds.[40] But the difficulties that invest his earlier treatment of law

36. Maine (1875).
37. Vinogradoff (1959), p. 119.
38. ibid., ch. vi; Allen (1961), pp. 64-152.
39. Durkheim (1947).
40. Durkheim (1957); (1959), ch. 8.

persist in Radcliffe-Brown's emphasis on 'constituted authority, political, military, or ecclesiastical', as the agent disposing of legal sanctions. Radcliffe-Brown makes no attempt to elucidate the constitution of authority. The attempt might have led directly to a formal theory of corporations.

In developing the ideology appropriate to institute and guide and legitimate the modern bureaucratically centralized state, with its unified form of legal administration, political philosophers and lawyers alike had logically to exclude recognition of independent or antecedent corporations; hence arose certain peculiarities of social-contract theory. By these means they denied the legal existence of corporations, save those derived from the imperium. Any other course might simply have permitted the perpetuation of feudal elements such as fiefs or guilds, which it was necessary to eliminate in law and state if the requisite centralization and uniformity were to obtain. In Britain, Maine reopened this subject by directing attention to the historical priority of corporations aggregate over corporations sole. In Germany, the status of pre-civilian Teutonic corporations was keenly contested during the process of drafting the Civil Code of 1898, following the work of Savigny and Jhering. It was in this context significantly that Tönnies contraposed *gemeinschaft* and *gesellschaft*, and Gierke undertook the historical analysis of natural law in Europe, seeking thereby to reinstate as legal units the ancient Germanic corporations, fraternities, local communities, and the like. The curious convergences on the subject shown by syndicalism, by the Fascist theory of the corporative state, and by advocacy of intermediary corporations, are also significant. In different ways and for different ends, these were all attempts to reintroduce corporations as units of legal jurisdiction, after their virtual elimination as autonomous units from the legal systems of modern states.

Malinowski, in his attempts to redefine and analyse primitive law, reacting against the presumption of central power, began by looking for 'rules regarded as compulsory obligations of one individual or group towards another'.[41] He found that

the whole structure of Trobriand society is founded on the principle of legal status. By this I mean that the claims of chief over commoner, husband over wife, parent over child and vice versa, are not exercised arbitrarily or one-sidedly, but according to definite rules, and are arranged into well-balanced chains of reciprocal services . . . Social relations are governed by a number of legal principles . . . mother-right . . . succession to rank, power and dignities, economic inheritance, rights to soil and local citizenship, and membership in the totemic clan[42]

In short, legal relations are embodied in and expressed by social structure which analytically reduces to a distributional network of

41. Malinowski (1959), p. 15.
42. ibid., p. 46.

reciprocal jural rights, privileges and obligations. The primacy of corporations as units of this social structure is owing partly to their qualities of persistence, to their estates which include rights in the persons of their members, to their external unity and identity, to their internal jural autonomy, which defines the essential conditions of membership, and above all to the fact that together, and in their interrelations, they constitute the society and the policy. Given these characteristics, the procedural features which writers like Roscoe Pound or Radcliffe-Brown have stressed as essential pre-requisites of law cease to be meaningful. The primitive corporation is simultaneously a unit of social structure and of social procedure; these two aspects cannot be separated.

Thus, when Hoebel defines law as a social norm, the neglect or infraction of which 'is regularly met, in threat or in fact, by the application of physical force by an individual or group possessing the socially recognized privilege of so acting'[43] two comments are in order. First, the unit of reference and authorization is a corporate group of some kind, and the authority varies with regard to issue and as the corporation is autocephalous or heterocephalous. Secondly, binding obligations are law, even where physical force is rarely or never applied, provided that their breach effects some alteration in the jural status of the corporation or any of its members.

The appeals of legal uniformity, coherence, and efficiency for lawyers and theorists are quite understandable. We should not, however, allow these normative qualities to lead us astray. Regularity and effectiveness in legal operations have directed attention to the efficiency of sanctions in the process of law; hence there is stress on centrally administered coercive sanctions to enforce decisions made by authorized tribunals. Certainty in the application of sanctions is one but not the only characteristic of 'perfect' — that is, predictable — legal process. Such certainty may be irrelevant when law consists in skillful guesswork, or in the words of Judge Holmes, 'prophecies of what the courts will do'. Here, near perfection of predictable regularity in the application of sanctions fails to compensate for irrationalities in legal decision-making. In this situation, the routine, predictable administration of sanctions is clearly no adequate basis for identification of law.

In societies that are imperfectly centralized, we may expect an imperfect or irregular application of sanctions, and perhaps even of judgment also. These are both quite consistent with the presence of law. Difficulties arise only when we accept the ambiguous ideals of perfect law, that is, of routinely enforced judicial decision, which is clearly a lawyer's desideratum, as the basis for a minimum general definition of law. It is clear that this ideally perfect law, the derivative of natural law theory, represents an extreme of legal development in which many differing levels and types of imperfect

43. E.A. Hoebel (1954), p. 28.

law are also important. In simple societies, legal imperfection obtains, both as to recourse to law and in regard to the enforcement of decisions. Typically, the tribal law is unwritten, and judgment considers many particulars which Western rules of evidence would exclude. Such systems of law have predominant commitments toward rationality of substance rather than form, using these terms in Max Weber's sense. One basic reason for this difference is that the primitive law normally operates without the overriding sanction of central political institutions, and accordingly requires consensus and support among members of the corporate groups it affects. Where overriding repressive sanctions are available to enforce judicial decisions, lawyers and judges are free to pursue formal rationality and coherence at the public expense.

Undue attention to substantive rules and their codification, coupled with the assumption that only perfect law is law, has diverted the attention of sociologists from the significance of procedure in defining legal events. Even the catalogue of Radcliffe-Brown, despite his procedural concept of law, does not include the sanction of nullity, which is essential for valid legal form. Sir Paul Vinogradoff identifies this sanction when he says that 'unless certain rules are observed, an intended result cannot be achieved'.[44] The effect of this sanction is to distinguish jural from other types of social procedures and rules, whether recorded or not. Feud, compensation, arbitration, appeals to divination, ordeals, oaths, councils and the like are all procedures institutionalized within social units to publicize, regulate and resolve intercorporate disputes.

Only when writers, having assumed a very specific procedural basis, define law substantively and as a perfectly effective system, are these imperfect modes of procedure theoretically problematic. Thus Weber, having initially identified law as an order 'externally guaranteed by the probability that coercion (physical or psychological), to bring about conformity or avenge violation, will be applied by a staff of people holding themselves specially ready for that purpose'[45] soon has to admit that 'not all law is guaranteed law', and thus to recognize 'indirectly guaranteed' and 'unguaranteed' law, where enforcement staffs are absent.[46] The distinction Weber makes here corresponds closely to the differences between perfect and imperfect law mentioned above. But there is also a special normative quality of perfect law which derives from its basis in the programmatic theory of natural law, and which, aiming at a perfectly coherent, formally closed, and independent system of law, directly excludes all that might obstruct its objective, and rejects the

44. Vinogradoff (1959), p. 23. On the distinction between perfect and imperfect law, see ibid., p. 31. Nullity (*butlan*) exists in Muslim law; in *'urf* it exists in the sense that omission of 'economical' nullifies the binding character of the act.

45. Rheinstein (1954), p. 5.

46. ibid., p. 13.

incorporation of all elements extraneous to the imperium with which it identifies itself.

5.

We can provisionally test and refine this analysis by a brief review of the framework of legal development in certain African colonial societies. For this purpose, I shall consider only three bodies of legal tradition — French, Muslim, and British — which interacted with native African society and law. In various parts of Africa these foreign systems were established by treaty, force, or other means as the law of the dominant group, in 'territories which never showed signs of national life ... and where the principle of unity is fundamentally due to the action of the dominant group'.[47] In all such situations the native society and legal tradition were officially subordinate to the foreign law. The new state was constituted by its rulers in the context of their own legal tradition, and the forms of law familiar to them served to limit or regulate their relations with native institutions. We have seen that these three dominant traditions differed significantly in their development and constitution. They differed also in their accommodations to the common situation of African overrule. It is therefore worth asking to what degree their differing theories of law and government may have guided or limited the adaptive capacities of these ruling groups to the colonial condition.

We may regard French law after the Code Napoléon as a fine expression of systematic legal rationalism developed and advocated by theorists of natural law. The sole and ultimate source of this law is the imperium of the French state. It is not directly crucial for this theory of law how the imperium is distributed among the central corporations that constitute the state, providing only that there is a definite, recognized procedure by which all laws are instituted and applied. In theory and fact alike, this body of law begins with a systematic coherent code, which is subsequently modified and supplemented by statute, including rules made by particular organs of state in the exercise of powers delegated by statute. The result is a formally perfect legal tradition which excludes all units, relations, and processes not directly or indirectly represented in the statutory law. In this system procedure and substantive law are both well defined, the distinction between public and private law is central, and there is great refinement of form. High levels of certainty obtain in regard to both adjudication and the application of sanctions. The code expresses a classical tradition aimed at perfection in law. The state itself has as legal basis a written constitution, and all the organs of government are defined and identified by law.

Muslim law, like Islam, derives from Muhammad's mission. Its base

47. Moreira (1957), p. 502.

is the Koran and the Sunna. Its object and limits are Islam, as both the Faith and the community of the Faithful. In theory, this law expresses God's *religio* (or binding ordinance). In practice the sources of law are heterogeneous, and the *sharī'a* is furthermore mixed with or supplemented by regulations derived from *'urf* or *siyāsa*. In theory, then, legal procedure and substance are well defined. In practice both are somewhat ambiguous in various spheres. Muslim law as we actually encounter it in Africa embodies all these elements, some directly at odds with the Koran and the *sharī'a*, others supplementing their prescribed procedures or substantive rules. In this legal tradition there was initially no legitimate place for statutes, other than those contained in the Sunna or the Koran, although they may derive legality from the ruler's authority as sanctioned by the Koran. In a word, the tradition is one of theocratic pragmatism with a predominant focus on substance or content.[48] In this system uncertainty attaches, *ceteris paribus*, both to judicial decisions and to the application of sanctions.

British common law is almost equally complex. Besides custom, its sources include precedent, judicial decisions, legislation, equity, and various rules made by subordinate units with autonomous powers.[49] It is equally consistent with an imperium based on organic historical growth and expressed in an unwritten constitution, or with one defined by a formal document, such as the American and Australian constitutions. Where, as in Britain, there is an unwritten constitution, the legality of law ultimately reduces to the observance of certain accepted procedures by legislature and courts alike. In such a system, if it merits that term, the traditional diversity of sources of law is linked with and maintained by rejection of systematic codes. In consequence, conditions conducive to conflict of laws arise, and uncertainty attaches to legal decisions on both formal and procedural grounds, though the application of sanctions is sure. In keeping with this secular empiricist tradition, periodic compilations of the current law are undertaken as part of a more or less continuous process of adjustive activity in which legislature, courts, jurists, and others are involved. In general, the law of procedure exceeds substantive law in clarity and certainty.

Indigenous African law varied widely in procedure and substance, in sources, theory, and scope, perhaps as an expression of differences in social organization too numerous to catalogue. The extremes of this variation may be illustrated by the Bushmen and the Baganda. In Buganda, Muteesa I (1856?-84), following Kabaka Mutebi, exercised an absolute and despotic power, the autonomous jurisdictions of clans having been circumscribed, hereditary chiefs and officials eliminated, and the ruler's orders enforced as supreme law. During these developments, the political constitution and legal procedures and

48. R. Levy (1957), p. 502.
49. Allen (1961), chs. 3-7.

content underwent simultaneous complex changes which we may summarize as the modification and replacement of an old corporate structure by a newer highly centralized despotism. These changes were partly legitimated by the Ganda theory of the Kabaka as the sacred personification of their unity as a nation.[50]

Within a Bushman tribe, bands are the only corporate groups, and band headmanship, which is often held by infants and occasionally by women, is the only corporation sole. Band and headmanship are identified with each other and with certain properties, such as water holes, *veldkos* areas, and the like. Both persist, with their estates, even when the band has ceased to exist. Jural rights over property — that is, over Bushmen resources — vest entirely in bands, and the Bushman's habitat is divided accordingly. There are no legal tribunals, unless the flurries of excited collective jabber in which members of a band engage to 'talk' some offender into retribution are so regarded. But crimes such as theft, though rare, are recognized, and violent punishment by the injured person is sanctioned, no protest arising even though the thief is killed.[51]

Between these extremes we find a wide variety in the corporate constitution of African societies: age-sets, age-regiments, age-villages, lineages, clans, local communities, associations, secret societies, castes, offices, and various types of chieftainship. In all instances an individual derives his jural status and rights from membership in some corporate category or group, or from tenure of some corporation sole. Thus the subordinate Hutu in Ruanda, like the slaves in West Africa, shared the jural disabilities attaching to the corporate category to which they belonged. These corporations, in their differing constitutions, bases, ideologies and interests, provide the sociological framework of indigenous law. As Gurvitch points out, 'the real collective units only, e.g. groups, give birth to the frameworks of law', the legal system of a given society 'representing already the syntheses and the equilibria among different kinds of law'.[52] Moreover, as corporations defined the scope and the source of the law, they embodied its theory and procedural forms, and established the frame within and through which legal relations and processes obtained. The nature, form, and content of these jural relations and processes will therefore change with the identity and characteristics of the corporations involved, directly or indirectly. In this context law provides the medium for expression and adjustment of the corporate relations which constitute the framework of society.

Perhaps the most important structural difference among the French, Muslim, and British legal systems lies in their treatment of corporations. In English law, corporations emerged as independent juridical personalities endowed with continuity and exercising legally

50. Southwold (1960); Richards (1960), ch. 2.
51. L. Marshall (1960, 1961).
52. Gurvitch (1947), p. 156.

valid powers. The law accordingly admitted the existence of a certain type of unit which may or may not have been formally acknowledged by the state. In the developing English law of corporations, the legal capacities of these units were taken to include powers of rule-making for their membership, where not inconsistent with the laws of the land. In short, common law, with its feudal basis and heterogeneous sources, accepted corporations constituted on various principles as relatively autonomous legal units.[53] The position in Muslim law seems curiously similar. Muslims were free, through the *siyāsa* and the doctrine of *'urf*, to suspend application of Islamic rules in favour of local practice, and could thus recognize and use the corporate organizations of those they ruled. They could also, with fewer procedural problems than the British, institute new corporations, both group and sole, as social or political conditions seemed to warrant. In the French legal system corporations exist as juridical units only by virtue of specific recognition or acknowledgment by the state. The French legal framework, being logically coherent, complete, and closed, cannot admit the logical or historical existence of native corporations independent of or antecedent to the colonial regime. On this basis the French theory of law denied recognition to African custom and polities. Inevitably this consequence follows from the French view of law as a statutory code, properly authorized by the French state or by some other state that France recognizes. Only by special legislation could such law admit the existence of other old or new units. Even then it had difficulty in recognizing custom. With these bases the French had little alternative except 'to regard their oversea territories as an integral part of the national community'.[54]

One case discussed by Delavignette makes the position plain:

For a long time African customary law was not legally recognized, since the situations to which it applied did not fall within any of the categories provided for by French law. Supposing a Chief tried to establish in the courts, in accordance with the Code, the traditional rights exercised by a village over its own land. . . . The magistrate inquired in what capacity the Chief appeared. As representing the village — true, but what, according to the Code, is the legal status of the group known as a village? Is it a public utility company, a society, an association, a syndicate, a corporate body, an association of owners? The magistrate searched through the Code and found nothing. The African village exists in fact but has no means of proving its existence in law. It exists within the framework of customary law, but has no power to act within the framework of French law . . . Now on 3 November 1934 the Court of Appeal at Dakar, the supreme court of French West Africa, for the first time took cognizance of the nature of customary law in its own legal practice . . . The court decided two questions: first — what was the legal basis of the African village? The court's decision was that the French legislature, by proclaiming its recognition of local custom, placed the village on a legal basis entirely distinct from anything provided for in French law . . . In order to recognize the legal status of the

53. Maine (1905), ch. vi; Vinogradoff (1959), pp. 54-60.
54. Delavignette (1950), pp. v-vi.

village and of the land rights it asserts, the court must define custom and legislate in accordance with it. The second question was, who is qualified to represent the village in law? ... The decree of 3 November 1934 [points] ... the way to a solution of the conflict between Code and custom by means of a development of French law.[55]

This involved a major modification of French legal theory.

The British, with their inadequate theory of law, and the Muslims, with a religious conception liberally modified by and adapted to circumstance, escaped the difficulties that faced the French because of the logical closure of their system and the extreme integration of legal theory with the theory of the state. Common-law willingness to accommodate corporations allowed the British to deal freely with tribal units whose forms and boundaries they could identify. Given prior experience with custom in common law, in Africa the British were well equipped to incorporate traditional social units and custom· within the framework of their colonial administration, both legal and political, under the general rubrics of native authorities or native law and custom. Moreover, again on the basis of common-law experience, the British were well placed conceptually to admit that customs have a capacity for change, and thus tapped an essential source of adjustive development. As native law and custom changed, the British were therefore free to admit changes in the boundaries, character, and identity of the representative native corporations.

For Muslims, Islam imposed the obligation of *jihad* and thus legitimated their conquests. Under the Koran, the Muslim ruler also enjoyed a discretionary power of pragmatic accommodation to secular conditions. The adaptive capacity of *siyāsa* has enabled Muslim law to harness the regulatory powers of custom and local corporations to the service of Muslim rulers. In practice, only those who identified themselves by the essential religious observances as Muslims had access to the *sharī'a*, all others being subject to the poll tax (*jizya*) and irregular levies or demands, as well as to effective official disenfranchisement, although under *siyāsa* and the doctrine of *'urf* they were free to maintain their traditional custom and social groupings.

6.

I draw two conclusions from this review. First, as a rule of method, in the comparative sociology of law, it seems as essential to examine the history of legal theories as to observe the operation of legal systems themselves. In a very special sense, these theories and ideologies, however imperfect they may be, as in modern Britain or ancient Rome, serve to define the framework within which law proceeds. It is furthermore possible, given suitable data, to refine an

55. ibid., pp. 91-2; see also Hailey (1938), pp. 185-206, 484-91.

initial analysis of the special properties and assumptions of differing systems of law by comparing their adaptation to a common situation such as African pluralism provides. Perhaps only by some such procedure are we likely to develop a culture-free notion of legal facts significant for theory and practical affairs alike.

My second conclusion relates to the theory of law itself. We have found that the critical element in three traditions — Muslim, British, and French — is their treatment of corporate bodies other than the state. Muslim law apparently ignores the question, but thereby permits great adaptive freedom; British law explicitly provides legal recognition for autonomous corporations; French law as explicitly excludes them. It seems possible that law is both the process and the product of processes by which corporations emerge, acquire definition, and articulate with one another within a wider unit. In Muslim theory, the most inclusive corporation is the House of Islam; but when dominant, Muslims are legally free to acknowledge the corporate organization of their pagan or *dhimmī* subjects, whose traditional customs are accordingly recognized as valid in regulating their internal affairs. Without any overriding religious commitment or classification, British law permits equally flexible accommodation. *Per contra*, French law, which most perfectly expresses the dominant rational Western theory of law, assumes a primary sovereign corporation, the state, and accordingly denies the legality of prior or independent units unless the latter are expressly recognized by the state. In their common African situation, the responses of these dominant legal traditions inevitably differed; and their relative capacities to absorb native legal and political institutions into their framework varied inversely with their logical closure and formal completeness, that is, with the specificity of their political presuppositions. If this conclusion holds, its pertinence for sociologists concerned with the general problem of law and social control may lie in its stress on corporations as modal units of social and legal structure.

5.

Pre-Industrial
Stratification Systems

Societies that rely primarily on human or animal sources of productive power are usually regarded as 'pre-industrial'. This label involves no expectations about their future. Although pre-industrial societies vary greatly in their structure and developmental level, at this stage we need only distinguish traditional pre-industrial societies from the 'national' units in which they are currently incorporated. Even when both these units are equally pre-industrial, they differ sharply in structure, boundaries and orientation. Industrialization appeals to few traditional pre-industrial societies as a desirable programme. To 'national' pre-industrial societies, it may be a structural necessity, and in emergent nations, industrialization is always a national programme, even where its impact on local units is greatest.

1.

The nature of stratification is more complex and critical for our discussion. The common distinction between concrete and analytic structures, that is, between membership units and generalized aspects of social process,[1] suggests parallel distinctions between analytic and concrete concepts of stratification. Since the approach presented here differs from others in current use, I should try to indicate these differences at once.

Stratification is often conceived as the evaluative ranking of social units. Some theorists regard it as an abstract necessity of all social systems. Concretely, it refers to empirical distributions of advantages and benefits in specific societies.[2] Analytically, it connotes the abstract possibilities of evaluative rankings on any number of special scales.[3] As observers, we can construct as many stratification scales as we wish by employing any criteria we choose, separately or together; but we should not confuse these abstract possibilities or analytic artifacts with empirical systems of social stratification. The significance of any analytic scale depends on its meaningful correspondence with a concrete system of stratification; and, as Smelser and Lipset suggest, these concrete stratifications may be

1. M. Levy (1952), pp. 88-9.
2. Smelser and Lipset (1966a).
3. M. Levy (1952), pp. 343-7; H. Kuper (1947), pp. 6-7.

identified by the differential distribution of social advantages.

Stratification is a process as well as a state of affairs. Of these two referents, the first seems more fundamental, since the state of affairs is both a product and condition of social process. As an institutional order, the process of social stratification must be regulated by some principles which can be derived by analysis of the social structure; and, on the basis of structural analysis, I shall argue that stratification consists in the principles that regulate the distribution of social advantages. Thus, the unit to which my argument refers is the society rather than its various components, the concept of society being that presented by S. F. Nadel and Marion Levy, Jr.[4]

Being highly differentiated, modern industrial societies may accommodate considerable diversity of evaluative scales in their systems of stratification. None the less, these scales must be functionally consistent and related if they are to be simultaneously institutionalized. In less differentiated pre-industrial societies, the theoretically possible variety of scales is severely restricted by structural stereotyping of social units and individual life-cycles. When the more complex pre-industrial systems institutionalize two or more stratification scales, relations between them are usually well-defined.

Since the social evaluations reflecting stratification are neither random nor contingent, the criteria on which they rest must be institutionalized within the social structure, and for this reason evaluative rankings express underlying structural principles. The logical alternative involves such randomness, contingency and discord in the aggregate of evaluations that it cannot constitute a ranking system at all. But if the actual ranking of social units expresses structural relations, the differential distribution of sanctions with which this rank order is identified will also be governed by structural principles. Such differential distributions of benefit and deprivation are no more random and contingent than the evaluative rankings that reflect them.

With these considerations in mind, while reviewing stratification in pre-industrial societies, I shall also explore relations between the prevailing distributions of advantage and the structural principles that regulate the processes of distribution. I shall also try to show why these principles are more significant for the analysis of social stratification than the mere distribution of advantages.

I approach this discussion of pre-industrial stratification systems as a social anthropologist, conscious of the divergences between sociology and social anthropology, especially in their conceptions of social structure and stratification. Despite personal involvement in a few small-scale societies, a social anthropologist is committed to comparative analysis; and in these comparisons his primary concern is with the particular combinations of structural principles under-

4. Nadel (1951), pp. 187-8; M. Levy (1952), p. 113.

lying the observable variety of social processes and forms. For such analysis, the anthropologist's concept of social structure facilitates identification of these principles and their combinations. Thus, while the lineage principle is common to all lineages, these vary structurally as this principle is modified by others. In like manner, structural changes are modifications of structural units and relations that involve some rearrangement or alteration of the principles which constitute them. For this conception of social structure, the view of status as a bundle of rights and duties is critical. In static terms structure can be conceived as an arrangement of such positions, some held by individuals, others by corporate units. Dynamically, structural change involves modification or rearrangement of the underlying principles. With this background, social anthropologists conceive societies positionally, as systems the key units of which are statuses, related to one another by their particular distributions of privilege, duty and right. Social action, change and stratification are understood by reference to the social structure.

In sociology, as I understand it, structure is often viewed as a set of 'directional tendencies', or purposive processes of institutional action, which seek to satisfy the 'functional prerequisites' of social order. In effect, the strategic concept for initial analysis is the role, usually defined by reference to normative expectations; and the society, as an action system with sufficient internal order to ensure its persistence, is identified as a normative consensual system. In analysing congruent or incongruent role expectations, the sociologist relies heavily on such notions as norms, values, and value-orientations.

Many differences between sociology and anthropology flow from these divergent orientations, and some of these find expressions in conflicting disciplinary approaches to the study of stratification. For many sociologists, 'no society is "classless" or unstratified';[5] 'social inequality in human society is marked by its ubiquity and its antiquity. Every known society, past and present, distributes its scarce and demanded goods unequally.'[6] Stratification is 'a particular type of role differentiation, that is a requirement for any society'.[7] 'Social stratification is a generalized aspect of the structure of all social systems.'[8] This being so, sociologists attempt 'to explain, in functional terms, the universal necessity which calls forth stratification in any social system . . . The main functional necessity explaining the universal presence of stratification is precisely the requirement faced by any society of placing and motivating individuals in the social structure.'[9] Though these views are not

5. K. Davis and W.E. Moore (1956), p. 242.
6. Tumin (1953), p. 337.
7. Aberle et al. (1950), p. 106.
8. Parsons (1953), in Bendix and Lipset (1953), p. 93; see also Parsons (1940).
9. K. Davis and W.E. Moore (1956), p. 242.

shared by all sociologists[10] they represent the prevailing sociological approach to a theory of stratification. The point of view they express contrasts so sharply with the social anthropological approach that in preparing this paper I have had to seek some common ground between the two in order to relate anthropological materials on pre-industrial societies to the framework of current sociological theory.

One can contrast the assertion that 'no society is classless or unstratified' with representative anthropological statements. For Landtmann, 'one of the most remarkable facts ascertained and elucidated by sociology [is] that a condition of almost complete equality reigns among peoples in the lowest degrees of culture'.[11] According to *Notes and Queries* (6th edition), '*some* societies are stratified in social classes or, where these are closed, castes . . . Social classes entail differences in status and civic rights, often conditioned by descent, in the access to positions of power, influence or wealth, and also in occupation and habitual modes of living.'[12] For Nadel, stratification is identified by the presence of social strata. Only

when a society is divided into large aggregates of individuals who share, in relevant respects, the same status and are marked off from other such aggregates by different status [may] we speak of social strata . . . Clearly the various age groups in a society, or the two sexes, may also be collectively differentiated by status; yet we should not in that case speak of social strata.[13] . . . Power and authority would seem to be more relevant criteria of social stratification than the varying access to other commonly valued benefits.[14]

By status, Nadel understands

the rights and obligations of any individual relative both to those of others and to the scale of worth-whileness in the group . . . 'Rank' is a more highly formalized version of status . . . 'Prestige' . . . a more fluid version. By status we mean . . . status in the widest relevant group . . . the politically effective corporation, so that status means political status.[15]

Sahlins, having asked, 'What is egalitarianism and what is stratification?' replies:

Theoretically an egalitarian society would be one in which every individual is of equal status, a society in which no one outranks anyone. But even the most primitive societies could not be described as egalitarian in this sense. There are differences in status carrying differential privilege in every human organization . . . [but] the qualifications are not everywhere the same. In certain societies, e.g., Australian aboriginal communities, the only qualifications for higher status are those which every society uses to some extent, namely sex, age and personal

10. Bottomore (1963), pp. 38-40, 195-6.
11. Landtman (1938), p. 3.
12. Royal Anthropological Institute (1951), p. 93. My italics.
13. Nadel (1951), p. 174.
14. ibid., p. 175.
15. ibid., pp. 171-2, 174.

characteristics. Aside from these qualifications, there may be no others. A society in which the only principles of rank allocation are these universals can be designated 'egalitarian', first, because this society is at the stratification minimum of organized human societies; second, because, given these qualifications, every individual has an equal chance to succeed to whatever statuses may be open. But a society unlike this, that is, one in which statuses are fixed by a mechanism beyond the universals, e.g. [by] inheritance, can be called 'stratified'.[16]

For Bohannan,

stratification . . . implies not merely a ranked hierarchy, but also a homogeneous quality in each of the various strata. This quality . . . is certainly absent in . . . 'situs' systems . . . and minimal in 'caste' systems.[17]

While anthropologists conceive stratification concretely, as a feature of some, but not all, societies, sociologists tend to stress its universality as an abstract necessity of all social systems, whether these are conceived analytically or not. Underlying these differing orientations is the anthropologist's emphasis on status as the primary concept for analysis of social structure, and the sociologist's emphasis on role. I suggest that this difference also explains why sociologists are keenly concerned with a theory of stratification, while anthropologists are little concerned about it. Because anthropologists conceive social structure as a status structure, in their view an inclusive theory of stratification would represent a general theory of all forms of social structure. On the other hand, because sociologists regard societies as systems of roles, they need a theory of stratification to analyse the articulation of these roles.

No discussion of 'pre-industrial stratification systems' that fails to resolve these differences can provide a useful basis for their comparison or for the study of their re-stratification. Any general comparative survey of social stratification presupposes an acceptable notion of stratification. In seeking to arrive at this, I shall have to deal with the following questions, among others: (1) In what sense does an unequal distribution of advantages indicate stratification? (2) Whether 'functionally requisite' or not, is stratification universal and coextensive with society? (3) How useful is the dichotomy between ascription and achievement for an analysis and typology of status systems? (4) How valid is the assertion that stratification expresses normative consensus? (5) How valid is the thesis that 'positions which are combined in the same family cannot be made the basis of stratification'?[18]

16. Sahlins (1958), pp. 1-2.
17. P. Bohannan (1963), p. 165.
18. K.B. Mayer (1955), p. 5.

2.

Various sociologists identify stratification with prevailing inequalities in the distribution of social advantages or benefits. 'If the
rights and prerequisites of different positions in a society must be
unequal, then the society must be stratified, because that is precisely
what stratification means . . . Every society, no matter how simple or
complex, must differentiate persons in terms of both prestige and
esteem, and must, therefore, possess a certain amount of institutionalized inequality.'[19] Being general, this formula neither attempts to
distinguish types of social advantage, nor examines the distribution
that identifies stratification. Here, the critical question is whether
this distribution or the principles which regulate it is the relevant
object of study. Current social theory seeks to handle the second
alternative by distinctions between systems in which status is
ascribed and achieved, but the results are hardly satisfactory, first
because all systems of stratification combine both principles, but
more importantly because this device signally fails to answer the
critical question, namely, in what sense is the unequal distribution of
advantages evidence of stratification? Doubtless this obscurity is
essential to the theoretical claim that stratification is a universal
response of society to certain functional prerequisites; but if this
assumption obstructs discriminating analysis and comparison, it can
scarcely provide a sound basis for the sociology of economic
development. Especially, perhaps, because the theory based on it is
said to represent such 'a higher degree of abstraction [that] . .˙. it is
impossible to move directly from the kind of proposition we were
making to descriptive propositions about, say, American society'.[20] A
more pedestrian but operational scheme is needed.

Inequality seems to be the heart of the matter. It is with this in
one form or another that sociologists identify stratification; but they
generally leave obscure the sense in which these unequal rankings or
distributions of advantage are crucial for stratification. And though
these inequalities are conventional and institutionalized, being
regarded as necessary on theoretical grounds, all their forms are
treated as equally appropriate and legitimate. 'Social inequality is
thus an unconsciously evolved device by which societies ensure that
the most important positions are conscientiously filled by the most
qualified persons.'[21] It is difficult to show that the 'most important
positions' are always held by the 'most qualified persons', or that
they are always 'conscientiously filled', but if we accept these
assumptions, the regimes of Adolf Hitler, Trujillo and Franklin
Roosevelt are all equally appropriate and legitimate.

19. K. Davis and W.E. Moore (1956), p. 243.
20. K. Davis (1953), p. 394
21. K. Davis and W.E. Moore (1956), p. 243.

Since positional inequality is identified with stratification, it is useful to consider briefly what the diametrically opposite condition implies. Little effort has been made recently to see what such perfect equality involves.[22] A condition of perfect equality of social positions is admittedly hard to conceive, and its duration over any period of time even more so. The reasons are evident. Such perfect equality involves the systematic elimination of all socially relevant differences, biological or structural, with the result that, except perhaps for their differing locations, all persons simultaneously hold identical positions, rights, duties and relations. In consequence, none hold any. Child and father, ill and hale, sane and insane, all are positionally identical. Clearly no such aggregate could survive midsummer, since this perfect equality eliminates right, obligation and relation as well as individuation, and institutes the preconditions of the Hobbesian 'war of all against all'. Such total elimination of positional differences automatically dissolves society, since society can only be defined by reference to differentiation, whether this is conceived relationally or in terms of action.

In a condition of absolute positional identity, individual organisms are the only possible units, but despite their biological differences, they are *ex definitione* identical. Such total antithesis of differentiation is of course biologically impossible. Populations being biologically differentiated, societies inevitably consist in differentiated positions and roles, with their correlative rights and duties. Such differentiation inherently involves the differential distribution of rights and duties, simply because this is what the differentiation consists in; but clearly stratification is only one mode of social differentiation and not identical with all its forms.

The point here is simply that in any society, at any point in time, the current distribution of social positions and advantages must always be unequal, because they are differentiated; and not merely because these 'advantages' are highly various, but because the members of any society are heterogeneous as regards age, sex and personal qualities. Even in social systems subsumed by kinship, this will be the case, since mother and child are an indispensable asymmetrical pair. Instead of simplistic references to the universality of unequal distributions of right, duty and advantage — that is, to social differentiation of status and role — we must seek to discriminate the principles regulating and institutionalizing varying modes of distribution. Some of these modes may constitute a stratification, others may not. Not inequality, but the modes of its institutionalization, its bases and forms, are the relevant materials for identifying and analysing stratification systems. We have to take inequality for granted, since total equality in any indispensable

22. For valuable discussions, see Jean-Jacques Rousseau, 'Discours sur l'origine et fondement de l'inégalité parmi les hommes' (1753), cited in Vaughan (1915). Also Tawney (1961).

relation such as parent and child is merely inequality once removed and intensified.

In studying institutionalized inequality, two questions are essential, and a third perhaps even more important. Descriptively, we must ask: 'In what does inequality consist? What is its form, degree and scale?' Analytically, we must ask: 'On what is this distribution based, and how does it relate to other features of the social order?' Historically, where data permit, we should ask: 'How did the present system come into being? What changes has it recently undergone, or is currently undergoing?'

Whereas sociological theory regards answers to the first, descriptive, question as proof of stratification, anthropologists generally rely on the second for the data by which they classify systems as 'stratified' or unstratified. For them, simple inequality in the distribution of advantages is inevitable on grounds of biology and kinship, and therefore cannot provide sufficient evidence of stratification. In their view, the principles by which observable inequalities are institutionalized are the critical data. These principles differentiate systems in which inequalities are temporary, random or contingent from others in which access to advantageous positions is differentially distributed, so that, whatever the grounds, some persons are privileged and others disqualified. Systems of the latter sort may be stratified if the differential distribution of opportunities characterizes ranked strata having some internal homogeneity and external distinctness. Excluding biologically given differences — without which human society is of course impossible — inequality in the distribution of access to favoured positions is decisive for societal classification as stratified; only some societies having differentially distributed opportunities may in fact be stratified; and stratification never consists in the mere existence or occupancy of these differential positions, but in the principles by which the distribution of access and opportunities is regulated.

Even when all members of a society enjoy equivalent opportunities to obtain positions of social precedence and advantage, at any given moment and over time, these must be distributed 'unequally', in the sense that some persons hold them while others do not. 'Photographic' accounts of current distributions fail to provide an adequate basis for social classification or analysis, simply because they assimilate sharply different types of society on the basis of superficial similarities.

Where access to the highest positions and advantages is equally open to all, these positions usually form an indefinite series, coextensive in space and time with the society their dispersal identifies. They are accordingly highly standardized, and functional differentiation is limited thereby, the society concerned being typically acephalous. In intensity and span, integrative centralization corresponds with the degree of functional differentiation attained by a society; in form, with its structural differentiation. Under conditions of centralization, equivalence of access to the highest positions and advantages will be limited in the first place by the small number of such positions relative to the size of the population. Since the chiefdom may only have one paramount at a time, and few in any individual life-span, most members cannot reasonably expect to be chief. In Athens, where offices were filled by lot, a conscious effort was made to maintain this ideal equivalence within a clearly defined stratum by devices combining the principles of divination and roulette.[23] Neither achievement nor ascription adequately describes this mode of recruitment.

3.

Given the preceding discussion, it will be useful to describe various types of unstratified society, to clarify their variety and institutional mechanisms.

The political structure of many East African societies consists in a hierarchy of male age-sets. Organizational details vary widely as between societies; but in all, age-sets are ranked by seniority, and in most the different sets have differing roles, rights and duties. Age-mates are social and jural equals, and each set exercises jurisdiction over its members. Seniority regulates relations between successive sets. At regular intervals, new sets are instituted in tribal ceremonies that move all senior sets forward into the next higher grades. Rights to marry, to beget children, to establish a homestead, to participate in civil or judicial councils, to officiate at rituals, to go on raids, are all variably integrated with this age-organization. At any given moment an unequal distribution of rights and advantages obtains among these peoples; but the mode of institutionalization guarantees the automatic transfer of positions and advantages to junior sets at determinate intervals, and thus ensures equality of access over time. The seniority principle, basic to age-set differentiation, regulates this distribution of social positions and access to them. Inequalities are always temporary, and each individual in turn automatically moves through the same series of positions by virtue of his compulsory identification with an age-set. Despite their internal homogeneity and external distinctiveness, given their ceaseless progression, it is patently ridiculous to designate these cohorts by the same term used for castes, estates, slavery or social classes. In age-organization, mobility is identical with the system, in its rhythm and limits. The principles by which differential advantages are institutionally distributed in these age-systems are directly opposed to those constituting stratification. These conditions occur in varying form among the Galla, the Nandi, Kipsigi, Terik, Masai, Turkana, Jie,

23. Warde Fowler (1952), pp. 166-7.

Karimojong, Kikuyu, Kadara, Hidatsa, etc.[24]

Stratification is scarcely possible below a certain minimum level of differentiation, but even where a number of asymmetrical roles and units are differentiated, these may be so distributed as to preclude stratification. According to Lauriston Sharp, this is the condition of the Australian Yir Yuront, where 'a hierarchy of a pyramidal or inverted Y type to include all men in the system is an impossibility',[25] since each individual participates as superior and inferior in an exactly equal number of dyadic relations. Since the 28 Yir Yuront kinship relations embrace virtually all institutionalized roles, despite their asymmetry, their distribution enjoins social equality by restricting inequalities to individual relations, and by so distributing these that no individual lacks 14 superiors and 14 inferiors simultaneously. Few systems achieve this mathematical perfection. That of the Yir Yuront gives such extreme stress to specific asymmetrical relations that even the concept of *situs* seems excluded, much less stratification.

Different patterns appear among the Ituri Pygmies and Bushmen, whose bilateral kinship institutions differentiate fewer roles and pattern them less strongly. These peoples are so weakly differentiated that stratification is impossible for them. Pygmy bands lack effective leaders and any differential distribution of sanctions or privileges among their members, above the level of the household. Individuals are free to leave or enter a band, unless members oppose their entry. Since all Pygmy households are equally self-sufficient and interdependent, the distribution of household and inter-household roles is ·constant and uniform. Pygmies approach the Durkheimian model of the primitive undifferentiated society that excludes stratification, whether on grounds of ascription or achievement. Neither in ritual, hunting, kinship nor band relations do they exhibit any discernible inequalities of rank or advantage. In the familial sphere, the apparently unequal distribution of rights and duties has a simple biological basis in congruent inequalities of capacity.[26]

Pygmies are not unique. !Kung Bushmen evince similar patterns. !Kung live in bands, each with its component families and fixed resources of water rights, *veldkos* areas, mangbetti woods, etc. Each band has a headman, normally recruited by descent, who exercises symbolic custody of band resources. Among !Kung, bands cannot exist without headmen, but these may or may not reside in their bands. A 'stranger' seeking water first asks the headman's permission before visiting the band's water-hole; but the headman will only refuse if the band members object — a rare event. Band headmen

24. Huntingford (1953, 1955); Prins (1953); Peristiany (1939); Pamela and P.H. Gulliver (1953); P.H. Gulliver (1953, 1958); Bernardi (1952); Lambert (1956); Dyson-Hudson (1963); LeVine and Sangree (1962); Lowie (1949), pp. 273-82; Fosbrooke (1948).
25. Sharp (1958), in Ray (1958), p. 5. See also Lloyd Warner (1958).
26. Turnbull (1961).

may be children or women, where men are unavailable for succession; apparently nobody wants the role. Headmen have no advantages that distinguish them from other !Kung. Band members hunt in small teams of their own choice; they are obliged by various institutions to distribute the meat of the hunt rather widely. Very few men are polygynists and these may or may not be headmen. When away from their bands, headmen have neither special statuses nor obligations. With the exceptions mentioned above, this is also their position within the band.

Certain devices of fictive kinship ensure the extension of kinship terms and behaviour to non-kin, so that in effect all !Kung are related to one another directly or indirectly in ways entailing specific rights and obligations; but the roster of differentiated relations is short by comparison with the Yir Yuront. In some relations, real or fictive, each !Kung will enjoy some advantage; in others his role is inferior; in the remainder the relation is symmetrical. The narrow bilateral kinship system by which kin are dispersed, mainly through marriage, provides no basis for gerontocracy; nor do !Kung allocate status on grounds of age. As among Pygmies and Andamanese, !Kung bands hold frequent rituals in which all adult members take part. All men are shamans. They share identical ritual status and collective duties. In no sense can the !Kung be said to exhibit stratification above the level of the family.[27]

Descent provides another basis on which distributions of differential position and advantage may be so organized that equal access and automatic transfers prevail. Here also, societies vary: some trace descent through the male, others through the female line, and others through both lines, together or separately. In societies of the last type, all individuals simultaneously belong to their father's patrilineage and to their mother's matrilineage. In each, they hold different rights and obligations and enjoy a different status. These differences are balanced, and thus distinguish the complementary lineage forms.

Lineages, as these unilineal descent groups are called, vary widely in their depth, span, scale, form, functions and other attributes. Some incorporate sizable tribes, such as the Gusii, Tiv, Lugbara, or the issue of Abraham. Where this occurs, the component lineages are distinguished in a hierarchic series of corporations having an explicit segmentary organization corresponding to the genealogy. Social distance is then defined by the range of collateral kinship. Hierarchic relations of descent indicate jural identity. Close lineage kin share exclusive solidary obligations and identical jural status. As the range of kinship extends, jural differentiation increases, the relevant units being groups rather than individuals. The segmentary lineage is a system of corporate groups organized in a hierarchy of co-ordinate

27. L. Marshall (1957, 1959, 1960, 1961, 1962).

divisions of differing depth and span, and unified by an ideology of common descent.[28]

Long ago Radcliffe-Brown isolated the principles on which these corporate lineages are based, namely the unity of the sibling group as seen from without, and the equivalence of same-sex siblings.[29] Given the tradition of tracing descent through one sex to the exclusion of the other, these principles, if observed, inevitably promote corporate unilineal descent groups with a segmentary internal structure. Duplicated, they develop a system of double descent. Modifications that deviate from these principles produce structures differing from the segmentary model in direct correspondence. Some illustrations of this are mentioned below.

For its emergence and continuity, the segmentary lineage presumes the jural, ritual and social equivalence of siblings in the direct line of descent. Accordingly, it classifies different sibling groups as units of co-ordinate status, each internally undifferentiated, thereby excluding jural inequalities among its members, even though at any given moment the senior men enjoy superior social and ritual advantages as family heads and custodians of lineage rights. The equivalence of lineage members really consists in the equal distribution of rights and access to such positions among them, as they mature. Thus, the segmentary lineage, a rather widespread social form, excludes internal stratification, despite the inevitable inequalities in the current distribution of advantages inherent in its generational and familial composition. In place of horizontal strata, the lineage principle establishes vertical divisions between lineages as units of corporate status, as befits Durkheim's segmental model. The effect is to restrict lateral or inter-lineage mobility, while instituting vertical or intra-lineage mobility. The status system of the corporate lineage is thus diametrically opposite to hierarchic ranking; and all men are status peers in societies organized on these lines, since all lineages are co-ordinate at some level of the organization.

4.

Despite the differential distribution of rights, duties and advantages within Pygmy or Bushmen families, I do not regard them as stratified, for two reasons. First, these differentiations do not go beyond what is essential for the definition and maintenance of the family as a unit of husband, wife and offspring. Secondly, the differentiated positions are equally open to all in due course. Without these differentiations, the family could not be constituted or identified. Children would have no fathers.

Whether the family everywhere exhibits this lack of internal

28. Gluckman (1948), pp. 5-8; Fortes (1953); M.G. Smith, Chapter 1 above; Harris (1962). For an excellent collection of lineage studies, see Middleton and Tait (1958).

29. Radcliffe-Brown (1930-1, 1941, 1950, 1952*b*).

stratification is surely an empirical matter. If we regard 'hierarchical sex and age grading'[30] as stratification, then we must recognize the internal stratification of families in all societies where such grading occurs. Siblings who belong to different age-sets ranked as senior and junior are distinguished within as well as beyond the family. Conversely, if we do not regard families as internally stratified, these age and sex distinctions should not be represented as stratification. Some writers, however, simultaneously hold that stratification is universal and deny that families are ever internally stratified. Since societies such as the Bushmen or Pygmies lack any supra-familial organization, if their families are unstratified, then they lack stratification also. Thus, the postulate of the unstratified family contradicts the asserted universality of stratification, both being advanced by the same writers, with relevant functional explanations. In fact, the data show that social stratification is not universal, and that families are not universally exempt from it, on any definitions of society and the family one cares to fashion.

For Kingsley Davis,

those positions that may be combined in the same legitimate family — viz., positions based on sex, age and kinship — do not form part of the system of stratification. On the other hand, those positions that are socially prohibited from being combined in the same legal family — viz., different caste or class positions — constitute what we call stratification. With reference to the class hierarchy the family is a unit: its members occupy the same rank. This is because one of the family's main functions is the ascription of status. It could not very well perform this function if it did not, as a family, occupy a single position in the scale. Children are said to 'acquire their parents' status', with the implication that two parents have a common status to transmit, and that the child gets this status automatically as a member of the family. In the same way, husband and wife are treated as social equals.[31]

The convenience of this doctrine for the analysis of Western industrial society has encouraged its acceptance without much effort to check its validity. Evidently it refers mainly to the nuclear family in monogamous societies, but since the thesis is unqualified it is now being applied to polygynous societies also.[32] I shall therefore discuss its validity with reference to systems of either type. Even in monogamous societies, where siblings have differential rights to inheritance and succession, this generalization may not hold. The variety of organizational problems and solutions that such conditions present is illustrated by the coexistence of gavelkind, primogeniture, and 'borough English' in medieval Britain.[33] Where wives and their offspring are differentially ranked in certain polygynous societies, these differences are often integrated with extra-familial stratification. Under such conditions the family functions quite efficiently

30. Aberle et al. (1950), p. 106.
31. K. Davis (1949), p. 364; partly cited in K. Davis (1953), p. 394.
32. Bohannan (1963), pp. 166, 180-2.
33. Vinogradoff (1959), pp. 122-3; Homans (1962), pp. 148-55, 161-5.

as a mechanism of status placement by meticulously differentiating members instead of assimilating them.

Among the Swazi,

the clans are graded into a rough hierarchy, and the rank of a clan is measured by its position in the national structure. The entire clan as such does not hold this position, but only certain lineages . . . In every large clan there are a number of parallel lineages . . . linked up with the senior lineage at irregular points of the family tree . . . In every lineage members are graded by their distance from the head.[34]

Wives of a polygynist hold unequal status; during his lifetime they are graded primarily on the basis of seniority, the first taking precedence over the second, and so on, but after his death the children's rights to inheritance and succession are determined by their mother's rank and mode of marriage . . . The fundamental principle underlying the selection of the main heir of a polygynist is that property and power are inherited from men and acquired by them, but are transmitted through women, whose rank, more than any other factor, determines the choice. 'A ruler is ruler by his mother". . . The tie between sons of the same father undoubtedly depends largely on the status of the wives, and it is over succession and inheritance that cleavages between half-brothers come out sharply and bitterly . . . The main heir receives far and away the major share.[35]

Among the Tswana,

there are three separate classes, nobles . . . commoners . . . and immigrants . . . Within each class there are further distinctions. Among nobles, the more closely a man is related to the chief, the higher does he rank . . . Among commoners . . . the head of any group is senior to all his dependents, among whom his own relatives are of higher status than the others.[36] . . . The children of paternal uncles are differentiated according to the relative status of their father . . . If senior to one's father by birth they are entitled to obedience and respect; if junior their services can be freely commanded. The saying that a man's 'elder brother' is his chief, and his 'younger brother' his subject, summarizes adequately the accepted relation . . . But disputes sometimes occur owing to arbitrary exercise of authority and rival claims to property and position, and it is not fortuitous that most accusations of sorcery are made against one's relatives in the same ward.[37]

Among the Zulu,

the closer a royal prince was (and is) by birth to the reigning king, the higher his social status . . . The same rules applied to the ruling families within the tribes.[38] . . . The status of sons depends on the status of their mothers in the compound family.[39] . . . Wives are graded. One, the chief wife of the great house, who may be married late in life will produce the main heir. She has placed under her a number of subordinate wives. Another wife is head of the left-hand house, which also contains subordinate wives; and another group of wives, in very big families, for the right-hand huts . . . The junior wife and her children are under the authority of the senior wife and her children . . . The sons' rights and positions in their father's home and in their agnatic lineage are determined by the positions

34. H. Kuper (1947), p. 111
35. H. Kuper (1950), in Radcliffe-Brown and Forde (1950), pp. 93, 96, 98.
36. Schapera (1953), pp. 36-7; (1963), pp. 159-73.
37. Schapera (1950), in Radcliffe-Brown and Forde (1950), p. 104.
38. Gluckman (1940), in Fortes and Evans-Pritchard (1940b), p. 34.
39. Gluckman (1950), in Radcliffe-Brown and Forde (1950), p. 186.

of their mothers. Some of the main sources of litigation among the Zulu are disputes between half-brothers about their rights arising from the respective status of their mothers . . . The positions of the wives' huts in the village, their status in the tribe, the order of their marriage, their wedding ceremonial, the source of their marriage cattle, are all considered in evidence.[40]

Among the Kachins of Highland Burma, few of whom have plural wives, ultimogeniture prevails and 'elder sons today usually move to another village', to escape their high-ranking youngest brother. 'A man's rank is in theory precisely defined by his birth', but since 'an intolerable psychological situation is likely to arise' if he stays at home, the elder brother generally moves to his wife's village as 'bond slave (*mayam*) to his *mayu* (wife's kin)'. According to Leach, this 'mechanism of lineage fission is closely linked with ideas about class status, and the process . . . is at the same time a process of social mobility up and down the class hierarchy. The choice that an individual makes about his place of residence affects the class status and prospects of his descendants.'[41]

Polynesia provides some of the most elaborate examples of a unitary stratification system that ranks family members as well as families:

The mode of succession is primogeniture; the eldest son succeeds to the position of his father . . . Not only is he differentiated from his younger brothers, but so also is every brother differentiated from every other, in accordance with their respective order of birth and the consequent prospects of succeeding to the position of their father . . . The seniority principle in the family is a microcosm of the ramified social system . . . As a consequence of seniority, the descendants of an older brother rank higher than the descendants of a younger brother . . . *Every individual* within this group of descendants of a common ancestor holds a differing status, one precisely in proportion to his distance from the senior line of descent in the group . . . People descendent from remote collaterals of the common ancestor are lower in rank than those descendent from a more immediate relative of the chiefly line. People with the lowest status are those who have descended from younger brothers through younger brothers *ad infinitum*. The process of primogenitural succession and its consequent implication of seniority results in a ranking structure which encompasses the entire society . . . In every ramified society one can recognize groups of statuses or status levels which are functionally significant in terms of differential socio-economic prerogatives. These different levels are normally present in all the larger ramages.[42]

Among the Muslim Hausa, besides his legal wives, a man could have slave concubines. Under Muslim law a concubine who bore her master a child became freed on the master's death, when her child inherited with those of the four legal wives. Several Hausa emirs in the last century were born of concubines. In this case, free and slave, the master and the concubine, are joined in the same family; but only on the former's death is the latter freed.

In Hausa families,

40. ibid., pp. 183, 195-6.
41. Leach (1954), pp. 109, 160, 167-8.
42. Sahlins (1958), pp. 140-2, 147. His italics.

differences of marriage order take precedence among co-wives over other
differences, such as age or parentage, but outside the household these other
differences may have more significance . . . The average Hausa woman probably
makes three or four marriages before the menopause . . . Under such conditions of
marital instability, spouses cannot share the same social status. Indeed, the status
differentiation of co-wives by reference to marriage order precludes their status
identity with the common husband. Legally and politically this identity is also
impassible[43] . . . [since] authority over women is divided between their husbands,
to whom they are subordinate, and their kinsmen, who are their legal guardians.
Thus the wife is not identified with her husband as his ward.[44] . . . [In Hausa
society] the status gradient produced by rank and lineage is finite and steep . . .
Inheritance . . . facilitates the economic differentiation of descent lines . . .
lineages include descent lines of widely differing status.[45]

These data show that even within nuclear families, for example
those of Hausa men and their concubines or wives, spouses may not
share the same status, nor siblings the same rank, as among the
Kachin, Polynesians or Bantu. In all the cases cited, the differential
ranking of family members extends beyond the family to rank them
and their descendants differently in the wider society. Thus the
stratification within the kin group supports and corresponds with
that outside it, and this is an important feature of the political
organization of these societies. For the Southern Bantu, Hoernlé
generalizes that 'among the children a strict hierarchy prevails, based
on the seniority which serves as a fundamental principle of . . . Bantu
society. The elder brother always takes precedence between brothers
. . . and so too between sisters . . . Outside the intimate circle of the
immediate family, the same principles of kinship and seniority hold
sway.'[46] According to van Warmelo 'Bantu social structure knows
no equals, as with whole sibs, so with individuals. The first-born of
the same parents is always superior to those born after him, and this
superiority is extended to his descendants, with varying consistency.'[47] This is the type of rank-differentiated unilineal grouping
that Kirchhoff identifies as the 'conical clan'. In his words, 'it is
precisely the nearness of relationship to the common ancestor of the
group which matters . . . [This] principle results in a group in which
every single member, except brothers and sisters, has a different
standing.'[48] As our data show, Kirchhoff erred in ascribing equivalent status to siblings in these units. If siblings shared equivalent
status, the conical clan could not emerge. In short, when societies
rest their stratification on principles that differentiate descent lines
in status by seniority, they do likewise with family members.

It is clear that many societies exhibit a stratification which
differentiates family members as well as families. Thus, neither of the

43. M.G. Smith (1959), p. 244.
44. M.G. Smith (1961), p. 59.
45. M.G. Smith (1959), p. 241.
46. Hoernlé (1937), in Schapera (1937), p. 71.
47. van Warmelo (1931), p. 11.
48. Kirchhoff (1959), in Fried (1959), vol. 2, p. 266.

two general assumptions on which the functionalist theory of stratification rests are empirically valid. Neither is stratification universal, nor are families universally exempted from it.

If we ask why, given their inconsistency, these postulates of universal stratification and the unstratified family are combined, the answer seems to be that on this basis it is easy to distinguish different types of stratification system by reference to the family. The reasoning might be summarized as follows: (1) All societies are stratified. (2) In all societies, families are homogeneous units of status placement. (3) Stratification systems differ in the ways they treat families; some restrict opportunities to a limited number of families, others· distribute them to all member-families equally. Systems of the first type are ascriptive and particularistic, while those of the second stress achievement and universalistic criteria. (4) Since systems of both types exhibit both stratification and familial status unity, a single general theory is applicable to all.

Ethnographic data show that these assumptions, and the theory that seeks to justify them, are invalid. The 'universal necessities' imposed by functional prerequisites are simple misapprehensions. If my argument holds, the critical sources of difficulty for this functional theory are twofold: first it seeks to explain structure by function, when the reverse is the wiser procedure. Structures are highly differentiated and complex, while functions tend to be generalized and rather abstract. Just as Malinowski failed adequately to account for the known range of variation in the family by his very general functional theory of the family, so it is probably impossible to 'explain' the known variety of social structures by· a single functional theory of stratification. Secondly, in seeking universality, this theory creates difficulties for itself by regarding any set of observable inequalities in the distribution of advantage as stratification, irrespective of the mode of their institutionalization. Given this, the errors regarding relations between family and stratification seem inevitable. But in segmentary lineages, which are political structures despite their familial components, and in age-set systems, though positions of unequal advantage and responsibility are general, the mode of their institutionalization involves an automatic serial rotation of these positions, since the modal life-cycle and life-chances are equal and standardized. Stratification consists in institutionalized differentiations of access to positions of differing advantage, rather than in the mere fact of social differentiation.

When unilineal descent principles are combined with internal differentiation of rank between siblings, on grounds of either matrifiliation or seniority by birth, the resulting internal stratification of the lineage group precludes the status equivalence of siblings, and the co-ordinate status of segments descended from them. As a direct effect of these principles of status differentiation, and in exact correspondence with their intensity, the structure of the unilineal descent group diverges from the pure model of the segmentary lineage as a hierarchy of levels, the members of which are all co-ordinate. In similar fashion, the ascriptive universalism of the age-set will be modified by principles that impose status inequalities among its members on other grounds. Similarly, band organization varies societally as a correlate of the differing principles on which the bands are constituted. However important, stratification — the differential distribution of access to advantageous positions — is only one of these modifying principles.

5.

There are two sides to my argument. Negatively, I seek to show certain inadequacies in the current theory of stratification. Positively, I am suggesting that the principles that regulate access to positions of advantage also define political units such as age-sets, bands, segmentary lineages, ramages, etc. In short, I wish to stress the political basis of social stratification. Unstratified societies are acephalous, and in these units status consists of membership in the modal political units. Stratification is correlated with hierarchical political organization, which may or may not be fully centralized. Like other principles and modes of social differentiation, stratification has political bases and implications. Whether restrictive or egalitarian, differentiation is a condition of political organization. Some highly differentiated societies may not exhibit determinate strata; others do; but even systems with primary stress on situs will gravitate towards stratification unless certain principles prevent it. Stable situs systems may thus represent an arrested intermediate type between the formally stratified and the unstratified. The differences between the latter pair are fundamental.

I fail to see in what sense it is useful or accurate to describe personal status differences in bands, segmentary lineages or age-organized societies as either ascribed or achieved. Neither term seems meaningful here. The utility of either presupposes some hierarchic differentiation of positions and some principles by which access to them is differentially distributed. As these principles vary, status is usually said to be ascribed or achieved. The utility of this dichotomy is also doubtful on other grounds.

Munro Edmondson illustrates some of the operational difficulties in his distinctions between ascribed, achieved, and associational status. In his view, statuses differentiated on age, sex, and kinship are ascribed, while achieved statuses include differentiations based on religion, economy or politics. By associational status, he indicates differentiations based on membership in such voluntary or compulsory organizations as dance societies, ceremonial associations, fraternities, religious orders, clans or *gentes*, phratries, bands, villages, tribes, age-grades or stratified ranks.[49] The inconsistencies of this effort are apparent.

An important theme of the following paragraphs is that ascription and achievement of status are regularly concurrent in stratified societies. Wherever secular stratification is overtly or formally ascriptive, positions are achieved or held by competitive struggles. Wherever the conditions of stratification formally stress individual achievement, ascriptive factors are crucial. Ideal-type analysis of these complex and very varied systems is not merely inadequate but misleading. Even an analysis in terms of dominant and subordinate value systems fails to deal adequately with their structural complexity and variety.[50] We must always seek the structural particulars, resisting reductionist temptations inherent in value theory until the essentials of a given system have been isolated as a particular complex of principles, and compared with others of similar and differing character. Quite probably such inquiries may require somewhat less ambiguous categories than ascription or achievement; attention to restriction, sponsorship, competition and personal or impersonal selection may be more useful.

Stratification consists in the restriction of access to positions of varying advantage. If uninstitutionalized, such 'restriction' can only be random, unprincipled, contingent and temporary. Not to be so, it must be institutionalized on the basis of certain principles, whatever these might be. Such institutionalization always involves a historical selection of the relevant principles. Where the various principles that regulate this differential distribution of opportunities are mutually conflicting and obstructive, dissensus is generated, and the system may break down. Thus adequate institutionalization involves mutual accommodation of the relevant principles into a congruent scheme. These principles may and do vary widely; so do the positions and rewards to which they relate, and so does their mutual congruence and interdependence. Where the relevant principles regulating opportunities and defining the structural significance of positions are loosely integrated, a situs system may emerge, and such a system may enjoy adequate consensus. While the resilience of a stratification system depends on the consensus it elicits, this consensus itself depends on the character, congruence and inclusiveness of the principles that establish the stratification. Even though its constitutive principles are congruent and mutually reinforcing, a stratification may lack adequate consensus if these principles are not sufficiently inclusive. The political nature and implications of stratification are directly evident here.

To postulate a consensual normative basis for all forms of stratification is an unnecessary error which may be traced to the

49. Edmonson (1958), pp. 8-9.
50. Kluckhohn and Strodtbeck (1961), pp. 32-5.

influence of Weber and Durkheim.[51] It is also very common nowadays, and recurs at various levels of specificity as an indispensable premise for the analysis of society by reference to values. Thus,

regardless of the type of stratification and authority system, a normative scale of priorities for allocating scarce values (precedence, property rights, power, etc.) is . . . always vital.[52] . . . Human society achieves its unity primarily through the possession by its members of certain ultimate values and ends in common.[53] . . . Stratification *in its valuational aspect*, then, is the ranking of units in a social system in accordance with the standards of the common value system.[54]

Normative consensus expressed in agreement about standards relevant for ranking persons and positions is perhaps the most efficient basis for a system of differentiated access; but it is neither the only one, nor self-generating; and its principal conditions, ethnic homogeneity and identification by birth with a unit having a continuous history, are not general among underdeveloped nations currently engaged in industrialization. In consequence, as Shils observes, 'consensus' may have to be 'coerced'.[55] This empties the notion of any positive meaning. Furnivall succinctly described some of these societies in their colonial phase as 'plural societies'. Perhaps this pluralism persists into early independence. In the plural society, 'as a whole, there is no common social will. There may be apathy on such a vital point as defence against aggression. Few recognize that in fact all the members of all sections have material interests in common, but most see that on many points their material interests are opposed.'[56] In these colonial and post-colonial societies, the system of stratification is one of the most fertile sources of discord. Its continuity often depends on constraint rather than consensus.

Schwab provides an illuminating application of consensualist theory and procedure in his discussion of stratification in Gwelo, a Rhodesian mining town of 7,000 Europeans and 25,000 Africans, mainly Shona, Ndebele, etc. Having defined social stratification as 'the differential ranking of functionally significant roles in terms of a common set of values', he asks, quite correctly, 'What are the functionally significant roles?' and 'Is there a shared and common value system by which these roles are evaluated?' His answer follows immediately:

Clearly, in the African urban social system in Gwelo, which is marked by extreme heterogeneity and fluidity in norms and social behaviour, there is no

51. For representative statements by these writers, see Durkheim (1957), p. 61; Weber (1947), ch. 1, sec. 5 and p. 298.
52. Aberle et al. (1950), p. 106.
53. K. Davis and W.E. Moore (1956), p. 244.
54. Parsons (1953), p. 93. His italics.
55. Shils (1962), pp. 14, 16, 35, 58, 64, 70.
56. Furnivall (1948), p. 308. For comparative materials, see also International Institute of Differing Civilizations (1957).

single system of values by which individuals are ranked higher or lower according to their various roles and activities. Therefore what we must ask is whether there is one common set of values which predominates in the urban context, over all other value systems and which then may serve as a source of differential evaluation.

In short, having failed to find evidence of a common value system, we must postulate one; and this follows duly in the next paragraph:

In any society, a person holds numerous roles, any one of which could be used as a basis for evaluation. Here I shall consider that the relevant roles for evaluation in the system of stratification in Gwelo are those that are socially functional within the urban context, and require . . . full time participation . . . In Gwelo, this means the roles an individual has within the urban industrial economic system.

The illusory quality of this 'common value system' is almost immediately apparent:

The most striking feature of the Gwelo social system is the discrimination in roles between Africans and Europeans. By custom and law, occupational categories have been stereotyped.[57]

In short, the stratification is political in base and ultimately rests on force. Although among the Africans, 'tribal affiliation is a primary category . . . of differentiation', Schwab regards such differentiation as secondary to 'the socially functional roles in the urban industrial system which I have taken to be the primary basis for the system of social stratification'.[58]

Schwab's frankness may be unique, but his assumptions and procedure are not. One major weakness of current sociological studies of stratification is their commitment to this postulate of a normative consensual basis and integrative function, even where the stratification is forcibly imposed. History is full of dead and overthrown stratification systems – e.g. that of eighteenth-century France.

Consensual normative bases can hardly be claimed for systems that were overthrown by popular revolt or subverted by new religious ideologies, or which provoked extensive withdrawal, such as the migrations to America beginning in 1620, or a series of unsuccessful revolts, such as New World slavery. Simply to say that 'stratification systems may in fact endure for considerable periods without causing rebellion or revolt, but because of the differential distribution of power (including knowledge), this is neither surprising nor to the point',[59] is merely begging the question. This confession admits that stratification may rest on other bases than 'a common system of

57. Schwab (1961), in Southall (1961), pp. 128-9.
58. ibid., p. 131.
59. W.E. Moore (1963), p. 83.

values', and likewise social order. It is also a direct contradiction of the same writer's earlier thesis.[60] As I have pointed out elsewhere:

Social quiescence and cohesion differ sharply, and so do regulation and integration but, if we begin by assuming that integration prevails, it is virtually impossible to distinguish these conditions . . . It is especially difficult to isolate the positive effects of common values in culturally split societies that owe their form and maintenance to a special concentration of regulative powers in the dominant group.[61]

The evidence shows that while some societies have integrated consensual normative systems, others have not, but depend on coercion for establishment and continuity. While stable acephalous societies lack stratification but are consensually integrated, stratified societies may or may not have consensual bases. Ubiquitous cleavages between groups labelled Conservative, Liberal, Communist, Fascist or other, indicate how widespread dissensus about the current stratification may be.

In the following sections, I shall therefore contrast stratification systems whose stability varies as an effect of differences in the inclusiveness and congruence of the structural principles which define them. All the systems discussed below are mixed in the sense that they combine institutional arrangements for the ascription and achievement of status. By considering their differing stability, we can explore the relations between the structural principles on which these systems are based and the levels of consensus or dissensus that they exhibit.

This is not the place for a formal discussion of stability. By a stable system, I merely mean one that does not generate internal movements aimed at radical structural change. By an unstable system, I mean one with a history of violent internal movements for such change. By comparing systems of different degrees of stability, I merely wish to show how consensus varies as a function of the structural basis of their stratifications, and thus to suggest that instead of simply postulating normative consensus as the basis of all social order and stratification, we should analyse the structural conditions that regulate its incidence, intensity and scope.

6.

Opinion varies as to appropriate units for stratification analysis. Some writers stress positions, others roles, others individuals, groups or social categories. All agree that stratification consists in status rankings. Each of the statuses ranked has an absolute value, that is, its constitutive rights and powers; each also has a relative value in comparison to some or all others. This relative value varies with the

60. K. Davis and W.E. Moore (1956), pp. 244, 246.
61. M.G. Smith (1960c), in Rubin (1960), pp. 775-6.

units compared. The absolute value also varies as the rights and powers of the status are latent or manifest. When these are latent, the absolute significance of the position or incumbent is of less interest than its relative significance in the system of positions. In a rigid, well-defined stratification, rankings are always constant and clear, despite the latency or relativism of the units, and this means that the system must observe certain laws of economy. It must be based on one or two very simple general principles, such as birth and ritual status, or birth and jural status. Where the system rests on several principles, ambiguities of relative status are almost unavoidable, and the system loses its rigidity as well as its definition. I can illustrate this by reviewing some familiar forms of stratification.

In a consensually based society, the unequal distributions of opportunities that constitute its stratification are accepted as part of the normal order of things, as for instance in Hindu India, medieval Japan or Europe. Such differential distributions of opportunity may have differing bases and may relate to ritual, material or social values. Several such systems of differentiation may coexist without any single one being clearly primary. While some societies exhibit only one stratification scale, others exhibit more. In either event, the consensus on which the stratification rests also supports the political order. Systems lacking an adequate consensus differ in their properties, problems and potential.

Indian caste is an instance of a rigorously ascriptive system of ritual status, which enjoys such profound support that modernization makes limited headway against it. Caste being primarily ritual in its base, ranking and referents, it easily accommodates variable local secular rankings based on wealth, power, knowledge, etc. Its immutability simply means that ritual status is absolute, even when latent; and this condition restricts realignments and individual mobility to the secondary secular sphere. Although individual movement between castes is virtually nil, within limits people may change their occupation and residence and, by changing their ritual observance, they can also seek to elevate their ritual status and that of their issue. But since personal status is identical with caste status, individual mobility on this level is minimal, though *jati* (sub-castes) may change their relative status over the generations by internal fission, relocation, and by adopting new external ritual symbols. Given the deep consensual basis of caste, such enhancement of *jati* status corresponds to the more stringent observance of ritual norms. The system evokes this intense support through its identification of the social and religious orders. The religious principles that regulate caste differentiation legitimate the entire structure as a religious order.[62]

62. Hutton (1946); Stevenson (1954); Srinivas et al. (1959); Basham (1959); ch. 5; Leach (1960); Zinkin (1960); Gerth and Mills (1947), pp. 396-615; Marriott (1955); A. Mayer (1960); Beidelman (1959); Bailey (1960); Kalenda (1963).

The feudal organization of medieval Europe and Japan also rested on fairly general consensus and habituation. Despite their institutional cleavages, these populations shared common cults and community membership, much as the Brahmans and *harijans* do. In differing places and periods, the rigidity of these feudal orders varied; but all based their differential distribution of opportunities primarily on birth. Some were born free, others serf, some noble, others villagers, merchants, and so on. Even guilds sought to restrict membership by descent from members. In both areas, only such religious structures as the Catholic Church or the Buddhist mon-asteries, by their celibacy rules, excluded recruitment by descent, thus implicitly presenting alternative structures. None the less church recruitment for offices of varying rank was qualified by the candidate's birth status. In these systems, the principal avenue of individual mobility was physical transfer and relocation, usually in a town. Only thus could one escape the direct implications of one's birth status.

None the less, these estate systems differ sharply from caste. Ritual heredity differentiates castes, but in estate systems, hereditary differences are secular in base and referents. While caste can accommodate secular ranking as a secondary local stratification, in medieval Europe, ritual stratification was itself indirectly dependent on birth differences of a secular nature. Under caste, secular relations among ranked castes are rather variable; and instances of Sudras acquiring Kshatriya status by virtue of their territorial and military dominance are well known. In the secular estate system, the political bases and correlates of stratification are fixed and clear. Members of superior strata exercise jurisdiction over members of inferior ones, individually and collectively. Short of rebellion, the only hope for the subordinate strata to improve their lot is by physical withdrawal — to the town. In Europe, besides strata differentiated by birth and political status, the nobility was also divided between church and state. In the secular sphere, nobles competed for titles, land and power against rivals also qualified for this competition by birth; in the ritual sphere, birth status was qualified by secondary emphasis on learned clerical skills.[63]

This baronial competition has numerous parallels in other intermediate societies. In India, Kshatriyas were rivals or allies; in Buganda, Anuak, Zulu, Swazi, etc., royals fought for the throne while eligible commoners, recruited restrictively, competed for lesser offices open to them. Among the Hausa-Fulani, royals competed for the throne, noble lineages for reserved office, clerics for clerical office, slaves and eunuchs for theirs also. In Japan, *daimyo* were recruited mainly from *daimyo* and *samurai* competed with *samurai*.

63. Sansom (1962); J.W. Hall (1962); Reischauer (1956), in Coulborn (1956); Bloch (1961); R.J. Smith (1963); Ganshof (1952); Bennett (1960); Pirenne (1963, no date); Weber (no date); Postan, Rich and Miller (1963); Coulton (1959); J.P. Davis (1961).

We cannot simply write off these combinations of restriction and competition as transitional phenomena, as Nadel would have us do.[64] The combination of competitive achievement and restricted eligibility is too variable and widespread to be glossed over lightly. Examination may show that it is in one form or another a universal feature of all stratification systems. Certainly such mixed systems vary widely in their particulars, and merit detailed study. Even modern industrial societies whose ideologies explicitly stress universalistic and achievement orientations exhibit restrictive particularisms which, despite their educational and financial bases, effectively preserve racial and social inequalities. Without this structured contrast with ideology, the conflicting interpretations of American stratification by such writers as Parsons, Mills and Warner are incomprehensible.[65]

Recent studies of the Chinese bureaucracy warn us against classifying mixed systems loosely as ascriptive or open, and also against overlooking the critical analytic differences between ideal and actual patterns. Though in theory recruiting its officials by competition — and so encouraging social and economic mobility — positions in the Chinese bureaucracy were often acquired on other grounds, and though the Chinese stratification was notoriously static, movements between the gentry, bureaucrats, peasants and commercial class were apparently continuous. Despite Confucianism and these institutional provisions for social circulation, this stratification also lacked a religious ideology adequate to maintain general consensus, as the various revolts that punctuated Chinese history show.

In any centralized society of moderate scale, the number of highly rewarded positions will be small by comparison with the number of eligible candidates, however restrictive the conditions of eligibility. Technical qualifications may be stressed, but unless the opportunities to acquire them are uniformly distributed throughout the society, its stratification has a restrictive base, and the achievement of individual status by competition is qualified accordingly. Unequal distributions of educational and occupational opportunities may thus generalize ascriptions by birth and effectively maintain these long after they have been formally repudiated. Under such conditions, the stratification cannot be accurately represented either as an open system or an ascriptive one, or as a transitional form; its particulars require detailed analysis; and to distinguish the conditions and consequences of its combination of principles, we must ask what regulates the range and scope of the competition, and the recruitment of competitors, and what differential rewards and disabilities are involved. In India, where inter-caste competition is ruled out, ritual heredity is the principle of recruitment, and differential ritual status

---

64. Nadel (1951), p. 171.
65. Parsons (1953); Lloyd Warner, Meeker and Eells (1949); Lloyd Warner and Lunt (1941); I.L. Horowitz (1963), pp. 23-71, 305-23; Mills (1959).

the explicit reward. In feudal societies, descent is the basis of a differential distribution of jural status, including rights to land, jurisdiction and political office, these being the main rewards. In systems where 'technical' qualifications prevail, such as Imperial China and the modern West, differential educational opportunities are the mode of restriction, and occupational status the main reward. Various combinations of these arrangements can be found in historical and contemporary societies, industrial or other.

7.

A consensualist theory of stratification tends to overlook conquest states, despotisms and slavery, which usually evince clear stratifications. Conquest and its consolidation establishes a stratification explicitly based on force, as for instance in Norman Britain, among the Swat Pathans, or in Aztec Mexico.[66] Accommodations developed during the process of consolidation may establish a solidary stratification on consensual or symbiotic bases,[67] or they may not. In Ruanda until recently, various writers believed that the subject Hutu accepted the 'premise of inequality' on which Ruanda stratification was based. The introduction of democratic electoral processes has shown the error of this view.[68] Despite a common ideology of divine kingship, Hutu expelled their Tutsi rulers with amazing efficiency and speed. In Hausaland (Northern Nigeria), where conditions are comparable, the ruling Fulani, whose power rests on conquest legitimated by Islam, are exposed to no such threat. The differences here are rather interesting. Tutsi consolidation in Ruanda instituted 'caste endogamy' and a perpetual exclusion of Hutu from positions of social advantage in ritual, political, military and other fields. Fulani intermarried with Hausa, adopted their language and political institutions, and provided ample opportunities for mobility into important positions. Whereas the divine kingship of Ruanda remained the property of the Tutsi 'caste' and identified with it, in Northern Nigeria Fulani domination is expressly identified with Islam and its faithful observance. In line with this, Fulani stress Islam as an indispensable qualification for political office, descent being secondary though highly strategic. Hausa subjects accept this mixed regime, with its unequal opportunities, partly because it is legitimated by Islam, partly because the commercial context provides opportunities for the pursuit of compensatory values, and partly because the distribution of power discourages protest.[69]

Until 1900, slavery enjoyed official sanction in Hausaland; in some Hausa states, perhaps one-half the population were slaves, but to my

66. Barth (1959); Soustelle (1962); Moreno (1962); Bernal (1963).
67. Nadel (1938, 1941); M.G. Smith (1965a).
68. Maquet (1954, 1961); Kagame (1957); d'Hertefelt (1960a, 1960b, 1962a, 1962b).
69. Hogben (1930); M.G. Smith (1955, 1960a, 1964a).

knowledge the Hausa never experienced any slave revolt. In the West Indies and Brazil, where slavery was widespread, revolts were frequent and often serious.[70] Haiti owes its independence to such a revolt.[71] In Surinam, Jamaica and the Guianas, large groups of slaves withdrew to settle in inaccessible jungles or mountains, where their descendants presently remain. The contrasting responses in these Muhammadan and Christian slave systems illustrate how consensus may vary even in systems that are formally very similar. While some systems of slavery excite revolt, others do not. I have shown elsewhere how the assimilation of slave and free through religious and kinship institutions inhibits revolt, while the reverse obstructs satisfactory accommodations.[72]

The traditionalist Latin American societies present varied phenomena: revolts followed by aquiescence, competition within restrictively defined circles, political nullification of subordinate strata, and a universal Church identified with the social structure, both as critic and sanction. Systems of this sort may endure despite evident inequalities, dissent and apathy, partly through force, partly through inertia, partly because their organizational complexity and structural differentiation inhibits the emergence of effective large-scale movements with coherent programmes. Castros are, perhaps, not only exceptional but limited in their effect.[73]

Latin American societies vary greatly in their particulars, but all display certain common features. Cultural and social pluralism prevails with racial stereotypes or classifications and correlative value divergences. Mobility is restricted, though individual Indians 'can move, albeit slowly, into rural mestizo classification':[74]

In general, South American countries impose fairly rigid barriers to both horizontal and vertical movement out of Indian society . . . There is considerable reason to believe that some very distinctive rural mestizo cultures are also plural societies, as rigidly demarcated as are Indian cultures . . . In Mexico, large masses of rural mestizos have substantially the same culture as many Indians, but do not form distinctive plural societies, although there is a high degree of localism and regionalism. The only countries where the feudal class system and, more particularly, feudal class attitudes have disappeared to any extent are the Europe-oriented countries and Mexico.[75]

The resilience or immobility of Latin American stratification may thus be in part a function of the cultural diversity of the large subordinate strata. This reinforces community closures among mestizos and Indians alike, each community maintaining its dis-

70. Ramos (1939), pp. 25-43; Parry and Sherlock (1956), pp. 72, 151, 163, 186; Herskovits (1941); M.G. Smith (1953b); Elkins (1963).
71. Leyburn (1941).
72. M.G. Smith (1954b).
73. MacGaffey (1961); Adams et al. (1961).
74. Beals (1953), p. 338.
75. ibid., p. 336.

tinctive status system. An individual's status is thus derived from his community. Such ethnic heterogeneity generates 'racial' structures of discrimination which perpetuate the structure of inequality as a base for cultural and social differences, even where the populations thus segregated are overtly similar in race, as for instance in Haiti or Guatemala.[76] Beals's conclusion that 'the use of strictly economic or economic and political criteria for class analysis of Latin America is the least fruitful approach'[77] may hold for other societies in which 'the significant feature of the stratification is its bifurcation',[78] with many segments among the subordinate strata.

Simple increases in market opportunity will not usually alter these stratifications, for two reasons. In many cases these economic differentiations are integrated with the system of stratification as conditional or dependent factors; in others, as India, they may be simply irrelevant. Geographical mobility, especially to the large anonymous cities, may offer an opportunity to escape one's given status; but this is only significant where one wishes to escape, or where ritual conditions permit it. In secular systems, unless individual levels of aspiration and expectation are adjusted to the conditions of stratification, dissent and protests are likely; but to be effective, these presume that the subordinate strata are not vertically divided into closed communities. In these unstable systems, with more or less dissensus, ascription and competition coexist, and in the most extreme form of this system, the plural society, the closed community is often represented by occupationally specialized ethnic groups, such as the Jews, Chinese, etc.[79]

8.

I summarize my argument as follows. Stratification is a mode of social differentiation, and though social structures may be viewed as status systems, only some of these are stratified. All such systems display observable unequal distributions of advantage, but they fall into quite distinct categories. Some societies institutionalize equal access to positions of advantage; this involves uniformity in the positions and in the modes of recruitment. Such societies lack stratification. Other societies institutionalize unequal access to positions of advantage, and display stratification in various forms and degrees. In all cases, unstratified societies are politically decentralized, and the political and status structures are coincident. Units, the members of which share an identical status, are the corporations on which political and administrative order rests. These units of

76. Tumin (1952); Gillin (1948, 1951). For Haiti, see Lobb (1940), pp. 23-4; Leyburn (1941); Simpson (1941, 1962).
77. Beals (1953), p. 339.
78. Sjoberg (1952), p. 233.
79. Broom (1954, 1960b); Benedict (1961, 1962); van Lier (1950); Furnivall (1948), pp. 304-12.

public order and regulation are mutually distinguished and related by the same principles that regulate the distribution of status. Nor could it be otherwise, since status is a jural and political condition. These acephalous unstratified societies vary quite widely in structure, but if stable they all rest on general normative consensus.

Stratified societies also vary in many ways. Some, with diverse bases of distribution, emphasize situs to the virtual exclusion of ranked strata; others distinguish ranked strata of varying kinds, some being defined jurally, others ritually, yet others racially and culturally. In all cases, the principles that differentiate and regulate this unequal distribution of opportunities are identical with those that distinguish and regulate publics as corporate units of internal order and external articulation. That is to say, the principles of stratification are basic to the political order. Nor could it be otherwise, since the differentiated statuses have jural and political connotations, directly or indirectly, as Max Weber recurrently observed.[80]

The principal criteria of status differentiation are linked directly or indirectly with the various types of reward, and these criteria may vary from ritual or jural capacity, from race, culture or wealth to education and occupational qualifications; but in all cases the widest span of the status system coincides with the limits of the widest effective political unit, as Nadel points out; and its basis and significance lie in the political sphere. For this reason, stratification cannot be adequately studied in terms of underlying value-orientations; it represents an order interdependent with the political order, based on certain concrete structural principles. In consequence of these principles, people might develop adjustive value-orientations, or protestant ones; but we must explain the values by reference to the structural principles that generate them, rather than the reverse.

If my argument holds, economic variables cannot have unconditional priority in the allocation of status unless uniformly open conditions of occupational recruitment are institutionalized, so that expansive market opportunities will generate increased mobility. In such conditions, one would expect that market contraction would stimulate institutional barriers to mobility; in no society known to me, however, have economic or occupational differences served as unconditional criteria of status allocation. Restricted eligibilities are always important, though often covert. So far as economic and occupational opportunities or achievements are regulated by other principles of status allocation such as ritual, birth, race, cultural difference, etc., market fluctuations may leave the structure unaffected; but any general process of re-stratification is always political.

While stratification systems vary in stability as a function of their normative consensual structure, this consensus is itself dependent on

80. Gerth and Mills (1947), pp. 160-1, 163-4, 171, 179, 191-3, 259-60, 276, 283, 298, 300-1.

the character, congruence and inclusiveness of the structural principles on which the stratification is based. Some stratified societies, despite high inequalities, develop a consensus that legitimates the order. Others, with similar or lesser inequalities, do not. The source of these differences seems to lie in the nature of the principles that regulate the systems rather than in the scale of inequalities as such. The wider the consensus and the more inclusive the legitimating ideology, the more absolute may be the tolerable differences between ranked strata and the wider the span of the stratification. India, China, feudal Europe, Japan and Latin America illustrate this. Situs structures correspond to narrow spans of differential advantage and diverse or competing legitimating norms. History shows many examples of political orders, that is, status structures, which endure for more or less time despite popular dissent. European absolutism, New World slavery or peonage and modern colonialism are merely the most obvious examples. To regard stratification as universal, and as always based on common values, is doubly mistaken. In societies lacking consensus, stratification is explicitly political in base, function and form. In societies with consensual foundations, the status structure, whether stratified or not, is at least implicitly political in function, basis and form, and generally explicitly so. Where present, whatever its bases, stratification is a condition and focus of the political order as well as a product of political history. In societies with 'bifurcated' or plural stratifications, such as Latin America, India, China, colonial Africa, South Africa, the Middle East and the West Indies, the re-stratification requisite for adequate economic mobility to support industrialization may thus develop only through explicit political action that seeks to rearrange the relations and categories forming the structure.

If an industrializing 'emergent nation' is a territorial association of diverse indigenous societies, the 'national' stratification inevitably differs from that of these indigenous units; hence the generality and political basis of plural or 'bifurcated' systems. Moreover, the process of industrialization pursued at the national level itself intensifies the differentiation of these two types of stratification. The local distribution of these industrializing efforts also differentiates their structures from the pre-industrial systems around them. When tribesmen move to industrial towns, they may or may not lose their tribal identifications, wholly or in part; but in either event they enter a different milieu with its own logic and organization. In various urban industrial situations, such immigrants encounter differing structures of opportunity, incentive, restriction and sanction; and if they remain, they must accommodate to these as best they can. Normally, these structures of opportunity and restriction are politically determined and enforced; the events of this American summer (1964) or the processes of decolonization are patent evidence. This constraint may also be true of the movement to town.

While canalizing the accommodation of their urban proletariats, such social structures generate divergent responses according to the particulars of their situation. Amerindians in Tegucigalpa, Bantu in Johannesburg, Ibo in Enugu, Gonds in Orissa, Mende or Temne in Freetown, face rather different structures of opportunity and restriction, and, partly for this reason, they react differently.

6.

A Structural Approach to the Study of Political Change

1.

In the absence of appropriate conceptual and analytic frameworks, the theoretical study of political change remains undeveloped despite current interests in the processes and conditions of 'political development' and 'modernization'. To excuse this deficiency, we cannot plead lack of data. Indeed, the range, volume and variety of historical records of political change present social science with materials of unequalled richness and importance. Neither is it true to say that these questions have hitherto escaped attention. From Plato and Aristotle to the present, we can trace a long line of illustrious thinkers whose preoccupations with the conditions and forms of continuity and change in political regimes have inspired their working lives. Social anthropology, sociology, history and political science all derive from these analytic interests; but to date historians have probably done most to advance our understanding by furnishing those descriptive accounts of political units and sequences which are indispensable for any comprehensive, theoretical study of political change.

Historians differ in their interests, methods and objectives. Probably most direct their studies towards narrative reconstructions of the development of particular social units or selected institutions and situations. Besides the accuracy, relevance and comprehensiveness of their primary data, such narrative histories also differ in the cogency of their arguments, in the new light they shed on familiar topics, and in their general significance for other inquiries. Historical treatment of such institutional systems as the economy, the church, the constitution or law, requires more explicit analytical conceptions and procedures than narrative representations of past developments. In differing ways and degrees these institutional histories apply or expound conceptual schemes which derive from general theories of the institutional systems or processes under study. Thus legal historians employ concepts drawn from their theories of law and studies in jurisprudence. Economic historians employ or examine categorical relations which derive from economic theory. Historians of philosophy or science are also guided by the interests, conceptions and relations that distinguish these fields. Thus the analytic frameworks that organize these institutional histories have extrinsic origins and referents, and rarely emerge from the historian's consideration of specific historical processes.

Although this quality is often implicit, history is inherently comparative in its reference. History which is explicitly comparative has two principal forms: 'universal' histories or 'philosophies of history' such as those of Marx, Hegel, Gobineau and Toynbee; or comparative studies of more restricted phenomena such as feudalism, riots, revolutions, the classical city-state, archaic imperial systems and the like. Universal histories attempt to comprehend all ranges of social action within a single general framework, such as Toynbee's processual model of challenge and response, or Marx's theory of ultimate economic determinism. Neither alternative provides an appropriate basis for analytic studies of political change, since both assimilate political relations to other types of social relations and propose to 'explain' the development of these ensembles by abstractions of remote and historically contingent character. In any case, the formulas which universal history is said to demonstrate, whether processual or causative, are equally difficult to validate or to develop and refine for application in detailed studies of limited sequence and range. In effect, universal histories lack several essentials of analytic science.

Comparative studies of particular historical forms, such as feudalism or latifundia, or of specific processes such as colonization, bureaucratization, or dynastic decline, provide materials and insights of greater relevance for those students of political change whose interests are not restricted to contemporary problems of 'modernization' and 'political development'. However, the principal merits and shortcomings of these comparative histories arise equally from their analytic concentration on specific processes, forms or contexts to the exclusion of all else. In consequence, their approaches and conclusions are at best only casually co-ordinate, though often inconsistent. It would seem then that, despite the varied and important contributions historians have made to the theoretical study of political change, the form and character of their inquiries has diverted attention from the essential preliminary task of developing appropriate conceptions and procedures.

In contrast with such historical inquiries, a scientific study of political change seeks to develop generalizations that are universally valid, precise in their reference, verifiable, capable of further refinement, and logically linked by their derivation from a common conceptual scheme. Such a study presupposes clear definitions of its subject matter and scope. It also requires a system of discriminating operational conceptions and analytic procedures. Thus, before proceeding to set out its central conceptions and analytic procedures, we should indicate the scope and character of our inquiry as well as its specific subject matter.

2.

Whatever their differences of subject matter, scientific inquiries have uniform character and proceed by analysis and observation. They seek to formulate general statements concerning relationships that regulate the structures and processes of the phenomena under study. Such generalizations constitute a theory if they form a logically coherent body of propositions. The validity of such scientific theories is measured by their correspondence with empirical events. This correspondence may take two alternative forms. In laboratory situations, experimental techniques allow for the verification or disproof of scientific hypotheses and the theories to which they attach by replicative experiments. In such sciences the empirical validity of a theory can be determined by experimental tests of expectations or predictions inferred from it. In other sciences which, by reason of their subject matter or stages of development, lack suitable experimental techniques, the empirical validity of a theory is commonly assessed by its capacity to accommodate novel data within its categorical system, while illuminating their structure, relations and development. Parsons and Shils correctly distinguish these two types of scientific theory as categorial and predictive.[1] Categorial theories consist of logically developed conceptual schemes designed to order and comprehend all phenomena of a given sort without, however, generating specific hypotheses about their necessary relations which empirical research could verify. Predictive theory presupposes development of operational procedures to test specific propositions about given classes of phenomenal events based on abstract models of invariant relations within the categorical field. It is evident that scientific inquiry seeks to isolate invariant relations within particular fields of study, to formulate their logical connections, and to guide their further investigation. These objectives hold also for the scientific study of political change.

These objectives have certain implications. First, if 'invariant relations' are the principal goals of study, then scientific inquiries should range comprehensively throughout the fields in which such phenomena occur. Operationally, this means that generalizations must be validated by processes and relations observed at all levels of political action and within all varieties of political unit. In its indifference to such comprehensiveness, the theoretical structure of current studies in political modernization and development exhibits grave weakness.

If our object in studying political change is to formulate valid and verifiable general statements about it, then such changes are the sole

---

1. Parsons and Shils (1951a). See also Sheldon (1951), pp. 30-44.

subject matter of our study, and the generalizations we seek can only refer to relations inherent in the conditions and processes of political change. This objective has three implications. First, it necessitates generic criteria which will allow us to segregate political change from other phenomena in the social field. Secondly, it obliges us to distinguish as endogenous and exogenous those conditions or 'causes' of change that are intrinsic or extrinsic to the sequence of events under study, and directs our attention to endogenous relations and processes, that is, to those developed within the political unit or system. Finally, this objective identifies the inquiry as a search for invariant relations within the conditions and sequences through which political change occurs. Such analyses must initially exclude questions of causal determination, in order to investigate the formal properties of processes involving change. If we can adduce any invariant relations from the study of such processes, these generalizations should either specify uniformities in the relations of determinate political conditions or in the sequences by which these change. Such uniformities of structure and process can only express relations of logical necessity. No alternative foundation for such invariant relations is conceivable, given the enormous variability of political sequences, forms, contexts and units with which we have to deal.

To many, restrictions that focus our study on the formal features of sequence of change may seem unnecessary and mistaken, since they exclude the study of 'causes', or 'determinants'. Such objections are ill-founded for several reasons. First, although it is appropriate initially to exclude problems of exogenous causation in order to seek constant relations among the elements and processes of change, our framework neither denies the relevance of 'exogenous' causation, nor prohibits its study. Indeed there is a clear advantage in basing investigations of the 'causes' of change on detailed prior analyses of sequences that identify their critical initial events and distinctive forms. Moreover, given the specificity of the socio-historical contexts in which political change proceeds, causal explanations inevitably consist in specifications of historically derived sets of contingent variables and circumstances. By their nature, they accordingly exclude the invariant relations that scientific study seeks in such phenomena.

Causation is more complex in character and demonstration than the formal analysis we seek to develop. In some laboratory sciences it may be possible to isolate specific causal factors and relations for direct study by replicative experiments in which variables are controlled and manipulated. This is rarely possible in sociological study, and never in history, which provides much of the basic material for theoretical studies of political change. In consequence, substantive causal analyses of historical processes that specify particular or general determinants are rarely verifiable and normally problematic, since the relative significance and connection of the relevant factors in all the different situations that constitute the sequence cannot be demonstrated conclusively.

Of all factors which have hitherto obstructed the scientific study of political change, preoccupation with 'causal explanation' is undoubtedly the most important. Even today many scholars reject analyses of social events as inadequate unless they are cast in causal moulds. However, given the variety of conditions and factors necessary to the occurrence of any event, assertions that a single factor or set of factors determined a specific occurrence are rarely verifiable or analytically illuminating. This reservation holds whether the asserted 'cause' is an impersonal condition or force, or individual or collective motivations, imputed or actual. Unless such 'causal' analyses invoke an ultimate universal determinant, as in Marx's theory of historical materialism, the isolation of proximate 'causes' merely initiates an endless regression to identify their determinants and the antecedents of these determinants, indefinitely. This regression is logically necessary in order to demonstrate the causal principle or principles at work and their efficient conditions; but at each step in such regressive analyses the speculative component increases as the empirical declines, so that the initially problematic postulate loses its value as the derivative of this speculative chain.

In seeking to avoid these difficulties some writers postulate universal and ultimate determinants of social phenomena. However, it is then necessary to demonstrate the decisive influence of such ultimate factors in any particular sequence, either immediately or by regressive speculations. Alternatively, if regressive inquiries into the genesis of proximate causes are excluded, the inquiry is restricted to the identification of immediate determinants. 'Causal explanations' of this latter type must thus illustrate the determination of events and processes either by a single 'cause' or by a variety of 'causal factors' in similar and different situations. Once again, analyses of the first sort can rarely be restricted to the universal proximate 'cause', despite assertions to the contrary. Now while explanations of the second type, which appear to demonstrate the variability and multilateral character of 'causation' of similar and different events may possess superior plausibility, they exclude illumination by presenting apparently arbitrary images of contingent determinants. Moreover either type of causal explanation also leaves unresolved various substantive problems by predicating their uniform or diverse determinants in similar and dissimilar historical situations. Thus, neither model of causal explanation can justify its claims of necessity, nor does either possess any evident superiority to a strictly formal analysis that seeks to identify uniform relations among the elements, conditions and processes of change. Indeed, given the historic failure of 'causal' theories of political change, it is appropriate and necessary to approach this subject from a different angle and with differing questions and aims.

3.

To orient our inquiry, we must first examine with care the notion of change. Analytically, change and continuity are complementary and mutually exclusive concepts that serve to define one another. Empirically, continuity and change are often, perhaps typically, concurrent in social affairs, which appear always to exclude absolute novelty or perfect stasis. Thus, continuity and change are relative terms that indicate certain dimensions or aspects of social process.

Change may denote alteration in the state or relations of any object or objects, or it may denote the processual context and events in which such alterations develop and are manifested. The first meaning identifies change as observable modification, the second as the process through which such modification occurs. These altern-ative emphases are quite compatible and complementary, providing they share identical criteria of modification. However, uncertainties arise when modifications are latent rather than manifest, or when they proceed through events that imply, or even obscure, instead of exhibiting them. Such possibilities direct attention to the need for clear criteria and conceptions in order to identify change objectively.

Any event may be loosely identified as an instance of change, even if the only change involved is an expenditure of energy. Often routine transactions characteristic of a given system are plausibly treated as moments of change, since they effect redistribution of some components. For example, the replacement of one official or age-set by another may be perceived as change by the actors and by the communities involved; but if these are their only features, such events may also with equal or greater validity be cited as evidence of continuity in these societies. That it is possible and common to find two apparently opposing classifications of the same events as evidence of continuity and change, indicates the need for clear criteria to distinguish these conditions. In the situations just cited, to determine whether or not the event represents change or routine circulation, we need further data on the nature of the polities concerned, and especially on their operational processes. It is of course accepted that for the individuals involved these status movements do represent change; but this merely emphasizes that our unit of reference is neither the individual nor the community, but the system of social relations in which these events occur. By change, then, we mean either some alteration in the state of a system of social relations, or the processes by which those alterations occur.

This reformulation merely raises the question whether any and every modification in the 'state of a social system' constitutes its change. Since social systems have temporal duration, they commonly experience expansion and contraction of their memberships as well as the simple circulation of members in roles. We may therefore ask whether any alteration in the numbers or composition of the members or in the material resources and capabilities of a social unit constitutes evidence of its change. Concretely, this question requires distinctions between the social system as a system of social relations and its demographic, economic or technological dimensions, each of which can be conceptualized as an analytic system and examined for evidence of persistence or change. While it is likely that beyond variable limits, changes in their demographic, economic or technological bases and characteristics may destabilize or modify social systems, as yet we neither know these limits precisely, nor can we determine their implications without considerable information about the nature and ecological context of the societies in which these developments occur; but *prima facie*, mere changes in its number of members or gross domestic product or urbanization ratio need not directly entail modifications in the nature or structure of the system itself. They may indeed manifest its continuity and routine growth. We should accordingly distinguish such developments from others that entail or express modifications in the nature or structure of the social system, whether or not its population, economy and technology remain unaltered. To distinguish these developments from system change, we can classify the former as *extensive*. By change, then, we do not mean merely extensive alterations in the state of a system or the processes by which such alterations occur. Rather, we mean those alterations in the structure of the system which involve changes in its characteristic processes and operational conditions. In short, we seek initially to segregate structural change from those conditions or processes that involve mere changes of extent, while recognizing that in many contexts both processes go together. For us, the decisive criterion of change is modification or transformation of the structure of the system concerned.

By structure, we mean the set of units and their interrelations which gives a system its characteristic perduring form, boundaries, and operational modalities. The two critical components of structure are discrete *units* and the *relations* that hold within as well as between them. The precise character of these established units and their relations will vary with the unit or system under study. As a system, the family has a structure which articulates a complementary set of statuses and roles; but often such family units are minor components of larger aggregates, which constitute the major structures of their societal systems. In short, these conceptions of structural components are equally applicable at any level of social organization. In addition, these conceptions are closely connected. Systems conceived as more or less viable units composed of interacting parts depend on their structures for organization and boundaries. Structures, as persistent articulations of determinate parts, presuppose specific contexts and processes for their development, existence and modification. Structure and system are thus complementary abstractions through which the continuum of social processes may be conceptualized for analysis. Social structure consists in those enduring relations and units manifested in recurrent processes of social action; while by a social system I merely mean a set of interconnected social processes and the structures they engage and sustain or modify. Accordingly, changes in system structure develop and are expressed through changes in the processes and conditions that constitute these concrete units and articulate them to one another as operational structures.

These conceptions enable us to distinguish simple circulation of personnel through social positions from superficially similar movements which none the less involve or generate modifications in the criteria or procedures of allocation and in the scope, status and relations of the positions concerned. Circulation that does not express or entail structural modification illustrates the continuity of system routines. If the circulation of personnel directly or otherwise modifies the procedures, criteria, properties and relations of the statuses concerned, it manifests, initiates or implies some structural change. This change may be limited in range and discontinuous in time; or it may be otherwise. Change may thus develop in one component without immediate or wider effects. Change may be either episodic or continuous.

Structural change of any kind develops by processes or series of events through which initial structural arrangements undergo greater or less modification. Without at this stage attempting to specify exact criteria, we can usefully distinguish *transformations*, which involve major reorientations of structure, from other developments which may illustrate internal adjustments and/or external adaptation. *Transformations* may proceed abruptly, episodically or radically, with or without violence; or they may develop gradually through processes of some historical duration. In either event, a structural transformation may be challenged and revoked by counteractive processes. If the structure alternates between two contrasting poles, as for example the *gumlao* and *gumsa* regimes among the Kachin,[2] it illustrates *pendular* transformations. If the system recurrently develops a series of three or more differing types of structure, it illustrates self-generating *cyclical* change. If the alternative structures develop in fixed succession, as in classical models of ancient Greek polities, the cycle can be described as *stable*, even though its transformations proceed violently. *Unstable* cycles are those in which the structural alternatives succeed one another irregularly for various reasons. In both pendular and cyclical transformations, possibilities of structural change are limited to those alternatives which are consistent with the character and capacities of these systems in their specific contexts. In effect, though the decisive moments of

2. Leach (1954).

structural transformation in pendular and cyclical systems are episodic, structural change proceeds continuously with them, within limits set by certain ineluctable conditions and features of the systems concerned.

Without evolutionary or developmental implication, we can distinguish those courses of structural change which are neither pendular nor cyclic as *linear* or *vectorial*. These terms merely indicate that the sequence of such changes appears to trace a path distinct in outline from pendular or cyclical schemes, though generally irregular in its rate and direction. Phases in a process of linear change may form a structural series, or they may be episodic and discontinuous. Episodic change may either be institutionalized as a feature of a restabilized structure, or it may be nullified by some counteractive process. Systems subject to periodic restabilization after episodic changes may achieve transformation through such successive modifications. The events that express these episodes of change may be radical or casual, violent or peaceful, similar or dissimilar, unique or widely distributed. They may be generated within or outside the system.

Two terminal situations of structural change relate to the processes by which systems emerge as distinct units with clear boundaries and constitutions on the one hand, or dissolve, disintegrate and lose their distinctness, boundaries and internal cohesion on the other. As regards social systems, both alternatives may develop internally by the normal processes of structural change, or they may be mediated by historic events such as conquest and consolidation, the formation and dissolution of empires, or the political abolition or creation of units. Though these historic and genetic processes can be assimilated, it is useful to distinguish them, since the former operate abruptly and discontinuously to generate or dissolve systems by drastic revisions of unit boundaries, scope and autonomy. To the subjugated system, such terminal change is always exogenous; but to the dominant unit, the new system based on its domination is endogenous in generation.

As outlined, structural change is neither synonymous nor coterminous with political modernization or development. Indeed, history and ethnography illustrate many courses of structural change which involve neither modernization nor 'political development'. Political modernization I take to mean the processes by which regimes develop the administrative and party-political features and capacities characteristic of modern industrial states. In this form, the concept is especially unsatisfactory, given the variety of political and administrative institutions that are to be found in this ill-defined category of 'modern states'. Certainly, besides the stable and unstable democracies and pseudo-democracies of the West, we should have to include totalitarian regimes, such as Soviet Russia, Nazi Germany, Falangist Spain, confederations like Switzerland and Lebanon, racial oligarchies such as the Republic of South Africa and Rhodesia, military, familistic and personal dictatorships, and so forth. Objectively, I can find few characteristics common to such a heterogeneous assembly of states which might serve as analytical criteria for identification and study of distinctive processes of change. Evidently, also, the concept of modernization is intended to subsume the notion of political development; and this latter characteristically denotes enhancement of system stability and capacity by increasing the differentiation and interdependence of functionally specialized structures within the polity. However, historical evidence does not support the assumption that the stability of a political system increases in proportion to its internal differentiation or enhanced capacity. France, Italy and Germany indicate the reverse. It may be advisable, then, to restrict the notion of 'political development' to the enhancement of system capacities without assuming parallel increases in stability. Further, it is analytically useful to distinguish changes of system *scope*, that is, of the affairs routinely regulated and functions routinely performed, from changes in system *capacity*, redefined as potential for the performance of additional functions or for the better performance of existing ones. In this sense, capacity is conceptually latent in the current scope; and only in the limiting case is capacity identical with scope.

The notion of stability has differing connotations in studies of synchronic and diachronic systems. Synchronically, stability denotes system perpetuation with minimal change. Systems may be ranked as more or less stable on this criterion by reference to the incidence of structural changes within them. However, in diachronic studies which treat continuity and change simultaneously and equally, the stability of a system denotes the persistence over time of congruent and logically coherent structural conditions and processes generated within it. In this sense, diachronically France may be less stable than the United States, though synchronically the reverse may well be true. France, indeed, may represent a case of pendular change, whereas the United States appears to trace a vector, despite secondary pendular movements.

Since we are concerned with those preliminary clarifications which are necessary for a comprehensive and theoretically oriented study of political change, defined as changes in the structures of political systems, our discussion has concentrated on structures and processes within the system, while ignoring those without. However, though as yet unremarked, the political system clearly engages or generates beliefs, values, ideologies, knowledge and attitudes, among much else that is commonly described as political culture, together with such material conditions as population size, composition and distribution, economy and technology, historic experiences and contemporary socio-ecological contexts. These latter are perhaps the principal external factors that influence political action; and only by so doing can such factors influence the system to modify or preserve it.

Since change of state develops as a process, that is, by a series of events, some events will manifest or initiate change while others which are also relevant to the understanding of these developments may not reveal their import directly. We have, then, to treat events and conditions in which change is latent; and to demonstrate and analyse the structural implications of these events, we need discriminating criteria derived from appropriate conceptions of the system under study and from the processes of change itself.

In studying change, although events provide our data, the analytic units are processes or events of variable form, scope, span, simplicity, direction and length. Occasional sequences provide 'natural' units, as for example in revolutionary movements. Yet even in such cases, the criteria and value of periodization vary with the purpose and level of our inquiry; and it is advisable in analysing change to periodize an event, series of process successively into sequences of diminishing span and range for increasingly intensive analyses. If the processes by which political structures change are structurally uniform, being characterized by invariant relations among their elements, then such re-analyses of progressively smaller sections of a common sequence of change should yield sequences of identical analytic structure, despite substantial differences of detail. In chemistry or physics, such re-analyses of limited parts of process or substance provide important confirmations and further insights into their structures; and perhaps in studying social change, we may benefit likewise from a similar procedure.

4.

The generic unit whose processes of structural change we seek to analyse is the political system, which consists of those activities and relations by which public, that is political, affairs are regulated. Political events are the incidents by which this regulation of public affairs proceeds. The elementary components or principles of political action are authority and power, authority being the right and obligation to take appropriate actions in certain situations subject to conditions and procedures set out in precedents or rules, while power is the capacity for effective action, despite material and social obstacles. Though power presupposes the framework of precedents and rules which distributes capacities to secure support and compliance unequally among individuals and social aggregates at any moment, its bases, modes and application are not entirely circumscribed by these norms and rules, since these institutions retain their legitimacy for relatively long spans of time until superseded, whereas the distribution of power tends to be labile, instrumental in its bases, modes and objectives, and open to the influence of many variables, without prescriptive legitimacy.

Political relations in the strict sense are relations that mediate and express the distribution of power. Administrative relations express and mediate the forms and operation of public authority. Together these relations of power and authority, of politics and administration, constitute the regulatory processes of government that identify the political system and delimit its social boundaries. In short, all systems of public regulation combine forms of public authority with distributions of public power. Differences between political systems can thus be reduced to differences in the forms and scope of public authority within them, and in the distributions, bases and modes of their public power, together with the conditions produced by the combination of these two structures.

The social unit to which the political system attaches is generally described as a polity; but in its narrower meaning, this term denotes the political system as a discrete, continuous system of regulatory activities. From Aristotle's day to ours, the term polity has had these dual referents; to the form of the system of political action, and to the social unit such action regulates. Often a social unit maintains a particular system over long spans of time. In other cases, for example France, a continuing social unit may experience different political systems in fairly rapid succession. In yet other cases, such as the Tswana or Hausa, populations that share a common basic form of political organization maintain their boundaries by mutually exclusive political systems.[3] It is appropriate, none the less, to regard these Hausa or Tswana societies in some analytic contexts as having a common polity or type of political system. In another context, although their polities are centralized, Hausa and Tswana societies remain subdivided into a plurality of internally autonomous units comparable with nation-states in the modern world. Thus political centralization may unify a society or subdivide it into replicative segments; and it may also subordinate several societies to domination by one. It is thus inappropriate to equate centralized polities and societies, or to assume that politically segmented societies must always be stateless.

As a formally distinctive system of political relations and activities, the polity is coextensive with the society it incorporates and delimits. Societies conversely owe their boundaries and order to the structures and processes that distinguish their political organization. As indicated above, these structures and processes are closely identified, political processes being adaptive and articulative operations that are generated by political structures and modify or sustain them.

The primary units of a political system are identified by the exclusive regulation of certain affairs for their members. Such units are always *corporate groups* which, despite important differences in their bases, scale, organization and other qualities, all share certain

3. Schapera (1953); M.G. Smith (1959, 1964*b*, 1965*b*).

common features, being presumptively perpetual aggregates with unique identities, determinate boundaries and memberships, and having the autonomy, organization and procedures necessary to regulate their exclusive collective affairs. While some corporate groups or publics lack corporate subdivisions and may or may not form parts of larger groups, others often contain two or more such divisions, which may or may not differ in their bases, scope and organization. Thus, communities and nation-states represent corporate groups which include other corporate groups of diverse type and span. At the opposite extreme, in the simplest societies, the corporate band is a unicellular autonomous group that does not form part of a larger one. These examples illustrate extremes in the range of polities whose change we seek to study. In nation-states the polity embraces a public organized as an inclusive corporate group under a distinctive institutional system. In a society based on corporate bands, the polity contains a number of discrete units of identical form and character without any wider collective structures to co-ordinate them. While the 'centralized polity' is a self-contained unit, the decentralized polity, despite generic homogeneity, contains a series of homologous units whose articulation and boundaries derive from their similar structures, compositions and conditions of interdependence. To apply common conceptions and procedures to the analysis of changes in systems of either type, we must first identify and distinguish their structural components, and then examine the evidence of change in these structures at the widest or at any subordinate level of organization. This procedure applies equally to polities organized as corporate groups and to those decentralized polities constituted as *corporate categories.*

Polities, or any perduring social units that lack comprehensive organization and effective arrangements for the co-ordination and regulation of relations among their components, represent *corporate categories.* Having presumptive perpetuity, determinate boundaries, identity and memberships, such corporations are constituted as categories by their lack of the organization, procedures and capacity necessary to regulate the common affairs of their collective memberships. While corporate groups and categories are both 'perpetual' aggregates, groups possess the co-ordinative organization that categories lack, and in consequence they have the requisites for and the need of continuous regulative action. Unlike corporate groups, which are thus always units of public regulation, corporate categories, whether societal or sub-societal, are structurally incapable of common action to regulate common affairs, since both presuppose the comprehensive organization that would convert these categories into groups.

A corporate group such as a community or a nation-state may include members of different categories, for example the various caste categories that cross-cut Indian villages, or the jural categories that cross-cut feudal manors. Conversely, some categories such as clans, slaves, races or age categories, may contain a plurality of corporate groups without losing their categorical character. Decentralized polities illustrate corporate categories which are normally subdivided into a plurality of corporate groups.

Within corporate groups, we often find collegial units constituted as presumptively perpetual decision-making bodies in which only a minority of the group membership participates. Such *colleges* or councils are governmentally specialized corporations that should be distinguished from the corporate groups they regulate on various grounds. To organize and administer their collective affairs routinely, all but the smallest and most intimate corporate groups require specialized regulatory structures of corporate character, which must thus be determinate, unique, and presumptively perpetual. *Colleges* provide one possible agency of such public regulation, *offices* provide another.

Offices are corporations sole, which possess the four formal and four operational features that distinguish *perfect* corporations such as groups or colleges, and endow them with capacities for continuous regulatory collective action. Characteristically, the office, like the college, is attached to and embedded in some corporate group as a regulatory organ. Often, however, a single corporate group is simultaneously regulated by one or more offices and colleges, having more or less appropriate divisions of authority and function among them. Corporate categories lack colleges and offices as co-ordinative agencies, and thereby lack the requisites of corporate groups; but occasionally corporate categories may be converted into corporate groups by a charismatic leadership which mobilizes and co-ordinates their collective action; and even more rarely the category, under favourable circumstances, may constitute itself as a group by establishing a college to regulate its affairs.

Charismatic leadership illustrates one type of *commission*, another being represented by military, magisterial, ecclesiastical and bureaucratic commissions which are organized into 'perpetual' ranked series of identical and substitutable units of indefinite number and duration. Unlike such serially organized commissions, charismatic leadership is a unique self-authenticating organ of collective regulation, which accordingly lacks prescribed procedures, organization, spheres of action and authority. As Max Weber showed, a charismatic commission often mobilizes its own public and establishes its own procedures and structures which may later dissolve, fragment or be 'routinized' by conversion into an official hierarchy.[4] Yet a third type of unique discontinuous commission, characteristic of centralized polities, is a statutory commission created by presidential or parliamentary action to investigate or regulate a particular subject, or in republican Rome, to deal with a critical emergency. On completion

4. Weber (1947).

of its task, the statutory commission normally ceases to exist, though it is sometimes perpetuated by conversion into a college or an office. Until then, it generally enjoys a wide discretion to achieve its purpose.

Commissions, organized in ranked series of indefinite extent, are important units of administratively specialized corporate hierarchies under the direction of superior units; and in consequence these hierarchic structures have the characteristics of a corporate group. However, commissions differ from offices in certain ways. Precise rules, conditions and procedures of succession are essential components of office, to regulate the recruitment of successive incumbents and secure the unit's perpetuity, while maintaining its unique identity. The commission, however, lapses with the individual who creates or receives it, either on his assumption of office or on his promotion to a higher rank, as for example from captain to major. Moreover, while offices normally attach to specific corporate groups, serialized commissions operate as agents of the office or corporate group that creates and gives them authority. Unlike self-generated commissions, offices are subject to the rules and traditions that constitute and perpetuate them. Unlike statutory commissions, they operate continuously and routinely regulate recurrent affairs. None the less, there are many situations in which commissions operate like offices, for example in the direct administration of colonial territories by District Officers and/or District Commissioners. To the units administered, the commission, being apparently permanent, appears like an office, though in fact each attaches to the individual official who administers the area on behalf of the colonial government, rather than to the community itself. Indeed, administrative boundary changes are notoriously frequent in colonial administrations. Such ambiguities in the character and status of commissions amply illustrate their utility as organs of public regulation. However, autonomous discretion is normally restricted by rank in serially organized commissions, and by the allotted tasks of statutory ones. In simpler societies, self-proclaimed commissions such as shamanism may be institutionalized within corporate categories or groups, in which case they operate discontinuously, conditionally and in limited spheres without mobilizing the collectivity as a whole.

These corporate units of political organization may be classified in two ways: by the number of their members, or by their differential capacities. The first criterion distinguishes groups, categories and colleges as varieties of *corporation aggregate* from offices and commissions of either type which represent varieties of *corporation sole*. Under the second criterion, groups, colleges and offices are distinguished as *perfect* units endowed by their structure with capacities for continuous regulatory action from categories and commissions which lack one or more of these properties. All societies are politically incorporated as categories or as groups; and colleges, offices and commissions alike presuppose corporations aggregate as their contexts. For clarity we may distinguish these varieties of corporations as alternative *forms* or *types*, noting their possibilities for mutual conversion.

In synchronic studies of political systems, these various corporate forms, groups, categories, colleges, commissions and offices between them subsume all units whose properties and relations constitute the political structure. Whether the community under study is a polity or some segment thereof, and whether centralized or not, in diachronic studies these corporate forms and their relations also constitute the structure whose persistence or modification is under review. Accordingly, the forms of corporate organization institutionalized in a polity represent the primary units whose modifications of content, type and articulation or relationship provide the basic data in which invariant relations of process should be sought. It is therefore essential in every case to detail the particulars of this corporate organization before attempting a diachronic study of the structure and its transformation.

5.

To develop these conceptions of corporate organization in ways that may advance the analysis of change, we should first seek their general and specific *requisites* and *implications* by isolating the *principles* on which they are based. Corporate groups or categories may be based on descent, ethnicity, ritual and belief, locality, sex, age, occupation, property, jural status, or on association of persons for various purposes. Separately or in various combinations, these alternative *principles* constitute the logically possible *bases* of unit incorporation, since they govern the recruitment and differentiation of members and the exclusion of others. All corporate groups are based on some selection and combination of these alternative principles; and differences in the structures and operations of corporate groups are partly reducible to differences in their respective *bases of incorporation*, partly to the articulations with their social contexts. The conditions and criteria that govern the recruitment and standing of their members accordingly differentiate the major types of corporate groups in form, resources, interests and scope, organization, external articulation and capacity alike. This relation holds equally true for corporate categories and colleges. Within as well as between societies, similarities or differences in the structure and properties of corporations of the same class reflect identities or differences in their membership, bases and conditions on the one hand, and the external articulations of these corporations on the other. Because this is so, we are able to make systematic comparative studies of particular types of corporate units such as lineages or age-sets, guilds, professional associations, secret societies and economic corporations, cult groups and political parties in differing milieus; and since other classes of corporation, such as colleges, categories or corporations sole differ *inter alia* and *inter se* in the principles on which they are based and recruit their members, these may also be studied comparatively in structural terms. In such inquiries, having initially identified the type to which the particular corporation belongs by the formal and functional criteria given above, we should first analyse its structure and scope to isolate the specific principles on which it is based, that is, the minimal criteria that constitute and segregate it as a unit. These criteria are expressed in the rules and conditions that govern the allocation, tenure and loss of membership in the corporation. Accordingly, we should examine with care all procedures, rules and conditions that exclude non-members and regulate the admission and status of members, while prescribing and distributing their obligations, rights and privileges, uniformly or differentially in various ways. We expect uniformities in the conditions that regulate the recruitment and expulsion of members in corporations aggregate of any type, since this is essential to maintain the unit's boundaries, identity, continuity and form. However, uniformity in the criteria of membership is quite consistent with internal differentiation of members on other criteria.

Uniform conditions of allocation are also requisite for those commissions that are organized in ranked perpetual series of indefinite extension, since commissions of any single category in such structures are formally and functionally identical. Other commissions which are characterized by uniqueness and discontinuity in their incidence and operation can also be distinguished by differences in the principles on which they are based. Thus, charismatic leadership is based on its own claims to superior authority, while shamanism manifests its ritual base in specialized activities, and statutory commissions are clearly constituted for specific purposes by corporate bodies that have political authority to do so.

Office, the perfect form of corporation sole, is especially sensitive to change in its bases of allocation and in the conditions and spheres of its routine activity. An office is a corporation perpetuated through a series of single individuals who hold the position and exercise its functions in succession. Accordingly, the *succession* rules and procedures by which incumbents are recruited to offices bear critical relations to their structural persistence or change.[5] Yet notwithstanding the elaborate rules and procedures devised to regulate official succession uniformly, given their political significance and variable contexts of transfer, their bases, scope and relations with other units are frequently modified through succession struggles and processes. If such offices none the less persist with marginal change in their scope and character, despite changes in the formal principles

5. Goody (1966*a*).

that regulate their allocation, this indicates that their relations with other corporations in the system have not been radically altered by these changes in the conditions of succession. To legitimate such innovations, the ideology that prevails should translate and justify them as the restoration or fulfilment of some antecedent or superior norms. Hereditary offices are especially subject to structural change through modifications or adaptations of succession procedures; but perhaps such recurrent deviations are essential to the vitality of these regimes and, moreover, given the structural centrality of office and the differing situations in which succession proceeds, such variability is perhaps unavoidable over adequate time spans. Their systemic implications may be illustrated briefly by comparing the contrary cases in which non-hereditary offices are pre-empted by descent groups, a process by which patrimonial regimes are fragmented and multiplied, with those in which initially hereditary offices are appropriated on other grounds. Such changes in the principles of succession have equally important implications for the organization and continuity of the political unit in which the office is central, and for the character and operation of the office itself. Accordingly, these developments are important indices of processes of structural change in such regimes.

The *basis* on which a unit is incorporated can be represented as that *set of principles* which specifies the criteria that regulate the recruitment of members and exclusion of others. These criteria define the unit's boundaries, its essential interests, and the conditions of its continuity. Consequently, units constituted on different sets of incorporative principles differ in their *bases*, interests and requisites.

Any principle on which a unit is incorporated has certain logical *requisites* and *entailments* which can be identified by logical analysis. Logical *requisites* are those conditions which are logically or conceptually necessary for the formulation of a specific principle. For example, the principle of unilineal descent presupposes identification and differentiation of paternal and maternal relations and of genealogically successive generations. *Entailments* or *implications* are immediate logical consequences of a specified principle. For example, the principle of unilineal descent entails differentiation of some kind between kinsmen who share common descent and others who do not. It also entails the institutionalization of appropriate procedures for the identification of those who share common unilineal descent.

Though this is normally the case with corporate categories, I have not found any corporate group constituted on the basis of a single principle. Since corporate groups are the generic species of political unit, being inevitably concerned with the regulation of their own collective affairs, it is necessary to treat their bases and properties with particular care. Since corporate groups are constituted on a plurality of incorporative principles, whereas corporate categories may be based on one alone, it may seem that the fundamental differences between these categories and groups have their source in the number of principles on which units of either type are incorporated. Clearly, if a series of principles such as descent, locality and property are combined to demarcate and constitute the corporate unit, besides their *formal* or conceptual consistency with one another, their combination generates operational interrelations of a *substantive* kind. The *formal* and *substantive requisites* and *entailments* of each principle represented in the *set* that forms the basis of a unit must therefore be integrated with those that attach to other principles. In consequence, a *set* of incorporative principles as a set exhibits two kinds of entailments and requisites, the *substantive* as well as the *formal;* and these substantive requisites and entailments together define the operational conditions on which these principles can be viably combined to perpetuate a distinct unit. However, while the substantive requisites and entailments that attach to a specific set of clearly defined incorporative principles indicate their conditions of integration and continuity, they also appear to determine the *form* of the corporate unit based on that set. Thus, for example, unilineal descent, age differences, or locality may provide bases for the incorporation of units of differing form, such as categories or groups, each having distinctive requisites and implications; but such differences of corporate form inevitably qualify the specific principles selected and the mode of their combination. The differing properties and operational conditions of these corporate *forms* may therefore qualify the substantive accommodation of requisites and entailments of the principles that constitute them as corporate units and prescribe their relations to the wider system of which they are part. It is convenient to distinguish these substantive requisites and entailments and the alternative *forms* of corporation that entail or generate them from the *basis*, or set of principles, on which the unit is incorporated. The particular *form* of a corporate unit accordingly in part reflects its *mode of incorporation*; and provisionally, both *mode* and *form* prescribe certain substantive conditions that must be met by the combination of particular formal principles that constitutes the corporate unit.

Any set of rules or conditions has certain logical requisites and entailments, logical or conceptual requisites being those conditions or concepts which are necessary for the formulation of the rule, entailments being its intrinsic implications. Since the institutional components of social systems consist largely of rules and regulative procedures valid for all units within the system, the requisites and entailments of incorporative rules distinguish units of similar and different type, and regulate the collective and individual interactions of their members. Some of these implications and requisites refer to conditions *internal* to the units constituted by the principles to which they attach. Others refer to *external* relations of the unit concerned. Thus, the *requisites* and *implications* of determinate units can also be distinguished as *external* and *internal* by the relational spheres to which they refer.

For example, in a corporate group that recruits members by unilineal descent and forbids their intermarriage, special provisions are necessary to maintain the latter rule within the group and to arrange and regulate the marriages of members with non-members. Some of these provisions are *internal entailments*, others are *external*. Both sets of provisions are direct implications of the exogamous rule that binds the unilineal unit. It might be argued more remotely that this rule also implies the presence of nearby aggregates with whom the unit's members can intermarry; and that it also requires some rules to regulate the residence of spouses after marriage. However, neither inference involves an entailment. Connubium with others is not an implication but a *requisite* for exogamy as the characteristic of a corporate unit; and exogamy is neither requisite for nor entailed by unilineality, though very frequently associated with it. Moreover, unambiguous residence rules for married couples, however common and valuable, are neither requisite for nor entailed by exogamy or unilineal descent. To determine the foundations of these residence rules, we have to examine the forms and articulations of the intermarrying groups, paying special attention to the logical bonds between their internal constitution and their relations with one another.

It is analytically useful to distinguish the internal and external articulations of a given corporate form by segregating the internal and external requisites and implications derived from the principles that constitute it. *Articulation* simply denotes relations that hold between components within a given unit or between units in a given system.

Like its components, the system as a unit has its own incorporative principles, requisites and entailments, and its own internal and external articulations, which vary with its structure and context. Among the obvious *requisites of systemic articulation* are viability, boundaries, capacities for self-maintenance, structural congruence, and adequate levels of internal consistency and operational efficacy of its processes and parts. Systems, social or other, vary empirically in the degrees to which they fulfil these requisites; and they differ also in their forms, compositions, contents, characteristic operations and properties. Since political anthropology has to treat decentralized and centralized polities as varieties of a common general category, it clearly recognizes the variability of social systems. If we treat these systems and their components as units incorporated on differing principles and having diverse modes of articulation, we can analyse all as viable systems based on different principles and possessing different requisites and implications.

While the *external requisites of a system* vary with its nature and properties, they always specify its relations with its environment. So do the system's *external implications.* Together these external requisites and implications embrace the greater part of the continuing adaptive interactions or articulations that relate the system to its environment. For its operation and continuity, given a particular form and content, the system presupposes a minimal set of environmental conditions; and its operation generates others that may in turn react upon it, as Malinowski perceived.[6] Together, these external requisites and implications define the minimal external articulation of the system and its environment. Thus, unless specific developments in these external relations generate structural developments within the system, we may assume their provisional equilibrium and classify them as *exogenous* in order to segregate relations and processes within the unit for initial analysis. Moreover, even when external conditions do generate or restrict intra-systemic changes, these extrinsic relations should be segregated for analysis from the structural changes that indicate their effects upon this system.

The internal articulation of a system has certain operational implications for all its component units. Whether loosely or tightly articulated, the continuity of the system as a clearly bounded unit presupposes viable accommodations among its constituents and the complex triple congruence of their entailments and requisites with the principles on which these units are based, with the operational requirements of other units in the system, and with the viable external articulation of the unit or system as a whole. Systems vary in their coherence and viability with differences in the structural congruence and capacities of their components.

Clearly such conditions of systemic articulation have numerous implications for the units within them. However, without adequate data on these components and their properties, we cannot specify the precise implications entailed by their articulation in a single self-sustaining system. None the less, two points are clear: (1) on logical grounds, units of identical basis and form in a common system should have identical and mutually congruent requisites and entailments, while units with differing bases or forms should differ correspondingly; (2) systemic articulation has uniform and specific implications for all units of identical bases and form; accordingly, units of diverse bases and form are governed by different specific conditions of systemic articulation. Such uniformities and differences distinguish varieties of corporation as units of different status and scope within the system.

As indicated above, we can regard all units of identical form within a social system as systems whose immediate environment is the wider societal framework with which they articulate through their external requisites and implications. In this case, the internal

6. Malinowski (1944), pp. 1-144.

articulation of each unit consists in the relations between its components. These should be mutually congruent and harmonized with the requisites and entailments which attach to the unit as an operational system. It is thus evident that the same analytic model, conceptions and procedures apply equally to the most inclusive system, the society, and to all its corporate components. Accordingly, analytic procedures and generalizations appropriate at one level of organization should also hold at others.

6.

Relations between the principles on which a corporation is based, their requisites and their implications, are complex, but especially significant for the study of social change. A unit, U, having properties X^{1-n}, may be based on some specific set of principles such as locality, sex, descent and age, which might be written $Pa\text{-}d$, and which together involve certain requisites, R^{1-n}, and implications, I^{1-n}. Each principle generates its own specific entailments and requisites which must be integrated with those of others within the set to constitute the unit as a viable structure. Thus, requisites $1\text{-}n$ must be consistent with $Pa\text{-}d$ and with I^{1-n}, the entailments of the set. Moreover, as we have seen, some requisites and entailments govern the unit's articulation to its environment, that is, to the inclusive system, while others govern the articulations of the unit's component parts. We can therefore distinguish these two sets of conditions as *external* (E) and *internal* (I_n) respectively. An obvious internal requisite is mutual congruence of the constitutive principles on which the unit is based to form a viable set.

Thus, given $Pa\text{-}d \therefore R^{1-n} + I^{1-n} \therefore (RE^{1-n} + RI_n{}^{1-n}) + (IE^{1-n} + II_n{}^{1-n})$.

The state of stationary equilibrium for the unit UX^{1-n} based on $Pa\text{-}d$ requires the routine fulfilment of all these cónditions. Such a state indicates more than the mere mutual congruence of requisites and entailments. It also suggests their asymmetrical transitivity. By this I mean merely that external and internal requisites may stand in certain functional relations to one another and to their linked implications such that changes in either term may involve changes in the values of others without, however, prescribing their precise directions or proportions. It is thus possible that relatively minor changes in one sub-set of the series may be linked with extensive adjustments in one or more others. Such multilateral asymmetric responses in the set of implications and requisites may insulate the principles to which they attach from formal change by modifying certain properties of the unit, particularly its status or scope. We may therefore distinguish as major those changes in either of these requisites or entailments which generate changes in the form of the unit or in the set of principles on which it is based. Such changes may involve unit dissolution, absorption, or reconstitution on differing bases either by the amendment or repeal of a previous rule or by conversion of the unit into a different corporate type. In either event the unit's alteration of form or capacity will be expressed in its altered articulation with other units and the inclusive system of which they are part.

The major units of societal structure and articulation are corporate, as are the agencies that regulate them. Despite important differences and widely variable combinations, these corporations constitute societies as aggregates that have distinctive compositions, structures and modes of articulation. Societal articulations vary in looseness or tightness along distinct dimensions of centralization and functional interdependence. They vary also and more importantly in *mode* as societies are incorporated on *universalistic, consociational* or *differential* principles.

Corporations of any class have certain qualities, properties or conditions, namely persistence, unique identities, rules that regulate their membership, internal and external articulations. In addition corporate groups, colleges and offices possess set capacities for positive action to regulate particular affairs for particular aggregates by virtue of their organization and articulation in particular collectivities. Some commissions display autonomous regulatory powers while others are clearly subordinate agencies of the superior organization that creates and directs them. Of the five types of corporations and quasi-corporations described above, only categories lack autonomy, procedures, organization or common affairs reserved for their collective regulation. Even when subdivided into a plurality of corporate groups, a category lacks capacity for collective action as a comprehensive unit, being without the requisite means of inclusive or representative coordination. Being thus constitutionally incapable of undertaking routine actions to regulate any distinctive affairs, and whether or not subdivided into groups of variable scope and continuity, categories are either regulated by abstract rules which specify particular *proscriptions* or impose disabilities on the members, or they are subject to positive regulation by other units. A corporate category whose members by virtue of their categorical status remain subject to regulation by others is *differentially incorporated* in the society in which those who regulate it are characteristically organized as a corporate group. For example, conquerors commonly reconstitute the widest corporate groupings of the conquered people as categories by destroying their organization in order to incorporate them *differentially* into the wider society.

Categorical clans, which are subject only to regulation by abstract rules, though incapable of inclusive action, illustrate the opposite of such differential incorporation. The organizational incapacities shared by such clans indicate their equivalence as subdivisions of a society in which all individuals are incorporated directly and on identical terms. This mode of societal incorporation is explicitly *universalistic*.

A third, *consociational* mode of societal incorporation may be illustrated by societies organized in bands or segmentary lineages or as confederations. To enjoy the status of citizen, *consociational* modes of incorporation presuppose individual membership in one of several corporate groups of identical status and form whose union constitutes the common society. Individuals are thus incorporated in such societies indirectly and by virtue of their prior membership in one or other of these constitutive units. Individual affiliations are thus intermediate, indirect, and both formally and substantively equal under consociational structures, whereas under conditions of universalistic incorporation they are immediate, direct, and formally, though not necessarily, substantively equal; and under differential incorporation they are basically unequal in form and substance, intermediate and direct for some, but not for others. Briefly, under differential incorporation, the subordinate category is *in* the society but not *of* it.

Although analytically distinct and mutually exclusive as regards any particular regulative sphere, these three *modes of incorporation* may be combined in various ways to generate polities of differing structure and type. For example, *consociational* and *universalistic modes* of incorporation are combined in modern federations by arrangements that segregate the spheres of federal and state activity and simultaneously incorporate individuals in the federation and its member-states. Such regimes are structurally similar to those of the simplest societies organized in corporate bands, for example, Pygmies, Bushmen or Shoshoneans, since, although free to attach themselves to other bands, individuals can only participate in these societies as members of some band.[7] Such classic confederations as Switzerland, Ashanti or the Iroquois are correspondingly similar to societies based on segmentary lineages, for example, the Tallensi, Lugbara or Tiv, since in either consociational regime individual membership presupposes identification with one or other of the primary corporate groups.[8] In like fashion, societies based on universalistic modes of incorporation, such as France or the Plateau Tonga, share certain features, including the direct admission and formal equivalence of all individuals who participate in the collective life as members of the society.[9] Thus, universalistic and consociational regimes are equally compatible with political centralization or decentralization; but whereas all centralized polities as corporate groups maintain very clear boundaries, societies incorporated categorically on universalistic principles vary in this respect. With few exceptions, uncentralized

7. Turnbull (1965); L. Marshall (1965); Steward (1938).
8. Busia (1951); Morgan (1851), 1962 ed.; Fortes (1940); Middleton (1965); L. and P. Bohannan (1953).
9. Colson (1962).

societies that are incorporated consociationally are clearly demarcated, since their principles of incorporation exclude all who do not belong to a specific set of structurally identical units whose articulations establish and delimit the consociation. Although categorical in form, such societies are none the less sharply bounded aggregates, organized in units of identical basis and mode. In contrast, since decentralized societies based on universalistic incorporation assimilate individuals directly and without prior or intermediate affiliation, their boundaries are often ambiguous, since individual associations establish societal participation, while individual disputes indicate uncertainties about the norms, conditions and scope of societal membership. In such structural contexts, dispersals of power are marked, authorities restricted in range and scope, and the autonomy of individuals and of small, inherently labile groups is maximized. In consequence, the aggregate lacks effective structures of public. regulation capable of mobilizing members for such collective tasks as self-defence. The decentralized universalistic society accordingly invites attacks from other units on its borders, including consociationally organized regimes; and it may easily be incorporated in whole, in part, and differentially into a wider society by conquest. Such differentially incorporated societies are normally but not invariably centralized by their rulers to assure effective co-ordination and control of their subordinate categories. While many centralized polities have originated through the differential incorporation of subjugated elements under exclusive control of their conquerors, such structures may also develop in consociational systems if one unit or set of units extends its authority over the rest. Political centralization may also emerge when consociationally organized aggregates welcome alien immigrants among them as impartial mediators, judges, and leaders in ritual and military affairs.

It is evident that the differing forms and conditions of social stratification in all societies, pre-industrial or modern, correspond with these basic differences in the modes of societal incorporation. This is so, since corporations aggregate are the primary units for distribution of collective status. While unstratified regimes are generally consociational in their base, some universalistic corporations may institute formal egalitarianism, as in East African age-organized or matrilineal societies. The most rigorous stratification of corporate collectivities characterizes differential incorporation, while individually variable status placements are characteristic of centralized societies incorporated on universalistic principles. In brief, categorical aggregates incorporated universalistically or consociationally exclude corporate stratification, while centralized societies having similar bases combine individual status differentiations with arrangements for social mobility to meet certain operational requirements. By contrast, differential incorporation creates a structure of mutually exclusive collectivities ranked as superior and inferior by reference to their differential political status, and excludes intersectional mobility. The status structures of uncentralized consociations are thus radically different from systems of social stratification in which collectivities or individuals are the units of rank-differentiation. In the consociation, corporations of identical form are status equals, and so are individuals of the same generation and sex by virtue of their corporate membership. Thus the principal alternative forms of social stratification are directly correlated with those differences of mode by which societies are incorporated and constituted as groups under centralized administration, or as categories without it. Political centralization introduces stratification of individuals into formally unstratified consociational or universalistic regimes.

Differential incorporation automatically constitutes societies as amalgams of closed sections or segments that differ in rank, resource, obligation and privilege. It simultaneously proscribes intersectional mobility. Conversion of such an order into a universalistic regime can only proceed by eliminating these collective distinctions of rank and citizenship while individuating the criteria and distributions of status. Clearly, any changes in the modes of incorporation, or in the corporate status of an aggregate as category or group, entails many far-reaching changes in its political arrangements as well as in the forms and conditions of social stratification.[10]

Even societies that share identical bases of incorporation may differ widely in the complexity and character of their corporate organizations. Analytically, even the simplest societal system characterized by replications of a single corporate form presents at least two organizational levels that require detailed attention, namely that of the inclusive unit and that of its modal components. The internal articulation of such simple systems thus consists in the interconnections of these component corporations; and being identical in their bases, form, structure, resources and capacities, these units must also have identical requisites and implications, procedures, autonomy and scope — that is, those affairs and activities reserved for their routine regulation. In consequence, their relations with one another will be uniform and symmetrical, since all have congruent and identical requirements and entailments. Such uniformities necessarily prevail among all corporate units that have identical bases and modes of incorporation within the same milieu. Thus, units subject to differential incorporation differ correspondingly in their autonomy, resources, articulation and scope, even if they share identical bases, as in pre-colonial Ruanda;[11] and in so far as units having identical bases of incorporation articulate with one another asymmetrically in a common society, these differential relations indicate their status differences, which may also involve differences in

10. Southall (1956); Winans (1962).
11. Maquet (1961).

their modes of incorporation. Thus any event that initiates or expresses novel asymmetries in the relations of homologous corporations indicates or illustrates structural changes in the polities of which they are part.

Since units incorporated on identical bases and modes have identical requisites, properties and implications, they should also have identical types of relations with corporations of similar and different form, base and mode. Corporations accordingly differ in their articulative networks in correspondence with differences in their *form, bases* and *modes* of incorporation. Such differences in corporate units and their alignments will naturally complicate the structure of a political system and increase or decrease its cohesion in correspondence with their congruence.

The Yakö illustrate a polity that combines a variety of corporations, patriclans and patrilineages, matriclans and matrilineages, wards, ward-associations of various bases and types, age-sets, councils and offices in all these units, village associations of diverse bases, scope and character, and a village council under a ritually senior office. This Yakö village polity articulates its diverse corporations by distinguishing their criteria of membership, levels of organization and spheres of operation, and by segregating and ranking them casually by differences of scope, range and autonomy, while distributing offices and collegial memberships unequally among their senior members drawn from the different lineages and wards to form a graded structure of overlapping directorates that proves effective for village communication and control.[12] Kikuyu, Yoruba, Ibo, Cheyenne, Kipsigis, Hopi, Kwakiutl and Canella illustrate other combinations of diverse corporations, articulated as among Yakö, partly by the structural segregation of corporate memberships and their operational spheres; partly by assigning individuals multiple memberships in units of differing scope, type and level; and partly by hierarchic gradations that align corporations according to differences in their scope and range.[13] In such complex political organizations, units of identical basis, requisites and implications have identical status, autonomy, scope and articulations with one another, with differentially constituted corporations, and thus with the system as a whole. Conversely, units of diverse base differ in their properties, requisites, interrelations and articulation with the milieu. Inductively and *a priori*, the principles by which such structurally heterogeneous aggregates are co-ordinated include: (1) differentiation of corporations by basis, form, scope, range and status; (2) differentiations of regulatory spheres and their distributions among several agencies of diverse base, form, range and scope; (3) dispersal of individual

12. Forde (1964).

13. Lambert (1956); Middleton and Kershaw (1965); Forde (1951); Forde and Jones (1950); E.A. Hoebel (1960); Peristiany (1939); Eggan (1950), pp. 17-138; Boas (1940), pp. 356-69, 379-83; Nimuendaju (1946).

memberships in corporate groups and colleges, and simultaneous attachment of many persons to several units of differing base and type; (4) recognition of the validity of each unit's operation within its customary sphere; (5) simultaneous identification of all individuals with certain corporations such as lineages, age-sets and wards, as necessary conditions for societal membership and eligibility to enter others; (6) procedures for generating new corporations by collective action, subject to requisites of their compatibility with those already extant, and adequate congruence in their modes of articulation.

7.

The simplest human societies are identified by corporate units of a single uniform type. These societies are accordingly dependent for their internal order, cohesion, and continuity on the character and properties of their articulative structures. Characteristically, these articulative structures inhere in the symmetrical balanced requisites and entailments of the corporate units in which such populations are organized. In consequence they are diffuse, and contingent on individual interactions for expression and validity. Rarely are there any superior organs vested with responsibilities and resources for regulating the relations between these corporations; and where such organs as offices and commissions exist, there is generally little that they can do even in collective emergencies, given their lack of authority and resources. Thus, in the normal case, the societal structure represents a fine but discontinuous network of individual ties channelled by criteria of kinship, locality, generation and sex across unit boundaries. Individuals are normally free to transfer their affiliations and residence from one unit to another; and, being status peers, individuals of the same age and sex are members of corporate units with formally identical rights and properties. Social order is thus pervasively egalitarian, despite individual differences of status based on kinship, generation and sex, and less clearly on relative seniority within generations. Authority and power are thus dispersed with hardly any differentiation among individuals, even though the adult males may be organized in age-groups, or, as among Turkana and Karimojong, primarily in categories.[14] In consequence, individuation of this undifferentiated authority and power inhibits endogenous changes in the political structure, since differences in their distributions remain individual, situational, and therefore unstable. Even in situations of collective crisis, this distribution normally frustrates collective action under local leadership, since individual authority is equalized in type and span within corporate groups. While such categorical modes of organization may permit sporadic collective action, they inhibit institutionalization of differential roles among individuals. Since individual autonomy is

14. P.H. Gulliver (1958); Dyson-Hudson (1963).

preserved through freedom to transfer from one group to the next, responsibilities and authority remain vested in individuals, despite the structural requirement of group membership. Accordingly, despite individual mobility, groups are invested with residual and legitimating rights, and so provide enduring frameworks for the societal structure and for individual action alike.

Such a system accordingly admits three possibilities for endogenously generated change. Either some individual may establish his superior authority within a group by subordinating the autonomy of his peers on some continuous basis, or one or more groups may dominate others; or groups may dissolve, together with the societal requirement of prior individual membership within them. Either of these two last developments alters the mode of societal incorporation from the original consociation to a differential incorporation in the one case, and to a universalistic incorporation in the latter. Moreover, given the emergence of a dominant individual capable of imposing his will on other members of his group by ritual or other means, three courses of development are possible. Either the group may dissolve or be reduced below its viable threshold by the departure of those who question the validity of this personal domination, though unable to avoid it as members; or the leader may stabilize the group and his authority without further repercussions during his lifetime; or on various contingencies the group may engage in conflict with others, leading either to stalemate, to dissolution of the leadership, or to further and perhaps progressive extensions of its domination in variable forms and degrees.

In the normal case we should expect the authority of a gifted individual in such a context to operate discontinuously, contingently, situationally, and with reference to specific spheres such as ritual or hunting. It should also proceed by persuasion and consent rather than constraint. Its range should thus be limited by the context of grouping, and its span by the lifetime of the individual who generates it. These expectations are grounded on the egalitarian mode of individual incorporation which entails identical autonomies for persons of the same sex and generation in all spheres not subject to kinship regulation. Thus the establishment of personal ascendancy or dominion under such conditions must either restrict individual autonomies, thereby contravening the norms of this status structure, or the leader must extend the range or scope of activities and relations for the members of his unit without thereby reducing their traditionally individual autonomy.

Extensions of range in social relations will normally involve expansion in the scope of social action for at least some individuals and units. However, extensions of scope without range would seem to require cultural innovations that increase the set of individual interests and capacities, and may thus be difficult to develop and institute. None the less, since its social organization presents the readiest field for creative innovation at this rudimentary level, it is possible that gifted leaders might institutionalize extensions of scope and range, for example by introducing new forms of social relations such as trade or ritual partnerships, formal friendships or ritual brotherhood, patronage, clientage or some new types of fictive kinship, which might permit individuals to extend the range and variety of their social relations without surrendering their autonomy. Such innovations presuppose acceptance for institutionalization. Accordingly they depend on intrinsic appeal and collective support rather than on individual authority or power for their adoption. If institutionalized, they may enrich and complicate the old status-structure with new elements while leaving its incorporative bases undisturbed. In contrast, if individual domination increases the status roster without expanding the scope and range of social relations, it can only involve direct or indirect reductions in individual autonomy and corresponding changes in the political and social structure of the component unit or the wider society.

These developmental alternatives, open to the simple monocellular system represented by band-based societies, illustrate fundamental features of many processes of change in political structure. At any moment a political structure, societal or subsocietal, consists in a finite set of relations among or within corporate units of determinate form, basis, scope and number. The hypothetical equilibrium of such a structure consists in the relations that harmonize the requisites and implications of its individual units, thus preserving their autonomy, forms, and relations without change. If the system actually exhibits such an equilibrium, so will all its component units, since their articulations will integrate the requisites and entailments of the principles on which each is based.

In corporate groups, colleges and offices, as already observed, there are recurrent occasions and specific procedures by which regulatory roles are transferred, and there are often also special provisions for altering institutional arrangements. Such arrangements are commonly validated by a mixture of elements, by the unit's organization and history, by its current internal and external relations, by beliefs in the appropriateness of such changes, by correspondences between these forms and the duties and capacities of the unit, by correspondences of such alterations with the practice of other units of identical basis, status and type, and by their objective or perceived instrumental values. In turn, such constitutional arrangements, developments and procedures authorize and modify the current distributions of role, responsibility and resources within the unit, and its corporate relations with other units of similar or different type. Any alterations in these internal or external relations that are effected by and consistent with the institutional procedures of the corporation are thus legitimate and authorized. They accordingly express the continued vitality of the unit's structure even when they modify this. By contrast, routine unit operations that involve no structural modification do not belong in the study of change. Thus simple circulations of office or collegial roles illustrate unit maintenance, unless they involve some material alterations of procedures or rule. However, where the rules and procedures that affect the structural relations of a social unit are altered by institutionalized action or otherwise, then these events, their antecedents, contexts and consequences, are directly of interest to the student of change; but mere redistributions of power or influence among the members of a group which involve no modification of the prevailing framework of procedures, relations and rules, nor any change in the unit's scope, range, or in the validity of its operative particulars, illustrate its structural continuity and do not concern us.

At the most elementary level, changes in the political structure of a unit must always involve one or more of the following developments: (1) alterations in the conditions and categories of membership of some corporate unit, which may include dissolution or changes in the bases of its incorporation; (2) alterations in the scope of unit activities, which modify its internal and/or external articulation, resources and collective status; (3) those alterations of unit procedures and rules which are linked with either of the preceding developments.

Developments of these three types represent changes in the structure, status and capacities of the units that undergo them, even if they follow prescribed procedures and observe unit rules. Moreover, if such changes develop outside or in violation of the constitutional framework, they clearly challenge or reduce the validity of the previous structure, while altering it. Normally also either of these modifications involve substantial changes in the rights and conditions of at least some members of the unit, and perhaps changes in its scope and capacity also.

Redistributions of power and influence that precede or accompany allocations of authority within a social group, without modifying its bases, norms, formal procedures or external status, merely illustrate the characteristic processes and routine operations of the unit. Such institutional processes of redistribution validate the unit-structure by upholding and manifesting its norms, and by demonstrating their validity and adaptive capacities. Reallocations of authority that proceed extra-institutionally or contra-institutionally indicate the inability of the antecedent institutional structure to restrain or accommodate these developments. Likewise, illegitimate deployments of authority by those holding institutional positions illustrate the inadequacy of prevailing procedures and norms which ensure or generate official immunities despite incompetence or misconduct. Developments of either kind tend to invalidate the antecedent corporate constitution and to evoke collective responses which may generate further changes in the unit's procedures, structure, scope and conditions of membership. Where such developments modify or contravene earlier institutional arrangements, these cannot directly validate them; and they must therefore owe their effects to other regulative principles, notably to the distributions and manifestations of power in the current context. Moreover even when structural changes are made in accord with the institutional norms and procedures of a unit, and are thus legitimized and authorized by these sources, such revisions of the previous structure, procedures, rules, scope and conditions of membership must either express the power alignments that prevail, or their reorientations to current and foreseeable conditions. This is equally true of structural changes induced within a unit by exogenous events or forces, such, for example, as the actions of other bodies that modify its status and external relations in the social context by altering its scope, autonomy and resources, with or without the unit's assent. All exogenous developments that generate structural change accordingly modify prevailing alignments of power or authority within the unit affected, and ensure its accommodation, conditionally or otherwise, and with or without its consent. Yet even if such structural modifications are instituted with the formal assent of the unit and in accord with its accepted procedures, they can only express the reorientations that prevail under its current distributions of power and authority.

For example, if corporate groups of identical form combine to institute a confederation for their mutual benefit and defence, each initially reserving the right to repudiate the laws and policies of their union, the changes of unit-status and relations that establish the association express their responses to changes in their political situation which appear to necessitate the union without necessitating permanent transfers of unit autonomies to some central executive. In such circumstances, the determination of the associated units to preserve their internal autonomy intact indicates their formal equivalence in status, capacity, modes and bases of incorporation. In consequence, the consociation is based on their symmetrical articulations. Despite such restrictions, the consociation none the less modifies the status and autonomy of its member-units while prescribing their identification in it with one another by proscribing their independent relations with foreign bodies. Thus, by its establishment the confederation changes the status and scope of its components significantly and uniformly. Thereafter the union faces three possible courses of development. It may either persist for generations without structural changes in the status and relations of the members and central agencies; or it may dissolve in various ways and under various circumstances; or it may be transformed, abruptly or cumulatively, into some structure of another type, for example a unitary or federal state, by the progressive extensions of central authority and scope through the development of new functions and activities by its central agency, or through its appropriation of other tasks and resources that were formerly lacking or reserved to member units. In the latter case, even if the original autonomy of member units remains formally unchanged, their dependence on the centre increases with its increased activities and capacities; and *pari passu* so does the political status of its central administration. Such redistributions of power that neither impair the validity of the institutional arrangements nor modify the status, scope, autonomy, membership conditions or external relations of a unit, manifest its structural persistence, adaptability and authority. Other developments that invalidate these institutional arrangements or alter the unit's status, scope, membership conditions and autonomy, whether endogenous or exogenous in their genesis, indicate its structural change and express other alignments of power with differing orientations and goals.

Of authority and power, the two basic elements in which political relations of any type consist, authority, being identified by and through institutional forms, procedures and relations, presupposes their validity and operates to conserve or enhance them, even when used to initiate or promote changes in the institutional structure. In consequence, relations of power that validate and conserve institutional arrangements must operate within and through the authority structure, even when initiating or promoting its modification. However, while authority is committed to structural preservation by the assertion or adaptation of institutional norms, power has two modes of structural expression. It may be employed either to uphold and maintain the system without change, or to initiate and institute its structural modification. In the latter case, power may be employed legitimately and in accordance with institutional arrangements; or it may be employed extra-institutionally or contra-institutionally to modify them.

Evidently then the processes of political change may involve certain necessary and therefore invariant relations at the level of the elementary principles that constitute political systems, namely authority and power; but all such changes in the structure of a political system must also be manifested by changes in the external or internal conditions of its corporate components. The conditions thus invariably linked may be listed as follows: (1) The political status of a corporate unit is manifested in the conduct of non-members towards its members as representatives; and such status is also shown by the form and articulation of the unit with other units in the system of which it is a part, that is, by its mode of incorporation. Together these conditions determine the unit's proper scope, autonomous activities, resources, operational requisites and implications, and appropriate relations with other units of similar or different kind within the system. (2) The internal organization of a corporate unit is expressed in those institutional procedures and rules that crystallize and order its structure of status and relations to form a viable coherent unit. The scope, autonomy and resources of the corporate unit will vary with its basis and mode of incorporation, and frequently with its range also. The basis of a unit's incorporation specifies the conditions that regulate its membership, and especially the admission, obligations and rights of members, but also their differentiation by status. The basis and mode of its incorporation also prescribe the unit's corporate form, and thus indicate the appropriate conditions for its internal and external articulations, given the composition and status of the system of which the unit is part.

The *bases* and *modes* of a unit's incorporation differ in their reference; the former denotes the criteria of unit membership, while the second substantially specifies the unit's external articulations. It seems logically necessary that these internal and external dimensions of a unit's organization should be mutually congruent and that each should also form a consistent and viable scheme. Given its form and the principles on which a corporate unit is based, the mode of a unit's incorporation accordingly defines its appropriate external relations and collective status within the wider system, by prescribing the appropriate autonomy, scope and internal articulation from which its members derive their corporate rights and status. The unit's operational *scope* is manifest in those routine autonomous activities which are simultaneously governed by its bases and modes of incorporation and which specify the collective obligations and rights of the members as a distinct 'perpetual' unit.

8.

Analytically, the corporations whose changing properties, relations and forms constitute changes in the structure of the political system of which they are part, are presumptively perpetual regulatory units whose differences of type, base, scope and articulation indicate and specify their differences of status. While the principles on which a unit is incorporated determine its immediate requisites and entailments and thus its minimal scope, its *corporate form* determines its minimally appropriate internal and external articulation, given the *mode* of its incorporation to its particular context. Thus in the limiting case of a perfect equilibrium, the extrinsic and intrinsic properties of the corporation must correspond perfectly, as should the requisites of its internal and external articulation, and its collective status with that of its members. In such conditions the unit's procedures, organization and scope should correspond perfectly with one another and with its formal attributes. Accordingly, its routine activities will then manifest its public status and external articulation. The exercise of corporate authority is thus restricted to those relations and activities that sustain the order by fulfilling its requisites and implications; and any material changes in the form, capacities or bases of the unit will modify its status and articulation correspondingly. Moreover, since such developments invalidate some institutional norms, they presuppose and express corresponding changes in the alignments and orientations of power within and beyond the unit. Invariably also, such structural developments modify the articulative networks in which the unit was formerly aligned, together with its juridical status and autonomy. More extensive or critical changes may invalidate some of the unit's requisites or entailments, and thus some conditions and features of its corporate organization. Whether such processes of change consist primarily in revisions of the external relations and status of the particular unit or in extensions or reductions of its scope, these consequences prevail. While changes of unit scale or range sometimes accompany changes of its structure, both may proceed independently; and the mere multiplication or reduction of the number of units, or simple extensions of their range, need not alter the structure of a political system, though either may clearly affect its capacity, unless some changes in the bases or modes of unit incorporation are involved.

Such structural changes in the conditions, context and articulations of a corporation modify the status and capacities of its members by altering the scope and conditions of their membership, that is, by modifying its distinctive rights, duties, privileges and relations, and sometimes by transforming the bases and categories of membership also. Such modifications of membership content commonly take either of three alternative courses. First, the content of membership and thus the scope of the corporate unit may be extended, for example by the acquisition of new collective functions and resources, conditionally or otherwise. Alternatively, membership content and collective scope may be reduced by loss or restriction of former capacity or autonomy. Finally the content of corporate membership may be altered, with or without any accompanying changes in the unit's autonomy and scope, by some revision of prevailing membership categories and by the redistribution of rights and duties among them, presumably on the basis of new criteria of differentiation. For example, tendencies to obstruct the circulation of executive roles summarized in the Iron Law of Oligarchy may materially alter membership contents by revising their distributions without corresponding changes in unit scope. So does the restratification of members in new or modified categories on new or modified criteria.

9.

The basis on which a unit is incorporated may be altered formally by the action of its members or their representatives through procedures that explicitly or implicitly revise relevant rules, with or without change in membership content. In either event the status, autonomy and external relations of the unit will be correspondingly affected, the particulars varying with the specific alteration and with the unit's initial form and scope. It is clearly possible to modify the principles on which a corporate unit recruits its members without directly affecting its corporate form as group, category, college or other. However, when its principles of membership recruitment are altered, the unit's collective status and external articulation are directly affected. Thus any changes in the basis of incorporation, irrespective of internal restratifications of membership categories and content, invariably involve changes in the unit's external articulation, and thus its public status.

As regards changes of status, scope and articulation, the relations adduced above also apply whether we deal with the status of members in a given unit, or with that of units in a given system. If the system retains its former scope and range, its structural change can only consist in modifications of the original articulation of its corporate components, which in turn involve revisions in the distributions of status, autonomy and resources among them, with correlative changes in their membership contents. Where such realignments proceed without any changes in the number or variety of these corporate units, the processes of structural change simply reallocate status and autonomy among the pre-existing units by redesigning their mutual relations, scope and status to correspond with altered distributions of power and capacity. However, since these changes always implicate the articulative structure by which such units are incorporated in the system, no changes of corporate form can proceed without them. Alternatively, without any alterations in the previous scope and the system, new units of differing base may emerge only by parallel realignments of collective relations and redistributions of capacities and membership. Finally, the scope of the system may change under the impact of endogenous or exogenous forces. These include victory or defeat, aggrandizement or conquest, imposed alliances, tributary relationships, the development of new technological or ideological structures, the desuetude of old arrangements, population changes, and many other conditions.

Systems or units may institutionalize limited changes in their scope without parallel changes in the articulative structure and relative status of their corporate components, providing only that these changes of scope are distributed appropriately among component corporations in complementary or proportionate modes. However such distribution may be possible only for systems with extremely simple corporate structures, and then only under stringent conditions. If alterations of scope invalidate the requisites or entailments of any particular class of corporations in the system,

they will modify its autonomy, status, relations and scope correspondingly, thereby generating a process of structural change which
may be episodic or continuous, until a new articulative structure is
stabilized for all. Thus, whatever the context and level of corporate
organization, structural change consists in the sequential modification of unit status and articulations and consantaneous alterations
of its autonomy, resources and scope. These two sets of changes
comprehend the form and substance of the system and its units
respectively. On grounds already presented, whether or not they
illustrate the decline or growth of the system, such structural changes
invariably presuppose and manifest new alignments of power
adequate to modify the pre-existing structure of corporate status and
relations.

We may distinguish as radical those processes of change by which a
systemic structure and its major corporate units are simultaneously
transformed by reincorporation on new bases and/or modes. The
more abrupt and inclusive the process of change, the more critical
the disbalances of antecedent corporate status and scope with
prevailing distributions of power and authority.

To illustrate our analysis, let us consider briefly a system with
various types of corporation: for example, localized lineages, local
communities, male age-sets, colleges or community councils, each
type of corporation initially having its own appropriate organization,
scope, resources, and internal and external articulations. If hypothetically we assume that the system undergoes structural change
without any change of scope, then its structural alteration requires
some realignment of these corporate components which must be
expressed in complementary redistributions of autonomous
capacities among them. Alternatively, similar realignments and
redistributions may be confined among the corporations of any
particular category, such as its age-sets or lineages. The fewer the
units affected, the less extensive the structural changes involved, the
simpler the process, and the more likely that it will be episodic,
restricted and easily stabilized. However, if the scope and capacities
of lineages as one class of corporations increase or decrease, this
affects their articulations to other units of differing type, for
example the age-organization and/or community council, as well as
their articulations with one another. Alternatively, if the community
unites with others to establish a wider confederation of identical
scope, thereby extending its range, its prevailing distributions of
status, relations and capacities may remain unaffected. On the other
hand, if one or more lineages extend their autonomy at the expense
of others and thus appropriate dominion, the status and relations of
all units involved are correspondingly modified, together with the
modes of their articulation and collective autonomies. In systems of
this complexity, the pre-eminence of any class of corporate units
inevitably affects the structure and functions of the community

council, and perhaps those of the age-organization also. Clearly, any alteration in the autonomy or status of a given corporation directly affects the rights, obligations and status of its membership, and those of other units and their members contingently. The varieties of corporate unit in this hypothetical case provide the principal political structures, while their articulation constitutes the framework of the political system. In consequence, changes in this political structure proceed by rearrangements in the bases, forms and interrelations of these corporations.

The assumption of new capacities or the loss of old ones by the political system as a unit illustrate the generality of the relations adduced above. Either the new capacities are appropriated to a novel type of unit whose accommodation modifies the pre-existing articulative structure and increases its complexity while instituting new relations with older units; or the new capacities must be distributed in proportionate or complementary modes among the original units, or at least among all units of a given corporate class, normally that with the largest prescriptive membership and widest scope. Unless there is an objectively symmetrical distribution of these capacities among corporations of all types, changes in their status and interrelations are inevitable, and thus changes in the structure of the total system. It is also possible that the institutionalization of these new systemic functions might modify the bases on which some of these corporations recruited their members; but in that case, such changes in their systemic articulations will probably modify the modes of incorporation of these units correspondingly.

If a political system as a whole suffers some loss of former function, its structural responses to this reduction in scope and capacity demonstrate identical relations, since in so far as they are structurally significant, these substantive losses will find structural expression in revisions of membership status and contents in all those corporations that are directly or indirectly affected, with parallel revisions in the properties and interrelations of these units. Such loss of systemic capacities will also affect preceding distributions of power among these units and will therefore modify the structures of corporate status and articulation associated with this distribution. Accordingly reductions in the scope and capacity of any corporate unit, including that of the political system itself, will normally generate disbalances of its requisites and entailments that destabilize its articulation and may modify its mode. The status of the affected unit *vis-à-vis* others will then change correspondingly. Moreover, if the system as a whole loses the capacity to insulate its internal structure from further change, such losses must either fall equivalently on all classes of units, a remote possibility given initial dissimilarities in their form, bases and scope, or they will fall unequally and primarily on those corporations of greatest significance and scope in the original system, thus subverting it further by weakening its most fundamental units.

These few examples are enough to show how the concepts and propositions set out above may be tested and refined in analyses of empirical situations and courses of political change. They accordingly illustrate a method to disconfirm or develop this theory of political organization by applying it to particular situations of change. Briefly, having fashioned a set of concepts that allows us to analyse political aggregates at any level of complexity by isolating the logically necessary elements and relations of their structural components, we can readily construct an accurate model of any political unit whose operations or change we wish to study. By logical analysis we can then determine the bases and forms of all corporations that constitute our model and the modes or conditions of their interrelation. In this way we can specify the formal and substantive requisites and entailments of each of the diverse kinds of corporations whose properties are known; and from this refined model of these structures, we can deduce precise hypotheses about their alternative responses to specific events and conditions of change, which may then be compared with historical or contemporary situations to test or correct them. Thus, having first selected empirical situations whose components, processes and outcomes are known or can be studied, we may attempt to derive the latter by deduction from our model of the unit or units involved. In this way we can test those general ideas of the form and substance of political units that underlie our specific models, and hopefully we may refine and clarify these ideas to yield progressively closer and fuller approximations of the empirical courses of change.

Naturally we cannot anticipate the nature, time, form, intensity or source of all external stimuli that may affect the unit whose change we wish to study, but, given certain essential information about its external context and relations, we should be able to indicate the associated sequences of internal development or change. Likewise, while we cannot anticipate the nature, locus, intensity, form and time of all endogenous events that may modify the structure of a unit, given an adequate account of the aggregate and its properties, and assuming that its external context and relations remain unchanged, we should be able to indicate alternative probabilities in some detail by analysing the articulations of its corporate components in the light of their bases, requisites and entailments.

Such invariant relations as we may ultimately seek among the elements of our general model of political units should be revealed by their recurrence in all the empirical sequences we study as elements of a constant order that underlies the modifications of those corporate organizations. Naturally at this stage of inquiry we cannot say how the invariant relations of the logical elements in our general model may be affected by the various combinations and differing intensities of empirical factors. None the less, in so far as we have correctly identified the formal and substantive properties, requisites and entailments of its corporate components, we should have a sufficiently detailed and accurate model of any aggregate to enable us to deduce the precise nature and order of its responses to any particular elements or influences that bear upon it. Thus, by examining our model of the aggregate, we should be able to say whether its structure would change in response to specific conditions, and if so in what specific ways and degrees, and in what order. We may then compare these deductions with the data on the empirical situation, and re-examine our model and deductions to identify any errors of construction or reasoning that may account for the discrepancies we find, thereby facilitating the progressive correction of the model and refining our general ideas to improve our understanding of political organization and the actual sequences of political change. Clearly if this procedure enables us to formulate hypotheses that are confirmed empirically, such confirmations imply that those logically necessary relations among the elements of our general model of polities, as orders of corporate organization having specific properties and conditions, may provide some invariance in the structures of the processes by which such units change.

Finally, although as elsewhere in these essays I have often referred to the aggregates under discussion as 'systems', this loose descriptive usage should not be taken to mean that I regard them as 'systems' in any theoretically significant sense. At most my usage is heuristic, and the term 'organization' could be substituted. Thus instead of discussing the functional unity, stability, closure, feedback circuits and other properties of these units as systems, I have dwelt on the bases, forms, requisites, entailments and articulations of these aggregates and their components, all being conceived as structures of the same general kind, namely corporations, whose properties and relations are logically implicit in the conditions and forms of their incorporation. Thus instead of treating these aggregates or their components as functional systems, I have tried to isolate those structural elements and conditions which are sufficient and necessary to define and maintain them, in order that we may deduce their alternative responses to any events or forces that may affect their properties or relations. In effect we could substitute the terms 'organizational aggregate' for 'system' in almost every instance without any loss of meaning. However, following convention, I have first described these political units as 'systems' to facilitate identification, and then proceeded to abstract their structures as the central object of study.

7.

Institutional and Political Conditions of Pluralism

Pluralism is a condition in which members of a common society are internally distinguished by fundamental differences in their institutional practice. Where present, such differences are not distributed at random; they normally cluster, and by their clusters they simultaneously identify institutionally distinct aggregates or groups, and establish deep social divisions between them. The prevalence of such systematic dissociation between the members of institutionally distinct collectivities within a single society constitutes pluralism. Thus pluralism simultaneously connotes a social structure characterized by fundamental discontinuities and cleavages, and a cultured complex based on systematic institutional diversity. In this essay I try to isolate the minimal conditions essential and sufficient to constitute pluralism. I try also to show how such conditions generate and sustain social cleavages that distinguish pluralities, while other combinations of institutional and social differences differ in their structural expression. Having summarily indicated some of the principal forms that social pluralism may take, I review briefly the modes and conditions by which it may be stabilized or transformed.

Pluralism may be defined with equal cogency and precision in institutional or in political terms. Politically these features have very distinctive forms and conditions, and in their most extreme state, the plural society, they constitute a polity of peculiar though variable type. Specific political features of social pluralism centre in the corporate constitution of the total society. Under these conditions the basic corporate divisions within the society usually coincide with the lines of institutional cleavage, reinforcing and generally converting them into deep and rigid inequalities in social and political life. The enforcement and maintenance of these corporate divisions and inequalities are then normally identified with the preservation of social order and stability. Any modification in the political and social relations between these corporate divisions involves corresponding changes in the conditions of social structure. To seek out the conditions essential for this coincidence of corporate boundaries and institutional discontinuity, we have therefore to discover the minimal degrees and forms of institutional divergence which are required to facilitate, promote, or enjoin the sectional closures that plural polity incorporates; and conversely, we need to inquire how various alternative forms of corporate organization may establish, preserve, or foster institutional differentiation, or reduce or deny its public significance, while permitting its persistence or dissolution equally. In effect, we need first to determine the circumstances and ways in which these modes of corporate organization and institutional differentiation interact to support, reinforce, dislocate, or modify one another, and then to identify the conditions requisite for their stabilization or transformation.

1.

To analyse the institutional and political conditions of pluralism, it is first necessary to distinguish pluralism from its principal alternatives, and to indicate how its variable range governs its structural significance.

Since institutions are collective modes of action, organization, and orientation, both normative and cognitive, institutional differentiation correspondingly distinguishes collectivities that differ in organization, standardized procedures, norms, beliefs, ideals, and expectations. Quite commonly, all the members of a distinct society share an identical system of institutions. The boundaries of such societies are defined by the maximum span of the institutional system on which their social organization and cohesion are based. Such conditions of institutional homogeneity, which are characteristic of simple societies, represent the polar opposite of the systematic institutional diversity that constitutes pluralism.

Many societies, including the most highly developed industrial societies, seem to stand midway between these extremes. In these societies the entire population, or at least the overwhelming majority, share a common system of basic institutions, while being systematically differentiated at the secondary level of institutional organization in which alternative occupational, political, and religious or ethnic structures predominate. Societies with this combination of common and exclusive institutional affiliations are properly distinguished by their pervasive heterogeneity from the conditions of homogeneity and pluralism already described. These types of societies differ significantly in structure, complexity, modes of integration, and in their capacities for self-generated development. Though institutional homogeneity and high levels of organizational complexity are mutually exclusive, and no industrial society is ever institutionally homogeneous, social heterogeneity or pluralism is equally consistent with industrial or pre-industrial levels of economic and technological organization. Thus the institutional classification is independent of economic or technological criteria.

The most extreme and politically significant expression of pluralism is to be found in the 'plural society', as J. S. Furnivall appropriately labelled internally autonomous and inclusive political units ruled by institutionally distinct numerical minorities.[1] The subjugated majority of the population in a plural society may or may not share a single common system of institutions; often the people are internally subdivided by their differing institutional allegiances; but in all cases they simultaneously differ in their political status and in their institutional practice and organization from the discrete minority who rule them. In their colonial phase, all recently independent African states were plural societies;[2] and despite independence, most of these ex-colonies retain their plural character with marginal alteration. Thus pluralism and colonialism are not homologous. Colonialism is merely one mode of pluralism, characteristically instituted in the form of a plural society. However, pluralism is by no means confined to plural societies, although it is in those units that it has its purest expression and most profound effects.

One of the major problems that faces emergent nations with a recent colonial past consists in effecting the transition from pluralism to the heterogeneity requisite for their transformation into cohesive national units. Such transformations have not yet occurred in several Latin-American societies, despite relatively long histories of independence. Of European states that faced a similar predicament at an earlier date, we need merely mention Spain, Portugal, Russia, Germany, and France to indicate the various difficulties, processes, and outcomes involved. One of our concerns in this paper is to detect as best we can the most general conditions requisite for those processes of societal transformation and enhanced political integration on which 'modernization' directly depends.

2.

A society is a self-sufficient, self-perpetuating, and internally autonomous system of social relations. Such a system distinguishes a population occupying a specific territory; but as a system of social relations, the society is clearly distinct from territory or population. The society is the structure of relations through which the population of members is internally organized as joint occupants of a given area. Changes in population mass or composition, or more obviously in territory, do not themselves directly constitute changes in the social system, although they undoubtedly affect it in many ways. It is with differences in the systems of social relations which constitute societies that the distinctions between pluralism, homogeneity, and heterogeneity are directly concerned.

Social relations are either institutionalized or optional in their base, individual or collective in their form. The range and conditions that govern optional relations at both the individual and collective levels are themselves institutionally prescribed and regulated. Thus

1. Furnivall (1945); (1948), pp. 304-12.
2. Balandier (1965); Moreira (1957).

the inclusive autonomous system of social relations which constitutes a society is directly or indirectly institutionalized. If the members of the society share a common system of institutions, then they will also share a common framework and pattern of social relations; and their internal differentiation by corporate and personal status will be governed by uniform criteria and principles. If the aggregate is institutionally heterogeneous in its base, then the system of institutionalized relations in which its society consists will be correspondingly heterogeneous in character and form. In consequence, members will differ in the significance they attach to those criteria and principles that regulate their corporate and personal identity and status placement. If the society consists of collectivities divided by fundamental institutional differences, then, within the corresponding corporate divisions whose interrelations constitute the societal level of organization and integration, there will be corresponding diversity of institutionalized relations. In such conditions, members of differing social sections occupy significantly differing positions in relations with one another. In consequence, societies with homogeneous, heterogeneous, and plural institutional systems differ correspondingly in character and structure.

3.

Following Malinowski, Radcliffe-Brown, Nadel and others, we may define institutions as 'standardized modes of co-activity',[3] characteristic of social collectivities. Individual habits are subject to institutional regulation but, being personal and optional, even when common among a given primary group, they differ sharply from institutions which are essentially normative, standardized, and sanctioned modes of collective procedure. It is by virtue of sharing common institutions that an aggregate becomes an organized collectivity; and it is precisely because they are neither the only nor the majority of the collectivity that shares common institutions that local communities are not discrete societies but merely sub-groups thereof. In short, its institutional foundation transforms an aggregate into a distinct collectivity even in the absence of any inclusive common organization. Only in consequence of the structural uniformity and functional coherence that a single system of shared and coextensive institutions provides are the acephalous societies familiar to anthropologists analytically or in their members' eyes identified as distinct societal units. Lacking inclusive organization for the collective regulation of their common affairs, these acephalous societies are constituted as institutionally distinct and closed perpetual categories in consequence of their uniform institutional base. Such internal cohesion and external distinctness as they

3. Malinowski (1944), pp. 52-74; Nadel (1951), pp. 108-44; Radcliffe-Brown (1952*d*), pp. 197-203.

possess, these acephalous societies owe directly to the distinctiveness and homogeneity of their institutional fabric. However, as we shall see, not all homogeneous societies are acephalous; nor are all acephalous societies institutionally homogeneous. While acephalous societies retain their constitution as functionally coherent corporate *categories*, other societies having a representative central organization for the direction of common collective affairs, including external relations, are accordingly constituted as corporate *groups*.

The decisive characteristics of all corporations, categorical and other, are their presumed perpetuity, closure, determinate identity, and membership. A category lacks the coextensive organization that is requisite for its constitution as a group. The corporate group, in addition to the features already listed, possesses this inclusive organization, a set of distinctive common affairs, and the procedures and autonomy necessary to regulate them. Societies unified as corporate groups have common political institutions and regulative organs, thereby enhancing the functional integration derived from shared institutions by specializing a single collective structure authorized to administer certain common internal affairs and to represent the unit externally. This structure is itself corporate in basis and form, being presumptively perpetual, closed, with determinate identity, membership, and form, and possessing the authority, organization, and procedures to discharge its collective regulatory functions.[4]

The authority, responsibility, and resources required for this collective regulation may be vested in a corporate office or structure of offices, or in corporate colleges such as councils, parliaments, or senates. Members of these colleges and official structures exercise political functions over the collectivity and on its behalf since these regulatory corporations are institutionalized as the appropriate agencies for political regulation and integration of the whole. If the 'centralized' society shares a common system of basic institutions, and continues to derive its primary underlying cohesion and unity from this condition, the central political agencies serve merely to co-ordinate, mobilize, and direct collective actions and resources as various exigencies require, and to preserve the institutionally requisite conditions for an orderly collective life. Such modes of political organization and activity presuppose the integration of the society concerned by virtue of the symmetrical or complementary interdependences of its corporate elements derived from their shared institutional foundations and modes of action.

Per contra, in a plural society where the rulers form a culturally distinct numerical minority, the aggregate depends for its formation, unity, order, and form primarily on the concentration and active employment of regulative powers by the ruling section through the

4. See above, Chapter 3.

political framework, in consequence of the institutional cleavages within it, and the exclusive asymmetrical relations that such cleavages entail. In addition to this primary institutional bifurcation between rulers and ruled, there may be several secondary cultural divisions among the subjugated; but in either case, in the plural society the rulers typically maintain their organization as an exclusive corporate group in order that they may collectively secure and control the political institutions on which the internal order and unity of the aggregate depend, together with their own privileges of status and opportunity. Further, to minimize threats to their regime, the dominant section, through its political organization, actively discourages or suppresses extensive organizations by which the subject population could convert itself from an acephalous, institutionally disprivileged category into a coherent corporate group capable of effective political and social action. Thus the institutional and regulative responsibilities and powers of the central political agencies differ sharply in aggregates of differing institutional base and composition.

The contrast may be summarized most cogently by comparing plural societies and nation-states, the political forms and contexts of modernization. As Broom says, a 'nation is the antithesis of plural order. A nation implies common ancestry and cultural homogeneity; a state refers to a dominant political unit, regardless of the variability of its components. A state may contain a plural society.' [5]

Ideal-typically we may express the contrast as follows: (1) A nation is usually a single inclusive corporate group whose members — or the majority of them — share common traditions, institutions, history, and ethnic identity. (2) In the nation-state, the state is the derivative political expression of the nation's cohesion and unity. The members of the nation are citizens of the state, which provides all with equal representation, protection, and regulation. Equality of access and obligation to the political organization, and equality of opportunity for participation in the political process, are essentials of national identity and citizenship.[6] Democratic, totalitarian, or dictatorial philosophies of the nation-state all assume these basic relations, although construing them very differently. (3) Regulatory corporations of the nation-state are equally representative of, binding on, and accessible to all members of the nation as a corporate group.

In the plural society the state is the representative political organ of the ruling section organized as a corporate group, its exclusive and ultimate instrument for the internal domination and corporate control of the institutionally distinct subject populations, who are simultaneously denied political rights, citizenship, and opportunities for their own organization by prescriptions of state, and are accordingly paralysed as disunited corporate categories. Thus in the

    5. Broom (1960*a*), in Rubin (1960), p. 889.
    6. T.H. Marshall (1965), pp. 71-134; Aristotle, *Politics*, bk. 3, ch. 6 (ed. Jowett, 1943, pp. 136-8).

plural society the mass of the people are not citizens but subjects; a..d the state, instead of being the collective political expression of the inclusive aggregate, is merely the external political form of the dominant corporate group, the instrumental framework of its domination, and the ultimate source and expression of prevailing sectional inequalities. Indeed, the political institutions and ideology of the plural society are almost complete antitheses to those of the nation-state, whether democratic or totalitarian. In place of the systematic congruence of representation, access, and accountability which characterizes the nation-state, within the plural society, centralized or acephalous, accessibility, representation, account-ability, and power are systematically restricted; and the foundation and primary feature of the polity is its basic division between the rulers, organized as a corporate group, and the ruled, constituted as a leaderless, disorganized residual corporate category, often segmented by its own deep institutional divisions.

Political and social inequalities are as pervasive and fundamental in the plural society as they are ideologically inconsistent with the organization of a modern nation-state, whether democratic or totalitarian. Whereas the citizens of the nation-state, or at least the majority of them, normally share many other common institutions besides the government, in the plural society differential subjugation to the government is often the sole common condition that delimits the aggregate as a unit; and since such a society is established by specifically political action, its boundaries, composition, form, order, continuity, and developmental capacities are all politically co-determinate.

4.

As collectively standardized modes of coactivity, institutions have several interconnected dimensions: activity, social groupings and relations, norms, ideas, values, and orientations. Each institutional system also requires a material base, a social locus, and appropriate resources.

Analytically, the major institutional systems common to all societies, whatever their developmental level, consist of marriage, family and kinship, education, religion, economy, law, and govern-ment. Each of these systems may distinguish and integrate several specific institutional patterns, such as inheritance, property, marketing, bureaucracy, military organization, courts, divorce, adoption, contract, and the like. The form and content of these institutional systems vary widely among societies; and so do their differentiation and interconnections. In the simplest societies, kinship institutions virtually embrace the economy, cult, govern-mental agencies, modes of social control, education, and law; indeed, in the extreme case there may be no separate agency other than the kinship group which is specialized to discharge these functions. At the other extreme, kinship, marriage, and family are segregated from formal economic, political, and religious planes of action, and, to an increasing degree, from education also. Whereas in the simple undifferentiated society, kinship subsumes these latter institutional relations and activities, in the highly differentiated society, each institutional sphere has its own characteristic modes of organization, procedures of action, resources, aims, rules, values, membership, and ideology; and the higher the level of institutional differentiation and specialization, the greater the complexity of these specific structures and thus of the total social order.

All institutions have two analytically distinct, intimately connected aspects: the cultural and the social. Whether culture is restrictively defined as the symbols, norms, values, and ideational systems of a given population, or more inclusively as their standardized and transmitted patterns of thought and action, all institutional organization has a cultural coefficient, since each institution involves collective norms, ideas, and symbols as well as standardized modes of procedure. But since institutions prescribe norms of social grouping and relation, as for example in law, government, cult, or family, all institutions have prominent sociological aspects in the groups they constitute, and in the structures of status and role which they enjoin.

In consequence of this duality, culture and society are equally rooted in the institutional system on which each human aggregate depends for its inner cohesion, distinctive identity, membership, and boundaries. It follows that an institutionally homogeneous aggregate is also socially and culturally homogeneous; institutional heterogeneity likewise involves social and cultural heterogeneity; and social and cultural pluralism are equally rooted in institutional pluralism.

However, these social and cultural dimensions of heterogeneity and pluralism neither necessarily nor always correspond. This is so for two major reasons. Besides ideational and procedural correlates of social relations, culture includes such systems as language, aesthetic styles, philosophies, and expressive forms which may be transferred across social boundaries easily and with little social effect. Conversely, systems of social relations may perdure despite substantial shifts in their cultural content or explicit orientations. Thus, despite their common institutional basis and tendencies to congruence, culture and society may vary independently; indeed, their divergent alignments have special importance in contexts of pluralism, as indicated below.[7]

5.

Those institutional systems that are common to all societies whatever their developmental level are evidently basic conditions or

7. M.G. Smith (1965c), pp. 68-73, 81, 84-5, 175.

requisites of any societal organization. These systems include law, cult, economy, socialization, kinship, and government. Even in the most extreme context of pluralism, each aggregate is identified as a unit by its subjugation to a single common government. Beyond this, their institutional divergence may be almost total. In a heterogeneous society the majority of the members share all or most of the common basic institutions, namely, kinship, education, economy, government, law, and cult, despite institutional differences of a secondary level in the economic, educational, occupational, and even religious spheres. Such secondary differentiations are implicit in the functional specializations with which the complexity and development of these societies is inseparably linked; but as Durkheim and others point out, these institutional specializations are functionally interdependent, with the result that, given a shared institutional base, the aggregate derives cohesion from its internal differentiation at the secondary level of institutional development.

Perhaps Holland and the Scandinavian countries best represent this simple model of the heterogeneous society; such countries as Britain or Belgium contain added ethnic differentiations in consequence of their histories. Other heterogeneous societies such as the United States, the Soviet Union, Mexico, or Brazil embrace many plural features which further complicate their organization but do not alter their basic character since these differences only involve demographic minorities of the wider society.

In this context we should distinguish two modes of pluralism which may be combined with predominant societal heterogeneity. In the first and simpler case, the institutionally distinct minority or segments thereof constitute territorially discrete enclaves, as for example do the various tribal remnants on reservations in the United States or the Indians of Chiapas and other areas in Mexico. In such cases the heterogeneous society merely contains a number of plural enclaves whose members form dependent minorities.

Alternatively, a heterogeneous society may contain several plural communities, as notably in the Southern United States. In their internal organization, these plural communities satisfy all the conditions necessary to distinguish plural societies except that, lacking political and cultural distinctness and autonomy, they remain dependent and subordinate local segments of a wider society; and, lacking the corporate closure with which institutional distinctness provides societies, they are continuously subject to the various pressures and influences developed within the society that surrounds them. In short, as United States political history shows, these plural communities of the South are structurally peculiar local segments of the heterogeneous American society that incorporates them, but neither separate nor independent societies.

We should therefore distinguish heterogeneous societies with plural features from those without, and in the first category, those with plural enclaves from those with plural communities, or from others with both.

The essential criterion of the heterogeneous society is that the majority of its members share a common system of basic institutions, together with systematic differentiation at the secondary level of institutional and organizational specialization. In the plural society, a politically autonomous unit ruled by a culturally distinct and politically privileged minority, the sole institutional framework that incorporates the aggregate is government, which normally has the form of a state. Whether it is redistributive or market-based, the economy of such a unit includes the population differentially.

Plural societies vary in the institutional heterogeneity or homogeneity of their ruling sections. The dominant whites in the Republic of South Africa are institutionally and socially heterogeneous, while the Tutsi of traditional Ruanda[8] or the Muslim Paktuns who ruled Hindus in the Swat Valley[9] were rather the reverse. Only if the ruling section of a plural society is institutionally homogeneous, as in Swat, will the unit remain uncentralized — a polity unified by a common structure of corporate domination, but lacking the forms and integration of a state. Wherever the ruling section in the plural society is institutionally heterogeneous, as in Latin America and the Caribbean colonies, in feudal Europe or the colonial Far East, the plural society is always incorporated within the framework of a state.

6.

In addition to the distinction between centralized and acephalous societies, we should also distinguish societies with reference to their ideological basis and majority orientations as sacred (theocratic) or secular.

In the sacred centralized society, typical for example of Islam, differences of cult and belief divide believers and non-believers into two distinct religious and political collectivities. If Jews or Christians are also present in substantial numbers, these *dhimmi* are also segregated as separate collectivities. Islam prescribes the political exclusion of non-believers and their subordination to the community of the Faithful, and in this respect it merely systematizes the orientation that characterizes all theocratic regimes, including Hinduism, Buddhism, and Christianity. Islam further prescribes the organization of the Faithful into a political community with the form of a state under a ruler and a hierarchy of officials. Thus, where devout Muslims constitute the dominant minority, as in many parts of traditional India, Northern Nigeria, and the Niger Bend at various historical periods, the result is a theocratic plural society in which religion provides the basic legitimation and principle of corporate

8. Maquet (1961); d'Hertefelt (1965).
9. Barth (1959), pp. 7-30.

cleavage, irrespective of other shared institutions, such as kinship or economy.

In all theocratic polities the religious bases and conceptions of society as a divinely prescribed order enjoin pluralism solely on religious grounds wherever the dominant congregation is a minority, irrespective of racial, linguistic, or institutional communities across religious boundaries. Normally each ritually ordained social organization is so distinctive in its form and content that differences in religion usually entail corresponding differences in other institutional spheres. However, this was not always true of Protestants and Catholics, whose religious conflicts during the sixteenth and seventeenth centuries promoted the secularization of European society. Nor have religious differences within the Buddhist or Muslim communities always involved parallel differences in secular institutions. Often rather minor differences of ritual or belief serve to set co-religionists against one another; but unless contraposed groups are also differentiated institutionally, pluralism has no place in their conflict.

7.

We can now begin to examine the relations between institutional divergences of differing degree and type, and pluralism or heterogeneity. Our basic question concerns the minimal combinations of institutional or political difference which are necessary and sufficient to incorporate collectivities as separate sections of a wider society. More precisely, we must also try to show how these differing combinations of institutional or political differentiations come to take such effect. These questions are equally central to our understanding of the social processes and structures of plural and heterogeneous societies.

It is true that differences in the basic institutional systems of two collectivities constitute pluralism and establish plural societies where the minority, by reason of its superior resources and organization, dominates the majority, whose institutional organization and resources reduce their capacity for resistance. The ensuing domination may be based on conquest, negotiation, enslavement, indenture, or ideological ascendancy, separately or together. It may be instituted as serfdom, helotage, peonage, slavery, or colonialism, or through restrictive political franchise. In some cases the structure of domination takes the form of caste, although, as we shall see, such 'caste' differs profoundly from the Indian institution. In all contexts of pluralism, the dominant section distinguishes itself from the dominated, both politically and by means of their institutional differentiae; and where these social and cultural differences coincide with differences of 'race', corporate exclusions and oppositions are frequently expressed in racial terms. Indeed, 'racial' coefficients of institutional and political division are often invoked as stereotypes despite their objective absence or their marginal biological significance. The social validity of these racialist classifications and interpretations of social cleavage is obviously unaffected by their scientific status. Where institutionalized, such racial categories are generally local developments of modes of thought that formed part of the traditional culture of the dominant ethnic group.

A strictly demographic typology of pluralism is unsatisfactory because it predicates that which it should explain; explicitly, it makes no attempt to identify the particular types, degrees, or combinations of institutional difference which distinguish conditions of pluralism from heterogeneity. Empirical materials cannot directly resolve this problem. It is therefore necessary to proceed to a theoretical analysis of the implications of institutional differences and continuities of various types for the integration of the social systems in which they appear. In this analysis simple demographic ratios are initially irrelevant.

Meyer Fortes' distinction between the kinship and politico-jural domains of social organization is especially useful in this inquiry.[10] We may generalize this to distinguish the familial or *private* domain and the collective or *public* domain. Fortes, who applies this distinction to the analysis of descent, kinship, and affinity in segmentary lineage societies, shows clearly that in these relatively undifferentiated systems, the same institution may figure prominently in both domains of social life, though typically in different ways. Thus, to cite his own example, in tribal societies with a lineage base, marriage is simultaneously a relation between exogamous corporate lineages and the institutional basis of family life.[11] It thus falls equally in both domains, and in either its position and implications are qualified by its role and place in the other. In centralized societies, marriage is likewise regulated by laws of the state, while retaining its pivotal place in the private domain. As regards divorce, inheritance, paternity, family law, adoption, and the obligations of maintenance, all pre-eminently centred in the private domain, the position is essentially similar. These relations form part of the law by which the inner organization of the collectivity is regulated. In effect, the elements and organization of the private domain are common to all members of the collectivity that observes uniform institutions of marriage, kinship, family, and domestic organization. Likewise the institutionally homogeneous collectivity owes its integration and distinctness to the communities of procedure and organization which constitute its distinctive and common public domain. Among these elements of the public domain, collective organizations, forms, and modes of action are generally institutionalized in corporate form, whether in law, government, or

10. Fortes (1959).
11. ibid., pp. 194-7, 206-8.

economy. In addition, such institutions as property, markets, occupational associations, education, labour organizations, and cults are all explicitly collective phenomena which simultaneously serve to regulate relations within the collectivity and to organize and integrate its members as a structurally distinct and bounded aggregate.

Most of the basic institutional systems are represented in either domain, though unequally so, and variably, as societies differ in their modes and levels of institutional development and specialization. For example, in simple societies, routine economic action, education, and basic patterns of ritual action may be almost exclusively centred in the private domain. Commonly, in simple systems, the collective government is also based on kinship groupings. In heterogeneous differentiated societies the position differs sharply; there it is normally possible to consider collective organization and institutional structure with minimal attention to the level of family organization. None the less, all societies, even the simplest, depend for their boundaries, organization, and internal order on the scope and character of their corporate structure, which is explicitly centred in the public domain. Together the corporate forms that the system includes constitute the collective frameworks of social organization for the people concerned. Thus, for example, if the unit's corporate structure includes appropriate modes of grouping for leadership, it will enjoy an explicit political unity under a representative central organization; otherwise, the prevailing corporate organization constitutes the aggregate as an acephalous body whose unity is implicit in its common institutional framework at both the private and the public levels, though without expression in a single corporate form.

8.

Another feature of institutional systems which requires explicit recognition is their variable interconnection and autonomy. Alternative modes of relations within and between the several institutional sectors of a common system include compatibility, inconsistency, and incompatibility of structure; divergence, complementarity, or equivalence at the formal and functional levels; asymmetrical dependence of one institution on another; interdependence or indifference and autonomy; symmetrical or asymmetrical reinforcements; feedback, congruence, coherence, co-determination, and integration; and conflict or contradiction. These are only some of the more familiar modes in which the institutions of a given system may be interlinked.

Some institutions such as family or cult may have several diverse types of relationships with other institutions in the common social system; but clearly, unless there is a tolerable margin of consistency or coherence among these institutions, they can scarcely combine into a self-perpetuating system capable of supporting an orderly collective life.

To illustrate the variability of institutional interconnections, we may briefly compare certain processes in American and Soviet society. As evidenced by their space programmes, these countries have attained similar levels of technological and scientific development. Such equivalence implies substantial convergences in the Soviet and American structures of science and education. None the less, the Soviet Union and the United States differ sharply in the political and economic institutions on which the technological capacities and educational organizations of their several space programmes depend, equally though in differing ways. Interestingly, both the Soviet and the American economic systems, despite frequent assertions to the contrary, likewise depend, historically and structurally, for their institutionalization, development, maintenance, and regulation on political institutions that date from creative revolutions. Although substantially similar modes and levels of scientific, technological, and educational organization are equally compatible with the differing Soviet and American economic and political frameworks, Soviet economic collectivism is no more compatible with the American form of political organization than is individualist capitalism with the Soviet political regime. It would seem here, despite Marx, whose practice supports our interpretation against his theory, that instead of the 'economic system' or, more specifically, the mode of production, determining the forms and levels of social organization, a specific political structure is prerequisite for the particular economic form, since in this comparison each mode of political organization excludes the alternative form of economy. Thus, although similar scientific and educational institutions may prevail under these radically different social regimes, and though their technological and economic systems may have comparable capacities, these economies, being structurally dependent on the political organization, differ correspondingly in form. Comparable variations characterize the relations between religion and polity in these two industrial states.

This example illustrates the point that while each institutional complex such as kinship or cult tends to form a reasonably coherent and autonomous sub-system, the integration of these several sub-systems with one another is normally more variable and indirect than the integration of elements in each. For example, the connections between marriage, family, and domestic organization are more direct and pervasive than those that link familial organization to cult or government, especially in highly differentiated heterogeneous societies. As a corollary, institutions of the same kind drawn from societies with differing cultural traditions are likely to differ in their structural requisites and in their implications, wherever they differ in their elements and inner organization.

If the elements of two societies were hypothetically shuffled together like two decks of cards, the institutional correspondences and interdependences on which either system initially relied for its inner coherence and efficient sequences of action could scarcely be reproduced by transference to other sectors of the alternative system. The connections between institutions within a system are far too specific and complex for such substitutability, equivalence, or transfer of connections to be generally possible for institutions drawn from historically differing systems. In two societies, specific relations between family, economy, and cult can rarely be the same, given structural differences in either of these sectors. For such transferability to be generally feasible without institutional dislocation and disjunction, the interconnections within and between the different sectors of either system must perfectly replicate and correspond with one another. This is a remote probability on analytic and statistical grounds alike.

A simple imaginary experiment demonstrates that, besides the specific elements that appear to constitute each institutional subsystem, we must also give special attention to their essential interconnections and structural requirements in order to determine their relative autonomy or interdependence within the system as presently constituted or under specific but variable conditions. This condition indicates that when two or more peoples having differing institutional systems are 'shuffled together' by historical circumstances into a common inclusive aggregate, the probabilities that an immediate functional correspondence can be established between their several institutional systems is rather low, unless indeed these collectivities, falling at the same level of social development, also belong to a common wider tradition, as did the European immigrants to the United States, and thus already share a sufficiently broad frame of institutional correspondences in substance and form to permit relatively simple assimilation and inter-systemic accommodations of their several distinct patterns.

Systemic tendencies towards institutional integration themselves preclude or obstruct facile substitutions and accommodations of the same or complementary institutions drawn from structurally different systems. Further, while some consistency and symmetrical reinforcement between institutions in the private and public domains of any collectivity are essential for the effective and orderly operation of its social system, institutions in either of these spheres require adequate levels of internal autonomy in order that their adjustments to developments in other institutional sectors of the social system may be effected smoothly. The higher the level of institutional differentiation and specialization within the system, the greater the specialization of each institutional sector and the greater the autonomy and flexibility requisite in each sphere to accommodate change generated elsewhere.

9.

Societies vary in the institutional differences that characterize the collectivities they incorporate. These lesser collectivities may share similar institutions of kinship, marriage, and family, while differing in their several public domains; or they may differ in both domains; or, while sharing a common mode of public organization, they may differ in other institutions of the public domain and also in their private domains. Alternatively, the collectivities may initially differ in particular public structures, such as government or cult, while sharing common patterns of organization in other areas. We must now try to determine analytically how such variable combinations of institutional continuity and discontinuity affect the organization and character of the inclusive society.

All politically unified societies possess common governments that exercise jurisdictions within them and on their behalf. This is equally true of colonies and of metropolitan states; but an autonomous exclusive jurisdiction is inconsistent with membership in an effective federation. Thus, in so far as an institutionally diverse aggregate forms a distinct and autonomous polity, whether acephalous as in the Swat valley or Kachin hills,[1,2] or centralized, as is more usual, all its components will be subject to a common government, although often differentially so. In consequence we may exclude the common political system from initial consideration in seeking those specific combinations of institutional divergence and community which distinguish pluralism and heterogeneity.

Employing Fortes' distinction between private and public domains, and recalling the important but variable connections among institutions in these spheres, let us consider certain specific alternatives: for example, situations in which two or more ethnic groups incorporated in a common polity do or do not share common or similar organizations of their private domains in the institutions of kinship, family, and marriage. If continuities in kinship and marriage prevail, then intermarriage and consequent social assimilation are facilitated to the degree that the associated private institutions such as domestic organization, divorce, inheritance, and the like are also common or symmetrically congruent, and in so far as such connubium is not obstructed by geographical separation or by collective regulations in either group, or proscribed in the public domain of the inclusive unit.

European immigrants to America, sharing sufficiently common institutions of kinship and marriage and recognizing American common law as the appropriate standard to regulate these relations, are subject to no national proscriptions against intermarriage. Such

12. Leach (1954).

groups are, however, influenced by their own collective regulations and by accidents of circumstance, location, and the order in which they entered American society. Religious barriers to intermarriage with outsiders are institutionalized in the public domains of various religious collectivities. Further, strictly ethnic considerations limit the incidence of outgroup marriage. It seems unlikely that, despite the national ideology of assimilation and the absence of any legal proscriptions on this matter, outgroup marriage ratios exceed ingroup ratios, even in the third generation of immigrants among American Catholics of differing ethnic collectivities or among American Jews.

In America, marriage between whites and Negroes or Indians is also restricted, and collective proscriptions are often present. However, in these cases initial differences in the kinship institutions of white, Negro, and Indian Americans are not in themselves wholly sufficient to account for these collective restrictions. Native Indians were originally excluded from American colonial society as enemies or as allies; societal segregation was then mutual; but, as the Indians were overrun, the status of the Indian declined until connubium between the two groups came to be disapproved. The Negro, imported as a slave, was by status initially precluded from marriage with a free person, though not from concubinage.

Among the Tutsi and the Hutu of traditional Ruanda and Burundi, kinship institutions were sufficiently similar for fictional assimilations of Hutu and Tutsi patrilineages to develop. However, Hutu and Tutsi may not intermarry. Tutsi, the ruling section of these plural societies, proscribed such unions and thereby constituted themselves and the subject Hutu as closed perpetual endogamous castes. By these proscriptions the Tutsi maintained their sectional disassociation from the Hutu around them, and avoided compromising their relations of dominance by ties of kinship and affinity. Caste-endogamous marriage served also to reinforce the closure and the internal cohesion of the Tutsi as a corporate group controlling the administrative and political structure; for the Hutu, constituted as a corporate category under Tutsi regulation, caste endogamy merely perpetuated conditions of servitude.[13]

The Fulani of Northern Nigeria fall into two distinct categories: pastoral nomads, who are nominally Muslim, and their settled cousins, who provide the Muslim intelligentsia and ruling aristocracy of most Central Sudanic emirates. The nomads and their sedentary cousins share identical kinship institutions; and settled Fulani aristocrats often marry girls of pastoral stock, though the reverse rarely occurs. However, the two Fulani communities remain quite distinct by virtue of differences in their respective public domains. Their separation persists despite long traditions of military and political symbiosis and the formal overrule by settled Fulani of the

13. Maquet (1961), pp. 46, 64-7; d'Hertefelt (1965), in Gibbs (1965), pp. 414-19.

nomad communities. Special institutional arrangements were maintained by ruling Fulani to accommodate the pastoralists to their regimes without alienation or forced assimilation. In this case, divergences in their public domains served to segregate two branches of a common ethnic stock despite shared familial institutions and formal freedoms of connubium.[14]

Evidently, while shared familial institutions permit the assimilation of separate groups by facilitating connubium, they do not necessarily promote or entail this result; and where the aggregates concerned are systematically differentiated in the political sphere, as by dominance and subordination in Ruanda, or by institutional differentiation among the Fulani, collective boundaries persist even without formal proscriptions of intermarriage.

On the other hand, where there are initial divergences of content, form, basis, and scope in the familial institutions of two collectivities, intermarriage is virtually precluded; and in such conditions intergroup mating typically proceeds by illicit affairs with ambiguous paternity obligations, by enforced concubinage in slavery or other forms of servitude, or by institutionalized or illegitimate hypergamy.[15] Given divergent familial institutions, these appear to be the sole alternatives to collective endogamy, which perpetuates corporate divisions and is easily transformed into 'caste', especially if the separate collectivities are ranked hierarchically as corporate units and maintain separate and unequal public domains. In such cases, an asymmetrical connubium may be institutionalized as hypergamy or concubinage; but either alternative merely serves to underline the corporate division and inequality. In either case, collective differences in the private domain seal off each aggregate as a separate self-reproducing unit having its own familial and cultural traditions, a segregated collective organization in its public domain, and distinctive contexts of socialization.

The factors that underlie patterns of collective endogamy in such conditions are reasonably clear. Given divergent norms of marriage and family, symmetrical intergroup marriage generates numerous problems of personal and collective status and rights, which exacerbate and often mobilize collective hostilities and actively contrapose the two groups. Whenever such unions are legitimized, these conflicts of collective norms and organization are directly evident. In consequence, juxtaposed collectivities that differ in the structure and scope of their familial institutions are generally segregated as biological and social units whose separate cultural traditions are thus preserved and entrenched in the separate contexts of socialization that each maintains.

14. Stenning (1959, 1965); see also M.G. Smith (1965*b*).
15. M.G. Smith (1965*a*), pp. 175-7, 182-8.

10.

Such corporate closures are basic to the Indian system of caste. None the less, as Hutton remarks, caste in India differs from pluralism.[16] First, caste is an essential dimension and organizational framework of the religion and culture all Hindus share. It identifies and unites these Hindu communities by dividing them on sacred bases. This differentiation is prescribed by a religious framework common to all castes. Secondly, as an effect of their occupational stereotyping, all local caste groups (*jati*) are directly and indirectly interdependent in the economic and ritual spheres; the various castes accordingly share several common institutions in their common public domain.

Familial institutions of the several castes in any region are also generally identical in form. Inter-caste relations are contractual, individual, and of various kinds. These relations simultaneously differentiate the members of any given caste, and link men of different castes in elaborate contractual networks that cut across collective boundaries, dispersing personal loyalties and interests by individuating members of each caste. Such institutional arrangements all belong, like caste itself, in the common public domain. Besides *jajmani* relations, they include tenancy, wage labour, political alliances and factionalism, clientage, representative village councils (*panchayats*), and certain common village rituals, as well as common scales of ritual pollution, marriage and family ceremonies of similar form, and common dependence on Brahminical rites. Further, in most rural areas the dominant caste is also the most numerous, and generally employs its numerical preponderance in the village *panchayat* to preserve its local dominance and control of local land. Thus in neighbouring areas, local dominance is often exercised by differing castes; and frequently these locally dominant groups are ranked low in the ritual hierarchy.

Such elasticities in the structure of secular status are quite consistent with the theoretically immutable ritual stratification of the various castes, since the ritual and secular status scales are only loosely connected and remain relatively independent of each other. As an effect of these conditions, Indian caste institutionalizes communities of action, norms, and social relations based on primary divisions of the people into a series of ranked endogamous categories whose separate autonomy is limited by their prescribed interdependence in the common public domain. In any caste, socialization to Hinduism and to the social order proceeds simultaneously with the inculcation of caste-specific norms and roles.[17]

16. Hutton (1946), p. 117.
17. A. Mayer (1955); Hutton (1946); Leach (1960); Marriott (1955); Beidelman (1959); Kalenda (1963); Srinivas et al. (1959).

Indian caste shows that, although continuities of institutional organization in the private domain permit the easy association and assimilation of collective groups by eliminating intrinsic obstacles to common connubium, these continuities are not in themselves sufficient to assure symmetrical intermarriage or the dissolution of collective boundaries; they are indeed unlikely to have such effects wherever the two collectivities are differentiated formally by their differing status and relations in the public domain of the inclusive aggregate. Conversely, as in the United States, ethnic groups and religious congregations may remain relatively endogamous despite similar familial institutions, and despite the absence of any formal proscriptions against connubium, while their members enjoy equivalent status in the inclusive public domain. However, if either collectivity is segregated spatially, its own public domain tends to become specialized, together with its relation to the inclusive society. Under such conditions, and especially if one collectivity is subordinate to the other as in Ruanda, or subsumed by its neighbour as among the Fulani, pluralism prevails through pre-emption of the societally regulative institutions by one unit to the exclusion of the other, with consequential differentiation of their collective domains and relations.

11.

We can learn most about the specific combinations of conditions which constitute or prevail under pluralism by examining further the varying combinations of institutional and structural diversity in American society. Among American whites, Jews, distinguished by religion and descent, form an internally divided, relatively endogamous group. Adherents of the Orthodox and Catholic faiths are likewise religiously differentiated and internally divided into a number of relatively closed ethnic groups, each distinguished also by its own specific religious organizations, by deep-set tendencies towards endogamy, by ethnic traditions, and sometimes by alternate languages. Protestants, subdivided by denomination and sect and also by ethnic group, probably have the lowest general tendencies towards ethnic and religious endogamy of all major divisions in the white American population. We have to ask in what ways do these parallel Jewish, Orthodox, Protestant, and Catholic differentiations differ, if at all, from the conditions of pluralism.

White Americans of Jewish, Orthodox, Catholic, or Protestant faith may participate freely and equally in common economic, educational, and political institutions; they are legally free to marry or to worship as they please; and in consequence, such closures as these ethnic and religious collectivities separately exhibit are optional and not societally prescribed. Given the institutional continuities in religious and familial institutions shared among these collectivities, individual mobility and assimilation are greatly facilitated so that uniform dissociations are restricted to such specific spheres as ethnicity or cult, where individual affiliations are also optional. Thus, neither the Orthodox nor the Jews nor the Catholics nor any of the various ethnic segments in 'White America' are permanently or effectively closed. Indeed, within each group the members are extensively differentiated by various and often contraposed alignments with individuals and groups of differing kinds outside the collectivity concerned. In effect the secular organization of United States society treats religion as one of several institutional spheres in which personal affiliations are optional, expectably diverse, and formally indifferent to the central organization of the common public domain. In consequence, intra- or inter-ethnic and denominational marriages or associations have limited significance in themselves for the wider society, or for the placement of individuals within it. The social identities and capacities of white Americans are not determined by their religious or ethnic affiliations; and, despite their undeniable significance to the individuals and religious or ethnic collectivities concerned, institutional identifications as Catholic, Orthodox, Jewish, or Protestant, or as Irish, Swedish, or Italian, are formally and substantively equivalent alternatives accommodated indifferently to the secular organization of the inclusive aggregate. By themselves, such ethnic and religious affiliations entail no direct or systematic differentiations or inequalities in the public sphere, in the educational, economic, social, and political systems, although they provide effective bases for the organization of corporate groups in pursuit of common interests.

These patterns of social heterogeneity among white Americans presuppose equally effective and uniform segregations of the several institutional spheres — kinship, cult, polity, economy, and education — so that differentiations among the population in kinship or cult do not necessarily entail corresponding differentiations or incapacities in other spheres. Thus, given the formal equivalence in familial institutions and the uniform segregation of religious organizations required by law as a necessary condition of secular equality, collective or individual differences in family and/or cult neither entail, presume, nor systematically correspond with parallel differences in other fields of individual or collective activity. Only by rigorous prescriptive closures such as Amish or Hutterites maintain can religious enclaves achieve a truly autarchic corporate differentiation in this society. In consequence, the structural significance of these ethnic or religious divergences and corporate affiliations for the total society and for the placement of individuals within it remains limited, conditional, and variable. In effect, such differentiated collectivities are equally consistent with the free participation of their members in the common heterogeneous society, and can neither disqualify nor differentiate individuals by status or by capacity in the public sector, being themselves by the law and conditions of the secular society together incapable of subsuming and prescriptively regulating the major institutional interests and needs of their members. Thus, these institutional differentiations and collectivities are segregated as equivalent alternatives at the structurally secondary levels of national organization and personal affiliation. They fall primarily within the private domain of the wider collectivity.

12.

It is revealing to compare these white American patterns with others found among Negroes in the United States. Such a comparison shows how corporate divisions, once instituted as structural and institutional disjunctions in the public domain, are internally and externally reinforced and may perpetuate primary cleavages, irrespective of later institutional continuities across their boundaries and discontinuities within them.

Franklin Frazier shows how the Negro's social situation in the United States has tended to institutionalize deformities in all sectors of its private domain,[18] kinship, mating, family, paternity, and domestic organization alike. He shows also that, especially in Northern cities, where conditions permit limited Negro professionalization and property accumulations, although Negro family and other social forms have tended to approximate the models institutionalized among American whites, the public domain of Negro society remains equally separate and distinctive.[19] Comparable contrasts in the religious, social, and family life of whites and Negroes in the Deep South are familiar to all.[20] In the North, Negroes and whites are segregated residentially, occupationally, and socially by informal caste or colour-caste. The two racial divisions operate parallel but separate and distinctive organizations, and the Negro community characteristically remains economically depressed and dependent on the wealthier, more numerous, and more powerful whites. Thus, economic differentials and spatial and social boundaries interact to reinforce one another.

In the Deep South, despite recent tokenism in churches, courts, registration booths, and schools, caste divisions are basic, formal, and deeply entrenched as the fundamental conditions of Southern corporate structure. The requisite Negro subjugation is facilitated and maintained by their corporate exclusion as a residual category from the public domain of Southern white society. White control is pursued by various devices such as differential justice, denial of political rights, land control, tenancy, sharecropping, occupational and educational inequalities and insecurities, segregation of public

18. Frazier (1940).
19. Frazier (1949, 1962).
20. Dollard (1957); Powdermaker (1939).

facilities and residence, and the like. The recent rise of corporate organizations and public movements against this racial structure of inequality has evoked widespread hostile reactions in the South. None the less, in the Northern United States, where these movements won most initial support, parallel racial barriers persist with corresponding inequalities and tensions.

Negro acculturation in America has varied in degree and scope with differences of social circumstance. Negro and white professionals or bourgeoisie share many common institutional patterns; but these classes vary proportionately in both racial categories as a function of the prevailing inequalities of educational, economic, and political opportunity; further, the bourgeoisie and professionals in both races are structurally segregated and, with marginal exceptions, they are occupationally and socially restricted to their own racial categories. Thus, despite extensive institutional continuities across racial frontiers, Negro and white American professionals or bourgeoisie are not socially equivalent; rather, each group is isolated from the other within unequal, closed, and perpetual corporate categories which are racially defined and structurally contraposed. In consequence of this primary cleavage, Negro American professionals are defined first as Negroes, then as Americans, and only finally by occupation, in contrast with their white colleagues. How do the contexts and correlates of such phenomena illuminate the salient differences between pluralism and heterogeneity?

On their introduction to America, Negroes were racially, culturally, and socially distinct. Slavery categorized them as the property of their owners and systematically denied them civil, economic, political, and other social rights.[21] Following the abolition of slavery after deep strife, effective substitute controls were developed by the dominant whites in the Deep South to perpetuate the categorical exclusions on which Negro subjugation and social inequality were based.[22] All persons of Negro descent were identified as members of the category excluded from participation in the public domains of Southern white society. In the North, to which many Southern Negroes emigrated, residential and social segregation produced broadly similar effects by simultaneously excluding them from white society and by constituting them in urban ghettos as a residual corporate category, irrespective of their internal institutional and social differentiations. Given these structural contexts, institutional continuities across racial boundaries, or institutional discontinuities within either racial category, have limited relevance, in the wider society, in either corporation, or to the individuals concerned.[23]

Similar divergences between institutional and corporate boundaries are observed among the East Indians and Creole Negroes

21. Olmsted (1959); Elkins (1963); Phillips (1963); Stampp (1964).
22. Johnson (1934); A. Davis, B.B. Gardner and M.R. Gardner (1941).
23. Myrdal (1944).

of Trinidad and British Guiana.[24] In Trinidad, East Indians may identify many local Creole Negro dishes and other cultural items as elements of 'ancestral Indian culture'. Conversely, Negroid Creoles, having forgotten their cultural debts to East Indians for numerous items, including cuisine, ornaments, and so on, identify these as traditional Creole patterns. Such 'plural acculturation', cultural exchange, or assimilation merely highlights the distinction between strictly cultural and strictly social categorizations within this community. However incorrect these attributions may be in fact, the primary identification for any individual or cultural item as East Indian or as Creole Negro is prescribed by this corporate contraposition. Hybrids, distinguished as *doglas* (bastards), are excluded by East Indians from their collectivity. Though many middle-class East Indians and Negroes share common institutional forms and skills, they remain contraposed by their corporate identities.

Similarly, no American of either race fails to identify an American Catholic Negro bishop or bureaucrat as first and foremost a Negro — that is, by his primary corporate identity. In the United States, as in Guyana and Trinidad, the racial division is institutionalized as a specifically social boundary between two closed categories, irrespective of institutional continuities across boundaries or differences within either category. On either side of these corporate boundaries, each collectivity maintains its distinct 'public' organizations for internal and external collective action in matters of common interest. In all three societies, the contraposed collectivities participate unequally and differently, but primarily as units in the public sector that includes them. As in Guyana or Trinidad, so in the United States, following an initial situation of marked differences between two structurally segregated collectivities, institutional modifications and assimilations have left intact their social boundaries, and social pluralism prevails, regardless of strictly cultural continuities between or differences within either category. In Trinidad and Guyana it is probable that a majority in either category remains unfamiliar with the other's institutional system, and perhaps also in the United States. However, exclusive categorical incorporations are clearly independent of cultural assimilation or internal differences. Likewise, in Senegal, despite official French doctrines of assimilation and association, similar categorical exclusions contraposed European and *évolué*, despite their common institutional allegiances.[25]

The principal conditions that ensure such persistence of social pluralism despite the prevalence of institutional continuities across social boundaries are inherent in the corporate organization itself. If a social boundary rigidly separates two corporate categories, as in the Northern United States, both collectivities will then lack inclusive

24. Crowley (1957, 1960); Klass (1960); Skinner (1960); R.T. Smith (1962), pp. 98-143; Despres (1964, 1967).
25. Mercier (1965*a*, 1965*b*); Crowder (1962).

corporate organizations in which they participate as equals and to whose co-ordinated actions alone they can look for peaceful changes in the corporate structure. On the other hand, if one of the collectivities has categorical form, while the other is organized as a corporate group, as in the South, the latter is generally dominant, and by virtue of its organizational and other resources, can effectively contain pressures for the dissolution of the corporate boundaries on which its power, status, and privilege are based. Individual actions and alignments cannot demolish or transform these social divisions and corporate units; nor can the representative national government initiate such radical action without assurances of overwhelming support from both collectivities, and especially from the majority of the dominant one.

When two corporations are defined by virtue of a common boundary, this can be abolished only by their separate but joint determination, or by the radical action of one of them. Tokenism is the logical corporate response to external pressures by a national government for the elimination of inequalities by which corporate sections are mutually defined and segregated, as in the Southern states. Cultural continuities or variations can neither erode nor transform these corporate structures directly for the simple reason that sectional divisions and relations are based on other principles, such as power, race, or other criteria of exclusive corporate solidarity and autonomy.

All collectivities that are segregated as or within societies require special procedures and organization to co-ordinate and regulate their internal action and to guide their relations with external corporations. In consequence, the public domains of segregated collectivities develop specific modes of organization and action to handle their collective interests and problems. The more rigorous and institutionally extensive the segregation of the collectivity, the deeper and wider is its associational boundary, and the more exhaustively are its members socially identified with and dependent upon it. In the structural context of a plural society, each corporate section develops sectionally specific institutions, organizations, and procedures that constitute its distinctive public domain; and if the plurality contains two or more collectivities of equivalent or differing status, their segregation is further reinforced by these mutually distinctive collective organizations. If these social sections are also segregated spatially, as is often the case, then the public domain of either unit enjoys corresponding freedom from external competition or immediate internal challenge. In effect, any institutional development or systematic organization in the collective domains of either section in a context of pluralism tends to reinforce the already existing divisions and separatism of the sections as mutually exclusive, internally autonomous, contraposed corporations. Such structural developments proceed independently of cultural continuities or assimilation across sectional boundaries.

Thus in the Republic of South Africa, as in the United States, the 'black bourgeoisie' remain subject to the categorical identities and disabilities of their social sections.[26] In Trinidad, Guyana, and Mauritius,[27] Indians and Creole Negroes have each developed and retained specific sectional structures; and when these social sections were simultaneously enfranchised, their distinctive organizations were quickly converted into political parties, as also in Surinam[28] and Nigeria.[29]

In sum, it seems that the decisive conditions that constitute and perpetuate social pluralism consist primarily in differences of institutional organization in the public domains of segregated collectivities identified as the basic corporate units of social structure, and contraposed in consequence of sharp initial differences in their political status and in their several public domains.

Under such conditions, it is irrelevant whether the inclusive social order emphasizes the functional differentiation and autonomy of institutional spheres within either section. If collectivities are rigorously segregated, spatially or associationally, although the institutional structure may be highly differentiated within either collectivity, their separate public domains will each represent a sectionally specific and structurally distinctive organization. Under such conditions, the societally integrative effects of institutional differentiations and interdependences are restricted by and within the primary demarcation of collectivities as separate associational fields. Similarly, the opportunities for and implications of institutional assimilations or isomorphism are subject to the structural conditions and requirements of the prevailing corporate organization.

13.

Inclusion of subordinate sections in the representative political institutions of the wider society on terms of formal equality is quite consistent with the maintenance of social pluralism, provided that this plural structure antedates the introduction of 'democratic reforms'. In such cases, formal democratization of the political process may be merely the means for preservation and stabilization of the plural regime.[30] This implies structurally profound divergences between formal equivalence and substantial reality.

Normally, however, the political regime of the plural society is

26. L. Kuper (1965); Mitchell (1960).
27. Benedict (1961, 1962).
28. van Lier (1950).
29. Coleman (1958); Post (1963); Hodgkin (1961).
30. In this context, for the reforms of Appius Claudius at Rome, of Solon and Cleisthenes in Athens, and the Carthaginian constitution, see Warde Fowler (1952); Ehrenberg (1964); Cary (1945). For two rather different modern views see Heard (1961); W.A. Lewis (1965).

identified by an exclusive concentration of political and juridical resources and functions in a ruling minority organized as a corporate group. In consequence, all other sections of the population are excluded from these political spheres as local aggregates or categories lacking extensive independent political organizations and capacities. Only where popular legislatures or tribunals prevail, or where offices are filled by direct or indirect election, can the scope of the franchise formally indicate the range of these differential statuses as citizen or subject. In most historic societies, such electoral institutions are lacking, and the ruling group is identified by its monopoly of the central political and administrative offices to which recruitment is primarily by descent or patronage. In either of these regimes, intermarriage and the equal association of the elite with the politically ineligible are normally proscribed. Generally, such structures of domination are centralized under a supreme office or corporation, identified exclusively with the dominant section.

In acephalous plural societies such as Pathan Swat, two further conditions are essential: the collective domination of the ruling group must be secure beyond local challenge; and the dominant section must have special institutional procedures to mediate its internal disputes and to mobilize its dispersed segments for joint action whenever necessary.[31] In centralized pluralities that lack popular electoral institutions, the ruler, identified socially and institutionally with the dominant section, is often ideologically represented as a personification of the polity, a divine king, or other quasi-sacred societal symbol. In themselves, these ideologies are clearly insufficient bases for the sectional dominions they seek to legitimate and rationalize.[32]

The political structure of a plural society is always dependent on a systematic organization of political, administrative, and military means and inequalities for its establishment and maintenance alike. In traditional contexts, sectional monopolies of regulative public structures normally presuppose and entail hereditary recruitments to office, sectional endogamy, and sharply differentiated contexts of socialization. As a result, the dominant section is identified as a self-perpetuating biological and social group by its closure, by its unique organization, by the societal authority of its public domain, and by the imposition of its own institutional order on the aggregate that it rules. The result is a characteristically oligarchic regime based on systematic political and social inequality and designed to preserve and perpetuate the institutional conditions essential for the sectional dominance with which it is identified. Ideologies of differing kind and quality may be elaborated to rationalize such plural regimes; but beyond such antecedent religious prescriptions as Islam enjoins, these

---

31. Barth (1959).
32. D'Hertefelt (1964); d'Hertefelt, Troubworst and Scherer (1962); Maquet (1961). See also Hocart (1941), pp. 1-11.

ideologies generally misrepresent or sublimate the motivations, interests, and relations involved.

The structural stability of such a plural society has several important requisites. (1) There must be substantial continuity of the economic and ecological conditions in which the structure was first stabilized, involving either an appropriate population policy or a resource base capable of accommodating population increases over substantial periods. (2) There must be relative isolation of the aggregate from other societies of comparable scale and differing type. (3) By design or otherwise, the demographic ratios of the ruling and the ruled should be maintained or improved gradually in favour of the rulers. (4) Sectional identities and boundaries have to be maintained by generalizing the requisite inequalities and differences to all spheres — religious, familial, educational, occupational, economic, and other — with consequent restrictions on intersectional acculturation and exclusion of intersectional mobility. (5) Symbiotic relations, which provide primary compensations for the subordinate section and increase the stability of the regime, and religions that offer deferred compensations — for example, Christianity — should be encouraged in appropriate forms. (6) The cohesion, *esprit de corps*, and superior organization and resources to which the rulers owe their initial dominance should be maintained or enhanced. through collective action that preserves and develops their corporate exclusiveness. Internal dissensions in the ruling group are functional only if they can be institutionalized in forms that subdivide and mobilize the subordinate sections to support elite protagonists, as in two-party systems firmly controlled by the dominant group. (7) Ideally the regime should be legitimized by an inclusive cult that sacralizes the structure and leadership, as in Inca or Ruanda society, by one that offers basic compensation in another life, or by one that advocates withdrawal from the world.

14.

It is to be expected that in a plural society the dominant section will employ all the political and social resources in its control to stabilize and preserve its power and regime. To this end its members must simultaneously monopolize positions of power and immobilize the subject categories by suppressing or proscribing their collective political organization. To remedy this situation, the subordinate section needs first to develop an effective and inclusive corporate group, as, for example, the *consilium plebis* at Rome in 439 B.C.,[33] the Hussite congregation in fourteenth-century Europe,[34] the Parmehutu Aprosoma in Ruanda,[35] the Congress Party in India, and

33. Cary (1945), pp. 72-83.
34. Cohn (1957), pp. 217-36; Kaminsky (1962).
35. D'Hertefelt (1960*b*); see also d'Hertefelt, Troubworst and Scherer (1962).

so forth. Often the collective protest of a subordinate acephalous section takes the form of social movements, such as Lollardy or Chartism in Britain, Cargo Cults in Melanesia,[36] or the revolutionary movements in France and Haiti at the close of the eighteenth century.[37] In other cases a charismatic leader may direct this sectional revolt through a loosely structured corporate group or body of disciples as Gandhi did in India, Toussaint and Dessalines in Haiti, John Ball in feudal England, Shehu dan Fodio in the Central Sudan,[38] Miguel Hidalgo in Mexico, or the Mahdi and Bolivar.[39] At all events, as corporate categories, subordinate sections in plural societies lack the inclusive organization requisite for effective political action to challenge the organized and entrenched minorities that rule them; unless they can create and support such units, they remain immobilized by their internal divisions and common situation as residual subject categories.

If religious differences impose the primary cleavage on which the plural structure rests, as in India, the Sudan, and elsewhere, then conversion and assimilation are necessary to eliminate it. Like Marxism, Islam for example has spread by enforcing the conversion and assimilation of conquered communities. Notably it has encountered sharpest resistance in India, where the ramified categorical organization of caste fragments its pressure and appeals.

Another peaceful process by which the institutional and corporate conditions of pluralism may be dissolved requires the absorption or assimilation of the dominant group into the culture and society of the dominated majority. This course is feasible only where the mass of the people bear a common culture which is appropriate to the maintenance of the political regime and which is more elaborately developed than that of their rulers. Such assimilations occurred among the Liao, Mongols, and Manchu in China,[40] the Seljuk and Ottoman Turks in Islâm,[41] the Bulgars under Byzantium,[42] and the Fulani in Hausaland.

Symbiosis may preserve a plural structure with minimal modification by institutionalizing mutually satisfactory accommodations of the rulers and the ruled.[43] This presumes the maintenance of favourable internal and external conditions, together with adequate balances between population and resources. Institutionalized symbiosis excludes structural change by stabilizing relations of reciprocal interdependence on the basis of institutional and status differences between component sections of the plural society. It simultaneously

36. Cohn (1957), pp. 209-17; Thrupp (1962); Worsley (1957).
37. De Tocqueville (1955); Le Febvre (1957); Leyburn (1941); James (1963).
38. Arnett (1922).
39. McHenry (1962), pp. 75-85.
40. Wittfogel and Chia-Sheng (1949); Grousset (1952), pp. 231-47, 272-302; van der Sprenkel (1962).
41. Brockelmann (1962), pp. 163-80, 256-343; Gibb and Bowen (1950), vol. 1.
42. Runciman (1961), pp. 222-9; Vasiliev (1958), vol. 1, pp. 281-3, 315-20, 331.
43. Nadel (1938); M.G. Smith (1965a), pp. 11-13, 255.

represents the ideal resolution of structural tensions and a condition
of stationary equilibrium in such societies.

Clientage, the institutionalized association of men of sharply
different status in contexts of political competition, has often served
to integrate the members of differing social sections in plural
societies, such as the plebs and patricians in early Rome and Athens,
the Hutu and Tutsi in Ruanda, the Fulani and Hausa in Northern
Nigeria, and free men of every station in the feudal systems of
medieval Europe and Japan.[44] Such clientage may only erode
corporate divisions if it is sufficiently widespread and general, in
consequence of basic cleavages within the ruling stratum or insecurities in their external context, which require mobilization of
intersectional support. Further, to promote structural transformation, the institution should also legitimate and encourage intermarriage across sectional boundaries, and should facilitate or entail
structurally significant changes in individual status and political
identity. Clientage is institutionalized political symbiosis between
individuals and/or reasonably small groups. It may accordingly
enhance the internal stability of a plural order by establishing
valuable intersectional affiliations oriented to factional competitions
within the ruling group. By itself, clientage is unlikely to dissolve
sectional boundaries wherever differences of culture, religion, or race
are prominent. In feudal polities which rested heavily on such
relations, the servile majority remained beyond the range of
institutional clientage, which was restricted to men of free or noble
birth.

15.

Domination by the ruling minority in a plural society may be
exercised collectively through its political institutions, as at
Sparta,[45] in Ruanda,[46] among the Inca,[47] or in Pathan Swat,[48] or
by *repartimiento*[49] or the territorial segregation of the dominated on
'tribal' reserves under the supervision of the dominant groups, as was
general in settler societies in colonial Africa. Alternatively, segments
of the subordinate population may be placed directly under the
control of individuals drawn from the dominant group. In the latter
instance, servitude is personalized; in the former it is collective.
Personal servitude has many forms: serfdom, slavery, peonage,
indenture, bondage, and so on. It is normally ascribed by allocation,
birth, capture, debt, purchase, or lease. Personal proprietorship may

44. Bloch (1961), pp. 145-238; Ganshof (1952); Sansom (1962), pp. 270-96, 426-31.
45. Aristotle, *Politics*, bk. 2, ch. 9 (ed. Jowett, 1943, pp. 107-14); Ehrenberg (1964), pp.
33-9, 54, 96-7.
46. Maquet (1961), pp. 96-124; d'Hertefelt (1965), in Gibbs (1965), pp. 406-7, 420-30.
47. S.F. Moore (1954).
48. Barth (1959).
49. Chevalier (1963), pp. 66-9, 277-96; Holmberg (1960), pp. 67-84.

be acquired by descent and inheritance, by vassalage, purchase, or official allocations, separately or together.

It is evident that these two alternative modes of instituting sectional dominance, the individual and the collective, establish patterns of intersectional relation among individuals which differ notably in immediacy, intensity, continuity, variability, and scope, and in the opportunities for cultural and social assimilation which they provide. Any collective organization of sectional dominance segregates the dominated in local collectivities that foster their cultural distinctness and solidarity. Communally segregated Spartan helots, like the Russian serfs, maintained a spirited collective life apart from their masters, and repeatedly revolted, in vain, as did Negro slaves on New World plantations. In Europe and Japan serfs were subject to far more rigorous and personal supervision of their social life and lacked equivalent incentives and opportunities for revolt. In Ruanda, subject Hutu were simultaneously supervised by at least two hierarchies of officials;[50] and the Inca also institutionalized a dual system of collective administration.[51] In Grenada (West Indies), after emancipation, ex-slaves were habituated to servitude by symbiotic relations and by dispersal in discrete estate communities.[52] In nearby Barbados, sectional legislation explicitly forbade the ex-slaves to move about within the island, thereby tying them to the plantations as a dependent, immobile, landless proletariat, where they remain to this day.[53] In Mexico and other Hispanic New World territories, Indian communities were subjected to individual domination by Creole Spaniards and mestizos as field labour under various forms of peonage; and although violence was common, given the specific personal structure of control, in this context it was rarely generalized at this level of the society, except during wider struggles among superior social sections.

The structure of categorical subordination, organized and exercised collectively through locally discrete autonomous corporate groups, invites frequent revolt to the extent that its conditions are onerous and its supervision lax. This structure insulates the several social sections, and accordingly preserves their institutional differentiations by restricting opportunities for intersectional assimilation. In its most extreme form, it prescribes tributary relations between two politically distinct societies, the explicit antithesis of pluralism, which requires a common corporate organization of disparate elements in one society. By contrast, personal administration of discrete segments of the subordinate section brings corresponding increases in the range, intensity, and frequency of interpersonal contacts across sectional boundaries. Such increases of intersectional personal associations institute corresponding opportunities for

50. Maquet (1961), pp. 100-24, 129-31, 140.
51. S.F. Moore (1954).
52. M.G. Smith (1963), pp. 9-11, 22-9, 36-8; (1965c), pp. 262-303.
53. Macmillan (1938), pp. 90-1.

cultural and social assimilations consistent with the corporate requirements of the inclusive regime. Under structures of either type, maintenance or modification of intersectional boundaries and relations depends primarily on collective social action rather than on cultural assimilations as such. In consequence, acculturated members of the subordinate section are situationally condemned to frustration, dissidence, or revolt, or to alignment with their superiors as trusted but expendable servitors and aides. This is so because in plural regimes individual qualities are irrelevant for the determination of social identity, which is ascriptive and corporate in base and significance. In effect, intersectional social mobility is kept at a minimum.[54]

Unless the politically excluded category is systematically subjugated by these collective or personal structures of domination, sectional control of the total society remains ambiguous and uncertain, despite sectional monopoly of the political regime; such a situation generates tension and invites revolt. Notably, this is the modal form of social pluralism which prevailed in Western Europe from the dissolution of feudalism to the recent establishment of popularly elected representative governments. Characteristically, in this area until the mid-nineteenth century, peasants and emerging proletariats were denied political and civil rights under systems of legal immunity and privilege, sectional administration, and restrictive political franchise.[55] Besides their monopoly of government, commerce, land, law, church, and the officer corps, the dominant sections of these divided societies sought to enhance and preserve their institutional differentiation from the dominated majority by exclusive educational provisions for socialization of their young, and by restrictive control of occupational opportunities. In their heyday, as Disraeli, Mayhew, Marx, and others observed, such societies consisted of two broad categories, the masters and the servants; but under the prevailing frame of organization, servitude was a contractual alternative to unemployment, brigandage, emigration, or forced recruitment to the army, the mines, or the fleet.

Marx and Engels, observing these societies, interpreted their political structures as consequences of the economic inequalities inherent in their capitalist organization;[56] in this they systematically inverted the relations that held between the structures of political and economic inequality. Analytically and historically alike, the economic inequalities these writers observed were based upon antecedent conditions of political and jural domination and presupposed them. With subsequent enfranchisement of the previously unrepresented section, economic inequalities have steadily reduced as the implications of political equality were realized. Anticipating such

54. M.G. Smith (1965a), pp. 205-27, 258.
55. Cole and Postgate (1946); T.H. Marshall (1965), pp. 71-134; Rudé (1964).
56. Marx and Engels (1948).

effects of political and industrial reform, Marx, whose dialectic led him to look for radical transformation of European society by working-class revolution, condemned gradualism and advocated political polarization. In this he clearly reveals his recognition of the primacy of political relations and action in determining the forms and degrees of social inequality and the conditions of social and economic organization.

In Western Europe, during the nineteenth century, disenfranchised categories — Marx's peasants and proletariats — were institutionally differentiated and sectionally segregated from the ruling minority but were not prescriptively subordinated by organized collective or personal systems of domination. They were accordingly identified as masterless subjects, a residual category beyond the polity but subject to the state, which here as elsewhere was the corporate organization of the ruling group. In this context of sectional isolation, trade unions, workers' political associations, revolutionary movements, and ideologies of varying type flourished apace, repeatedly shaking the foundations of these plural societies and successively demonstrating the urgency of incorporating the mass as citizens and providing them with the essential resources of education and organizational access necessary to translate formal citizenship into active capacity. Established political parties representing the elite and its interests occasionally sought to incorporate some of the disenfranchised within their ranks to achieve party advantage, and also to frustrate the emergence of rival structures devoted to sectional interests of the subordinate class. These aims were variably realized; but, as the hitherto disenfranchised acquired citizenship, education, and effective industrial and political organizations, they simultaneously reduced the institutional gulfs that had formerly separated them from their rulers, until, after the Second World War, the distinctive institutions, organizations, and differences of political status which had once contraposed the social sections of these European nations lost their initial significance; and, with some notable exceptions, the plural societies of eighteenth-century Europe were transformed into heterogeneous nation-states. We can summarize these processes of national development and integration as the progressive elimination of corporate categorizations in the social structure through the extension of citizenship from the oligarchy to all members of the corporate group.

16.

Colonialism in Africa repeats these European developments with much greater clarity and speed. Once enfranchised in consequence of military disasters and/or changes of political orientation experienced by the imperial states, the African colonial populations could not long be denied autonomy. Having obtained it, the ex-colonial states pursue economic development and social modernization in different ways, by single or multi-party regimes and under ideologies of varying provenance or coherence.

The essential conditions that currently diversify the organization and orientations of these new African states seem to flow in approximately equal measure from their history and from their social constitutions, but their histories and social constitutions both identify these emergent states as pluralities of varying complexity and form. In some states the major political divisions are between regionally segregated ethnic collectivities. In others the primary cleavages are between the Westernized elite and the traditional mass, organized in several tribal societies and/or traditional states. In yet others these two modes of cleavage are variously and fluidly combined; and in both the older independent African states, Ethiopia and Liberia, despite striking differences in history and form, social pluralism is basic to the political regime and shows no sign of immediate disappearance.[57] When to these alternatives we add the variable presence of European settler communities, the wide variety in the constitution of plural societies in modern Africa is clear, and a corresponding variety in their political and constitutional forms and developments seems inevitable.

Clearly, to transform these plural societies into institutionally heterogeneous nation-states is no easy task, however desirable or essential it may seem to nationalists committed to ideals of corporate unity, identity, and consensus. Yet, if our analysis of the structural and institutional conditions of pluralism is correct, its transformation into the social heterogeneity that is prerequisite for 'modernization' involves the following conditions together: (1) Effective institutionalization of uniform conditions of civil and political equality throughout the country; this especially involves the elimi-nation of elite, sectional, or ethnic privileges in the public sphere. (2) Provision of equal, appropriate, and uniform educational, occupa-tional, and economic opportunities to all cultural sections of the society, and the principled recruitment of active participation in approximately equivalent ratios from all major ethnic groups. (3) Public enforcement of the fundamental freedoms of worship, speech, movement, association, and work. Such measures seem to be equally expedient and necessary for any ex-colonial government, African or other, which is intent on pursuing social modernization by initiating the structural conditions requisite for the progressive but gradual transformation of their rigid plural societies into labile heterogeneous ones.

In this context it is most essential to distinguish substance and form, function and ideology, reality and fiction. Statute books may contain numerous liberal laws which, if implemented systematically, would dissolve the exclusive and unequal corporations in which

57. Fraenkel (1964); Ullendorf (1965).

pluralism consists. However, unless these laws are scrupulously enforced, they merely signalize that pluralism persists in the public sphere under covert or overt pressure. There are also many subtler ways in which an appearance of political and social equality may disguise and perpetuate pluralisms founded on basic social and institutional differences, disabilities, and inequalities. For example, in the Jamaican two-party system based on universal suffrage, each party with its industrial wing may demand internal stability as a condition of economic viability or development. Where such systems entrench historically privileged social sections in control of national organizations, public or voluntary, they stabilize the plural structure under apparently liberal political regimes by restricting the scope for social mobility and intersectional change through their institutionalized corporate factionalism.[58] However, one-party regimes based on mass suffrage may differ very little, if they also place ideological purity, solidarity, internal stability, and economic development ahead of social equality, mobility, and assimilation, and on these platforms institutionalize elite or ethnic domination.

Our survey shows that public regulative structures are the central agencies for the preservation or modification of corporate divisions and relations in plural societies. This is equally true under independence or colonialism, one-party or multi-party regimes. Unless equal and adequate public facilities are provided in representation, administration, education, justice, industrial organization, and occupational mobility, those inequalities and sectional divisions with which the old structure was identified will certainly persist, irrespective of the leadership, organization, and ideology of the state.

58. M.G. Smith (1965c), pp. 314-19.

8.

The Comparative Study of Complex Societies

1.

Most of mankind now live in complex societies and most of these societies are at present experiencing processes of change that promise to enhance their complexity. Such societies, variously labelled complex, heterogeneous, developing, developed, modern, modernizing, emergent nations or new states, are of manifest concern to all social scientists, but especially to sociologists and social anthropologists whose capacity to elucidate their variable structures, modes of operation and courses of development is no less important for the practical management of their affairs than for the creation of an empirically relevant and appropriate conceptual framework which might furnish a theoretical basis for the integration of these increasingly convergent disciplines. Curiously, however, very few sociologists or anthropologists have as yet attempted to define the category of complex societies or to delineate their essential or general characteristics. Instead, as Schneider observed over ten years ago,

the treatment generally accorded 'complexity' . . . consists mainly in simply referring to 'complexity' and then ignoring the matter. The fundamental problem is that of dealing with the range of different kinds of societies within the framework of a theory of society.[1] . . . It is a major problem which social theory has clearly failed to cope with, yet one of the most pressing of the problems before social theory at this time.[2]

In reply to such comments, S. N. Eisenstadt, who had explicitly contrasted 'primitive' or 'tribal' with 'complex' societies, of which 'modern societies' were an imprecisely distinguished sub-type,[3] casually remarks that 'both terms, to some extent, constitute residual categories',[4] and says that his 'model' of the complex society 'was largely derived from Durkheim'.[5] Accordingly to clarify the position we should first consider Durkheim's radical contrast between the undifferentiated 'primitive societies' ordered by relations of mech-

1. Schneider (1961). See also Leach (1961).
2. Schneider (1961). See also Kushner (1970), in Siegel (1970), p. 81.
3. Eisenstadt (1961), pp. 204-5.
4. ibid., p. 220.
5. ibid., p. 220.

anical solidarity and the advanced, differentiated societies that
depend on 'organic solidarity' for their integration, since this
underlies so much subsequent work on the nature and development
of complex societies. For example, Ronald Frankenberg employs this
antinomy to contrapose rural society, characterized by its 'complexity', with urban society, characterized by its 'complication'.[6] In thus
generalizing and redefining Durkheim's contrasted models of primitive and modern societies as rural and urban, Frankenberg assimilates
Durkheim's typology to that which Louis Wirth and Robert Redfield
formulated in contrasting urban and folk societies as ideal-types.[7]
But clearly while most urban units, industrial and pre-industrial, are
highly complex in their organizations, institutional operations and
composition, such units by no means exhaust the range of complex
societies, which nowadays include the 'emergent nations', 'new
states', and developing societies of the 'Third World', among other
forms. Neither does its rural condition always or necessarily exclude
a sufficient degree of the organizational 'complication' which
Frankenberg identifies by diversity of both occupational and other
roles[8] to substantiate his radical contrast. However, since such polar
models are not disconfirmed by phenomena that contravert their
assumptions,[9] they continue to fascinate sociologists and anthropologists by their simplicity and dramatic oppositions, and thus
obstruct the development of alternative approaches to the comparative study of complex societies as units that differ substantially in
many particulars, despite certain common features.

Durkheim's powerful contrast between 'primitive' or 'undifferentiated' societies integrated through relations of mechanical solidarity,
and other societies with an advanced division of labour that derive
their integration from relations of organic solidarity,[10] has continued to exercise an unfortunate influence on theoretical and
comparative sociology. Durkheim presented those models as
extremes in the evolutionary development of human society; and, as
the title of his book indicates, in his view the most general and
decisive index of the development and complexity of a society lay in
its prevailing 'division of labour'. However, though inexplicitly,
Durkheim does distinguish 'the division of economic labour'[11] from
other forms of 'social labour' or functional differentiation, when he
cites Britain as a 'segmental' or relatively 'undeveloped' society in
which the 'division of economic labour' was none the less highly
advanced.[12] Frankenberg's representative equation of Durkheim's
concept of the division of labour with economic and occupational

6. Durkheim (1947), pp. 70-132; Frankenberg (1969), p. 288.
7. Wirth (1938); Redfield (1947).
8. Frankenberg (1969), p. 288.
9. ibid., p. 286.
10. Durkheim (1947).
11. ibid., p. 282, n. 30.
12. ibid.

differentiation accordingly misinterprets Durkheim, although understandably so, given the opacities and tortuousness of Durkheim's thesis and its exposition. Evidently by 'the division of labour in society', Durkheim sought to encompass the differentiation of institutions and roles in other social fields as well as the economy, for example, in education, government, religion, family and law. By 'the division of labour in society', he thus attempted to embrace all levels and types of functional differentiation, and included institutional segregations and specializations in spheres of social organization other than the economy. Parsons, Eisenstadt and other structural-functionalists have employed Durkheim's criteria of functional and institutional differentiation as central indices of societal complexity and development.[13] For example, Neil Smelser writes:

One point of contrast between simple and complex societies is the degree of differentiation of social structures. In an ideal-typical simple society, little differentiation exists between a position in a kinship group, (e.g. elderly men in a certain clan), political authority (since elderly men in this clan hold power as a matter of custom), religious authority (since political and religious authority are undifferentiated), and wealth (since tributes flow to this position). The social structures are undifferentiated, and an individual occupies a high or low position in all roles simultaneously . . . In complex societies, by contrast, a position in the age structure does not necessarily entitle a person to membership in specific roles in the occupational structure; a position of importance in the religious hierarchy does not necessarily give an individual access to control of wealth. Though some individuals may simultaneously receive great amounts of different rewards — wealth, power, prestige — these rewards are often formally segregated in a highly differentiated social structure.[14]

None the less Smelser observes that 'many colonial societies of the late nineteenth and early twentieth centuries were intermediate between the simple and the complex . . . An important structural feature of such systems is that economic, political and racial-ethnic roles *coincide* with one another.'[15] On strictly functional grounds such coincident roles should denote the absence of differentiation in these colonial societies; but by distinguishing them from simple and complex societies as intermediate, Smelser recognizes that structural conditions regulate the coincidence or dispersal of analytically distinct activities, resources and functions. For Talcott Parsons, however, 'the increasing complexity of [social] systems, in so far as it is not due only to segmentation, involves the development of sub-systems specialized about more specific functions in the operation of the system as a whole, and of integrative mechanisms which interrelate the functionally differentiated systems'.[16] Further, according to Parsons, 'the structure of a system is that set of

13. Parsons (1952, 1969); Parsons and Shils (1951b).
14. Smelser and Lipset (1966a), p. 10.
15. ibid., p. 10. Their italics.
16. Parsons (1966), p. 24.

properties of its component parts and their relations or combinations which, for a particular set of analytical purposes, can both logically and empirically be treated as constant within definable limits'.[17] Such structures, being segregated analytically by functional criteria, correspond closely to those 'analytic structures' which Marion Levy defines as 'patterned aspects of action that are *not even theoretically capable of concrete separation* from other patterned aspects of action'.[18] Levy contrasts such 'analytic structures' sharply with 'concrete structures' described as 'patterns of action that define the character of membership units involved in social action'.[19] Clearly one central problem in the development of a sociological framework adequate for the analysis of complex societies is the relationship between such concrete structures or membership units and the analytical structures of 'constructivst systems'[20] that social scientists segregate by functional criteria for intensive analyses of dynamic relations between phases, properties and parts of social units conceived as systems.

Durkheim, who perceived this problem, proposed a solution which, being either tautological or empirically invalid, is quite inadequate although widely accepted. To account for 'the progress of the division of labour', he asserts that

the segmental arrangement [of societies] is an insurmountable obstacle to the division of labour, and must have disappeared at least partially for the division of labour to appear. The latter can appear only in proportion to the disappearance of a segmental structure . . . The growth of the division of labour is thus brought about by the social segments losing their individuality, the divisions becoming more permeable . . . [This] gives rise to a relationship between individuals who were separated, or, at least, a more intimate relationship than there was.[21] . . . The division of labour develops, therefore, as there are more individuals sufficiently in contact to be able to act and react upon one another. If we agree to call this relation and the active commerce resulting from it dynamic or moral density, we can say that the progress of the division of labour is in direct ratio to the moral or dynamic density of society . . . But this moral relationship can only produce its effect if the real distance between individuals is itself diminished in some way. Moral density cannot grow unless material density grows at the same time, and the latter can be used to measure the former.[22]

Durkheim then discusses three processes that may generate this 'progressive [demographic] condensation of societies'[23] together with certain exceptions to his correlations of social volume (size, extent) and density, before concluding triumphantly as follows:

17. Parsons (1964), in A. and E. Etzioni (1964), pp. 83-4.
18. M. Levy (1952), pp. 199, 551.
19. ibid., pp. 199, 551.
20. Easton (1965), pp. 30 ff.; Parsons (1966), p. 25.
21. Durkheim (1947), pp. 256-7.
22. ibid., p. 257.
23. ibid., pp. 260 ff.

We say, not that the growth and condensation of societies *permit*, but that they *necessitate* a greater division of labour. It is not an instrument by which the latter is realized; it is its determining cause.[24]

Thus, for Durkheim, 'condensation' beyond the 'dynamic' threshold invariably reduces the integrity and autarchy of collocated segments and generates equivalent or corresponding differentiations of individuals, institutions and functions. Thus once their condensation crosses the 'take-off' point, according to Durkheim societies must evolve inexorably in organization, differentiation and the specialized integrative institutions such developments assume along universally predetermined lines of advance. Curiously, however, it was the historical uniqueness of the rapid, fundamental and progressive transformations of European societies and cultures following the Reformation that preoccupied Durkheim's great contemporary Max Weber; and if, like Parsons, following Weber, we accept 'the uniqueness of the original development of the modern societal type in the West',[25] then the grand evolutionary edifice to which Durkheim harnessed his societal models and causal explanation collapses like a house of cards, bringing with it most subsequent restatements and elaborations of his evolutionary-typological scheme. What remains of continuing relevance from Durkheim's theory is the problematic relation between the levels and forms of functional and structural differentiation within human societies. But since the condensation thesis is no less incapable of illuminating this than of explaining the course and 'progress of the division of labour', it seems more profitable to examine the conditions and properties of concrete structures in human societies as direct measures of their differing complexity than to manipulate artificial entities of our own construction, the functionally defined analytical systems which are currently so fashionable, as causal factors, if only on methodological grounds.

As the preceding quotation shows, Durkheim himself evidently perceived the significance of these concrete structures for the restriction or promotion of differentiation in individual roles and relations and the segregation of functionally specialized institutions. This awareness is implicit in his emphatic opposition of the 'segmented' and 'organized' societies, and becomes explicit in his call for the creation of new intermediate corporations in the celebrated Preface to the second edition of his important book,[26] a proposal that he argued extensively on another occasion,[27] being morally disturbed by the anomic effects of the division of labour in industrial societies. However, even then Durkheim's functionalist predilections make him unable to see that such disturbing effects were generated

24. ibid., pp. 262 ff.
25. Parsons (1966), p. 3.
26. Durkheim (1947), pp. 1-31.
27. Durkheim (1957), pp. 28-41.

by contemporary forms and articulations of corporate units within those societies, for example, trade unions, cartels, employers' associations, political parties, civil and military administrations, religious, educational, scientific and other property-holding bodies, all independently seeking to pursue or protect their interests in an imperfectly regulated arena that mediated transactions of similar and differing values and kinds. None the less, in advocating the deliberate creation of these intermediate corporations to mitigate the strains of industrial society, Durkheim implicitly admitted the inadequacy of his 'condensation' hypothesis and its underlying general assumption of the functional determination of social structures, their development and integration.

One of the most decisive considerations against Durkheim's criterion of functional differentiation as an adequate index and measure of societal complexity is the impressive evidence of structural divergence in complex societies of similar technological and institutional levels, such for example as the 'archaic' societies of ancient Egypt, Mesopotamia, Assyria and Iran, and the more complex societies of imperial China, Japan, India, Carthage, ancient Greece and Rome, Byzantium, the medieval Islamic empires, Carolingian Europe, Renaissance Italy and Flanders. Though societies in each category share similar technologies and levels of occupational differentiation, and although in each category at different times and places some societies exhibited comparable degrees of 'condensation', the structural convergences and divergences between European and Japanese feudalism, the oriental despotisms of China and Egypt, the Hindu caste society, the orientalized theocratic regimes at Byzantium, the Ummayad and Abbasid caliphates, and the republican city-states of ancient Greece, Carthage, Rome, Renaissance Italy and Flanders, indicate quite clearly the independent variation of concrete social structures from functional differentiation and demographic densities. The structural parallels of imperial China and ancient Egypt hold despite their differing forms and degrees of functional differentiation; so do the parallels between Florence and Athens on the one hand, and feudal Europe and Japan on the other. We simply cannot account for such radically divergent though comparably complex social structures as Hindu caste, Roman society with its various orders of free men and slaves, Chinese society, the Japanese and European feudalisms, Athens, Sparta, Corinth, Byzantium and medieval Islam, within the conceptual framework developed by Durkheim and espoused with various modifications and elaborations by contemporary structural-functionalists. Besides their comparable technologies, the most important features shared by all these societies were literacy, pre-industrial modes of production, stratification, and lability or dynamism, even in such apparently stable bureaucratic regimes as ancient Egypt, China and Byzantium. Yet were these societies in all particulars notably less complex than those of Russia and Latin America before their twentieth-century revolutions? And can we seriously pretend that the divergent structure of Hindu caste derives from rather than enjoins the prevailing forms and levels of functional differentiation in Hindu society? The Australian aborigines, Bushmen and Kwakiutl alike subsisted by hunting and gathering; but their social structures diverge radically, not merely in their forms but also in their levels of structural differentiation, without corresponding functional specializations. Likewise the Bedouin and the Tuareg herd camels and operate similar technologies in similar habitats; but again these populations differ sharply in the form and elaboration of their social structures, without complementary modes of functional differentiation. Ethnography could multiply such revealing cases a hundred times.[28] Only if we choose to ignore the concrete particulars of social structure, or decide to subsume these structures *in toto* under that term, can we agree that 'the division of labour' underlies rather than depends on the forms of units of social organization. We must therefore attempt to sketch some of the ways in which concrete social structures generate or inhibit further differentiation; and in doing so I shall try to show how the conditions of structural generation regulate the processes, forms and levels of functional differentiation in human societies of diverse base and composition.

2.

On behalf of Durkheim and his leading contemporaries, we must recognize the responsibility of our anthropological predecessors for their theoretical shortcomings. Durkheim, for instance, wrote at a period when the ethnographic and theoretical literature on simple societies effectively subsumed all forms of social organization under kinship and community. He accordingly lacked the evidence we now possess of the variety and significance of alternative types of social organization besides the hordes, segmental lineages or clans, castes and guilds, and modern forms of economic and occupational organization with which he was familiar. Today however we should take note as well of age-sets and regiments; military, political, recreational and ritual associations of differing sorts, both open and 'secret'; corporate social strata such as estates of nobles, clerics, freemen, serfs and slaves; universities, temples and schools, fraternities, trusts and banks; productive and trading associations of such differing sorts as the Aztec *pochteca*, the medieval manor, Japanese *shoen*, ancient Greek *oikos*, Diola or Hausa trading enclaves, West Indian plantations, Hausa slave estates, Efik and Ibibio 'canoe-houses', as well as orders of office, law courts, administrative departments, councils or colleges of diverse composition and

28. For some examples see Forde (1934).

function, commissions of various kinds, and such differing forms of local grouping as bands, pastoral or herding groups, dispersed or nucleated sedentary communities, districts, provinces, towns, cities and nations.

All the units just listed — and this catalogue is far from complete — are corporate in their character, or 'segmental' in Durkheim's terms; and all involve or prescribe distinctive forms of social relations among and between their members and others. Most emphasize some set of functions or interests as primary, though few pursue these exclusively. All exploit some collective resources or privileges and rely on collective criteria for the recruitment of members, while most possess directorates to administer their affairs by procedures regarded as effective and appropriate. Those that lack such regulative councils or offices are thereby constituted as categories, collectively inert and accordingly subject to regulation either by other units or by traditional prescriptions and proscriptions, unless mobilized by some self-appointed charismatic leaders in situations of crisis. Collective structures of the kinds just listed present variably formidable obstacles to the differentiation of functionally specific relations and institutions within the societies of which they are part. None the less, in differing combinations and circumstances they may also facilitate or generate such differentiated units as concrete structures in Marion Levy's sense, endowing them with particular attributes, resources, personnel and functions. It seems appropriate then to look closely at such concrete units of social organization in our efforts to account for the development and diversity of complex societies; but before proceeding with this task, we should surely attempt to define both these terms, and at least provisionally to delineate the complex society by listing some of its central characteristics.

3.

According to Parsons, 'a society is relatively the most self-sufficient type of social system' in that it 'internally integrates more of the requisites of independent existence'[29] than does any other type of social aggregate organized as a distinctive unit. As 'a self-sufficient, self-perpetuating and internally autonomous system of social relations'[30] a society also organizes a determinate population over successive generations. In so far as the types of social unit and relations it involves are diverse in their basis, nature and range, the society is correspondingly complex. In so far as the units and relations through which the population is organized are uniform in their type and properties, a society may be described as simple.

29. Parsons (1966), p. 2.
30. See above, Chapter 7, p. 207.

However, simplicity and complexity constitute a continuum with several levels rather than a dichotomy. Parsons, for instance, like Smelser, distinguishes societies as primitive, intermediate or modern.[31] Within the primitive category he further distinguishes the simple from advanced types; and within the intermediate range he distinguishes such 'archaic' societies as ancient Egypt and Mesopotamia from such 'historic empires' as China, Rome and the Islamic empire, and the two 'seed-bed societies' of ancient Israel and Greece.[32] To this series we should certainly add medieval feudal societies, the many intermediate units created by colonialism, and the developing, modernizing or emergent societies that decolonization initiated; and at the modern pole we should distinguish the collectivist and individualist types of industrial society illustrated by the USSR and the USA.

Probably few would object to the following preliminary list of characteristics common to complex societies:

(1) Sufficient levels of structural differentiation to ensure significant differences in the distribution of differentiated roles among adult men.

(2) Some nucleated settlements with relatively large and heterogeneous populations.

(3) The institutionalization of production for exchange, whether this is transacted by markets and money or by other means, with complementary specialization of some productive units.

(4) Forms and degrees of social stratification that significantly differentiate the life-chances, experiences and orientations of categories within the society.

(5) Differentially distributed opportunities for lateral (spatial) or vertical (social) mobility within the population.

(6) Relatively clear separation of the private and public domains of social life.[33]

(7) Some traditions of literacy.

(8) The allocation of an increasing number of public roles on criteria other than sex and age.

(9) A significant number of impersonal and instrumental forms of social relation.

(10) Significant areas of social relations and activity formally open to individual choice and initiative.

(11) Diversity in the forms and units of social grouping.

(12) An increasing number of alternative forms of secondary group in which communications are mediated through some intervening link or set of links.

31. Parsons (1966), pp. 3, 26.
32. ibid., chs. 3-6.
33. Concerning the distinction between private and public domains, see above, Chapter 7, pp. 216-17.

Some commonly assumed attributes or conditions of complexity not listed above include political centralization, scale and size. However, we can neither deny the complexity nor affirm the political centralization of feudal Europe, Heian and Kamakura Japan, the Mozabite towns, the Swat Paktuns or Tuareg tribes.[34] Further, as employed by various authors, the term 'scale' corresponds so closely in its components and implications with Durkheim's ideas of functional differentiation that, having rejected the latter, we should avoid the former.[35] In addition, 'scale' is used to assimilate complexity and size, as in the contrast between 'small-scale' and 'large-scale' societies. The term is thus doubly ambiguous in its referents, and best avoided. Whether measured in territorial extent or population numbers, and although commonly associated with both, 'size' is neither a sufficient nor a necessary condition of structural complexity and functional differentiation,[36] if only because the development and co-ordination of large units presupposes these features. Certainly many small units such as the Mozabite cities, eighteenth-century Montserrat[37] and contemporary Iceland and Cyprus greatly exceed the Tiv, Gusii and Somali in societal complexity. None the less, given its relevance, the relations of size to complexity are discussed further below.

Of the twelve characteristics listed above, six — numbers (1) to (4), (11) and (12) — refer directly to concrete social units such as groups and categories; and another six, namely (1), (4), (5), (8) to (10), refer directly or indirectly to individuals; while five — numbers (1), (3), (6), (11) and (12) — relate to differentiation, mainly in the forms and units of social organization. The distinction between private and public domains isolated in item (6) of this list turns on the segregation of those interests, activities and relations which are matters of collective concern and regulation from others which are left for individuals and families to handle themselves.[38] Only one of these twelve characteristics, namely literacy, appears detached from all others; yet, like Parsons,[39] I believe that some level and form of literacy, indigenous or exogenous, is universally associated with complex societies, whether as an effect, correlate or condition of their development, I cannot pause to consider.

From this review of the characteristics listed above, it is evident that the two decisive foundations of social and cultural complexity are respectively the institutionalization of a sufficient number and variety of alternative types of social unit to ensure substantial

34. Bloch (1961); Sansom (1962), pp. 185-347; Allport (1954, 1964); Barth (1959); Nicolaisen (1963), pp. 137-54, 209-71, 393-452.

35. G. and M. Wilson (1945), pp. 24-44; Benedict (1968); Durkheim (1947), pp. 260, 287 ff.

36. Durkheim (1947), pp. 261, 263-6.

37. Lowenthal (1960a).

38. See above, Chapter 7, pp. 216-17.

39. Parsons (1966), pp. 26-7, 51-2.

diversity in the careers, life-chances, social networks, relations, orientations, rights, statuses and obligations of their members; and secondly, a sufficiently differentiated series of constraints, incentives and opportunities to oblige and permit an adequate and increasing number of individuals to select or to change their affiliations and occupations as circumstances suggest, even though these individual initiatives are distributed differentially among the various social categories and strata. Two correlates of such individual options are the individuation of adults by empirically distinctive combinations of social roles and interests, and individualism as a derived orientation and ideology. Yet even though such options are always unequally distributed within a human society, they assume and ensure corresponding measures of individual mobility, both lateral and vertical, and corresponding varieties of types of social unit that differ in their bases, functions and forms. These conditions in turn generate corresponding diversity and contingency in certain types of social relation, and, unless restrained, a progressive increase in the scope, resources and organizational complexity of the public domain which is the focus of collective interests and regulation, following its initial segregation from the private domain reserved for individual and familial action. In consequence of these associated characteristics, complex societies generate a competitiveness at individual and collective levels which in turn emphasizes the value of uniformity in their legal and civil administrations and in their criteria for the allocation of important public roles.

It is neither necessary nor useful at this stage of inquiry to attempt to indicate the approximate modalities or ratios of the various quantifiable characteristics listed above, since their combination defines societal complexity as a continuum, with the differing forms and degrees that reflect the variable values of these several components. Thus in the absence of one or more of these criteria, others might have effects disproportionate to their intensity, and may thus generate distinctive patterns and modes of complexity. What we can do at this stage, given the primacy of multiple concrete structures and individual autonomy in the genesis and organization of these complex societies, is to sketch a conceptual framework that may enable us to explore the relations of these two variables while reviewing the alternative courses by which societies of differing base and composition have historically developed complex structures of differing capacity and kind. However, before proceeding to these topics, let me stress that the entire discussion thus far has been based on the assumption of ethnic homogeneity as a general feature of complex societies. Historically, such ethnically homogeneous units are probably a fortunate but significant minority of complex societies. None the less, under Durkheim's influence, they have axiomatically furnished the ideal-typical contexts for theoretical discussions of their evolution. Thus, having sketched the evolution of homogeneous societies, we shall consider some alternatives and their development briefly below.

Of the criteria listed above, dense, heterogeneous settlements, regular and variably specialized production for exchange, some degree of spatial and social mobility and the allocation of public roles on criteria other than sex and age, are subsumed or entailed by the two generic conditions of multiple alternative concrete structures and individual autonomy. The functional differentiations of social units and relations, on which so much has been written, are simply inevitable correlates or consequences of increases in the number and variety of social units, that is, in the elaboration and differentiation of the societal structure. However, only beyond a certain indeterminate level of elaboration can a social structure generate conditions, incentives and opportunities that permit or require men to exercise choice and assume individual responsibility for establishing or maintaining social ties with other individuals and units; and on theoretical and empirical grounds it is clear that even under the most Utopian conditions all individuals in a given society can never be equally free to exercise such choice about all the categories of social relationship that their society permits, simultaneously or seriatim. The most we may reasonably expect is that many or most individuals may routinely be able to make certain choices in certain situations, while a progressively decreasing number of increasingly privileged persons will have opportunities for an increasing number of such decisions. In short, societies differ significantly in the affairs they open to individual initiative, in the scope and significance of the choices they enjoin or permit, and in the distribution of such constraints and opportunities among their members. Such differences simply reflect the definition and dispersion of alternatives created by the coexistence of differing and competing concrete structures in the public domain of the society. The more complex the society, the greater the number and variety of alternatives it opens to individual choice in the formation, maintenance and termination of social relations, and the greater the proportion of its population that can exercise such choice at equivalent phases in their life careers; but the number, distribution and scope of such individual choices themselves reflect the nature and articulation of the alternative concrete structures. The less complex a society, the greater the proportion of its members who are immobilized from birth till death by incorporation in social units of a single type, whether or not they are formally free to transfer their affiliation to some other unit of identical kind, as in those types of band-organized society discussed below. Not only do societies with such monotonous structures, which furnished the models for Durkheim's undifferentiated segmental type, restrict the freedom of individuals to alter their social relations and affiliations. They operate more importantly to obstruct the creation of new types of social unit and forms of interpersonal relations, thereby preserving their undifferentiated character. Yet if these component units, or segments as Durkheim calls them, effectively restrict individual freedom and initiative, they can do so only because they subsume all the functions and interests that are essential for the populations they organize. In consequence, in such societies no individual can either flout the rules of such units, or survive independently outside them. And since they regulate and provide all the culturally approved interests of their members, such units together subsume responsibility for routinely meeting all the functional requisites of human society, and are accordingly not merely multifunctional, but perduring social structures, with diffuse interests, resources and orientations manifested in the multiple role structures and interpersonal relations through which they organize and discharge their normal activities. Further, since all social structures rely for their perpetuation on perduring units of some sort, it is surely at this level that we must seek the conditions that generate or obstruct the development of societal complexity and differentiation.

4.

Besides roles, the dyadic relations they constitute, and the institutional statuses to which they are attached, social structures include various primary units such as the family, or groups of friends and workmates, which are ephemeral in that they dissolve with the death or withdrawal of their members. Though formally subject to regulations emanating from the public domain, these and other forms of transient primary groupings are clearly anchored in the private domain. In addition, all social structures normally include some variably institutionalized classifications of the population they organize by discriminating categories of male and female, infants, children, youth, adults and elders, the married, unmarried, social classes, and so on; and some of these categories may provide the basis for a patterned distribution of collective roles.

As societies normally depend on internal reproduction to persist, they are always heterogeneous in age and sex; and sex differences being immutable and central to reproduction, their elaboration provides a universal though variable basis for the division of labour, women commonly being privatized by their domestic and maternal functions, while men dominate or monopolize the arenas of public action and decision. Naturally societies differ in the ways and degrees in which they formalize such sex differences. They differ even more strikingly in the ways in which they pattern and emphasize differences of age, which only a few elaborate as frameworks of collective organization.[40] In most societies maturation is periodized and celebrated ceremonially on an individual rather than a collective

40. Eisenstadt (1956).

basis; but in many societies seniority by birth-order differentiates the statuses and life chances of same-sex siblings and their descendants in a progressively intricate organization by rank.[41]

Those perduring units that positively and/or negatively regulate human interactions and activities provide the frameworks and boundaries of societal organizations. They may be described as *corporations*: and, following Maine,[42] we can distinguish initially two grand classes of corporations, namely those that require several members, the *corporations aggregate,* and those that can only have one member at a time, the *corporations sole,* each a unique and presumptively perpetual status that integrates a complex of differentiated roles. Corporations of either type are characterized by their unique identities, by the presumption of perpetuity, by precise rules of recruitment and closure and thus determinate memberships at any given moment.

However the two classes separated by Maine must be further subdivided to yield a comprehensive discriminating typology of corporate units. To this end we should distinguish two major types of corporations aggregate, one of which is adequately described by the preceding list of corporate characteristics. We may call such units *corporate categories* to distinguish them from *corporate groups,* which possess, in addition to the characteristics already listed, representative or inclusive modes of organization, common but exclusive affairs that include their organizational and other resources, determinate procedures for the handling of these collective affairs, and sufficient autonomy to regulate them. As organized corporations aggregate, corporate groups have capacities for collective action that corporate categories, which lack the organizations essential for mobilizing and co-ordinating their members and resources, do not possess. None the less these categories are distinguished from other social categories as corporations by virtue of their closure and modes of recruitment, their presumed perpetuity, unique external identities, and determinate memberships which imply lifelong identifications of populations enrolled in such units, even though, as slaves, some might be manumitted, and as serfs, in opportune circumstances, some could seek the freedom of anonymity by flight to towns, as bilingual Indios in contemporary Guatemala convert to Ladino status by relocating.[43]

As institutional agencies for their representative organization and administration, corporations aggregate may employ councils and offices, separately or together. If such councils are constituted as permanent organs within the collectivity, they will then possess the ordinary attributes of a corporate group, but should none the less be distinguished as a separate class of corporations which, following

41. Sahlins (1958).
42. Maine (1905), ch. 5; Durkheim (1957), chs. 13 and 14, pp. 145-70.
43. Tumin (1952); Beals (1953).

Weber, we can designate as *colleges*,[44] since they are always a minority of the group whose affairs they regulate.

Besides the age-categories mentioned above, societies may institutionalize classifications by occupation, by social class, or on other grounds; but only if individuals are prescriptively and involuntarily enrolled for life in such categories can we designate them as corporate. Thus corporate categories preclude voluntary changes of social identification by their members. Accordingly in so far as individual optation and mobility prevail, as in regimes of class rather than orders of estates and caste, social categories, however important and institutionalized, are open rather than closed to individual movements, and allow some scope for individual initiative. In such cases one frequently observes those divergences between the subjective and objective identifications of individuals that correspond to Marx's distinction between true and false consciousness. Such divergences are absent or minimal among the members of corporate categories. However, as such categories lack the organizational preconditions of positive collective action, they also lack any common and exclusive affairs, any common regulatory procedures, and the autonomy requisite for such collective action. They must thus remain subject either to regulation by representatives of other units, as for example the manorial serfs and plantation slaves administered by their masters' agents, or they are governed by collective prescripts and proscripts of a traditional kind such as the rules that enjoin exogamy on categorical clans and endogamy on castes or on racial-ethnic and religious categories. Thus the regulations that govern the relations of members in corporate categories are generally imposed either by conventions and law or enforced by their superiors, by co-ordinate categories, or by the spontaneous action of some of their members. None the less even the prescriptive endogamy of serfs, plebeians, slaves and castes does not constitute such categories as corporate groups since it alone cannot furnish an appropriate and inclusive organization.

As bounded, presumptively perpetual units with determinate memberships, all societies, including those encapsulated or created by recent colonialism,[45] are corporations aggregate. If centrally organized under inclusive or representative institutions such as councils and offices, they are thereby constituted as corporate groups, whether fully or partially autonomous. Otherwise, and whether polycephalous or acephalous, such 'stateless societies' are simply the most inclusive kinds of corporate category. In either event, centralized or not, as the widest membership units with common organizational frameworks and institutions, societies derive their structures and perpetuity from the corporate organizations whose discontinuities demarcate their boundaries in space and time.

44. Weber (1947), pp. 360-73.
45. Geertz (1963); Worsley (1964); Lloyd (1971a); Almond and Coleman (1960).

Maine illustrated corporations sole by the example of office; but to this we may add a variety of quasi-corporations best described as commissions. Of these only one type requires notice here. As a unique perpetual status with specific conditions, rights, resources and procedures, an office is a unit that includes the criteria which govern its operations and transfer, and its relations with other units, corporate or non-corporate. By contrast, commissions of the type under discussion are normally asserted by individuals independently, even though the form of such assertions may be familiar and even institutionalized within their society. Thus the 'big men' of Melanesia, war leaders among the Cheyenne or the Iroquois, shamans among the Eskimo or the Tungus, prophets among the Nuer, Bakongo or Masai, marabouts and holy men in various Muslim societies, gurus in India and saints everywhere, all assert and establish their individual commissions to exercise certain distinctive types of regulatory power and authority on the basis of their charismatic qualities and performances. However, such individually asserted commissions are neither unique, presumptively perpetual nor transferable by collectively regulated procedures and rules, without their simultaneous conversion into offices. Moreover, while offices and colleges are always anchored in corporate groups as their regulative institutions, commissions of the kind instanced above commonly appear in corporate categories or other loosely structured aggregates. In some extreme situations such commissions may mobilize and co-ordinate these categorical units, thereby converting them into corporate groups at the same time that they themselves become offices.[46] Conversely, when the central regulative agencies of a corporate group are dissolved or proscribed, the group loses its organization and status and becomes a category, dependent for its corporate boundaries on external conditions in its social environment.

Together these five types of corporation and quasi-corporation furnish the major units of the collective organization that encompasses and structures the public domains of human societies. It is their variety, bases and relations that constitute the organizational frameworks that order and delimit societies. It is also their resilience and perduring qualities that assure sufficient continuities of social structure across the generations to preserve the collective identity, form and boundaries of human societies. Further, it is within and between the corporate members of this societal framework that the various impermanent and primary groupings and relations occur, as elements of the private domain under conditions and limits set by the interests and requisites of the prevailing corporate structure. And finally, it is in response to chronic or situational inadequacies of these corporate units that the unsanctioned, uninstitutionalized and

46. For an example see M.G. Smith (1966).

random conduct generally described as 'collective behaviour'[47] normally occurs, and commonly precipitates or crystallizes new forms of corporate grouping through social movements directed by leaders who assert and exercise regulatory commissions. Thus the incidence, forms and scale of collective behaviour within societies can only be understood by reference to the perceived inadequacies of their corporate organizations in the situations that precipitate such phenomena,[48] and while it is undeniable that the forms, occasions, scale and incidence of collective behaviour in primitive societies are significantly different and less than in modern industrial societies, we can hardly illuminate such societal differences by invoking the pattern-variables or 'four functional imperatives' that inform the analytic schema of current structural-functional theory, but must instead examine the articulations and capacities of the concrete macro-structural units to which these movements respond. In short, the conditions, situations, character, scope and limits of collective behaviour, and individual capacities for choice and innovation in social relation and actions, alike are set by the prevailing forms of corporate organization, and particularly by the variety, scope, bases and articulations of the corporate units that constitute their frameworks. It is thus necessary to show how such alternative forms of corporate organization generate and determine the differing levels, types and conditions of complexity in human society. In doing so, we may indicate how a conceptual scheme that gives primacy to these concrete perduring units can be employed to furnish a useful framework for the comparative study of societal organizations and developments at any level of complexity.

5.

To be sure, all human societies include families, peer-groups, work-groups and various types of interpersonal dyads and networks, all ultimately reducible to combinations of specific statuses and roles. Such transient and primary relations and groupings constitute the micro-structure of human societies and characteristically fall within their private domains. Other units, such as neighbourhoods or social categories of differing kind and base, being relatively constant though flexible features of the society, fall at the intermediate levels of its organization. But since these and other units depend heavily for their institutional articulation on the scope, basis and complexity of the prevailing framework of corporate organization, this dimension can be usefully segregated for analysis as the macro-structure of societies, since it represents the widest units of collective organization, deploys the widest regulatory powers and resources, and claims the greatest assurance of continuity. For example, families

---

47. Blumer (1959).
48. Durkheim (1938), pp. 3-12, 39-41, 65-73.

may or may not be formally incorporated in wider kinship units; neighbourhoods and age-categories may or may not be incorporated as units; peer-groups, dyads, work-groups, patrons, clients and factions can be found within as well as between corporations, or independently of them, and so on. But clearly the basis, variety, scope and articulations of the corporations within a society will significantly affect the autonomy and integration of these lesser types of social grouping, restricting their formations in some cases, their functions in others, or alternatively stimulating both, though invariably providing their conditions, means and objectives. Thus we need not dwell initially on the composition, autonomy and scope of these interpersonal dyads, ephemeral primary groupings and intermediate types of social units, since their range, form and significance are effectively governed by the conditions and necessities of the corporate organizations in which they are set. Accordingly to explore the criteria, determinants and conditions of societal complexity and individual differentiation, we should concentrate attention on the principal varieties of corporate organization that furnish the macro-structures and developmental moments of human societies. Only if the prevailing corporate organization permits or impels its members to establish novel forms of social grouping or relations can the society achieve levels of 'moral density' sufficient to enhance its functional differentiation. Thus the conditions and sources of functional differentiation in human society, to which the differentiation of institutions and roles correspond, are anchored in their corporate organizations. In this respect, the extreme antitheses are presented by societies organized on the basis of one type of corporation only, and others that have so great a number and variety of such units that they continuously require and generate new forms of organization to integrate their components. As we saw, Durkheim himself recommended the creation of 'intermediate corporations' under such circumstances and precisely for these ends.[49]

Societies organized in bands and segmentary lineages furnish alternative instances of the simplest segmental type that approximates Durkheim's model of undifferentiated aggregates dependent on mechanical solidarity for their integration. In both cases, these corporations are residential units that hold and exploit inalienable estates; but while segmentary lineages, being characteristically exogamous and recruiting their members by unilineal descent, depend on intermarriage to persist, many bands recruit their members by residence rather than kinship, and are not exogamous. In consequence, such 'composite bands'[50] are theoretically capable of self-perpetuation by internal mating and by the incorporation of strangers. Yet although individuals are free to withdraw from one band and join another, since these units alone routinely fulfil all the

49. Durkheim (1947), pp. 1-31; (1957), pp. 1-41.
50. Steward (1955), ch. 8; Service (1962), ch. 3.

essential processes and conditions of life in such societies, no family or individual can exist outside them. By contrast, exogamous segmentary lineages enjoin continuous co-residence of one sex-category among their members, normally males, while depending on affinal relations with one another for the spouses on whom their continuity rests. In such conditions individuals of either sex have little freedom to change their residence or immediate associates. They are thus even more intensively subjugated by the prevailing form of corporate organization than are the members of composite bands who retain the freedom to relocate. None the less, of these two types of corporation, the composite band is functionally more diffuse than the lineage, since not only can it perpetuate itself independently from its own ranks, but it subserves all the domestic functions of subsistence, shelter, socialization and technology, as well as the public functions of policy decision and implementation, rule-making and enforcement, allocations of resources and privileges, collective ritual, the administration and defence of its members and estate, and the conduct of group relations with other bands. Though the lineage also undertakes to discharge most of these functions for its resident members, being unilineal and exogamous, its continuity depends on affinal relations with co-ordinate units, which systematically differentiate its members in terms of their non-unilineal affiliations and require the orderly integration of autarchic, homologous units through intermarriages based on standardized definitions of the reciprocal obligations and rights of affinal groups, each internally differentiated by correlative genealogical and residential relations. Thus, despite its narrower functional competence, the lineage is structurally more complex and differentiated than the composite band, and commonly requires and exercises a more effective, rigorous and continuous control over the activities and relations of its members to secure their conformity with its operational requisites. Such control is achieved partly by the elaboration of lineage cults and rituals, partly by the political and legal stress that lineages place on their own and one another's external unity and collective responsibilities as units, and, consequentially, by the lifelong, exclusive and immutable identification of individuals with their natal lineages, jurally, ritually and, for one of the sexes, residentially as well.

When a segmentary lineage constitutes the local community by exclusive occupation of a compact block of land, its local divisions may correspond so closely with its genealogical segments that social and spatial distance are integrated, each local segment being an autonomous and compact corporate group for certain purposes. The articulations of such segments within the wider unit will then consist largely of the situationally shifting alliances and oppositions that reflect their conflicting or converging interests as expressed in disputes or ties between their members. In such milieus, relations are more prescriptive and particularistic in base and form, more functionally diffuse or multiplex in scope, and more heavily laden with collective orientations and affect, than in composite bands.

When a number of such segmentary units are brought together in a common community, although each forms a discrete segment of identical base and type for religious, economic, educational and similar internal purposes, including the control of its members, relations between those genealogically discrete lineages cannot be exhaustively defined in terms of kinship, despite their partial integration by intermarriage, inter-familial and interpersonal links. Accordingly these inter-lineage relations must be regulated and justified by other means and on bases other than community of descent. Characteristically the central problem of such multilineal communities is the preservation of internal peace; and this must often be achieved without impairing the parity or autonomy of their lineage constituents in other spheres, including external relations. Two common responses to such dilemmas include the elaboration of communal shrines, rituals and priestly offices, particularly cults of the earth or community which taboo intra-communal violence, and the development of representative councils to co-ordinate communal interests, to adjudicate or arbitrate inter-lineage disputes, to allocate community land, and perhaps to regulate relations between the local unit as a collectivity and other units elsewhere. Other and complementary solutions include the development of one or more corporate associations that enrol, singly or together, men of all lineages, the development of a structure of age-grades or sets that incorporate the youth of all lineages, or the institution of a central office, whether predominantly secular or ritual; moreover, whereas in monolineal communities such alternative structures as age-sets may be simply assimilated and subjugated to the prevailing framework of lineage loyalties and identification, as for example among the Gusii and the Nuer,[51] in various pastoral East African societies, the scope and significance of lineage organization and loyalty diminishes in multilineal communities as the scope and significance of the alternative age organization expands. Such age-set structures characteristically assimilate youth irrespective of lineage and locality, regulate their relations with one another and with their seniors and juniors, adjudicate disputes, restrict or prohibit lineage feuds, provide the framework for collective rituals, individual security and freedom of movement, establish a permanent and well-defined framework of collective roles for successive sets, and furnish a broader, more efficient means for the rapid and orderly mobilization and direction of the unit's manpower for military or civil ends. In some societies such as the Kipsigi, Masai and Galla, these age-corporations also

51. Evans-Pritchard (1940*a*), chs. 5 and 8; P. Mayer (1949), pp. 9-10, 22-3.

generate sets of functionally differentiated offices to regulate community affairs.[52]

These sketches indicate that as societies generate new forms of corporations aggregate, differentiated in their bases, scope, resources, range, autonomy, requisites, entailments and articulations with similar and differing units, they correspondingly elaborate more complex role-inventories at both the individual and collective levels, distribute their functional tasks differentially between these corporations, and consequently enhance the scope for individual options in social relations by differentiating and dispersing autonomy, resources, personnel and responsibilities among the various corporate units within their organization, which then commonly require for their ·integration some structures of councils and/or offices that characteristically develop at the initiative of individuals or sub-corporate groups. For example when kinship and affinity cease to provide the sole adequate and indispensable basis for enduring social relations, exchange, relieved of these constraints, may be pursued in other channels and for other ends, including political support, ritual assistance, the pursuit of prestige and strictly economic advantage. Markets may thus emerge even before market-places, together with varieties of part-time occupational specialists serving one another and a common clientele. However, such developments may obtain only to the degree that the regulative authority for the performance of essential social functions and for the co-ordination of their members' interests are effectively dispersed among corporations of diverse base and kind within aggregates unified by such institutions as councils, offices, associations, age-set systems or structures of other base and kind, whose distinctive characteristics and articulations demarcate the boundaries of the collectivity they unite. If some collective structure manages to establish its pervasive dominance over the rest, as for example, the Poro or the Ekpe secret societies among the Mende and the Efik,[53] or if some bureaucratized central chiefship does likewise, these institutions will rapidly elaborate the complex internal organizations their resources and regulatory roles require at the expense of autonomous developments in the structures of the units they dominate. In consequence, individual initiatives and mobility will be redirected or repressed to fit the requirements of the dominant corporation. In such cases the denial of adequate autonomy to other social structures effectively restricts their capacities to increase the scope and range of their activities or to modify their internal organization and external articulations. In effect, the dominance of any single corporation or type of corporate structure, whether an office or a corporate group, effectively inhibits tendencies for new forms of social grouping and relations to develop independently in other social organs and spheres. Where such developments occur

52. Peristiany (1939, 1954); Huntingford (1955).
53. Little (1949, 1965-6); Simmons (1956); Jones (1956).

none the less, as, for example, with the creation of the chartered companies that pioneered European colonialism from the sixteenth to the eighteenth centuries, or the monastic orders and foundations of medieval Catholicism, they normally depend on the tolerance, support or enterprise of the dominant institution for their creation and/or continuity. Thus, in seeking to perpetuate and extend its scope and power, a dominant corporation may effectively arrest the further development of the society it regulates by eliminating or repressing significant alternatives outside its organization. The effect is to restrain individual options and initiatives by restricting opportunities for the creation of alternative structures and role differentiation to the dominant corporation. If successful, the dominant unit will stabilize its regime as a truly traditional order, as occurred in ancient Egypt, China and Byzantium, irrespective of demographic densities, dynamism and the high levels of differentiation and specialization these societies allowed in politically marginal or regulated spheres of action.

6.

Although most pre-industrial societies, including such large complex civilizations as China and India, rest on bases of unilineal kinship with its numerous prescriptions and mechanisms to regulate individual conduct, according to G. P. Murdock, about 37 percent of human societies lack unilineal descent and exogamy.[54] Most of these latter have variable rules of post-marital residence. The composite band instanced above illustrates nicely the conditions and implications of this familiar type of kinship system.[55] While some bilateral kinship systems restrict individual variations and direct individual initiatives by embedding nuclear families within more extended units, by instituting polygamy, or by other means, the formal equivalence such kinship structures normally prescribe for the relations of genealogically equidistant kin obliges individuals to choose between these competing claims and to define their contents appropriately in diverse situations. Thus bilateral kinship systems provide substantially greater scope and incentive for the independent action of adult males in certain spheres, primarily by reducing and dispersing the kin-based collectivities that regulate individual choice and relations in unilineal systems. However, by the same token, bilateral kinship systems normally lack those mutually exclusive unilineal blocs whose competition as units for autonomy and parity of status generates the mediating or superordinate alternative structures mentioned above. In consequence, the egalitarian assumptions, emphases and supports for collective responsibility and parity that figure so prominently in undifferentiated unilineal societies are minimized in bilateral ones, where individual status differences and

54. Murdock (1957), p. 687.
55. L. Marshall (1960).

mobility accordingly have greater prominence and free play.

In such situations the general absence of corporate kinship groups facilitates nucleated settlements organized on other bases, namely through councils, headmen and their retainers, religious fraternities, associations of diverse base and function, or by some incipient stratification, separately or together. Unless restricted by conditions of political status, individuals are thus formally free to move socially and spatially as far as their fortunes permit or require. Frequently both types of movement concur, as for example when a man leaves his native community to become a client or trader in some other.

The principal reasons why many cognatically based populations remain undifferentiated, despite possession of an adequate technology, are first, their failure to form corporate units at and above the level of the community; secondly, their failure to institutionalize a chiefship or central regulative agency; and, finally, their adoption of forms of social stratification and succession to status that emphasize individual seniority, rank and mobility rather than collective solidarity and status differences. However, under favourable conditions, the intrinsically individualistic orientations and alignments generated in these kinship systems facilitate instrumental exchanges of goods and services, unequal distributions of power, influence and wealth, relations of patron and client, master and bondsman, and the incorporation of alien individuals and families, in differing degrees and ways. Such developments all enhance the structural complexity and heterogeneity of the aggregates concerned. Tendencies for corporate strata to crystallize in such bilateral societies are intensified by conquest or defeat, by commercial exploitation, and by such institutions as debt-bondage among the ancient Greeks, punitive taxation as in Nara Japan,[56] enslavement by purchase, individual appropriations of public resources, and by other means.

Given favourable ecological and demographic conditions among sedentary populations, bilateral kinship facilitates individuation, stratification or ranking; and a sufficient concentration of political power in the hands of a minority to stabilize hereditary inequalities of wealth and prestige. In these respects, which are crucial for the development of societal complexity, bilateral kinship contrasts sharply with segmentary unilineal structures in its implications. However, certain other types of unilineal and ambilineal descent systems that differentiate individuals and 'descent lines cumulatively by seniority and rank lend themselves readily to stratification and commensurate degrees of political centralization, although simultaneously restricting the options open to individuals by criteria of kinship and status.[57] Unfortunately we cannot pause to consider the developmental implications of these latter structures here.

56. Sansom (1962), pp. 158-74.
57. Goldman (1970); Bacon (1958).

7.

Instead let us briefly consider how three dominant characteristics of complex societies, namely, increasing impersonality in social relations, increasing reliance on secondary communication, and increasing volume or size, typically relate to the unilineal and bilateral alternatives sketched above. All three characteristics presuppose extensions of the social aggregate well beyond the level of the local community to incorporate relatively large areas and numbers of people. Alternatively, enforced concentrations or 'condensations' as in the synoecisms of Mesopotamia or ancient Greece, may generate impersonality and secondary communication structures, provided that the populations thus condensed are neither unilineal and exogamous nor unilineal and endogamous in advance. When people organized in unilineal exogamous groups are obliged by military and other considerations to concentrate in large multilineal settlements, they will probably develop some mixed consociational regimes, as among the Yoruba or the Baganda.[58] On the other hand if the compacted population was originally organized as a series of unilineal endogamous groups, then this condensation may precipitate a structure of caste or caste-like orders as in ancient Rome, India or among the Wolof.[59] In either event, such demographic compressions may merely reinforce the mutual exclusions of the original segments, thus maximizing the rigidity of the mass, while generating secondary communication structures, interests and interdependence without corresponding impersonality in social relations. The effect of such developments is thus to restrict severely the opportunities and scope for innovations by individuals and small groups to channels that are fully consistent with the consociational or stratified order. An alternative illustrated by the Zulu, Chinese and Arabs is for one unit to establish its superordinate status by dominating the others, thus generating a regulative structure which canalizes individual mobility and initiatives within itself. None the less, in so far as such compressed aggregates require various integrative structures to diversify and co-ordinate their segments, some structural and individual differentiation is unavoidable and necessary to the degree that the consociated components cannot maintain their former autarchic levels and cannot therefore regulate the activities of their members uniformly, totally and exclusively. Any selectivity and internal stratification of the concrete structures that accompany or follow such synoecisms accordingly introduces corresponding differentiation and complexity in the social structure; and in all contexts of this kind, some such developments cannot be avoided.

58. Lloyd (1971*b*); Southwold (no date).
59. Gamble (1957).

As the secondary groupings and communication structures that promote impersonality in social relations presuppose relatively large populations or multi-community aggregates, the demographic and/or territorial size of societies correlates positively with their complexity, although the relationships involved remain contingent. Of the four routes by which societies may achieve extensive volume, whether territorial or demographic, namely, through natural increase, through the assimilation of immigrants recruited freely or otherwise, through voluntary and negotiated union with other units, or by conquest, the latter, as Spencer and others have stressed, has been historically the most common and important process in the formation of massive population units or extensive territories.[60] However, with moderate populations and · area, such new countries as the USA, created by immigrants, were already complex before conquest extended their territories. Likewise, sundry other European colonies in the New World, such as Barbados, Jamaica, Martinique or Surinam, owed far less of their complexities to conquest than to combinations of voluntary and forced immigration.

As implied by the preceding sketch of alternative courses of structural development among populations ordered by differing types of kinship systems, by itself sheer natural increase or territorial expansion contributes indifferently to the complexity of the social organization, even in sedentary societies. Nomadism, which emphasizes heavily the advantages of patrilineal groupings and virilocal marriage, further inhibits the development of differentiated impersonal super-community structures of communication, even in such ramified rank-differentiated societies as the Mongols.[61] Further, as we have seen, synoecisms of exogamous or endogamous unilineal populations are likely to generate less structural development than those that concentrate bilaterally organized aggregates in which case stratification, centralization, and their ancillary institutions should elaborate rapidly.

8.

However, thus far, following Schumpeter's example, we have restricted our discussion to ethnically homogeneous societies.[62] We have further excluded units differentiated by religion, culture and social organization, even within a common ethnic bloc, the phenomena of Hindu caste being congruent with these self-imposed conditions. By contrast, conquest and immigration, whether voluntary or forced, commonly generates a population which is heterogeneous as regards its ethnic and/or racial composition, native languages, cultures, and, at least initially, religion. Commonly the

60. Spencer (1969), pp. 159-327.
61. Bacon (1958).
62. Schumpeter (1955a).

amalgamated stocks operate technologies of differing capacities and kind, and differ also in the forms, levels and capacities of their social organizations. Perhaps the most frequent issue of a consolidated conquest is the *differential incorporation* of the conquered as a subject category under the exclusive, direct and rigorous control of their masters. This necessitates the elimination, suppression and proscription of any autonomous organization among the conquered, thereby converting them into a corporate category, typically fragmented under several jurisdictions. Alternatively, as was the case of Greek Orthodox *dhimmi* administered by the Ottomans through the agency of their church, or the Muslim emirates of Northern Nigeria under the Indirect Rule of Lord Lugard, the corporate organization of the defeated is preserved as an instrument for the victors' manipulation and control, thus creating two tiers of officials, of whom the superior commonly exercises authority on secular, the inferior frequently on ritual grounds. A third alternative that conquerors may adopt on the margins of their homelands is to affiliate the conquered as tributary or satellite states under their ultimate control; but this arrangement excludes the conquered from the society of the conquerors by preserving their distinctive organizations.

Forced immigration, outside contexts of synoecism, normally involves the recruitment of immigrants by purchase or by nominally free contract, but it may also proceed by the assimilation of individual captives into the families and kinship groups of their captors. Alternatively forced immigration may proceed by collective enslavement, as among the Hausa, Ibo, Efik and Fon of Dahomey, the captives being organized under private or corporate ownership and settled in villages or on estates.[63] Certain forms of voluntary indenture and contractual labour recruitment differ mainly from slavery in being formally time-limited, while serfdom differed primarily in the inalienability of the serf from the land. Two further alternatives, although inadequately known in their full particulars, are the debt-bondage of ancient Greece and the clientage that bound plebs as *famuli* to patrician lineages in early Rome.

One consequence of either of these two latter modes of societal increase, conquest and forced immigration, is the crystallization of relatively rigid and exclusive collective barriers within the society, mitigated only by relations of clientage and asymmetrical connubium. Each section, the rulers and their subjects, is thus constituted as an endogamous, biologically and culturally discrete unit of radically differing status. Naturally, in such situations, unless collectively restrained, males of the ruling stratum exploit females of the subject category. Characteristically, the rulers also maintain the essential organization of a corporate group to secure and extend their

63. For Hausa slavery, see M.G. Smith (1965c), ch. 6; for the Efik see Jones (1956), pp. 148-57; on Dahomey see Argyle (1966), pp. 142 ff.; on Ibo slavery see Horton (1954).

dominance over the ruled. Frequently racial and/or ethnic stereo-typing develops, illustrates, rationalizes and reinforces these social exclusions; and so do the all too familiar forms of collective exploitation, disenfranchisement, denial of literacy and education, non-payment or underpayment for services, forced labour, and restrictions of movement, marriage, association, property ownership, religion and arms, and of autonomous collective organization. The effect of such differential incorporation is thus essentially to amalgamate within a single society two or more social sections as distinct orders of humanity, the rulers organized as a corporate group, their subjects as one or more corporate categories. As an effect of their differing statuses as humans and sub-humans, relations between representative members of either section, the dominant and the subordinate, are typically depersonalized, the superior commonly treating the inferior as sub-human and an animal while the latter regards his master as inhuman and a beast. Dehumanization rather than impersonality accordingly characterizes inter-sectional relations in these plural societies unless muted by clientage or concubinage. Naturally where racial characteristics differentiate such blocs, being immutable, they furnish efficient boundaries that are easily main-tained by proscribing or restricting miscegenation; but religious, linguistic or cultural differences readily lend themselves to similar elaborations; and in Ulster today the contraposed religious com-munities sometimes classify one another in racial as well as religious terms, though both are predominantly Celtic. Likewise in Panama, Catholic Negroes reserve the latter term for Protestant Negroes.[64] Objective racial or cultural features may thus have less significance for social relationships than the collective stereotypes generated by sectional differences of situation, experience, organization and interest. However, one must distinguish here the hierarchic structure of superior and inferior sections from the manifest contraposition of co-ordinate ones, such as obtains for instance among the Negroes and (East) Indians of Guyana, between Greek and Turkish Cypriots, and currently between Catholics and Protestants in Ulster.[65] When contraposed as co-ordinates, each segment is mobilized as a corporate group by a representative or inclusive organization which is often explicitly political. By contrast in a hierarchic structure only the dominant section is normally organized as a group, while intercalary and subordinate sections are aligned vertically or hori-zontally as discrete categories under the common administration of the dominant group.[66] Clearly, either of these alternative forms of inter-ethnic accommodation will greatly increase the complexity of a society at the collective level by rigorously differentiating its

64. For information on use of racial designations by religious communities in Northern Ireland I am indebted to Dr. Rosemary Harris, personal communication. For the Panamanian parallel, see Pitt-Rivers (1967).

65. Despres (1967).

66. van Lier (1950).

component aggregates, juridically, occupationally, ethnically, and in other ways. However, as Smelser remarked in the passage cited earlier, such complexities in the collective organization normally immobilize the subordinate sections as units and restrict the individuation of their members by excluding or restricting the development of significant alternative structures, contexts and forms of social relation among them. In consequence, and particularly among the subordinate sections who typically form the majority of these plural societies, individual scope for the exercise of initiative and choice is generally restricted to those spheres of social action allocated by the rulers as appropriate for subordinates while marginal to the stability or further development of the inclusive society.

It is apparent that societies with such compositions and structures present a different type of complexity from those which are ethnically homogeneous even though stratified; for in such plural societies, even while the dominant section may exhibit high levels of internal differentiation in structural and functional terms, as for example in South Africa, differentiation within the subordinate sections is repressed, together with their organization and capacities.[67] In consequence the dominant section in such societies is obliged to elaborate and specialize various regulatory institutions and agencies that frequently extend their interference into the private and public activities not only of the subordinate majority, but also, by witch-hunting for dissidents within its own ranks, among the rulers as well. Thus in certain respects plural societies that commit themselves to the perpetual subjugation and dehumanization of the subordinate section exhibit various significant structural distortions and institutional specializations that distinguish them as a class from comparably differentiated societies of an ethnically homogeneous base, with the possible exception of those in which some institutional group such as a dynasty, church, or totalitarian political party seeks to aggrandize its scope and to entrench its unchallengeable domination over the mass.

9.

It will be obvious from this review that the levels and forms of societal complexity correlate with the diversity of collective structures and with the distributions and degrees of collective autonomy to pursue interests of the same or different kinds in similar or different ways. Further, such dispersions of collective autonomy simultaneously determine the limits and spheres within which individuals or transitory groups are free to initiate new types of social relation and action, and reflect the conditions of the prevailing corporate organization. Finally, it is evident that the autonomy these

67. L. Kuper (1965); van den Berghe (1967); UNESCO (1969).

corporations enjoy, severally and together, ensures complementary differentiation of their members' relations, resources, activities and interests while reflecting the bases, scope, internal organization and external articulations of the corporate units themselves as the concrete perduring and regulatory bodies whose relations constitute the macro-structure of human societies. Thus the diverse bases, scope, range, resources, autonomy and articulations of such corporations decisively define the options that are open to individuals, the available alternatives, and the resultant complexity of societal structure. These dispersals of corporate autonomy and resources themselves reflect the bases, form, articulations and scope of these units. Such distributions normally express the effects of struggles within and between these corporations for autonomy, resources, control and dominance.

Notably, as South Africa illustrates, a Spartan society of masters and helots may replicate the organizational capacities and complexities of ethnically homogeneous modern industrial societies within its dominant section; but only by rigorously excluding the subordinate from participation in such activities.[68] Cases of this kind also refute the general thesis of Durkheim and other functionalists that social differentiation proceeds inexorably under the pressure of functional forces that replace inappropriate antecedent structures by more appropriate ones, particularly in modern industrial societies.[69] Again, as contemporary Holland and Britain illustrate, the antecedent organization of an ethnically homogeneous industrial society is considerably complicated by its incorporation of substantial alien minorities of differing language, culture and race. As our familiar assumptions that equate complexity with functional differentiation are unable to illuminate these phenomena, to develop an objective comparative study of the variety and characteristics of complex societies that will elucidate the conditions of their development and organization, we should concentrate instead on the bases, properties and articulations of their concrete structural units; namely, at the macro-level, on the corporations that order the domain of public affairs; and at the micro-level, on the variety and distribution of interpersonal relations and roles available for individual selection. We need also to determine the congruence and relations of the structural elements at either level with one another and with those of institutionalized intermediate units. To this end we may first isolate the preconditions and implications of the maintenance of units at each level, and then explore their congruence and their contributions to the persistence or development of the actual social structure.

It will be noticed that throughout this discussion there has been no need to assume that societies or their structures constitute systems, whether analytical or constructivist, natural, moral or

68. Blumer (1965).
69. Durkheim (1947), pp. 181-3, 222-4, 374-88.

symbolic, open or closed, homeostatic or other, nor to what degree or under what conditions. Such metaphysics are only essential in functionalist analyses of social situations and processes; but instead of furthering our understanding of concrete social phenomena, those conceptions merely obscure them.

9.

Race and Stratification in the Caribbean

It is said that the Caribbean includes over fifty societies;[1] and perhaps there are almost as many ways in which we might discuss their interracial patterns. Since David Lowenthal's recent account of these patterns[2] cannot be faulted, I shall try to carry forward the analysis by seeking to isolate those conditions or factors which have regulated the allocation of differential status among racially distinct stocks within Caribbean societies. Although the data and discussion concentrate on Creole societies, I shall cite sufficient materials from Hispanic units in this region to indicate that the analysis applies to them also. To pursue these goals I shall first indicate the nature of stratification and race, and then outline the variation and development of Caribbean societies with special attention to their population compositions and histories. In conclusion I shall briefly relate these data and findings to the general theory of social and cultural pluralism.

1.

To investigate the relationship between differences of status and differences of race in Caribbean societies, we need equally objective conceptions of stratification and race. Stratification is often identified as an evaluative ranking of social units; and some writers assert that, being an institutionally necessary response to a requisite of any social organization, it is a universal feature of all social systems. However, such assertions appear to be unfounded and at variance with ethnographic fact.[3] In any event, since the evaluations that constitute a stratification are neither random nor contingent, their criteria must be institutionalized within the social structure, and for this reason evaluative rankings will express principles that underlie and regulate social organization.[4] We may therefore defer this ideological conception of stratification in favour of one that is more concrete and empirically demonstrable.

Concretely, stratification is manifest by and in the differential

1. Lowenthal (1960*b*).
2. Lowenthal (1967).
3. See above, Chapter 5.
4. See above, Chapter 5.

distribution of resources, opportunities, rewards and sanctions among the members of a society. Where institutionalized, for structural reasons, these differential distributions of resource, opportunity, reward and sanction normally correspond and thus reinforce one another, thereby distinguishing ranked strata within the population, each characterized by internal and external similarities of social situation, advantage and disadvantage. Inevitably, in systems of this sort, the most privileged stratum enjoys the highest prestige and rank, the most disprivileged stratum the least. Inequalities in the distribution of social assets, opportunities and values are thus central to stratification; but the concrete empirical distribution of these inequalities presupposes some principle or principles to regulate, integrate and order the differentiation. Analytically, then, the stratification can be reduced to a set of specific principles that generate and organize the prevailing distribution of resources and opportunities. In racially heterogeneous societies such as those of the Caribbean, racial identity and racial difference are generally prominent among these bases of stratification; but, as we shall see, this is neither necessarily nor always the case. Moreover, since we are concerned to determine the precise conditions under which racial difference is institutionalized as a principle of stratification, we shall initially exclude race as a criterion or determinant of status in order to investigate these relationships objectively in different Caribbean milieus.

To isolate the relationships between race and stratification in Caribbean societies, we must therefore seek to determine the objective distributions of social assets and disabilities in quantitative terms among racially distinct sections of their populations. Moreover, to this end, we should review the historical development of these units as well as their current racial structures. It is clearly impracticable to attempt an adequate or exhaustive review of such materials in this essay; and indeed the data we seek are distributed unevenly by topic and period for any single unit, much less for the entire range of Caribbean societies. To proceed methodically under these conditions, we therefore need a typology of Caribbean units which will facilitate comparative generalizations for societies of each category while forestalling unsound extrapolations between them; but we can only attempt to elaborate this societal typology after reviewing the variations of scale and racial composition these units display.

In these agrarian societies with their long colonial histories, the social assets and values of most immediate relevance for study of the social stratification include differential distributions of civil and political rights, land ownership and access, distributions of educational opportunities and facilities, of income, occupation, employment and social status. The distributions of these resources and opportunities among racially distinct categories can be objectively illustrated where data are available by distributions of land, income, professional and managerial roles, educational experience and qualifications, political representation, office and disbursements, employment and social status. They could also be instanced at greater length by data on the differential rates of fertility, infant mortality, marriage, illegitimacy, literacy, tenancy, house values, crime, wages, salaries, overcrowding, disease, sanitation, and other indices of living standards and life chances among racially distinct sections of the populations; but since these two sets of indices are clearly associated as conditions and effects we may employ distributions of either type to describe historic and prevailing patterns of racial stratification within these units.

However, stratification is not the inevitable and only possible mode of interracial accommodation. Interracial accommodations are institutionalized relationships between racially distinct components of heterogeneous societies that regulate the adaptation of each component to its social environment. In a racially heterogeneous society, the stratification of racial stocks is a very general mode of interracial accommodation; but this enjoins the active and continuous participation of the ranked strata in a common system of interaction. Without such functional and jural interdependence, racial sections of a wider society would approximate discrete collectivities aligned solely by ties of political alliance or subordination. In such a case, the racially distinct collectivities may also be spatially separate, endogamous, and bionomically self-sufficient; and under such conditions, these racially distinct populations will normally differ in culture, perhaps in language, and in their systems of social organization and value, since each segment will constitute an exclusive context of reproduction and socialization. It is appropriate then to distinguish the societal alignment of racial segments ranked externally by criteria of numbers and dominance from systems of racial stratification which presuppose the incorporation of racially different stocks within a common system of action, even where both structures overlap. As we shall see, the Caribbean contains several societies of either type.

Granted their membership in a single society, whether *segmental* or *stratified* in its structure, the accommodation of racially distinct populations has a limited number of primary alternatives. If the racial segments are bionomically and spatially discrete, their accommodation may either be stabilized as a hierarchy; or it may be non-hierarchic and symbiotic, and take the form of a consociation in which the various segments collaborate externally with one another as units of equivalent status. Alternatively, racial stocks may either be incorporated into a single system of action by subjugation to a dominant group, or on an egalitarian basis which permits individuals to associate and cooperate freely, irrespective of their racial or ethnic identities. Each of these four alternatives represents a particular mode of collective accommodation; and each of these modes assumes certain specific conditions for its stability. Any event or condition that invalidates the requisites of a prevailing interracial accommodation will destabilize it, in proportion to its salience. Thus either a stabilized segmental symbiosis or a stabilized racial stratification may be converted into contexts of collective uncertainty and conflict by unsettling events. Alternatively, racial identities and exclusions may lose their earlier significance under the influence of changing conditions. Recent developments in Caribbean societies illustrate these alternatives nicely.

2.

Besides residual Amerindians in the Guianas, Dominica, St. Vincent, Aruba, and British Honduras, Caribbean populations include whites of varied nationality, Negroes, Chinese, East Indians and Indonesians (Javanese). I shall treat these six stocks as racially distinct since they 'are distinguished from each other . . . by the relative commonness within them of certain inherited characters'.[5] The hereditary characters that distinguish these six stocks are such prominent physical traits as skin colour, hair type, facial features and stature, which receive general notice in Caribbean societies. As traits these characters are gross and variable though none the less modally distinctive; but being transmitted biologically from parents to children within each racial stock, they are highly stable collective differentiae that possess objective validity. Accordingly they serve to distinguish children begotten by parents of the same racial stock from others begotten by parents of differing races through miscegenation; and these objective physical differences between hybrids and genetically unmixed stocks validate that biological conception of race which hybridization itself presupposes.

Since race is a biological term that may be used to distinguish populations by objective and biologically transmitted features, its relations with nationality are indifferent and variable. In classifying Amerindians, Chinese, Negroes, whites, East Indians or Javanese as racially distinct, it is irrelevant whether they belong to the same nation or many. However, in many Caribbean societies, for political and social reasons that reflect the interests of dominant groups, nationality and race have been long and variably confused. Thus, in the British West Indian census of 1943-6, resident whites were divided into the following 'races'; locally born (Creole) whites, English, Scotch, Irish, Italians, Germans, French, Jews, Portuguese and others. Such classifications clearly invoke criteria of national origins, language and culture rather than race to group whites in political categories of interest to the colonial power. Even so, these categories are not always consistent. Thus, even locally born Jews

5. Dunn (1958), p. 17.

and Portuguese are segregated from 'locally born whites'.[6]

In Trinidad the West Indian census of 1960 distinguished the following racial categories: Negro, white, East Indian, Chinese, mixed and Lebanese-Syrian. The Jamaican census of that year supplemented these categories with one for 'other races, unspecified', and broke down the mixed class into four divisions as follows: coloured (Afro-European), East Indian coloured (Afro-East Indian), Chinese coloured (Afro-Chinese), and Syrian coloured (Afro-Syrian).[7] Thus, if we employ these successive censuses to identify local races, we shall have to conclude that Trinidad and Jamaica had experienced profound racial transformations between 1943 and 1960. In practice the differing racial classifications of these successive censuses merely reflect differences in the political statuses of the territories concerned, and in the political identifications and interests of those who designed these censuses, that of 1943 being directed by Britons under Crown Colony rule, while those of 1960 were directed by native Trinidadians and Jamaicans on the eve of decolonization. By illustrating how variably people of different national identity and social status may classify themselves and others in racial terms, these census classifications indicate the inadequacy of those analyses of race relations which are based on folk schemes of racial classification. If we seek objectivity, we cannot rest a comparative study of these phenomena on the current sociological view that a race is any 'group of people who are regarded and treated in actual life as a race',[8] since this casually assimilates racial, ethnic and national blocs, and destroys in advance the necessary conditions for isolating the objective relations of race and society by enjoining acceptance of all societal classifications of race as equally valid even where these directly contradict one another. For example, according to some, in Cuba 'a man with some white ancestry is not Negro';[9] whereas in the USA anyone with Negro ancestry is a Negro. Moreover, as our West Indian census categories illustrate, folk systems of racial classification are often inconsistent, unstable, and differ for different reference groups. Thus though relevant as descriptive data, they cannot furnish a reliable base for the comparative analysis of objective relations between differences of race and social stratification. To investigate such relations we need equally objective and verifiable empirical conceptions of race and stratification, which should facilitate our identification of the variables under study despite their obfuscation by local stereotypes and ideologies. Such conceptions should also permit objective diachronic analyses of changing interracial accom-

6. Eighth Census of Jamaica, 1943, part 2, pp. xlix-li, 92-6; West Indian Census, 1946, part A., pp. 12-17, 95.

7. Eastern Caribbean Population Census, 7 April 1960, Series A, Bulletin no. 1; Francis (no date), ch. 4, pp. 4-6.

8. Blumer (1955), in Lind (1955), pp. 4-5.

9. MacGaffey and Barnett (1965), p. 59.

modations, even though current ideologies obscure the boundaries and relations of racial units.

As the 1960 Jamaican census indicates, besides primary stocks, Caribbean societies contain a variety of hybrid types derived from the crossings of whites, Chinese, Negroes, East Indian, Amerindian and Javanese, within or without wedlock. Setting aside these patterns of miscegenation for later discussion, the 1960 census classification of hybrids in Jamaica also shows that most of these hybrid varieties and populations are coloured or part-Negro.

Historically, most Caribbean societies were constituted by European colonists who dispossessed local Amerindians and imported African slaves in variable quantities and rates for the mines or plantations. Given the unbalanced sex ratios among these immigrant stocks, and the prevailing social organization, miscegenation proceeded between free white men and black women whose status as slaves excluded marriage. The hybrid offspring of such unions constituted a fast growing mulatto or coloured bloc, some being free and others slaves. Various factors differentiated these coloured hybrids from the white and Negro stocks to which their parents belonged; but differences of personal status further divided the coloured into two exclusive categories, the free and the slave. As Negro slave majorities increased with colonial development, white dominance increasingly relied on the support of free and slave coloured people. For generations the colonial populations were enumerated as whites, free coloured, free blacks (that is, manumitted or self-redeemed ex-slaves), and slaves. In some territories resident Jews, who lacked civil rights until 1832, were also distinguished from nationals of the colonial power. Thus when slavery terminated, most of these mixed societies recognized three racially distinct categories — white, black and coloured, the latter internally differentiated by decreasing Negro components in their genetic mixtures as sambo, mustafino, mulatto, quadroon and octoroon. Although emancipation eliminated the distinction between slave and free, these racial classifications persisted together with this quasi-genetic differentiation of Negro-white hybrids. The socially and physically heterogeneous category of coloured hybrids accordingly stressed its difference from Negroes while seeking to assimilate to the dominant white minority; and thereafter this heterogeneous category of coloured hybrids has remained structurally distinct from whites and Negroes in most Caribbean societies.[10] However, since coloured people vary rather widely in physical type, the phenotypical limits of this category remain indeterminate, so that at both extremes blacks and whites whose associates and qualities are predominantly coloured are easily assimilated to this social category:

The line between 'coloured' and 'black' fluctuates with the bias of the census

10. Lowenthal (1967), pp. 597-601; Broom (1954); M.G. Smith (1965c), pp. 60-6.

taker and the mood of the populace. The 'coloured' proportion of Dominica was reported as 30 percent in 1921, 75 percent in 1946, and 33 percent in 1960 – variations explicable only by changes in local evaluations. Jamaica exhibits similar anomalies. Between 1943 and 1960 the 'coloured' population of Kingston declined from 33 to 14 percent of the total, while that of one rural parish rose from 11 to 19 percent. Change in names doubtless played a part; Kingstonians were less chary of being called 'African' in 1960 than 'black' in 1943.[11]

Despite the uncertainties that attach to the boundaries and relative size of this hybrid category by virtue of its interstitial social and biological position, its objective existence and significance in Caribbean societies remain undeniable. None the less, this hybrid population has undergone various changes in social status, recruitment patterns, and composition over the generations, with consequent increases in its physical and social heterogeneity. It is also identified very differently in Hispanic and non-Hispanic societies. In the Dominican Republic (Santo Domingo) whites were estimated at 13 percent and Negroes at 19 percent of the population in 1942, the remainder, classified as mulattoes, being mainly of 'lower class'.[12] In Cuba while officials estimate that 72 percent of the people are white and 12 percent black, one unofficial estimate gives '30 percent white, 20 percent mestizo (coloured), 49 percent Negroid, and 1 percent Oriental'.[13] In Puerto Rico there has been a steady transfer of mestizo and coloured folk to the white category in successive censuses since 1860.[14] Thus, whereas in British territories the difference between coloured and black fluctuates situationally, in Hispanic areas this is true of the difference between coloured and white. In Cuba 'racial antagonism between Negroes and mulattoes is often sharp, for according to the proverb, one Negro may harm another but a mulatto will do worse!'[15] Similar tensions characterize relations between the middle-class coloured and lower-class black throughout the West Indies; and, as in Cuba, these social categories are often contraposed in racial terms.

Another distinction to persist from slavery which requires notice is that between locally born folk and others from abroad. Natives of Caribbean societies, whether white, black or racially mixed, are called Creoles or Criollos. The Creole category should therefore include Amerindians, East Indians, Jews, Javanese, Chinese, Lebanese and Portuguese who have been born in this region. However in practice these latter populations are designated by specific names, though their hybrid issue by black or coloured mates are normally classified as Creole. Thus, in Guyana, Surinam and Trinidad where Asiatics are numerous, the older Negroid sections reserve the

11. Lowenthal (1967), p. 600.
12. Tannenbaum (1946), p. 7.
13. MacGaffey and Barnett (1965), p. 34.
14. Hoetink (1967), p. 185; Lowenthal (1967), p. 600.
15. MacGaffey and Barnett (1965), p. 39.

designation of Creoles for themselves, thereby indicating the socio-
cultural nature of this category. Particularly in Guyana and Trinidad,
Creoles describe East Indians by the pejorative term 'coolie', while
East Indians describe their Creole hybrids as *doglas* (bastards,
outcasts). 'To the Trinidadian [free Creole], the Hindu East Indian
has always been a "coolie" regardless of status, never a Creole.'[16] In
short, generically, Creoles are native West Indians of black, white or
mixed racial stock.[17] To distinguish Negro-white mixtures from
hybrids begotten by unions of Amerindians and Spaniards, it is
therefore convenient to use the local terms, coloured and mestizo.

In Table 1 I set out the reported population and approximate
racial compositions of those Caribbean units for which reasonably
recent data are available. Unfortunately the table excludes the
French and Netherlands Antilles, together with Aruba, Bonaire and
Curaçao, British Honduras, Cuba, Haiti, Puerto Rico and Santo
Domingo since I failed to find recent data on their racial compositions. As indicated above, the reported ratios of coloured may err
in differing degrees and directions in different territories. We should
therefore regard these ratios as indicative rather than exact.

3.

Besides the West Indian ·archipelago, at the minimum the
Caribbean region includes Surinam, French Guiana, and Guyana
(British Guiana) on the Atlantic shoulder of South America, together
with British Honduras in Central America. These four mainland
territories with a joint area of 172,000 square miles and a population
of 1.1 million belong to this ethnographic zone by virtue of their
histories, colonial experience, cultures, racial composition and social
organization. In 1963, the islands contained about 22 million people
in a total area of 91,200 square miles. Of these 23 million West
Indians, 7.2 million live in Cuba, 4.5 million in Haiti and 3.3 million
in Santo Domingo, which together occupy 73,363 square miles or
four-fifths of the archipelago. The remaining 7 million West Indians
are dispersed among forty-eight island societies, which range in size
from Redondo with one square mile, or Saba with 5.4 square miles,
to Jamaica with 4,400 square miles; in population from Mairo in the
Grenadines with 250 to Puerto Rico with 2.35 million; and in
density from Dominica with less than 200 per square mile to
Barbados with over 1400.[18]

These gross physical variations have parallels in social and cultural
spheres. Caribbean societies divide into two major classes which may
be labelled Creole and Hispanic or mestizo, according to their
derivation from Spain or other West European countries. Excluding

16. Rubin (1962), p. 444.
17. M.G. Smith (1965c), pp. 307 ff.
18. Lowenthal (1960b), p. 788; Pearcy (1965), pp. 131-4.

Table 1

Racial composition of selected Caribbean populations in percentages

	White	Negro	Coloured	East Indian	Chinese	Other Amerindian	Carib	Indonesian	N/S Other	Total
Antigua	1.3	92.4	3.5						2.8	54,060
Barbados	4.3	89.6	5.9	0.2					0.6	237,732
Cayman Is.	18.5	17.3	63.6						0.6	8,456
Guyana*	1.5	31.1	11.9	50.1	0.7	4.7			0.8	638,030
Jamaica	0.5	78.1	18.3	1.7	0.6				1.5	1,609,814
Montserrat	0.4	95.7	2.4						1.5	12,167
Dominica	0.4	66.1	32.7				0.7		0.1	59,916
St. Lucia	0.6	68.7	26.9	3.5			0.2		0.1	86,108
Grenada	0.8	52.6	42.2	4.2					0.2	88,677
St. Vincent	2.3	70.3	21.8	3.2			1.6		0.8	79,948
Surinam**	1.7	46.2		34.3	1.6	1.2		15.0		316,184
St. Kitts, Nevis, Anguilla	0.9	89.4	8.7					1.0		56,793
Trinidad and Tobago Is.	2.1	43.5	16.2	36.4	1.0				0.8	827,957
Turks and Caicos Is.	1.3	93.9	3.8						1.0	5,669
British Virgin Is.	0.6	93.4	4.7						1.3	7,921
U.S. Virgin Is.	16.7	64.3	19.0							33,099

*Guyana returns are based on estimates for 1964
**Surinam returns are for 1962
Excluding these two countries, all figures refer to 1960

Cuba, Santo Domingo, and Puerto Rico all other Caribbean societies can be classified as Creole, whether derived from France, Holland, Britain or Denmark. The great majority of these societies are racially heterogeneous; however, we should distinguish three categories in racial terms: the racially homogeneous, the basically bi-racial and those multi-racial units that contain three or more distinct stocks. Provisionally also we should distinguish societies of moderate size, that is, with more than 15,000 people, from those miniscule units with less, most of these being political dependencies of their larger neighbours. From the data on racial compositions set out above, we can classify the Caymans, Turks and Caicos Islands, Montserrat and the British Virgins as miniscule units, of which only the first is clearly bi-racial. We can also identify Guyana, Trinidad-Tobago and Surinam as multi-racial societies, all other units being bi-racial in base and of moderate size.

To generalize about societies exhibiting such diversity of composition and scale, we have first to distinguish their major varieties and then to proceed comparatively. As indicated above, all racially homogeneous Caribbean societies are economically marginal units of miniscule size, while all Caribbean societies of moderate size are bi-racial or multi-racial. The overwhelming majority of these bi-racial units are highly stratified, while Caribbean multi-racial units all exhibit a segmental alignment of segregated racial stocks. In addition, all Caribbean societies are poor, weakly industrialized, heavily dependent on agriculture, forestry or mining; and in most the effective density of population on arable land is high. All were established as European colonies, and all have histories of slavery. In the general decolonization that followed the Second World War, most of the larger units have acquired internal autonomy, and some are now formally independent.

4.

Since 'the explanation of race relations must be sought in social conditions and historic experiences',[19] I shall now sketch the historical development and organization of Caribbean societies, paying special attention to their racial composition.

On discovery and settlement by Spaniards, Cuba, Hispaniola, Puerto Rico, and Jamaica were occupied by Arawak and Ciboney Amerindians. Despite initial intermarriage of Spanish men and Amerindian women, these native populations were rapidly eliminated by disease, overwork, and oppression. African slaves were imported from 1510 to replace them but, with the conquest of Mexico in 1521 and Peru in 1554, Spanish interests focused on the wealthy mainland colonies and these four Antillean territories became way-stations that serviced the shipping between America and Seville.

19. Blumer (1955), p. 9.

For example, in 1550, Cuba contained only twelve hundred Spaniards, three thousand Amerindians and a few African slaves.[20] While Spain concentrated her manpower on the conquest and settlement of her mainland territories, Carib Indians retained control of the lesser Antilles, until Holland, France and Britain, in search of colonies, dispossessed them and one another as occasion allowed. By 1655 the British had seized Jamaica from Spain, and had colonized Surinam only to lose it to Holland in 1667. Thirty years later France established its colony of Saint Dominique in the western half of Hispaniola by dispossessing Spain.

While the Spaniards initially sought precious metals by setting Indians and African slaves to mine, they also ranched and cultivated some tobacco and sugar on a small scale. The Dutch, French, and British proceeded to develop plantation economies based on slave cultivation of sugar for export to the metropoles under mercantilist regulations. Seamen sought wealth by transport, piracy and smuggling. Loggers colonized the coast of British Honduras. In St. Vincent and Dominica, as described below, the beleaguered Carib Indians welcomed escaping Negro slaves with whom they interbred to produce a hybrid people, the black Caribs, Negroid in appearance but Carib in culture and language.[21] Elsewhere Amerindian inhabitants were eliminated from the islands and replaced with African slaves by the colonizing French, British and Dutch.

In 1645 when Barbados contained 40,000 whites and 6,000 Negroes, most of the whites were indentured Britons recruited to cultivate tobacco. Under Dutch inspiration Barbados abandoned this experiment for sugar cultivation by African slaves; and by 1685 the island contained 20,000 whites and 46,000 Negroes.[22] In 1673, eighteen years after Britain had seized it, Jamaica contained 7,700 whites and 9,500 Negroes. By 1700 Negroes outnumbered whites in all British Caribbean colonies; in 1723, Jamaica contained 74,000 Negro slaves and 7,700 whites. As the slave trade continued and the sugar economy boomed under mercantilist protection, population increased by importation of African slaves throughout the non-Hispanic Caribbean, until by 1810, two years after Britain had formally prohibited further slave imports from Africa, the British Caribbean contained 568,000 slaves who represented 80 percent of its population.[23] Most of these slaves were natives of Africa. Of locally born slaves many were coloured.

Population structure varied colonially and also over time. In 1805, while 8 percent of the people in Trinidad were white, 24.5 percent were free coloured. In 1816, of 3,824 persons in British Honduras, 149 (4 percent) were white, 933 (24 percent) free

20. MacGaffey and Barnett (1965), p. 4.
21. MacRae Taylor (1951), pp. 15-35.
22. Parry and Sherlock (1956), p. 69.
23. West Indian Census 1946, part A, p. 5.

coloured, and the remainder were slaves. In Jamaica and St. Vincent by 1820, there were equal numbers of free coloured and whites, while about 10 percent of the slave population were also coloured.[24] In 1838 slavery was terminated in British possessions by an act of Parliament; in 1848 France did likewise; in 1863 the Dutch followed suit.

Throughout the seventeenth and eighteenth centuries, when these West Indian territories ranked among the richest and most profitable European colonies, France, Britain, Spain and Holland contested their possession in a continuous series of naval wars. Such territories as St. Lucia changed hands several times during these struggles. Others such as Saint Dominique, Barbados and Cuba escaped that fate. Meanwhile throughout the eighteenth century Cuba, Puerto Rico and Santo Domingo (the eastern half of Hispaniola) remained undeveloped by comparison with the colonies of Britain, Holland and France. In 1776, of 70,260 inhabitants in Puerto Rico, only 6,487 were listed as slaves.[25] Cuba, which may have contained 2,000 slaves in 1790, probably had a similar composition. However, by 1817, when the first Cuban census was taken, of 630,000 inhabitants, 291,000 were whites, 115,000 free coloured and 224,000 were slaves.[26] The remarkable changes in the composition and size of Cuba's population during these twenty-seven years followed the island's conversion from ranching and small-scale tobacco farming by free white residents to sugar production by imported slave labour. This conversion was stimulated by the collapse of sugar production in Saint Dominique, formerly the largest and richest plantation colony in the region, and by the rapid growth of a major sugar market in the newly independent USA.

Saint Dominique was ruined as a plantation colony by the revolution of Negro slaves and free coloured that began in 1791 and terminated in 1804. This revolution, which freed the country from France, was perhaps the most important episode in the history of Caribbean slavery. Set off by the Great Revolution in France, the successful Haitian revolt had rather special antecedents which merit notice.

Miscegenation of white males and black slave women characterized the slave regime everywhere. These unions proceeded outside wedlock, since their male participants were free, while the women were normally slaves. However, throughout the French colonies until 1674, since 'children received at birth the status of their father',[27] all issue of these interracial unions were free by birth; and, since Louis XIV had conferred full legal and political rights of citizenship on this increasing population of free coloured *affranchis* in 1658, another law

24. M.G. Smith (1965c), p. 93.
25. Mintz (1959), p. 276.
26. Parry and Sherlock (1956), pp. 127, 222 ff.; MacGaffey and Barnett (1965), p. 9; Mintz (1964), pp. xxi ff.
27. M.M. Horowitz (1960), in Rubin (1960), pp. 802-3; Brion Davis (1966), p. 277.

was passed in 1674 to restrict the growth of the free coloured populations which ruled that hybrids should take the status of their mothers.

Even so, the free coloured continued to increase in numbers and wealth, until white planters came to regard them as potential rivals. Beginning in 1758, the white planters who dominated the colonial legislature in Haiti passed discriminatory laws against the free coloured citizen. 'One by one his rights in the Code were abrogated . . . Law and religion were barred to him because of their honorific nature. Coloured women were forbidden in 1768 to marry white men. In 1779 began a series of laws designed to humiliate the coloured person in public.'[28] None the less, 'some say that in 1791 they [the coloured] owned a third of all the land in the colony and a fourth of all the slaves; others, more conservative, put the figure at one-fifth of each'.[29]

When the Third Estate convened at Paris in 1789, the white planters of Saint Dominique sent a delegation to seek colonial autonomy. They were met by radical demands for the forthright abolition of slavery as a direct implication of the Rights of Man. The resulting compromise formally re-enfranchised the free coloured of Saint Dominique, but left implementation of this measure to the colonial legislature, itself the instrument of white oligarchy. As the free coloured perceived that they would have to fight to secure their rights, they prepared to do so; and when the slaves independently revolted against their masters in August 1791, the free coloured aligned themselves with this revolt and sought to direct it to their own ends. Against this unprecedented combination the local whites were unable to offer effective resistance. Intervention by the navies of Britain and Spain merely consolidated the alliance of free coloured and slaves, who proclaimed their allegiance to revolutionary France with fervour. But when, in 1793, the Republic voted to abolish slavery in Saint Dominique and other French territories, 'the action [was] as distasteful to the free coloured people as it was to the whites; both groups wanted to own slaves'.[30] In 1797, after the surviving whites had been expelled from the colony, the free coloured under Rigaud fought the ex-slaves under Toussaint L'Ouverture, and were defeated. In 1801-3, when Napoleon, having removed Toussaint, attempted to reinstitute slavery in Saint Dominique, Christophe and Dessalines resumed the struggle until by 1804, all whites had been eliminated from the territory, and its independence from France was finally assured.

This sequence reveals clearly the central role of political relations in the racial order and social stratification of a Caribbean slave society. The revolt of Haitian slaves owed its success to the

28. Leyburn (1941), pp. 19-20.
29. ibid., p. 18.
30. ibid., p. 25.

antecedent persecution of coloured *affranchis* by white planters who feared the growing wealth and numbers of this hybrid category. This persecution forged a revolutionary alliance between the free coloured and the black slaves which had few parallels, even in the revolts led by the mulatto Fedon against the British in Grenada and by the Jacobin commissioner, Victor Hugues, in St. Lucia and Guadeloupe in 1794-5. For, on deciding to abolish slavery, the French Republican Government sent Hugues to implement its decree in the southern colonies, St. Lucia, Guadeloupe and Martinique. In response local French planters welcomed the British navies to protect them against the proclaimed emancipation. Hugues temporarily relieved St. Lucia but failed to take Martinique. However he did seize Guadeloupe and stimulated its slaves to assert their new freedom by revolt against their masters. In 1801, when Napoleon decreed the restoration of slavery, it proved necessary to re-establish the old regime in Guadeloupe by force and mulatto control was overthrown. The successful defence of slavery by French planters in Martinique, St. Lucia and ultimately in Guadeloupe contrasts sharply with its destruction in Saint Dominique (Haiti).

Spain's response to the revolutionary struggles that ruined the sugar production of Saint Dominique was to promote plantation slavery initially in Cuba, and, as Cuba prospered, in Puerto Rico, the only other West Indian island that remained under Spanish control, since the Haitians overran Santo Domingo from 1806 to 1844. Despite an Anglo-Spanish agreement of 1817 to suppress the African slave trade, Cuban slave imports increased steadily, until by 1837 they exceeded 12,000 per annum. By 1870 when the trade finally terminated another 200,000 Africans may have entered the island.[31] Only in 1815 did Spain begin to convert Puerto Rico to sugar production; but by then it was too late to secure the necessary numbers of African slaves since the Anglo-Spanish agreement of 1817 restricted these imports, while the Cuban slave market nearby offered better terms. In consequence Negro slaves never exceeded 15 percent of the Puerto Rican population; and in the absence of these and other supplies of foreign labour, the Puerto Rican government forced 'free but landless peasants to work on the plantations. A whole series of laws were passed during the period 1815-50 to exact more labour from landless freemen. Puerto Rico in this period presented the curious picture of a Caribbean colony where slaves were treated little worse than freemen.'[32] Thus, while their brief but vigorous careers as sugar colonies fuelled by black slave labour have given the racial compositions of Puerto Rico and Cuba a Creole complexion, this did not disturb their Spanish cultural foundations. In both territories Negroes have remained the minority. Only in Santo Domingo, following its domination by Haiti between 1806 and 1844, were

31. Parry and Sherlock (1956), pp. 224-5; Mintz (1964), p. xxv.
32. Mintz (1959), pp. 277 ff.

Negroes numerically preponderant in these Hispanic societies.

Although closely linked to the sugar plantation, West Indian slavery was not entirely restricted to it. In British Honduras slaves were employed in logging and 'worked side by side with their masters on similar terms to those of hired labourers'.[33] In Saba, where slaves remained a numerical minority, they worked alongside their masters in the field and at sea.[34] Curaçao and St. Eustatius, where Negroes predominated numerically, prospered through commerce instead of plantations. In French St. Barthélemy, slaves were marginal. On Grand Cayman, where sugar was not cultivated, they remained a minority. On the Turks and Caicos Islands, devoted to fishing, sailing and the production of salt, there were very few resident owners. There were also many small islands such as Barbuda, St. Maarten, and Carriacou in which Negro slaves employed in sugar plantations predominated heavily.

Caribbean societies with differing ecologies and economic resources responded differently to the abolition of slavery. Where all arable lands had been pre-empted by sugar plantations, as in Barbados, Antigua, and St. Kitts, emigration was the only feasible alternative that emancipation presented ex-slaves to tenancy and wage work on estates at rates dictated by the planters. Perceiving this, Antiguan planters eliminated the statutory period of apprenticeship and emancipated their slaves directly in 1834, without losing their labour. In Barbados, colonial legislation of 1840 effectively tied all labourers within the island to the plantations on which they lived.[35] But as the sugar market slumped with the repeal of imperial protection between 1846 and 1854, the Barbadian government encouraged emigration; and by 1920 over 100,000 people had left the island.[36]

In Haiti, despite Christophe, plantations were abandoned and broken up shortly after independence. The ex-slaves occupied themselves with subsistence cultivation. In Jamaica, British Guiana and Trinidad, where unused lands were available, emancipation permitted a heavy exodus of workers from the plantations to establish new communities based on subsistence farming. In Grenada some ex-slaves quit the estates to acquire their own small holdings, while others remained as resident labourers.[37]

Emancipation created a labour crisis in those plantation colonies that contained unused lands available for settlement by ex-slaves. This economic crisis was complicated and intensified by the withdrawal of protective tariffs in metropolitan states, and by the increasing supplies of cheaper sugar from Brazil and Germany. In this context, marginal sugar-producing areas, such as the Grenadines, the

33. Waddell (1963), p. 14.
34. Gorham Crane (1966), pp. 22, 25-7, 65-7, 103, 161.
35. Lowenthal (1957), pp. 453-4.
36. ibid., pp. 454-5; Mack (1967), in Bell (1967), p. 153.
37. M.G. Smith (1965c), pp. 151-2, 267-71; Farley (1954); Cumper (1954).

Virgin Islands, St. Maarten, Montserrat and Nevis, were abandoned to Negro peasantries as planters withdrew. Where territories had been entirely parcelled out in plantations as in St. Kitts, Antigua and Barbados, sugar production continued without serious decline in labour supplies since the ex-slaves had no practical alternative to plantation labour except emigration; but in St. Lucia, plantations were gradually abandoned over several decades; in St. Vincent they were converted to arrowroot, in Grenada to cocoa and nutmegs, in Jamaica to bananas; and in each case there was a sufficient turnover of management to facilitate the emergence of a coloured planter class, who were often the lineal issue of the last generation of white sugar planters. Alternatively, where planters decided to pursue sugar production despite the labour shortage that followed emancipation, foreign workers were imported at public expense under indenture contracts that ensured plantation control of their labour for several years. This response was adopted for different reasons in different measures and at different rates by planters in Guadeloupe, Martinique, Surinam, Trinidad, Guyana, Jamaica, St. Vincent and Cuba; and in general the largest numbers of indentured workers were imported by those units with the most expansive plantation systems.

Indentured workers recruited for these different territories came in different ratios from Africa, from Germany, Portugal, Madeira, Malta, the Azores and the Cape Verde Islands, from China, from India and from Indonesia, to Surinam, Martinique, Trinidad, Guyana and Jamaica. Cuba continued to import African slaves until 1870, following which it recruited indentured workers from China, and later from Yucatan. While these immigrations complicated and diversified the racial and socio-cultural composition of these Caribbean countries, they did not transform their social structures immediately, but facilitated their persistence.

In 1841, three years after emancipation had taken effect, Jamaican planters imported 10,000 free Africans, 1,000 Germans, 2,700 Britons and some Portuguese.[38] Between 1860 and 1893 the island also received 5,000 Chinese workers.[39] By 1871, Guyana had imported 14,000 Africans and 6,900 Chinese. Between 1835 and 1882 Guyana also received 31,600 Portuguese. However, by 1851 the Portuguese in Guyana had moved from plantation labour into shopkeeping, and owned 173 of the 296 licensed shops in Georgetown, the capital.[40] Such labour imports, financed from colonial revenues, varied territorially in volume, duration and source with the labour demands and profitability of the local plantations. Thus, Puerto Rico, which lacked the necessary capital and revenues, received few indentures, while Cuba needed none until her slave trade ceased in 1870. Barbados, Antigua and St. Kitts had no need of

38. M.G. Smith (1965c), pp. 151-2; Roberts (1957), pp. 103-32.
39. Roberts (1957), pp. 131-2; Black (1958), p. 165.
40. R.T. Smith (1962), pp. 8, 44; Despres (1967), pp. 56, 62-3.

foreign labour to work their plantations, while Carriacou, the Turks and Caicos Islands, the Caymans, Montserrat and other territories without operating plantations received no indentures. Jamaica, St. Vincent and Grenada, with inefficient and unprofitable sugar plantations, could neither finance nor absorb as many indentures as Surinam, Guyana and Trinidad, where plantations remained profitable and expansive.

The great bulk of indentured labour was drawn from India under schemes administered by the British Colonial Office. Between 1838 and 1917, when the Indian government terminated this programme, 'altogether about 548,000 East Indians came to the British, French and Dutch West Indies on official schemes . . . 239,000 to British Guiana alone, 134,000 to Trinidad, 78,000 to Guadeloupe and Martinique and 35,000 to Surinam'.[41] Another 36,400 went to Jamaica, 5,900 to Grenada, 4,400 to St. Lucia, and 2,500 to St. Vincent.[42] Though many Indians returned home on completing their indentures, the majority settled in the territories where they had worked; and, when immigration from India ceased, the Dutch indentured Javanese from the Dutch East Indies (Indonesia) to work in Surinam, much as Cuban planters had supplemented their Chinese imports by Spanish-speaking white and mestizo recruits from Yucatan.

While India furnished foreign labour, indentures declined and ceased elsewhere. By 1895 indentures from China had ended; but after 1910 other Chinese immigrated to Guyana, Jamaica and Trinidad at their own expense to seek their fortunes as traders and workers. During these years small groups of immigrants from Syria and Lebanon came to Jamaica and Trinidad for similar ends. These ethnic minorities have retained their occupational specialism and collective distinctness by endogamy and exclusive associations. In contrast, the earlier waves of indentured Chinese assimilated rapidly to the local population, as did many Portuguese.

The demographic history of British Honduras differs from other territories as an effect of its ecological situation. Following their revolt in St. Vincent and Dominica at the instigation of Victor Hugues in 1795, the black Caribs were deported *en masse* to the Honduran coast, and by 1802 had entered the colony. Between 1848 and 1851, another 4,000 Spanish-speaking mestizos and whites settled in the north to escape the Maya revolt in Yucatan. By 1861 these immigrants from Yucatan, totalling over 9,000, outnumbered the English-speaking Creoles who were then concentrated around Belize on the coast. At various periods during the past century Kekchi and other Maya tribes have also moved into British Honduras from Guatemala to settle empty lands in the interior; and in 1958 they were followed by 1,000 German-speaking Mennonites from

41. Newman (1964), p. 26.
42. Roberts (1957), p. 128.

Mexico seeking freedom from governmental regulations. Unfortunately the British Honduras census of 1960 does not indicate its racial composition. However, in 1946, 38 percent of the colonial population were black, 31 percent were 'mixed', 17 percent were Amerindians, 7 percent black Caribs, 4 percent whites and 3 percent Asiatic, mainly East Indian. It should be noted that the 'mixed' category in this census return is a composite of English-speaking Creoles, descended from Britons and Negroes, and of Spanish-speaking mestizos, descended from Spaniards and Amerindians. Classified by language, some 60 percent of this mixed category, and thus 18 percent of the colonial population, were Negro-white hybrids, the remainder being Spanish-speaking mestizos. At that date resident whites were almost equally divided between Spaniards and Britons.[43]

Emigration has also affected the racial composition of Caribbean societies differently, and at differing rates and times. For example, whereas Jamaica contained 35,000 whites in 1820, by 1946 there were less than 14,000. In Grenada, St. Lucia, Dominica, Nevis and elsewhere, as white planters withdrew during the latter half of the nineteenth century, they were succeeded by a hybrid class of coloured landowners who never formed more than 5 percent of the population, and who have since themselves withdrawn from such marginal areas as Carriacou, Union and Mairo, Barbuda, and some British Virgin Islands, thereby simplifying the social structure and racial composition of these abandoned communities. On the Cayman Islands, despite 'almost continuous emigration'[44] and very little immigration, population doubled between 1881 and 1943 with remarkable changes of racial composition. During these sixty years local Negroes increased by 10 percent from 972 to 1,051, while whites increased by 140 percent from 864 to 2,086, and hybrids by 185 percent from 1,230 to 3,518.[45] These figures suggest substantial rates of miscegenation and some emigration by blacks. Comparable patterns can be traced through census tabulations for South St. Elizabeth, Jamaica, where there are settlements of white peasants around Bull Savanna, and on Petit Martinique, near Carriacou, where the coloured descendants of former French colonists retain their ancestral culture, language, names and cult. On Saba, one of the Dutch Windward Islands, the white majority has been reduced by emigration, until now the population is evenly divided between whites and non-whites, very few of whom are hybrids. While 'poor whites' maintain exclusive peasant settlements in Barbados, Grenada, St. Vincent, Jamaica and elsewhere, on Saba by 1964 there was 'an almost completely random distribution of population'. All four villages contain white and black families.[46]

43. Waddell (1963), pp. 64-7.
44. *Handbook of Jamaica*, 1960, p. 719.
45. Eighth Census of Jamaica, 1943, p. 444.
46. Gorham Crane (1967), pp. 101-6.

Since the various immigrant stocks that entered the Caribbean were differentially affected by shortages of women, miscegenation, adult and infant mortality rates, migration and ecological context, they have declined or increased in numbers at differing rates in different countries and periods; but of all racial stocks within the region, East Indians everywhere exhibit the highest rate of natural increase and among the lowest rates of miscegenation and emigration. Thus, since indenture ceased fifty years ago, these Indian populations have increased disproportionately until they are now the second largest blocs in Surinam and Trinidad and the majority in Guyana. As indicated below, this rapid rate of natural increase among local East Indians has acquired political significance in Guyana, Trinidad and Surinam with the introduction of popular government, party politics and universal suffrage, following the Second World War.

5.

Miscegenation is an old and widespread feature of Caribbean societies which has generated two important categories, the mestizos and the coloured, while affecting all racial stocks differentially. Patterns of miscegenation illustrate prevailing modes of collective accommodation, and, for this reason, among others, they attract the attention of natives and observers alike. Miscegenation is not of course restricted to interracial mating. It may be identified wherever individuals belonging to mutually exclusive social categories establish sexual unions. Some examples of matings which controvert local norms and are therefore regarded as miscegenation, despite their avoidance of racial mixture, are cited below.

In polyglot societies characterized by the stable symbiotic accommodations of their racial or ethnic components, these will generally remain bionomically distinct, physically separate and mutually endogamous. In consequence the society will articulate discrete segments of parallel status but distinctive locations, memberships, organizations and cultures. The multi-racial society of British Honduras illustrates this type nicely. There, until recently, four racially distinct segments, speaking different languages and practising different cultures, coexisted under British rule in physical isolation from one another. Of these segments, the English-speaking Creoles were most numerous, followed by the Spanish-mestizo bloc, the Maya Amerindians, and the black Caribs. With the recent immigration of German Mennonites, the country now contains five segregated segments. Decolonization has placed British Honduras under the administration of coloured and Negro Creoles, since the Maya, Carib and Spanish-speaking mestizo segments are separately too small, isolated and remote from one another to challenge Creole leadership. However, repeated Guatemalan claims to the territory

threaten its precarious post-colonial accommodation and may reverse
the current relations and roles of mestizos and Creoles.

Other Caribbean multi-racial societies, such as Surinam, Guyana
and Trinidad, exhibit similar segmental patterns. In Surinam the
primary segments are Creole, Indian and Javanese, the native Bush
Negroes (Djuka) and Amerindians being without political representation. In Trinidad and Guyana until 1946, Creole and East Indian
peoples remained segmentally distinct, as do the Amerindians of
Guyana today. However, under the political economies of colonialism, although these Creole and East Indian segments were bionomically sufficient and discrete, they were articulated symbiotically by
their common subordination to the British, a condition expressed by
their differential disenfranchisement, differential civic rights, differential opportunities for education, public employment and access to
land, as well as by their racial segregation. As Britain proceeded to
decolonize, these colonial symbioses were destabilized, until the
Creole and East Indian segments were duly mobilized as blocs under
political parties competing for political dominance in both territories. This enhanced competition has reinforced and extended
their traditional segmental exclusiveness. The indirectly symbiotic
accommodation that prevailed under the colonial regime has thus
been changed by decolonization into relations of collective competition and conflict in Guyana and Trinidad. In Surinam, however,
where colonialism had stabilized a more effective symbiosis by
introducing the Javanese as a third bloc, decolonization has fostered
a consociational regime in which Creoles, Indians and Javanese,
organized by racially exclusive political parties, collaborate in the
territorial administration proportionately with their respective
numbers. Yet, even in Surinam, 'parties have become even more
racially oriented, and attempts to forge an interracial movement
have been up to now quite unsuccessful'.[47]

Differences in the racial compositions and proportions of the
populations of Surinam, Trinidad and Guyana have played a critical
part in promoting these diverse developments. In Surinam no single
racial segment can command a majority. In Trinidad-Tobago, where
the Creole (Negro and coloured) segment accounts for three-fifths of
the people, its present dominance seems secure. In Guyana, where,
although numerically the largest, the East Indian segment recently
formed less than half of the population, until 1964 the struggle for
dominance between Creoles and East Indians was violent and keen.

White and Negro populations of Saba in the Dutch Windwards
illustrate another type of segmental accommodation and its dissolution. Until recently Saba has always had a white majority. In 1863,
when Holland abolished slavery, Saba contained 704 slaves and a few
free Negroes. Following emancipation the two racial segments lived
apart in several villages, each securing its own subsistence by fishing,

47. Mathews (1966), in Mathews et al. (1966), pp. 96-103.

sailing, peasant cultivation and wage-work abroad. During the past century, population has fluctuated under the influence of successive emigrations. Whereas formerly black and white residents lived apart, in 1964-5 they occupied common communities. A report on Saba published in 1960 relates that:

Whites still stand firmly for complete segregation. In Saba whites are adamant and unanimous about this.[48] ... On Saba the tradition against intermarriage and even against extra-marital relations between members of the two races remains deeply entrenched; attitudes of whites towards race mixture are full of abhorrence and repugnance.[49]

These observations are invalidated by a later study which reports the situation on Saba in 1964-5:

Black and white children frequently play together, parents of both races frequently choose godparents of the other racial group for their children, people frequently use a phrase 'my good neighbour' in reference to a person of the other race, and there has been a slight increase, during the past thirty years, in interracial unions ... The majority of these unions, whether within marriage or outside it, are of the type opposite to those which formerly took place ... most modern unions are between black men and white women. Where there is no marriage and the child of a bi-racial union is brought up in the home of the mother, he usually shares in her social-racial assignation.[50]

These successive reports on Saba indicate that the formerly exclusive relations of blacks and whites have changed there quite significantly since 1955 from segmental symbiosis to an increasingly inclusive egalitarian accommodation. Although we lack relevant data, it seems probable that some black and white communities of the Cayman Islands may have experienced somewhat similar developments during the decades between 1881 and 1943.

Thus recent developments in Guyana, British Honduras, Surinam, Trinidad and Saba illustrate alternative transformations of stabilized segmental symbioses towards domination, strife, and consociational articulations, and to the dissolution of segmental boundaries in an inclusive social order. Comparably divergent accommodations of two identical racial segments may be illustrated by the fusions of runaway Negro slaves and Carib Indians on St. Vincent and Dominica between 1635 and 1763.

Under continuous attacks and harassment by French, British and Spanish, the St. Vincent Caribs first gave refuge to two boat-loads of Negro slaves in 1635; and by 1676 they had admitted about 3,000 Negroes, most of whom were males. These Negroes settled on the windward coast of St. Vincent, while the Caribs lived as before on the leeward coast. At that date the St. Vincent Caribs probably

48. J.Y. and D.L. Keur (1960), p. 204.
49. ibid., p. 200.
50. Gorham Crane (1967), pp. 161, 314.

exceeded 4,000. By 1700 when the Negroes approached 4,000 in numbers the 'red' Caribs had been reduced to 2,000 through continual warfare with the Europeans. As the population of Carib males decreased through slaughter, Negroes abducted Carib women to their settlements. By 1763 when Britain annexed St. Vincent, the 'black' (Carib) outnumbered the 'red' Caribs there by almost ten to one.[51] In adjacent Dominica, Caribs had also united with Negroes for common defence; but there they intermarried freely under 'the influence of French priests'.[52] Thus, whereas Negroes effected a forcible fusion of the two stocks in St. Vincent by seizing Carib women, in Dominica the union of these two peoples appears to have proceeded peacefully, under similar external threats, as fugitive slaves replaced Carib males slain in war.

With these data we can attempt to distinguish alternative patterns of interracial miscegenation as indices of collective accommodations among racially distinct stocks within Caribbean societies; but while miscegenation patterns are sensitive indicators of interracial adjustments, they are neither uniform nor transparent in their implications. Mutually exclusive racial segments are inevitably endogamous as, for example, the Negroes and whites on St. Maarten, St. Eustatius or contemporary Barbados. Where miscegenation is formally unrestricted, it must be symmetrical in the sense that partners of either sex and racial stock may mate by marriage or otherwise. In such a case, racial stocks participate as equals in a society defined by common connubium. Though rare, this pattern seems to be the direction of current developments on Saba, as earlier among the Caribs and Negroes of Dominica and St. Vincent. More commonly, miscegenation is either forbidden, in which case the racial blocs remain genetically discrete, or it is restricted in range and form. Wherever restricted, miscegenation is always asymmetrical and unilateral, in the sense that men of one stock or ethnic segment have access to the women of one or more others, without reciprocity. Such asymmetrical miscegenation generally expresses and presupposes relations of dominance and subordination among the stocks concerned, as for example prevailed between free whites and Negroes on West Indian slave plantations.

However, an asymmetrical and unilateral pattern of miscegenation may also prevail without the hierarchical alignment of inter-breeding stocks as a simple effect of complementary disbalances in the sex ratios of racially distinct populations. For example, the indentured Chinese and Portuguese workers who completed their contracts and quit the plantations for towns in Trinidad, Guyana, Jamaica and Cuba during the nineteenth century, acquired Negro and coloured concubines from the urban lower and middle classes, and the offspring of these unions were assimilated to the Creole population

51. MacRae Taylor (1951), pp. 24, 28-31.
52. ibid., p. 26, n.46.

as hybrids of distinctive type. Chinese communities in contemporary Cuba illustrate these processes very nicely.[53] In their turn these Chinese and Portuguese hybrids mated with persons of differing social level by marriage or outside it, thereby completing the assimilation process. Partly as an effect of these processes in 1946 only 8,500 Portuguese remained out of more than 30,000 who were brought into British Guiana between 1835 and 1882. In Trinidad, Grenada, and Jamaica also, most persons descended from indentured Portuguese are to be found within the coloured category. In Jamaica only 130 Portuguese residents were listed in 1943.[54] Likewise in Martinique 'several families have Chinese surnames and may have members who have distinguishable features, but do not otherwise differ from the bulk of the Martiniquians'.[55]

None the less, that mere imbalance in the sex ratios of an immigrant stock is not always sufficient to produce miscegenation is shown by the history of Indian populations in Surinam, Guyana, Trinidad, Martinique, Grenada, and, until 1943, in Jamaica also. Under institutions of caste, Indians practice endogamy to avoid ritual pollution. They accordingly ostracize their hybrids as *doglas* and anathematize the Indian parents, unless such unions can be assimilated to Indian notions of hypergamy, by which women of lower caste may in some areas mate with men of higher caste.[56] Their ritually enjoined endogamy 'has accordingly preserved the racial distinctiveness, culture, language and traditional social organization of Indian enclaves against rapid dissolution by Creole contacts and influences throughout the West Indies, while obstructing their assimilation to the Creole society.[57] In Surinam, the Javanese have been even more successful in resisting their ambience, and maintain their segmental isolation in the midst of diverse peoples.[58]

Until recently, unions between members of those ethnic stocks which were locally distinguished in racial terms despite their common objective racial identity were also described and treated as instances of miscegenation. As indicated above, Creole societies distinguished Creole (native born) whites of colonial descent from expatriate residents and nationals of other European countries in racial terms. Jews, Lebanese and Portuguese were also distinguished racially. On religious grounds Jews, who are one of the earliest immigrant groups to settle in this region, marry endogamously, though mating asymmetrically with Creoles outside marriage. As recent immigrants from Asia Minor, Lebanese are also highly endogamous; and so, until recently have been those Chinese who came to the area at their own expense after 1910 as traders and

53. MacGaffey and Barnett (1965), p. 41.
54. Eighth Census of Jamaica, 1943, pp. xlix, 92; Broom (1960*b*), in Rubin (1960), p. 883.
55. M.M. Horowitz (1967), p. 3.
56. A. and J. Niehoff (1960), p. 42.
57. Rubin (1962), p. 441.
58. Malefijt (1963).

craftsmen. However, unions of Lebanese, Portuguese, Jews, Spaniards or Italians with whites of British stock were locally classified as miscegenation until quite recently. Nor is such exclusiveness entirely restricted to groups of different ethnic or national stock. In Martinique:

Metropolitan whites [expatriate Frenchmen] are in the civil service and commerce. Almost all of them live in the capital city ... Economically and socially the metropolitans are on a par with the coloured native class. They are not accorded the status of *békés* [Creole white planters] whose exclusiveness is reinforced by endogamy ... Metropolitan whites arrive expecting to be accorded the deference they believe is due to their colour. They quickly learn, though, that their social position is determined by their occupation and by their birthplace. Marriage between coloured Martiniquians of either sex and metropolitans is common, especially among those who are educated in France ... Middle class *noirs* also marry metropolitans, but less frequently than do the *mulâtres*.[59]

Except that Creole whites are more heavily dependent on the metropole and thus less estranged from visiting expatriates in Guadeloupe, the pattern there is similar.[60] In Trinidad, the remaining French *békés* avoid intermarriage with local Britons; and in Jamaica, the members of Creole white planter families are no more willing to marry British expatriates engaged in commerce, industry or the civil service than are the *békés* of Martinique to wed their compatriots from France. Thus besides the norms of race and ethnicity, those of caste and class enjoin endogamy among Creole white planters as among immigrant Hindus. However, for white males, these taboos on intermarriage do not exclude miscegenation with women of other ethnic or racial stocks, notably Negro and coloured.

Some observers ascribe the absence of a 'mulatto social class in the Dutch Windwards' where white and black peasants have long been settled close together to the absence of a 'deeply entrenched, numerous or long enduring plantocracy'.[61] But similar patterns are also found at Mt. Moritz, Grenada, at Windward, Carriacou, at New Scotland, Barbados, and elsewhere in areas with long plantation histories. Moreover as data from Saba, Petit Martinique, and the Cayman Islands indicate, it is not always the case that contiguous black and white peasantries maintain sexual exclusions. Evidently, where Negroes and whites occupy similar socio-economic positions, the only alternative to symmetrical miscegenation is none at all. This principle explains why all perduring contexts of asymmetrical miscegenation between these stocks in Caribbean history have been characterized by the subordination of one to the other; moreover throughout West Indian history, with the sole exceptions of Haiti,

59. M.M. Horowitz (1967), p. 15.
60. Leiris (1955), pp. 168-87.
61. D.L. Keur (1960), in Rubin (1960), p. 798; J.Y. and D.L. Keur (1960), pp. 200 ff.

Grenada and Guadeloupe during the decade of the French Revolution, whites have dominated Negro and coloured folk.

Where coloured elites exercise dominance they replicate the asymmetrical patterns of their white ancestors and models. Coloured elites in St. Lucia and Dominica and Grenada taboo intermarriage with lower-class coloured or black folk, much as the Martinique *békés* taboo intermarriage with visiting Frenchmen or coloured Creoles. However, while the male members of these coloured elites mate freely outside marriage with lower-class women who are mainly black, coloured elite women remain taboo to men of deeper pigment or lower class. In Haiti, where the coloured elite numbered 150,000 in 1940 and formed 5 percent of the population they then controlled, elite males mated with Negro women by institutions of *plaçage*, while reserving marriage for women of elite lineage.[62] In consequence some sociologists were led to analyse relations between the Haitian elite and Negro peasants in terms of caste.[63] But those Haitian patterns have numerous parallels in the British Windward Islands, where coloured elites descended from white planters and black or coloured concubines observe similar endogamy. In contrast, black and coloured members of other socio-economic strata mate symmetrically by marriage or without it, thereby demonstrating that the asymmetrical mating of·black folk and coloured elites derives from collective inequalities of political and social status.

When the Spaniards first colonized Hispaniola and Cuba they simultaneously married Amerindian women and treated native Indians as heathen enemies whose subjugation was legitimate and imperative. Since intermarriage asserted the social equality of the races to which the partners belonged, being inconsistent with the racial stratification forged by conquest and exploitation, this practice lapsed rapidly, and Spaniards soon presented the Pope with the problem of deciding whether Amerindians were fully human and capable of divine redemption. As Negro slaves replaced the declining Amerindians, Spaniards mated with their women outside marriage, since slavery itself barred the latter relationship. Successive generations of British, Dutch and French colonists did likewise throughout the Caribbean, thereby instituting those asymmetrical mating patterns which persisted wherever some men administered others as unfree labour in plantation contexts.

H. Hoetink has recently interpreted these Caribbean modes of asymmetrical miscegenation as evidence of the inherent exclusiveness of the 'somatic norm image' of whites from north-western Europe, and he has argued that this image proscribes marriages between white and coloured or Negro folk. This interpretation overlooks the intermarriage of Frenchmen and coloured women in Saint Dominique until forbidden by law in 1768. It overlooks the intermarriage

62. Simpson (1941), pp. 640, 648; (1942), pp. 655-61; Leyburn (1941), pp. 186-93.
63. Cobb (1940), pp. 23-4; Leyburn (1941).

of white and Negro peasants such as Crane reports from Saba. It also overlooks the refusal of Creole white plantocracies to intermarry with members of their own national or ethnic stock; and it overlooks the endogamy practised by white ethnic stocks, by Hindu labourers, and by coloured elites who imitate their white predecessors. It also ignores historical patterns of intermarriage between coloured folk and metropolitan whites locally as well as in Europe. In short this thesis misinterprets endogamous patterns which subserve and express the political inequalities of differentiated social sections or classes by treating them as pure effects of directing racial archetypes. It is argued by Hoetink that these idealized racial phenotypes (somatic norm images) differ among Iberians and north-western Europeans in degrees that permit the former to marry coloured women while prohibiting the latter. However, Hoetink himself admits difficulty in distinguishing observable phenotypes of north-western Europeans and Portuguese;[64] and no one has ever yet observed, nor ever will, a 'somatic norm image'. Surely, as historical data indicate, indentured Portuguese, like the Chinese, being powerless, poor and in need of mates, were constrained by their circumstances to accept coloured or Negro women as intimates, whereas whites engaged in plantation management were equally constrained by their social circumstances to maintain social distance throughout these liaisons. If the 'somatic norm image' and its derivative, the 'somatic distance', regulates the matings of Negroes and whites, it should surely proscribe unions characterized by equality between Chinese and Negroes while facilitating close relations between East Indians and Negroes.

The data on Caribbean miscegenation presented above indicate that asymmetrical miscegenation is common among immigrant groups that have unequal sex ratios, as an adaptive response to their social situations. However, such unbalanced sex ratios are only found among the first generation of immigrants whose hybrid offspring must either assimilate to the host stock or be segregated socially by mechanisms of collective control. Ritual prohibitions may exclude both miscegenation and the problem of socially placing its hybrids; but wherever such asymmetrical mating is institutionalized among successive generations, it expresses and presupposes the political inequality of the racial stocks as a condition of their union. In contexts of collective parity, the alternative to symmetrical connubium between racial stocks is strict endogamy that excludes miscegenation between them. Thus, in seeking to isolate the critical factors that have regulated interracial status relations throughout Caribbean history, we should concentrate on the distribution of political resources and power among racial sections. The liberation of Haitian mulattoes and blacks by the elimination of resident whites illustrates the relevance of political relations for the racial com-

64. Hoetink (1967), pp. 166-74.

position and stratification of that society; and so does the continuing struggle between the coloured elite and the black mass that followed Haitian independence. Likewise, the violent protests of emancipated Negroes in Jamaica, Martinique and Dominica against their disabilities between 1865 and 1872 indicate their awareness of the political bases of the current racial stratification; and so do contemporary struggles between Creoles and East Indians in Guyana and Trinidad.

6.

To examine the hypothesis that collective alignments of power have determined the racial stratification of Caribbean societies, we should compare racial stratifications during periods of slavery, colonialism and since decolonization. We should also compare the racial distributions of social assets and disabilities in societies of different type and scale, for example, in segmentally organized multi-racial societies, and in bi-racial societies of moderate and miniscule size, distinguishing those with plantation foundations from others without. By a racial stratification we simply mean the differential distribution of social advantages and disadvantages among the racially distinct stocks of a given society. By comparing such distributions for selected societies of different base and type at successive intervals of time, we can test the thesis that the relationships between peoples of differing race in the Caribbean have always reflected distributions of collective power, without claiming to demonstrate it conclusively. However, if representative data from societies of differing base, type and periods support this hypothesis, the onus will rest on those who hold that interracial accommodations are governed by non-political interests and factors such as the maintenance of racial purity or the pursuit of economic gain to prove their case.

To locate reliable and comprehensive quantitative data on the differential distributions of social resources, advantages, and values among racial stocks in Caribbean societies is no simple matter. Of recent censuses, by far the most informative in this respect is the British West Indian census of 1946, and especially the Jamaican census of 1943, which provides a unique and invaluable account of the differing social situations of racially classified stocks. Some data from a study of social stratification in Grenada are also illuminating, although less comprehensive. Successive censuses rarely permit detailed comparisons of these distributions since they differ so widely in their categories and tabulations; and even within the same census, as illustrated above, we should not expect uniformity in criteria or tabulations. Comparative problems, compounded by the variable political statuses and affiliations of these Caribbean societies, are thus extended by our desire to compare the racial distributions of social assets within representative units at differing intervals of time.

Fortunately we need little quantitative documentation of the racial stratification of Caribbean societies for the centuries of slavery. During this period, whites exercised an unqualified authority over coloured and African slaves whose status at law was that of chattel property. In plantation colonies, if the owners were absentee, the slaves were subject entirely to the direction and control of the owner's agents. In colonies that lacked plantations, such as Saba, British Honduras, or the Turks and Caicos Islands, the lot of slaves was generally lighter, as shown by the relative absence of slave revolts or attempts at collective escape in these areas. In plantation colonies slave revolts and their suppression alike indicate the political basis of the social order. To police these plantation colonies, imperial states dispatched adequate military and naval forces, while local legislatures required all able-bodied white males to enrol in colonial militias and turn out as summoned to suppress slave revolts. These colonial legislatures provided representation for wealthy colonists from the imperial countries, while excluding other nationals, Jews, and the free coloured or free black population. Slaves were forbidden access to arms; slave evidence was inadmissible against white persons in colonial courts. Slave societies that lacked plantations lacked these or equivalent arrangements, but probably enjoyed greater internal security. For example, when the Spaniards invaded British Honduras in 1798, the local Britons armed their slaves who 'fought with considerable spirit' against the invaders.[65]

The freedom of proprietors or their agents to make innovations in the administration of their own slaves varied with the proprietors' influence, in plantation areas. In Carriacou, Sir George Maclean converted the labour system from daily tasks to weekly job work without protest in 1830.[66] In Jamaica in 1816-17, Monk Lewis, a British MP, was arraigned on charges of sedition and subversion by neighbouring planters for innovations that ameliorated the lot of his slaves while increasing their productivity.[67]

While plantations yielded high rates of profit on new lands, their profitability declined as the soil was exhausted under cultivation techniques then in use. By 1820 most of Jamaica's slave plantations were uneconomic. None the less, local planters resisted all proposals to modify the slave regime.[68] Like the planters, economists find it difficult to calculate the profitability of production under conditions of plantation slavery.[69] Thus in such conditions, the planters' insistence on the subordination of other strata could hardly be based on clear economic considerations. In Saint Dominique, pursuing

65. Waddell (1963), pp. 15 ff.
66. M.G. Smith (1962), pp. 22-4.
67. M.G. Lewis (1843), p. 113; see also M.G. Smith (1965c), pp. 96, 110-14.
68. M.G. Smith (1965c), pp. 111-15.
69. D. Hall (1962);

non-economic objectives, the white oligarchy had hastened its own elimination by driving the free coloured strata into a desperate revolutionary alliance with the slaves and the metropole. In Martinique and Guadeloupe, slavery was finally abolished by France in 1848 on the grounds that it cost her more to maintain the regime than to replace it.[70] In territories such as Saba or British Honduras, which lacked plantations and any significant external trade, it is doubtful whether slavery ever yielded any financial profits. Thus economic interpretations of Caribbean slavery vary in their validity for different areas and different periods.

In no Caribbean Creole society were rights of political representation conferred on slaves by their emancipation. Indeed except for the limited instruction by missionaries which planters warmly opposed, the ex-slaves had very little formal education; on liberation, they formed a landless, illiterate labour force with consequences mentioned above. Whites restricted their rights to participate at elections to the colonial legislatures as voters or candidates by property requirements that effectively disenfranchised all but a few of the black and coloured population. Colonial legislatures, dominated by planters who resented emancipation, predictably adopted policies to control the ex-slaves by imposing onerous tenancy laws that compelled them to labour under stringent conditions for low wages as the alternative to eviction. In Barbados, the Located Labourers Act of 1840 re-established planters' control most effectively. Planters also used their political power to import indentured workers from abroad with colonial revenues obtained by increasing excise and custom duties which transferred these costs to the Negro and coloured population. By admitting coloured men of property into the ranks, the colonial militia was expanded in anticipation of Negro revolts. Exiguous educational provisions were made for Negro and coloured people to meet the formal demands of imperial governments. While direct taxes on landed property remained negligible, and in many areas personal incomes went untaxed until 1938, revenues from excise and customs duties accounted for 80 percent of all indirect revenues in British territories, where indirect revenues often formed a similar ratio of government incomes.[71]

The general policy of these post-emancipation colonial regimes can be formulated simply: the propertied classes which monopolized the franchise employed their legislative power to levy revenues on the unenfranchised for the pursuit of policies designed to further their own collective interests and ends. Under onerous laws that regulated the relations of landlords and tenants, plantation management retained extensive control over resident ex-slaves. When disputes arose concerning wage payments, task measurements, task performance, tenancy conditions, evictions and the like, Negro complainants

70. Leiris (1955), p. 26.
71. West India Royal Commission (1945), p. 71 and Appendix D.

had to bring their suits before magisterial benches manned by white plantation personnel. This 'sectional definition and administration of justice which had been developed and employed by their former masters as a prime instrument of social control during the years after the abolition of slavery' finally generated a violent protest by the ex-slaves at Morant Bay, Jamaica, in 1865.[72] John Eyre, then Governor of Jamaica, authorized action in which 1,000 Negro homes were burnt and 600 individuals killed under martial law. Following this the colonial legislature, elected by a total of 1,903 voters, acting in 'the full conviction that nothing but the existence of a strong government would prevent this island from lapsing into the condition of a second Haiti',[73] decreed its own abolition, and transferred the government of the country entirely into the hands of the Crown. Revolts in Martinique and Dominica at this period encountered similar repression.

To justify their oligarchy, white planters had an armoury of racist arguments inherited from earlier apologists of slavery such as Edward Long; and at this period in Europe, Thomas Carlyle, Anthony Froude, Arthur de Gobineau, James Hunt and many others amplified this ideology with other arguments of diverse type that served merely to reinforce the sectional demands of West Indian whites. Understandably, despite periodic criticism by visitors, this colonial regime persisted with little change until 1937-8 when the politically inarticulate masses erupted in riots and strikes from Trinidad, Guyana and Barbados to Jamaica. At that period, registered voters formed 6.6 percent of the estimated population of Trinidad and 3.3 percent in Barbados. Even in 1944, when Grenada held its last election under the Property Franchise, only 14.8 percent of the people had a vote.[74] In 1915 — when 51.8 percent of the adult males in Guyana were Indian, 42.3 percent (Creole) Africans, 2.9 percent Portuguese, 1.7 percent Britons, and 0.9 percent Chinese — 46 percent of the Britons, 17.7 percent of the Portuguese, 12.3 percent of Chinese, 6.8 percent of the Creoles, and 0.6 percent of the East Indians qualified to vote. Even so, of the 4,312 voters in Guyana that year, 17 percent were Britons, 11.4 percent Portuguese, 62.7 percent Creole 'Africans', 2.4 percent Chinese, and 6.4 percent East Indians, Amerindians being without representation.[75] In 1936, when the Dutch finally initiated a common legislature for their six Antillean colonies, 'only 140 persons qualified as voters in all of the three Windward Islands . . . Only one member of the *Staten* was allocated from the three Windwards.'[76]

Throughout the region this pattern prevailed until the Second

72. M.G. Smith (1965c), pp. 152-3.
73. *Handbook of Jamaica*, 1954, p. 29; M.G. Smith (1965c), pp. 152-3.
74. West India Royal Commission (1945), p. 379.
75. Despres (1967), pp. 39-40; Ayearst (1960), pp. 112-13.
76. Gorham Crane (1967), p. 39.

World War when universal adult suffrage was introduced in British territories on the recommendation of the Royal Commission that followed the riots of 1937-8. In 1944 Jamaica witnessed the first election by popular suffrage to be held in the British Caribbean. In 1946 the French Republic decreed a new status for the French West Indian colonies of Guadeloupe, Martinique and French Guiana that reconstituted them as overseas departments of France, and simultaneously introduced universal suffrage. In 1948, the first elections by universal suffrage were held in Surinam and the Netherlands Antilles under a new constitution. Thus post-emancipation colonialism concluded, as it began, by political changes that significantly altered the antecedent distribution of power among racial stocks. But while emancipation had merely freed the Negro and coloured slaves from direct subordination to individual whites who finally replaced them with indentured Indians, given their overwhelming numerical predominance, universal suffrage made it formally possible for Creoles and Indians to strive for political control as a strategic condition of racial restratification in all territories except those under France.

To assess the significance of these recent political changes on the racial stratification of Caribbean society is not easy, given the numerous gaps in available data and the varied courses of 'decolonization' adopted by different metropolitan powers. Thus France technically decolonized Guadeloupe, Martinique and French Guiana by redefining them as overseas departments. However, despite the regionally exceptional allowances for social assistance that such integration has brought, until the race riots at Fort de France, Martinique, in December, 1959, the substance of colonialism persisted with its characteristic racial stratification at least as vividly in these areas as in the British or Dutch territories.[77] Perhaps our best guides to the significance of recent political changes are comparisons of the distributions of social assets under and since colonialism. In reviewing these distributions it is necessary to segregate the data on inclusively stratified bi-racial societies from those that pertain to multi-racial units with a segmental organization. It is also convenient to compare territorial data on the distributions of land, education, literacy, occupation, and incomes, for periods immediately preceding and succeeding decolonization before examining parallel data on politics, as far as our information allows. I shall, therefore, summarize the distributions of these indices within selected bi-racial societies, before presenting similar data on multi-racial units, following which we shall review briefly some data that indicate contemporary distributions of political attitudes and power.

77. Latortue (1966), in Mathews et al. (1966), pp. 148-83.

7.

In 1935-6, 73 percent of the arable land in Martinique was held in units of more than 100 hectares (247 acres or more), 40 percent of the registered proprietors holding units of 40 hectares (100 acres or more). In 1960, of 222 plantations totalling 42,275 hectares, all of which exceeded 50 hectares in size, 151 with a total area of 28,066 hectares were owned and administered by Creole whites who formed 0.70 percent of the Martinique population and controlled 66.41 percent of its capital. In Guadeloupe, according to the agricultural census of 1957, 51 farms of 100 hectares or more occupied 31.6 percent of the total area and represented 0.2 percent of all holdings. At that date, 13,813 holdings of less than one hectare occupied 14.8

Table 2

Landholdings of more than 100 acres in British Caribbean territories (excluding Jamaica), by race of owner, 1946[81]

		Black	White	Coloured	Other	Total
(a)	Windward Islands:					
	Dominica	1.5	8	87		110
	Grenada	36	20	51	6*	113
	St. Lucia	28	11	37	5*	81
	St. Vincent	8	12	24	—	44
	All with over 100 acres:	87	51	199	11*	348
	Total landholders:	10,682	477	7,023	800*	18,992
	Barbados	8	186	25	—	219
	Total landholders	3,525	612	738	6	4,881
	British Honduras	1	8	5	1	15
	Total landholders	840	53	618	1,941	3,452
(b)	Leeward Islands:					
	Barbuda	—	—	—	—	—
	Antigua	34	22	22	—	78
	St. Kitts	19	15	9	—	43
	Nevis	14	5	7	2*	28
	Anguilla	1	2	2	—	5
	Montserrat	12	8	4	—	24
	Virgins	14	3	4	—	21
	All with over 100 Acres:	94	55	49	2	200
	All landholders	7,441	133	673	14	8,261
	Trinidad and Tobago	119	94	112	113*	438
	All landholders	11,951	423	2,585	15,548*	30,571

* = East Indians

percent of the total area and represented 58 percent of all holdings. There also, the larger holdings are owned and operated by whites, the lesser by blacks, coloured and Indians. On both islands, agriculture engages one-half of the labour force and furnishes one-third of the Gross Domestic Product.[78]

On St. Vincent in 1946, 45 holdings of more than 100 acres each occupied 28,434 acres or 57 percent of all privately owned land.[79] Even in 1965 'practically all of the 24 large estates are exclusively held by the whites . . . All contribute through white ownership to white supremacy . . . In 1960, there were about 1500 agricultural workers on the island and about one-half of these were employed on the 24 estates.'[80]

We can compare the distributions of large land holdings among members of different racial categories within British Caribbean societies in 1946 by summarizing data from the census taken that year (Table 2).[81]

Except for Jamaica, comparable data on the racial allocations of land in these societies during 1960 are lacking. However, the Jamaican data are relatively complete and illuminating. In 1943, when 1,793,688 acres were under farms in Jamaica, 1,318 holdings of more than 100 acres accounted for 70 percent of this area. These large holdings were distributed by acreage and owner's race as follows (Table 3):

Table 3

Landholdings in Jamaica, 1943, classified
by size and landholders' racial status[82]

Holdings by Size	Whites	Blacks	Coloured	Others	Total Holdings	Total Acreage
100-199 acres	73	193	222	9	497	67,149
200-499 acres	89	99	170	23	381	120,074
500-999 acres	81	38	88		207	146,294
1000 acres +	168	36	125	4	333	921,203
Total large holdings	411	366	605	36	1,318	1,254,720
Total landholders	969	51,163	12,398	1,062	66,173	1,793,668
Large holdings as percent of total	42.2	0.07	4.9	3.4	2.0	70.0

At that date, of 1,237,000 residents in Jamaica, 1 percent were white, 1 percent Chinese, 2 percent East Indian, 17.5 percent coloured, and 78 percent Negro.

In 1943, when the total farms and buildings in Jamaica were

78. J. Benoist (1968); F.M. and S. Andic (1966), in Mathews et al. (1966), p. 109.
79. West Indian Census, 1946, part B, p. 44.
80. Wilwright (1966), pp. 45.
81. West Indian Census, 1946, part B, pp. 17, 35, 56; ibid., part E, p. 35.
82. Eighth Census of Jamaica, 1943, Table 200, p. 306, and Table 211, pp. 325-7.

valued at £17,930,000, the farms and buildings on units of 100 acres or more were valued at £9,218,000, or 51.5 percent of the total, although these were the most heavily capitalized units and 70 percent of the area. Such differential valuations of large holdings for taxation prevailed throughout the British Caribbean at that date.[83]

By 1954, Jamaican farmland had reduced to 1,788,660 acres, of which only 920,199, or 51.5 percent, remained in 1,213 units that exceeded 100 acres; but by 1960 this sharp fall in the area under large holdings had been partly redressed. Although the island then contained 1,706,560 acres in farms, a reduction of over 80,000 acres in six years, 1,130 units of 100 acres or more, representing 0.7 percent of all farm holdings, accounted for 955,165 acres or 56 percent of the total area in farms.[84]

In 1946 Barbados contained 88,580 acres in farmlands, distributed in 4,881 plots. Of this area, only 59,000 acres were cultivated, 41,000 acres with sugarcane in 4,078 plots.[85] By 1960, when the arable area had reduced to 83,000 acres, 85 percent was held by 260 estates of more than 100 acres each, almost all of them owned by whites, many of whom lived abroad. Of the 46,000 acres under canes in 1960, 36,000 were cultivated by these estates, the remainder being parcelled out among more than 30,000 peasants who held lots that averaged one-third of an acre each.[86] The racial composition and history of Barbados together ensure that the overwhelming majority of these cane-farming peasants were Negroes descended from slaves through generations of 'located labourers'.

Of 65,000 acres owned by private individuals on Grenada in 1946, 40,000 (61 percent) lay in 113 units of more than 100 acres held by 1.7 percent of 6,528 landholders. According to an agricultural survey of 1952-3, 10,000 plots of less than 25 acres each accounted for 18,600 acres together, while the remaining 100 estates of 100 acres or more totalled 34,400 acres.

In attempting to study the stratification of Grenadian elite in 1952-3, I investigated the relationship between social status and various conditions such as phenotypical colour, genotype, income, acreage owned, occupation, birth-status, and the like, and for this purpose employed a sample population of 403 prominent residents listed in the directory that was published in the *Grenada Handbook* of 1946. A panel of 19 residents ranked the personnel listed in this directory according to their relative status within the local society. By collation these rankings generated a single status scale with uniform intervals which ranged from 0.18 for the highest possible status to 1.00 for the lowest. As part of this inquiry four Grenadians also classified the directory personnel by phenotype as white, fair

83. West India Royal Commission (1945), pp. 81-3.
84. Agricultural Census of Jamaica, 1961-2, Bulletin no. 3, p. 26.
85. West Indian Census, 1946, part B, pp. 2-4.
86. Mack (1967), p. 149.

medium or mulatto, dark, and black. These qualitative ratings were converted into a decimal scale by assigning values of 0.2 to whites and 1.00 to blacks, with the fair, medium, and dark spaced equally between.' Phenotypical ratings of these sample individuals were then collated on this scale for correlation with their status scores.

An exhaustive scrutiny of the land rolls in all Grenadian parishes that year identified 76 landowners within this classified sample, for all of whom phenotypical values were available. Table 4 indicates the distribution of acreages among these 76 individuals, ranked by phenotypical scores that range from 0.2 for whites to 1.00 for blacks. The mean social status and acreages held by each phenotypical category are also tabulated to illustrate the distribution of status and land within this elite.

Table 4

Distribution of land among 76 Grenadian elite, classified by phenotype, 1953[87]

Phenotype	No. of Owners	Mean Status Scores	Total Acreage	Mean Acreage
1.00	3	0.67	1,822	607.3
0.9	1	0.87	81	81
0.8	6	0.59	1,241	206.8
0.7	8	0.49	1,779	222.4
0.6	21	0.44	4,770	227
0.5	9	0.41	3,159	351
0.4	8	0.33	1,189	148.6
0.3	5	0.30	1,484	297
0.2	11	0.21	3,834	348
—	72	0.417	19,359	278
Indians	4	0.57	2,425	606
Total	76	0.425	21,784	284

Of 72,000 Grenadian residents in 1946, 0.9 percent were white, the majority being peasants settled at Mt. Moritz and at Windward, Carriacou; 4.8 percent were Indian; 20.4 percent were coloured; and 73.6 percent were black. Of the 76 resident landowners in our sample, 14.4 percent were white, 5.2 percent were black, and the remainder, 76.4 percent, were coloured folk of varying hue. The steady decline in the social status of individuals as pigment deepens is nicely illustrated in this table.

These data on the distribution of land among the racial categories in Martinique, Guadeloupe, St. Vincent, Barbados, Jamaica and Grenada illustrate patterns that still prevail in bi-racial Caribbean societies. Parallel data on land distribution in multi-racial units will

87. M.G. Smith (1965a), pp. 142-7.

be cited below when describing the racial organization of those segmented societies.

8.

Since the distribution of minimal educational experience and opportunities is best revealed by the differential literacy rates of the various racial stocks, these rates are appropriate to introduce our review of the educational, occupational and economic dimensions of racial stratification in Caribbean societies under and after colonialism.

Of young men called up annually between 1946 and 1951 for military training, 21 percent were illiterate in Martinique and 42 percent in Guadeloupe, 37.5 percent in French St. Maarten, and 50 percent in Marie-Galante. Given the historic composition of these populations, Negroes and coloured folk predominate heavily among illiterates; but if their elders had been included the illiteracy rates would surely be higher.

Of school age children on Martinique in 1951-2, between 16 and 20 percent did not attend school; of those in Guadeloupe, at least 23 percent. In primary schools maintained by government, classes ranged in size from 80 pupils per teacher in the infant ranks to 20 in the more advanced. In Martinique, government public schools averaged 41 pupils per class as against 52 in Guadeloupe. In both islands, the Church operated fee-paying secondary schools with smaller classes for the children of Creole whites and wealthier coloured bourgeois. In both islands, the secondary school enrolment was then about 5 percent of the enrolment in primary schools.[88]

Excluding Jamaica, Table 5 describes the distribution of illiteracy among racial stocks in British Caribbean societies in 1946:

Table 5

**Illiteracy ratios in British Caribbean populations
over ten years old, classified by race, 1946 (Jamaica excluded)[89]**

Territories	White	Black	Mixed	Carib	Other American Indian	East Indian	Other Asiatic	All
Barbados	1.2	8.4	4.5	—	—	3.4	—	7.3
British Guiana	2.9	2.7	2.2	—	49.6	44.0	6.8	21.4
British Honduras	8.2	5.7	14.5	22.2	42.5	26.3	—	16.1
Leeward Islands	6.2	15.5	8.9	—	—	16.7	—	14.6
Windward Islands	7.1	29.3	28.0	42.9	—	46.2	—	29.1
Trinidad and Tobago	3.1	9.5	8.5	—	—	50.6	14.5	22.6
Weighted total	3.3	12.1	14.0	24.1	46.1	47.4	11.6	

88. Leiris (1955), pp. 73 ff.
89. West Indian Census, 1946, part H; p. 101.

While territorial illiteracy rates varied from 7.3 percent in Barbados to 29.1 percent in the Windward Islands (Grenada, Dominica, St. Vincent, and St. Lucia), the rates among East Indians, Caribs, and Amerindians are exceptionally high. By comparison, the rates among whites are exceptionally low, and those of blacks and coloureds fall between. However, Guyanese and Honduran rates for black, white, and coloured deviate from this British Caribbean norm by which literacy increases with pigmentation, perhaps as effects of the segmental contrapositions of Creole and non-Creole populations in these two colonies.

The Jamaican census of 1943 provides by far the most exhaustive documentation of the racial distributions of social assets and advantages available to us. At that date, illiteracy rates among the population over seven years old, classified by race, were as follows: whites, 3.2 percent, coloured 13.8 percent, blacks 28.1 percent, East Indian 48.6 percent, and 'other Asiatic' (mainly Chinese) 13.9 percent. Of the total population then in the island, 25.6 percent were illiterate.[90] The 1943 census also reports the distribution of educational experience among Jamaican residents over seven years of age by racial categories as follows (Table 6):

Table 6

Educational experience of Jamaican residents, over 7 years old, classified by race, 1943[91]

	Black	Coloured	White	Chinese	East Indian	Syrian	Total
Total	794,574	179,532	12,477	9,234	21,387	857	1,018,955
Percent illiterate	28.1	13.8	3.8	13.9	48.6	5.6	25.6
Elementary school only	70.5	75.1	35.0	73.6	49.1	46.1	70.4
Secondary or technical	1.1	9.8	48.1	12.0	2.1	46.4	3.4
Pre-professional or professional	0.3	1.3	13.1	0.4	0.2	1.9	0.6
Percent literate	71.9	86.2	96.2	86.1	57.4	94.4	74.4

These data speak so clearly for themselves that no comment is necessary.

In December 1942, of the 12 to 18 year age group, the ratios enrolled in secondary schools throughout the British Caribbean varied as follows: less than 0.2 percent — Dominica, British Guiana, and St. Lucia; 0.2 to 0.3 percent — Jamaica, Montserrat, and St. Kitts; 0.3 to 0.4 percent — Antigua, St. Vincent, and Grenada; 0.4 to

90. Eighth Census of Jamaica, 1943, p. lviii.
91. ibid., Table 108, p. 54.

0.5 percent — Trinidad-Tobago; 0.6 to 0.7 percent — British Honduras; over 0.7 percent — Barbados.[92]

At that date, fees for secondary education averaged £12 per annum per pupil throughout the area. In addition, governments gave an estimated £25 per pupil per annum to secondary schools, the overwhelming majority of whose pupils were drawn from the propertied white and coloured classes. Of children under 12 years old in British Caribbean territories in 1942, 90 percent were thought to attend primary schools. For these, almost all of whom were drawn from the then voteless black and Indian population, government expenditure averaged £4.50 per annum per child. Of children between 12 and 15 years old, it was estimated that only one half attended schools of any kind; and for those in government schools, the state contributed an average of £6 per annum per child.[93] At this date there were very few scholarships to secondary schools for children whose parents could not afford the normal fees. Thus government expenditures on education systematically favoured those children whose parents could pay the fees that currently averaged £12 per year per child. The parents of these privileged children had voting rights, and

used their political influence to secure high government grants for pupils at the secondary schools while keeping expenditure on elementary education very low. Thus the differential allocation of political rights which was based on educational and economic differences was used by its beneficiaries to maximize the sectional differences in education which underlay these economic and political inequalities. The educational system and the sectional order were integrated, and the one tended to perpetuate the other.[94]

In Haiti the situation was similar though more extreme. There the coloured elite are

aristocrats, partly (largely one might even say) because they are educated . . . Any programme which proposed universal education would cut the ground from under the present social structure by giving the masses equal opportunities to the elite . . . An ordinary degree of self-interest is quite sufficient to explain the lack of enthusiasm of the ruling class when the subject of general education is broached.[95]

The dramatic collapse of rural education in Haiti during the American occupation of 1915-31 illustrates elite policies on this subject nicely.

In British territories at this period almost all upper-class Creoles or whites sent their children to school overseas, preferably to Britain as their parents had done before them. In 1953, no member of the white upper stratum in Grenada had been schooled locally; one-

92. Hammond (1945), p. 18.
93. ibid., p. 25.
94. M.G. Smith (1965c), p. 167.
95. Leyburn (1941), p. 278.

Table 7

Provisions for primary and secondary education in selected Caribbean territories, 1957[6]

	Jamaica	Antigua	Barbados	Grenada	Trinidad	Cuba	Haiti	Puerto Rico
(a) Primary Education								
1. Government expenditure per school age child in shillings	208	155	338	120	241	267	29	418
2. Item 1 adjusted to equalize purchasing power on a century scale	91	59	166	57	106	70	14	151
3. % of 5-14 age group enrolled in any school	?	96	100	89.4	87.2	55	22	79
4. % of 5-14 age group in government schools	66.8	86.1	74.2	89.4	81.4	45.5	?	72.3
5. Attendance in government schools as % of their enrolments	69.5	70.0	78.1	75.6	84.5	?	82.5	82.6
6. Pupils per teacher average	54.5	36.8	32.2	39.2	35.7	31.8	43.0	49.0
7. Pupils per trained teacher	88.0	83.3	69.2	455.0	93.1	?	310.0	81.0
(b) Secondary Education								
1. Enrolment per 1000 pupils	10.9	29.9	38.7	14.9	21.7	23.7	3.4	71.9
2. No. of government scholarships per 100,000 of population	28	20	30	46	52	–	–	640
3. Pupils per teacher	19.6	26.6	25.0	21.4	22.2	17.2	22.0	36.5
4. Pupils per graduate teacher	41.3	129.0	95.8	75.0	49.4	–	–	136.7
5. Passes in School Certificate exams per 100,000 inhabitants	61	93	223	85.9	203	–	–	803
6. Students at higher institutions per 100,000 inhabitants	98	52	103	–	154	304	–	829
7. Scholarships to higher institutions per 100,000 inhabitants	9	5	10	2	6	–	–	?

96. *The Economist* Intelligence Unit (1959), Tables 24-32, pp. 83-96.

fourth of all persons in the three highest strata of the local society had been educated in Britain; and half as many again in Barbados.[97]

Comparative data for 1957 are tabulated above to illustrate the measure of change and continuity in British territories since 1943-6, and the extraordinary variation in educational provisions characteristic of the region (Table 7).

As decolonization proceeded, some British Caribbean governments initiated plans for educational expansion in 1956-7, and by 1960, though uneven and often ambiguous, there were evident signs of change. In 1960 the proportion of all school children who were enrolled in secondary schools ranged from 5.5 percent in the Windwards (Grenada, St. Lucia, St. Vincent and Dominica) to 21.4 percent in Barbados.[98] However, at that date less than 1 percent of the people over 25 years of age in any British Caribbean territory had attended universities.

In 1957 the Jamaican government initiated a programme of scholarships to secondary schools and undertook to meet half or all the educational and subsistence costs of children whose performances in an annual Common Entrance examination exceeded certain minima. Despite advice the government refused to restrict its awards to the children of poorer parents, ostensibly to avoid discrimination in reverse. The examinations were thus open to all children aged between 9-10 and between 12-14; in consequence those children who failed to secure scholarships or bursaries in their first attempt had a second chance to do so, while youngsters who received bursaries on their first attempt could seek scholarships by retaking the examination.

Between 1957 and 1961 the numbers that took these examinations increased from 15,000 to 18,000 per annum while the proportion who qualified for scholarships and bursaries declined from 15 percent in 1957 to 10 percent in 1961. Entrants were drawn from high (secondary) schools, from fee-paying private schools, and from government primary schools, in differing proportions and with differing results. These three types of school differed widely in the amount of government support they received, and thus in the quality of their educational arrangements and instruction. They differed also, not surprisingly, in the socio-economic classes for which they catered. The distribution of entrants and awards among pupils drawn from schools of differing type in the Common Entrance examination of 1959 is tabulated below to show how this scholarship programme actually worked (Table 8).

Official data indicate that high school entrants are predominantly children of professional, managerial, and clerically occupied parents. Private fee-paying and urban government primary schools cater primarily to the children of skilled and semi-skilled workers respectively. Two-fifths of the children from rural primary schools

97. M.G. Smith (1965a), pp. 219-27.
98. Roberts and Abdullah (1965), p. 145.

Table 8

**Entrants and awards in the Common Entrance examination,
Jamaica, 1959, classified by types of school[99]**

Types of School	Entries	Unit-percentage Awards
Government primary schools	81.1	54.7
Private fee-paying schools	9.5	16.7
Secondary (high) schools	9.4	28.6
Total	100.0	100.0

have skilled or semi-skilled parents, while an equal number are children of cultivators. Slightly over one-half of these scholarships and bursaries went to children whose parents paid income tax and ranked in or above the Jamaican middle-income range.

As we descend this parental scale of occupational status, the ratio of girls among scholarship winners increases steadily, being highest amongst entrants from primary schools. Thus under the scholarship scheme 'social mobility through the primary school system is largely a female affair'.[100] However, since males predominate heavily in Jamaican extra-domestic employment, and especially in its higher occupational levels, in commerce, management, the professions and government service, such sex-selective scholarship recruitment from the predominantly black 'lower class' will have little effect on the current distributions of executive occupational roles among Jamaicans of different racial stock in the immediate future.

In Trinidad the government's plan to build modern secondary schools and to fill them with successful candidates in the Open Annual examinations may actually increase prevailing educational inequalities of Creoles and Indians, given the historic educational disabilities of this Indian population.[101] It is by no means a simple matter to transform historically stable structures of economic and educational inequality that have served to differentiate racial stocks into substantively egalitarian distributions of opportunities. Colonialism systematically employed the unequal distribution of these facilities to sustain and extend the stratification in which whites enjoyed maximal advantages, propertied Creoles of hybrid stocks moderate benefits, and blacks, or East Indians and Amerindians where present, the minimum. Inevitably such regimes presupposed grossly unequal distributions of political power and rights among the differentiated racial categories. Inevitably they also generated correspondingly unequal distributions of occupational opportunities and incomes. The colonial distribution of occupations among racial and ethnic stocks is nicely illustrated by data from the Jamaican census of 1943 (Table 9).

99. Manley (1963), p. 58.
100. ibid., p. 71.
101. Government of Trinidad and Tobago, *Draft Second Five Year Plan, 1964-8*, p. 125.

Table 9

Male wage-earners and unpaid workers by occupation and race,
Jamaica, January 1943[102]

Occupation	Black	Coloured	White	Jews	Chinese	East Indian	Syrian	Other	All
Managers, farm	20	42	44	1	—	—	1	—	108
Managers, factory	11	36	45	6	9	—	—	—	107
Managers, construction	14	18	9	—	—	—	—	—	41
Managers, transport	26	31	25	1	—	1	—	—	84
Total managers	71	127	123	8	9	1	1	—	340
Trade, wholesale	6	27	49	9	21	—	5	—	117
Trade, retail	41	90	33	3	46	6	16	—	235
Total, commercial executive	47	117	82	12	67	6	21	—	352
Finance, managers	2	7	41	—	—	—	—	—	50
Teachers	626	324	49	1	6	5	—	2	1,013
Accountants	34	217	103	7	7	2	0.2	1	373
Other professionals	374	496	283	11	10	2	0.1	11	1,198
All professionals	1,034	1,037	435	19	23	29	3	4	2,584
Civil Service officers	34	118	54	4	—	1	—	—	211
Military officers	2	2	48	2	—	—	—	—	54
Total Public Services	36	120	102	6	—	1	—	—	265
Unskilled manual workers	38,426	4,151	48	2	27	794	2	8	43,458
Total workers	162,332	31,225	2,310	185	1,512	5,404	127	41	203,358
Total executives	1,190	1,408	883	45	99	37	25	4	3,691
% of all executives	32.2	38.2	24.0	1.2	2.7	1.0	0.6	0.1	100.0
Executives as % of all workers									

Table 10

**Percent distribution of wages earned in Jamaica
week ending 12 December 1942, by race of worker and amount[103]**

Wages in Shillings	Black	Coloured	White	Jews	Chinese	East Indian	Syrian	Other	All
0-10/-	58.5	32.1	1.8	1.7	6.1	49.7	2.5	24.0	52.4
10-20/-	26.35	21.7	16.2	11.1	13.3	35.1	9.2	13.3	25.6
20-40/-	10.65	19.8	9.4	15.1	41.0	10.9	18.5	24.0	12.3
40-60/-	2.94	11.2	11.1	14.1	24.0	2.3	27.6	22.0	4.7
60-80/-	0.94	6.3	10.2	15.1	7.3	1.1	13.5	6.9	2.1
80-100/-	0.33	3.2	8.9	9.4	3.4	0.4	11.0	2.0	1.0
100-150/-	0.23	3.8	15.1	13.8	3.8	0.3	11.6	2.0	1.1
150-200/-	0.04	1.1	9.2	9.4	0.4	0.1	3.7	—	0.4
200-300/-	0.02	0.7	10.0	6.9	0.4	0.05	1.8	2.0	0.3
300-400/-	—	0.1	3.8	1.7	—	0.03	0.6	2.0	0.1
400/- +	—	—	3.3	1.7	0.3	0.02	—	—	—
Total	100.0	100.0	100.0	100.0	100.0	100.0	100.0	100.0	100.0
Total workers	151,101	33,630	2,990	233	1,526	4,770	163	45	194,458

103. ibid., Table 125, pp. 220-1.

The West Indian census of 1946, though less detailed and informative, indicates that similar occupational distributions prevailed throughout all stratified bi-racial societies of moderate size in the British Caribbean at that time. Moreover, since distributions of employment opportunities and incomes correspond closely with the allocations of occupations, the highest ratios of unemployed and underpaid workers fell among East Indians and blacks, the lowest ratios among the whites and coloured folk. The distribution of wages among Jamaican workers classified by race and ethnicity at the end of 1942 illustrates this pattern in detail (Table 10).

To indicate recent changes, the wage distribution of employed males in Jamaica during April 1960 may be compared with that of December 1942 (Table 11).

TABLE 11

Male wage-earners in Jamacia, 1960, classified by weekly income in shillings[104]

Weekly Income /-	Number of Workers	Percent
-20/-	50,384	23.0
20-40/-	53,162	24.2
40-80/-	50,898	23.2
80-200/-	40,480	18.5
200-400/-	11,508	5.3
400-800/-	4,006	1.8
800/- +	1,045	0.5
Income not stated	7,668	3.5
Total	219,171	100.0

Although the Jamaican census of 1960 does not indicate the distribution of wage incomes among workers of differing racial categories, clearly the bulk of the most poorly paid workers and unemployed were black, while the majority of those receiving high incomes were white. In 1960, Jamaican officials estimated that some 15 percent of the labour force were unemployed.[105]

To compare these Jamaican wage distributions of 1942 and 1960, we must take note of the currency devaluation in 1951 and the subsequent steady decline in the purchasing power of money. In cash terms the average per capita annual income of Jamaica had risen from less than £50 in 1943 to over £110 in 1960; but this rise is largely offset by the fall in the value of the pound from $5 (US) to $2.80 (US) during this period. Money values accordingly overstate the growth rate of the Jamaican economy during this period; and perhaps we may compare the wage distribution of 1942 and 1960

104. Francis (no date), ch. 9, p. 19, Table 9.6.
105. ibid., pp. 7-19; Government of Jamaica, *Five-Year Independence Plan, 1963-8,* pp. 32-5.

more realistically by doubling earlier money values to adjust the real values exchanged as expressed in purchasing power. While 80 percent of the Jamaican wage-earners of both sexes received less than 40 shillings a week in 1943, in 1960 70 percent of employed males received less than 80 shillings ($11.20 US) per week, and another 18.5 percent between 80 shillings and 200 shillings weekly. By comparison with the data of 1942 which include all workers of both sexes, those of 1960 are also relatively inflated by the exclusion of female workers whose wage rates are on average lower than those of men. However, this comparison indicates that changes in the distribution of real incomes among the Jamaican workers of differing racial stock during this period were limited indeed.

In April, 1960, the character and stability of income distributions in Jamaica became the focus of a widespread controversy, following the calculation of E. P. G. Seaga, who later became Minister of Finance and Development that together with their household dependents, all who receive incomes above £300 per annum, or 120 shillings per week ($16.80), and paid income tax, represented only 7 percent of the population and 15 percent of the electorate. In the ensuing debate alternative calculations were presented to show that wage incomes had increased significantly in Jamaica since 1954, but this issue remained to influence the referendum and elections of 1961 and 1962 which overthrew the government that had taken office in 1954.[106] Since 1960, data from a random sample of households, budgeted for incomes and expenditures in 1958, have shown that 20 percent of Jamaica's households then received less that £50 per annum (20 shillings per week) while another 20 percent received between £50 and £99 per annum, and an equal ratio received incomes exceeding £300 per annum or 120 shillings a week, many of whom apparently escaped income tax. Of the island's households in 1958, 10 percent received 43.5 percent of the total income, while the lowest 70 percent received 27.3 percent. By comparison with other countries for which data on income distributions were then available, this Jamaican pattern appeared exceptionally unequal. 'Income accruing to the lowest 60 percent of recipient units [in Jamaica] is among the lowest recorded — 19 per cent . . . The percentage of incomes received by the 15 percent of units next to the top is higher than in all the countries listed.'[107]

In 1954, a survey of income distribution in Trinidad revealed that while 73.6 percent of the population, who received incomes of less than £250 per annum (100 shillings per week) shared 38.4 percent of the total income, the wealthiest 8.2 percent received 36.7 percent of all incomes between them. In 1956 a second survey reported that 71 percent of Trinidad wage workers received less than £250 per

106. G.A. Brown (1961), in Cumper (1961), pp. 12-22; *The West Indian Economist* (1961), pp. 4-7.
107. Ahiram (1964), p. 343.

annum, thereby indicating limited change.[108] When the Jamaican
and Trinidadian data for 1958 were compared, the poorest 60
percent of the Trinidad population received 27.1 percent of the
aggregate income while the top 10 percent received one-third.[109]
Evidently there was little change in Trinidad income distribution
between 1954 and 1958. By contrast, in Puerto Rico only 21 percent
of the workers received less than 72 shillings ($10.90) a week or
£186 per annum in 1967. Another 27 percent then received between
72 shillings and 144 shillings per week; while over half the labour
force received above 144 shillings ($20) weekly or £400 per annum.
While it appears that in Puerto Rico, 'distribution of taxable income
has become more equal during the period' (1955-67),[110] data
from Jamaica and Trinidad indicate little change. This implies that
despite increases in absolute value, the patterns of income distribution described for Jamaica in the 1943 census persist substantially to
the present as part of the persisting social order and racial
stratification inherited from the colonial period. Other indices of
such structural persistence which are reported above include distributions of land and educational opportunities even under the scholarship scheme of 1957.

On Martinique in 1938, whites controlled 85 percent of the export
trade. There, while over 1000 families, all of whom were white,
enjoyed annual incomes in excess of 200,000 francs, between 150,000
and 170,000 agricultural and industrial workers received less than
10,000 francs a year. 'Selon une estimation remontant à 1949 aux neuf
dixièmes de la population des Antilles françaises reviendrait la
possession d'un quart seulement des étendues globales, et, à la
Martinique moins de 5 pour cent des exploitations occuperaient les
deux tiers des terres.'[111] In 1955, after a period of inflation, an
economic survey estimated that 56 percent of the population on
Martinique and 59 percent in Guadeloupe had disposable incomes of
less than AF 350,000 ($700 US) per annum, though the total
disposable income of each island at that date exceeded AF 25 billion
($50 million US) per annum. In 1952, shop-girls, washer-women and
domestic servants in Martinique received AF 5,000 to 6,000 per
month ($10-12 US).[112] Recent quantitative data on the racial
composition of these two societies are hard to find, and data on the
differential distributions of social assets among the racial stocks even
more so. In 1961, Martinique contained 292,000 persons and
Guadeloupe 283,000. In both islands the bulk of the poor are of
Negroid and Indian stock, while the wealthy consist of Creole *békés*,
metropolitan Frenchmen, and the coloured elite.

108. *The Economist* Intelligence Unit (1959), pp. 43-9.
109. Ahiram (1966), p. 106.
110. F.M. Andic (1963), p. 75.
111. Leiris (1955), p. 33.
112. ibid., p. 45; F.M. and S. Andic (1966), in Mathews et al. (1966), p. 105.

9.

To illustrate some aspects of the racial stratification in a bi-racial Caribbean society of moderate complexity and size, I cite data gathered in 1952-3 on a sample of 403 prominent members of the colonial elite in Grenada. The status scores of those 403 individuals were determined from their individual rankings by nineteen local judges, as related above. Of the 403, I secured phenotypical classifications for 364, and genotypical values for 171 men from genealogical data on their family lines. These phenotypes and genotypes were reduced to colour scales that ranged from 0.2 for pure whites to 1.00 for pure blacks on either scale. Of these 376 prominent Grenadians whose phenotypes were known 57 (15 percent) were black, 94 (25 percent) were dark, 101 (26 percent) were mulatto, 85 (22.2 percent) were light-coloured, and 39 (11.1 percent) were white. On the status scale, these 39 whites had a mean score of 0.277, while the 85 light-coloured elite averaged 0.43, the mulattoes 0.52, the dark brown 0.7, and the blacks 0.752. On this scale, 'peasants' or non-elite ranked below 0.835.[113] Differences of personal status correlated closely with differences of phenotype − r being 0.682 with a probability 0.001. For those 171 males whose genotypes were known, correlations of individual status and genotype were even closer − r being 0.734 with the probability of 0.001.[114] Structural analysis identified four social strata within this elite, the three superior strata consisting of phenotypically similar families that intermarried more or less exclusively.[115] Except for immigrants of similar phenotype, culture, economic and social attributes and interests, these kin-bound social strata were virtually closed to penetration by mobile individuals from below.[116] All members of the higher strata, who were locally described as 'the planter class', although less than half were planters, had been educated abroad, as their fathers had been before and their children after them.[117] Those data described a series of highly impervious elite strata distinguished by mutual endogamy and differences of race, colour and social status.

Of 376 phenotypically classified sample members, I collected details of taxable incomes in 1952 from the Grenadian Income Tax Department for 230, and also for 9 Indians and 1 Chinese whose status scores were known. In Table 12, these data are presented for taxpayers classified by phenotypical score, so as to exhibit the numbers, mean status, and taxable incomes of these different colour categories.

113. M.G. Smith (1965a), pp. 158-63.
114. ibid., pp. 164-8.
115. ibid., pp. 168-204.
116. ibid., pp. 205-17.
117. ibid., pp. 217-27.

Table 12

**Distribution of taxable incomes and social status
by phenotype among Grenadian elite, 1953**

Phenotype	Number	Mean status score	Total tax-payers	Mean status of taxpayers	Total taxable income $BWI	Mean taxable income $BWI	Taxpayers as % of category
1.00	57	0.752	25	0.70	78,298	3,130	43
0.9	5	0.73	3	0.70	13,997	4,666	60
0.8	66	0.697	30	0.65	78,570	2,619	46
0.7	23	0.574	15	0.51	102,899	6,850	62
0.6	101	0.521	65	0.48	241,474	3,712	64
0.5	33	0.436	27	0.41	128,714	4,753	81
0.4	35	0.427	26	0.41	100,208	3,920	77
0.3	17	0.423	13	0.41	84,022	6,452	76
0.2	39	0.277	26	0.26	189,511	7,252	66
Creole sub-total	376	0.542	230	0.49	1,058,593	4,600	61
East Indians	—	—	9	0.62	72,819	8,091	—
Chinese	—	—	1	—	3,174	—	—
Total taxpayers —		—	240	0.494	1,134,586	4,720	—

In 1952 the Gross Domestic Product of Grenada was estimated as $15,000,000 (BWI) or $7,300,000 US. That year 2,348 individuals or rather less than 5 percent of the population were assessed for tax on incomes totalling $4,948,000 (BWI), or one-third of the GDP; but while these 2,348 taxpayers had a mean taxable income of $2,100 (BWI), the 240 taxpayers in the classified sample averaged $4,720, receiving together 7.5 percent of the GDP. None the less, this sample contained four individuals whose taxable incomes fell below $100 (BWI), and another 40 with taxable incomes below $1,000 distributed at all points of the phenotypical scale. While differences of phenotype and status were closely associated, the correlation between individual status and taxable income was only 0.31. None the less, as the table illustrates, there is a strong tendency for incomes and status to rise as pigment lightens across the phenotypical range of this elite. However, though whites and near-whites enjoy the highest mean incomes of Creole taxpayers, both receive less on average than the Indian taxpayers included, whose mean status is only a cut above that of Negro taxpayers.

Classified by phenotype and by the principal sources of their taxable incomes, these 240 taxpayers were distributed as in Table 13.

Of these elite taxpayers, one-half derived their income wholly or primarily from wage employment, and another fifteen from pensions as retired public servants. Phenotypical distribution of these employees and pensioners illustrates the expectable dependence of darker elite on wage work, particularly for the government. The various sources from which taxpayers of differing phenotype derived their incomes nicely illustrates traditional distributions of land, professions, and executive roles in commerce, government, or private enterprises by racial status in Grenada. Mulattoes predominate in commerce and private employment. For East Indians, land ownership provides the principal means of economic and social mobility. For dark or black Grenadians, so does government service. Given the prevailing distributions of land, literacy, occupations, income, and social status among racial stocks in Grenada at this time, the violent protests of Grenadian Negroes against the social order in 1951-3 are not surprising.

10.

As indicated above, we cannot validly extrapolate from distributions of social advantage within the Creole populations of bi-racial societies to distributions current among the non-Creole segments of multi-racial Caribbean units. However, we shall not find quantitative data of comparable specificity on the distribution of these assets within the non-Creole population segments. Such statistical gaps are themselves illuminating; but however imperfect or casual, such information as we presently have illustrates the division between Creole and non-Creole segments of multi-racial societies.

Table 13

Elite taxpayers in Grenada, 1953, classified by
phenotype and major occupational source of taxable income

Phenotype	Private employment	Government employment	Government pensions	Professions	Planters	Investors	Traders	Total
1.00	2	11	2	2	3	1	4	25
0.9	–	1	–	–	–	–	2	3
0.8	6	12	4	2	3	–	3	30
0.7	4	4	–	1	5	–	1	15
0.6	21	12	4	4	11	–	13	65
0.5	11	3	1	2	3	–	7	27
0.4	12	2	2	2	4	1	3	26
0.3	7	–	1	2	3	–	–	13
0.2	7	–	1	4	11	2	1	26
Creole sub-total	70	45	15	19	43	4	34	230
East Indians	–	1	–	–	7	–	1	9
Chinese	–	1	–	–	–	–	–	1
Total	70	47	15	19	50	4	35	240

In Surinam, the concentration ratio of 0.62 for the distribution of incomes indicates extensive inequalities, despite considerable tax evasion. In 1956, of those who paid income tax, 2.3 percent received 13 percent of all incomes taxed, while 34.2 percent received 16.3 percent of the total.[118] We have no indication of the distribution of these incomes among peoples of different racial stock.

In 1959, the distribution of Surinam farmland was equally concentrated. Of all holdings, 20 percent occupied 1.7 percent of the total area, while units exceeding 50 acres in size, although only 0.85 percent of all holdings, occupied 50 percent of the area in farms. 'Thirty enterprises alone accounted for 33,654 hectares or 32 percent of the acreage.'[119] Indians, who then formed 35 percent of the population, owned 50 percent of the farms and 45 percent of the land, while Indonesians, totalling 16 percent of the population, owned 38 percent of the farms but only 10 percent of the land. 'Creoles do not seem to play an important part in agriculture, though they do possess some of the larger plantations, which, however, are not being operated. The remaining ethnic groups possess 1 percent of the farms but 31 percent of the land.'[120] Presumably resident or absentee Dutchmen were prominent among these 'remaining ethnic groups'.

In British Guiana, the Bookers Company, a British corporation, owned 13 of 21 sugar estates that occupied some 155,000 acres of irrigated land. A second British syndicate had four estates, while another of less than 1,000 acres was independently owned.[121] Sugar accounts for half of the country's exports, and 45 percent of the government's revenue; bauxite for one-fifth of its exports and 10 percent of government revenues. Both industries are owned and directed by overseas whites in Britain or America. Rice, which between 1957 and 1960 provided 10 percent of the colony's exports, was cultivated by East Indians on 27,000 holdings that occupied 137,000 acres.[122] Only 1 percent of these rice farms exceeded 32 acres in size. Like rice, sugar cultivation, the major colonial industry, depended on Indian labour. Indians were 89 percent and 99 percent of all households and field workers on two sugar estates studied in 1956-7; and 73 percent and 92 percent of all workers on another two estates studies in 1960-1.[123]

The distribution of voting rights in 1915 among Guyanese of different racial stocks has been cited above. In 1940, of 34 government departments, 27 (79.4 percent) had British heads, 5 (14.7 percent) had Creole heads, and 2 (5.9 percent) Portuguese. East Indians, already more than 40 percent of the colonial

118. F.M. and S. Andic (1966), in Mathews et al. (1966), pp. 48-9.
119. ibid., p. 49.
120. ibid., p. 49, n. 7; Speckman (1963).
121. R.T. Smith (1962), pp. 60-1; Despres (1967), pp. 138 ff.
122. R.T. Smith (1962), p. 63; O'Loughlin (1958).
123. Jayawardena (1963), pp. 5-7.

population, occupied no departmental headship. At that date, of 629 pensionable civil servants in Guyana, 66 percent were Creole (African), 14.1 percent were British, 6.4 percent Portuguese, and 10 percent East Indian. By 1960 the colonial government included 57 departments of which 22 (38.6 percent) had British heads, 26 (45.6 percent) had Creole heads, and 6 (10.5 percent) Indians. Of 808 pensionable staff on strength in 1960, 12 percent were British, 16 percent Indian, and 58 percent Creole 'Africans', the remainder being Chinese or Portuguese.[124]

In 1931, of 6,202 'professionals' in Guyana, 746 (12 percent) were East Indian. At that date, of 1,397 teachers in Guyana, 7.2 percent were East Indian. In 1946 when Indians were 43.5 percent of the population, it is estimated that they held only 17.5 percent of the professional and senior civil service positions in the country.[125] In 1946, 86 percent of the illiterates in Guyana were East Indians, while 6.6 percent were Creoles. Until compulsory education was extended to East Indians in 1933, only 18.7 percent of the East Indian children aged between 5 and 15 attended primary schools; and even in 1960-1, a survey of five villages revealed that while East Indians at this date averaged 3.45 years in school, Creoles averaged 5.84.[126]

However inadequate, these data indicate that whereas East Indians remained marginal to the urban Creole society until 1946, they have increasingly oriented towards it since then. Some correlates and consequences of these reorientations are reported below.

Despite considerable concern with Creole-Indian relations, and an increased output of social and economic statistics, census materials, and other official data, quantitative information on the contemporary distributions of land, income, educational opportunities, occupational roles; and civil service positions among East Indians and Creoles in Trinidad are hard to find. Neither the 1946 census nor that of 1960 specifies these distributions clearly, except those cited above for literacy and large land-holdings. However, in 1931, of 42,000 East Indian males in Trinidad, 112 were employed in the government service, 10 in law, 8 in medicine, 5 in the police, 181 as Hindu or Moslem priests, 368 as teachers, 122 as merchants, and 1 as an engineer. By 1945, when 137 East Indians were either practising professions or training to do so, 53 in law and 48 in medicine and dentistry, they were still 'very poorly represented . . . in civil service jobs'.[127] In Trinidad, as in British Guiana, East Indians accordingly sought security in the acquisition of land; and by 1950 they were estimated to own over 100,000 acres.[128] None the less, they still formed the bulk of the rural proletariat. On one sugar estate, East Indians were 93.5 percent of the labour force and 83 percent of

124. Despres (1967), p. 163.
125. ibid., p. 130.
126. ibid., p. 129
127. A. and J. Niehoff (1960), pp. 42, 51-2.
128. Rubin (1962), p. 443, n. 35.

those who grew canes for sale to the local factory.[129] In 1946, 92.4 percent of East Indians in Trinidad lived in rural areas; but by 1960 one-fourth of the people in San Fernando, the second largest city on the island, were East Indians.[130]

Scholars have debated the scope and intensity of Indian 'Creolization' in Guyana and Trinidad in terms of Indian assimilation or exclusiveness.[131] Cultural transfers between Creoles and Indians have failed to erode segmental boundaries. East Indians restrict miscegenation with Negroes and coloured folk.[132] The two populations mate endogamously under strikingly different arrangements.[133] According to one observer, 'probably the greatest source of friction between the two groups stems from economic competition'.[134] However, criteria of individual and collective stratification rank high in the segmental disassociation and contraposition of Creoles and Indians. Creole conceptions of contemporary and desirable forms of stratification in Trinidad, as presented by Braithwaite,[135] a Trinidadian Creole, differ radically from those that Indians espouse. While Creole society elaborates differences of skin colour as indices and conditions of social status,[136] 'skin colour plays almost no part in the East Indian group as internal stratification. The primary determinant of status among rural Indians is caste membership.'[137]

The differences and incompatibilities of these East Indian and Creole status systems are summarized neatly by the Niehoffs:

The [Creole] status system can be reviewed as primarily based on colour with whites at the top and the Negroes at the bottom as is done by Braithwaite. This is logical from a Negro point of view, but it does de-emphasize the importance of other ethnic groups, particularly the Indians. From the Indian point of view, social differences are more often categorized in terms of whites, Chinese, Indians, and Negroes. The difference between coloured and Negroes, which figures importantly in Braithwaite's study, is comparatively unimportant to Indians. Pure Negroes, Negro-whites, and Negro-Chinese admixtures are all still Negroes to Indians . . . The middle class of 'coloured' (Negro-white) admixtures (Braithwaite: 1953, 92-120) has no clear-cut counterpart among Indians. Indians who become wealthy and educated do not tend to merge into this 'coloured' middle class, nor do they tend to establish such a class on their own. There are status differences among Indians, based primarily on economic position and leadership roles, but these differences can be viewed as a continuum more logically than as a system of classes. From the Indian point of view the most

129. A. and J. Niehoff (1960), p. 29.
130. Clarke (1967), in Schwartz (1967), p. 166.
131. Crowley (1957), pp. 817-24; (1960); Klass (1960); Braithwaite (1960); Skinner (1960); all in Rubin (1960).
132. A. and J. Niehoff (1960), p. 67.
133. Roberts and Braithwaite (1963).
134. A. and J. Niehoff (1960), p. 67.
135. Braithwaite (1953, 1954, 1960).
136. Braithwaite (1953), pp. 92-120.
137. Klass (1960), in Rubin (1960), p. 858.

clear-cut line of demarcation is that between whites and non-whites, and Indians and Negroes.[138]

A survey of racial attitudes among students at secondary schools in Trinidad also reports that 'in connection with their definition of the change in colour-class structure . . . the white student tends to regard all Creoles as Negroes, and does not make refined colour distinctions.'[139] Thus the central significance of colour differences rather than race is restricted to those elite hybrids who on these grounds claim 'ascendancy . . . concomitant with the withdrawal of the British'.[140] However, since these hybrids represent only 17 percent of the population, their sectional view of the social order and its stratification is hardly representative and merely serves as an ideological model to legitimize their minority rule. The divergence of this coloured status model from the views of whites and Indians indicates a source of profound disagreement between racial blocs in Trinidad about the nature of the society that their combination constitutes and their respective places within it. Several scholars have recently remarked this source of dissension in contemporary Trinidad, particularly as regards the contraposition of East Indians and Creoles.[141] The situation in Guyana is essentially similar but more advanced.

Critical emphases on colour as a basic condition of status are general among the hybrid elites of Creole societies. In bi-racial Grenada,

the hierarchy of status tends to correspond with the hierarchies of colour, power and wealth; but while the positions of whites and blacks in these overlapping hierarchies were well defined, that of the browns was far from clear. These conditions may explain why browns avoid those categorical concepts of race that whites and blacks employ, insisting instead on the relative scale of colour . . . The more problematic the significance of these colour differences, the greater the stress laid upon them.[142]

11.

As far as they go, these data on the distributions of social resources and values among racially distinct stocks of Caribbean societies identify two historic patterns of social organization that distinguish bi-racial and multi-racial populations. In bi-racial units there is a stratification that subordinates Negroes and coloured folk to a white minority whose forbears initially owned their ancestors as slaves and monopolized rights to land and political organization. In some of these bi-racial units coloured elites have now succeeded

138. A. and J. Niehoff (1960), p. 62.
139. Rubin (1962), p. 445.
140. ibid., p. 444.
141. G. Lewis (1962); Ryan (1966); Klass (1960); Rubin (1962).
142. M.G. Smith (1965a), pp. 158-9.

these white minorities as dominant strata, sometimes by inheritance from the old plantocracy, in other cases by appropriating bureaucratic and political positions. In Haiti, 160 years of independence have witnessed a continuous struggle for domination between the small but powerful hybrid elite and a succession of personalistic black leaders of the disorganized majority. In yet other bi-racial units such as Carriacou, St. Maarten, Saba, or the Cayman Islands, where the means and rewards of racial domination have no place, Negroes and whites live separately or interspersed, and mate endogamously or symmetrically without any evident stratification of racial stocks or differential distributions of social advantage.

In such multi-racial societies as Surinam, British Honduras, Trinidad, and Guyana, besides the Creole segment of Negro and coloured people socialized by historic domination to Europeans, there are also segments of Amerindians, Black Caribs, Bush Negroes, Indonesians, East Indians, and in British Honduras, the Spanish-mestizos, all of whom remained throughout colonialism aloof from the Creole politico-economic arena under various conditions. The processes of decolonization have affected these multi-racial units in differing ways; but nowhere have they promoted the dissolution of segmental boundaries or the assimilation of racial stocks. In Surinam, Javanese, Creoles, and Indians currently collaborate to govern the country by sharing political power on the basis of their numbers; but this political equivalence has reinforced segmental boundaries while inhibiting their stratification. As the Indian population of Surinam increases relative to that of other groups, this accommodation will become increasingly unstable. Already some Indian leaders in Surinam are seeking its amalgamation with Guyana where Indians are now the numerical majority, while Creole leaders seek to remove those constitutional restraints on local government that derive from the country's participation in the Kingdom of the Netherlands.[143] Likewise in British Honduras, Guatemalan territorial claims threaten the current Creole dominance, and may be expected to elicit the support of the large Spanish-mestizo bloc. Thus far, however, crises and confrontations between these segments have been avoided. In Trinidad and British Guiana, by contrast, decolonization has converted the traditional disassociation of Creoles and Indians into explicit contrapositions and struggles for segmental dominance. Both segments are acutely aware of the material and ideological issues at stake in their current struggles.

When universal suffrage was introduced to British Guiana in April, 1953, East Indians and Creoles combined to form a nationalist movement that sought to remove British control. Six months later the British government repealed the Colonial Constitution and placed Guyana under the direct administration of the Crown for nearly four years. During this interval, the popular movement split into two

143. Mathews (1966).

racial blocs of Creole-Africans and East Indians, each organized in a political party under leaders of appropriate race.[144] Since elective government resumed in August, 1957, racial alignments have dominated the Guyanese votes. In the election of 1961, the party led by Dr. Jagan, an Indian, polled 46.7 percent of all votes cast, while that led by Mr. Burnham, an Afro-Guyanese (Creole), polled 44.7 percent of the votes. 'These percentages are almost identical with the ratios of Indians and Africans in the population when the coloured are counted with the Africans. It would seem that very few voters crossed racial lines in the 1961 election.'[145] In 1962, the Creoles and Portuguese of Georgetown, Guyana's capital, directed racial violence against East Indian administration and residents and burnt down much of the city. In 1963, there were prolonged strikes against Dr. Jagan's government. In 1964, 'East Indian-Negro violence swept through the country. Before the proclamation of a state of emergency in July, 1964, over 170 persons had been killed in the racial conflict.'[146]

Despite these upheavals, the British government proceeded to decolonize, and conceded Afro-Guyanese demands for proportional representation in place of the previous single-member districts and simple majority rule. This change encouraged the Portuguese leader, Mr. P. D'Aguiar, to establish a third party based on the Portuguese and their affiliates in Georgetown. In the pre-independence election of 1964, Dr. Jagan's party, backed by Indians, received 45.8 percent of the total vote and 24 seats in the legislature; Mr. Burnham's party, backed by Creoles, received 40.5 percent of the votes and 22 legislative seats; the party led by D'Aguiar received 12.4 percent of the votes and 7 seats. The Creoles and the Portuguese then formed a coalition under Burnham's leadership to exclude Jagan's party from the government which led Guyana to independence in May, 1966. Late in 1967 it was officially announced that East Indians outnumbered Creoles by 54,000, and had achieved a clear majority of the country's population. The Premier, Mr. Burnham, duly appealed to West Indian Creoles resident in Britain to immigrate to Guyana at his government's expense;[147] thus far, his invitation has had few takers.

These Guyanese developments illustrate how decolonization has generated segmental struggles for domination between East Indians and Creoles and has encouraged resident whites to organize themselves separately for the protection and pursuit of their own interests. As in Surinam, so in Guyana, Amerindians remain outside the political arena.

144. Despres (1967); R.T. Smith (1962), pp. 163-80; Ayearst (1960), pp. 114-28; Moskos (1967), pp. 19-20.
145. Despres (1967), p. 8; see also Tables 20 and 21, pp. 172-3.
146. Moskos (1967), p. 21.
147. *Caribbean Monthly Bulletin*, 4, no. 11, p. 3; 5, no. 1, p. 2.

In Trinidad, where East Indians still number less than 40 percent of the population, although unable to frustrate Creole support for the West Indian Federation, which began in 1957 and dissolved in 1962, they were able to secure effective restrictions on further Creole immigration to Trinidad. In Guyana, then under the government of Dr. Jagan, the Indian majority opposed its entry into the West Indian Federation, since this would reduce their local dominance.

By 1960, Trinidad had a bicameral legislature, ministerial government under a Premier and cabinet, and two mass parties based on its Creole and East Indian segments respectively, each led by men of appropriate race, Dr. Eric Williams, the Creole Premier, and Dr. Rudranath Capildeo, an East Indian. Following their defeat in the 1961 elections, the East Indians were represented by four members in the Island senate, although the East Indians then formed 36.5 percent of the population. Of 23 senators nominated by the party leaders and the Governor, a Trinidadian Chinese, 7 were white or coloured, although together these categories accounted for only 18.2 percent of the population. 'Significantly under-represented, although by no means absent, are the two largest groups of the general population – Negro and East Indian.'[148] The Creole Premier, Dr. Eric Williams, none the less justified the unrepresentative racial composition of this nominated upper chamber as evidence 'that Trinidad is an open society with equality of opportunity'.[149]

Although 'the so-called racial politics [of Trinidad] may . . . actually be seen as socio-cultural politics',[150] these cultural oppositions have deep foundations in antecedent social and biological exclusions. For these reasons

East Indian national consciousness and East Indian population increase seem latent threats to the Creole elites; on the other hand the ascendancy of Creole elites, concomitant with the withdrawal of the British, poses a latent status threat to the East Indian upper-class and mobile elite. From their class vantage points Creole elites view East Indian traits in terms of socially undesirable and politically threatening exclusiveness.[151] . . . The East Indian tends to think in terms of the community because it is an East Indian community, the Negro in terms of the nation because he conceives it as a Negro nation.[152]

Thus recent development in the segmented multi-racial societies of Surinam, Guyana, and Trinidad substantiate the thesis that the alignments of racial stocks are regulated by political relations that express the conditions and distributions of collective power.

The history of slavery, indenture, and colonialism in these

148. Spackmann (1967), p. 82.
149. ibid., p. 85; see also p. 78.
150. Rubin (1962), p. 453.
151. ibid., p. 444.
152. ibid., p. 454.

countries illustrates white supremacy, which itself presumed and expressed the political predominance of different colonizing nations in different territories. That this social supremacy was restricted by political factors and reserved for nationals of the colonizing power is evident from the low status accorded immigrant Portuguese, Jews, and Syrians in these colonies, in this century as well as the last. In Guyana, on completing their indentures the Portuguese 'tended to move away as soon as possible and go into shopkeeping. So long as they remained small shopkeepers, they did not enjoy high prestige . . . Despite their colour . . . they tended to be despised, even by the Negroes . . . The identification of "Portugee" tended to become a fixed derogatory description.'[153] Their anomalous position as racial whites of relatively low status which parallels that of 'poor white' peasants in Barbados, the Dutch Windwards, Caymans, Jamaica, Grenada, St. Vincent, and elsewhere, demonstrates that whiteness in itself is insufficient to ensure high status in racially mixed Caribbean societies. While powerless whites have low status, dominant whites, hybrids, Negroes, or Indians enjoy the status that corresponds with their resources and power. In Trinidad the recently immigrant Jews and Syrians compete as peddlers, moneylenders and petty tradesmen. The coloured population does not care to distinguish between them. Both categories are disesteemed; and local Portuguese fare little better.[154] By contrast, in Jamaica, Jews and Syrians are sharply distinguished and rank high by virtue of the resources and power at their disposal.[155]

For bi-racial Caribbean societies, whether of Hispanic or north-west European derivation, the historical evidence demonstrates this political determination of racial stratification in unambiguous detail. Where prevailing stratification was reversed by revolt, as in Haiti, Guadeloupe, or Grenada in 1795, the conditions and processes of these reverses were unmistakably political; but so too were those collective withdrawals of African slaves, who evaded the racial stratification of colonial societies, and constituted autonomous communities of their own, in Dominica, St. Vincent, Jamaica, and Surinam, sometimes in alliance with Amerindians, sometimes separately. Reimpositions of slavery in Guadeloupe, Grenada, and St. Lucia, during or after the revolutionary decade, also illustrate the critical role of political power in ordering and maintaining these racial stratifications. So do the suppressions of numerous unsuccessful slave revolts that darken the history of these Caribbean plantation colonies from the sixteenth to the nineteenth century. As we have seen, after emancipation white planters maintained the preceding racial stratification by employing their political power to control the ex-slaves, to finance imports of foreign labour, to restrict education and political rights, and to suppress protests against their racial

153. R.T. Smith (1962), p. 45.
154. Braithwaite (1953), pp. 10, 78.
155. Broom (1954, 1960*b*).

oligarchy. Where these adaptations seemed insufficiently secure, imperial governments assumed direct control along with responsibilities for maintaining the racial stratification of these colonies. This era in Caribbean history was terminated by upheavals at the end of the Great Depression; and, following the Second World War, imperial governments introduced numerous modifications as necessary conditions of decolonization.

Having reviewed some consequences of decolonization in segmented multi-racial societies, we may indicate their parallels in stratified bi-racial units by citing data on recent distributions of political roles and attitudes in these units. As always, Jamaican data are the most precise and illuminating for illustrative purposes. Like Trinidad, Jamaica has a bicameral legislature in which the lower house is elected by adult suffrage while the members of the upper house are nominated by the governor and by the leaders of the two major political parties. In 1951, after two elections based on universal suffrage, the elected lower house contained 31 members of whom 28 were phenotypically classified as follows: white or near-white 3; light and medium brown 10; dark brown 12; black 3. Of 15 nominated and official members of the upper house at that date, 13 were white and one each light and dark brown.[156] In 1958, after further elections, under a government led by the opposing political party, the elected house contained 3 whites, 22 coloured, and 7 black members; while the nominated upper house contained 8 whites, 1 black, and 8 coloured members, of whom 5 were light and 3 dark brown. Indians and Chinese were conspicuously absent.[157] Evidently the coloured elite employed its leadership of both Jamaican political parties to restrict the access of blacks, Indians, and Chinese to the local legislature by election and nomination alike, while providing the white and coloured sections with disproportionate representation. It is equally characteristic of Jamaica during this decolonization phase that a sample of 72 'top leaders' in the country included 37 whites (52 percent) — of whom 8 were born abroad and 29 were Creole — 20 mulattoes (28 percent) and 15 others (21 percent) listed as 'dark brown and black'.[158] Such data demonstrate the persistence of colonial racial alignments in modern Jamaica, and indicate the widespread concern of its white and coloured elites to preserve their differential advantages and position in this overwhelmingly Negro country, despite universal suffrage, by managing the political parties, trade unions and government equally. Understandably, throughout 1959 to 1961, the black proletariat in Kingston protested against the persistence of the colonial order of racial stratification despite local self-government. Their protests generated considerable unrest and alarm and helped to discredit the current

156. Broom (1954), p. 125; Bell (1964), p. 83.
157. Bell (1964), p. 83.
158. ibid., Table 10, p. 84.

government and its support for the West Indian Federation.[159]

In 1961, a sample of 2,197 students, drawn from the fifth and sixth forms of 21 secondary schools throughout the island, together with 51 percent of the Jamaican students in the local university campus, was surveyed to determine their attitudes towards equality. Of this sample 2,091 students classified themselves by colour as follows: black 146 (7 percent); white 113 (5.4 percent); coloured 1,647 (78.8 percent). The remaining 185 students (8.8 percent) were self-identified as Chinese and Indians. Of the total sample, only 52.2 percent espoused egalitarian attitudes even at that critical phase of Jamaica's development. These egalitarian attitudes were expectably predominant among the black students (61.6 percent), marginally so among the coloured students (53.1 percent), and least common among whites (42.5 percent).[160] Neither the composition of this sample nor the distribution of political attitudes within it suggest that any major revision of the colonial system of racial stratification will occur by peaceful means in Jamaica for several decades.

Unfortunately these Jamaican correlations of phenotype and political attitude are representative of other British Caribbean societies. In 1961-2 a sample of 111 'top leaders' in Jamaica, Trinidad, British Guiana, Barbados, Grenada, and Dominica were interviewed to elicit their political attitudes. On the basis of interview data, these leaders were classified as 'democrats, authoritarian idealists, cynical parliamentarians, and authoritarians'. Of all the territorial contingents surveyed, the Jamaican leaders had the highest ratio of 'democrats' (39 percent) and the fewest 'authoritarians' (26 percent). If anything, these data suggest that the Jamaican political spectrum was rather more liberal than those of other British Caribbean territories.

Of equal relevance is the phenotypical composition of this leadership sample and the distribution of political orientations by phenotype within it. Of the 111 leaders, 38 were white, 20 light brown, 41 dark brown and black, and 12 'orientals' (Chinese and Indian). Of the 38 whites, 10 percent were identified as 'democrats' and 58 percent as 'authoritarians'. Of the 20 light brown leaders, 25 percent were 'democrats' and 60 percent 'authoritarians'. Of the 41 leaders classified as 'dark brown and black', 34 percent were 'democrats', 24 percent 'authoritarians', 10 percent 'authoritarian idealists', and 32 percent 'cynical parliamentarians'. Of the 12 'oriental' leaders, 8 percent were 'democrats' and 'authoritarian idealists' equally, while 42 percent were 'authoritarians' and 'cynical parliamentarians' equally.[161]

Clearly the historic structures of social inequality by which these racially mixed populations were bound have generated deep and

159. M.G. Smith (1965c), pp. 314-18; M.G. Smith, Augier and Nettleford (1960).
160. Duke (1967), in Bell (1967), pp. 119, 127, 131.
161. Moskos and Bell (1964), pp. 326, 328; see also Moskos (1967).

widespread commitments to inequality and authoritarianism within them, while discrediting parliamentary institutions among those racial stocks whose subordination was effected by these means. 'Il y a, écrit Tocqueville, un préjugé naturel qui porte l'homme à mépriser celui qui a été son inferieur, longtemps encore après qu'il est devenu son égal; à l'inégalité réelle que produit la fortune ou la loi succède toujours une inégalité imaginaire qui a ses racines dans les moeurs.'[162]

12.

It may seem rather trite to conclude from our review of racial stratification in Caribbean societies that race relations and alignments are normally mediated by political action and express differential distributions of collective power. However, others have interpreted these data very differently. According to Dr. Tannenbaum, cultural systems of religion and law may and normally do mediate race relations in stratified societies.[163] However illuminating, in order to apply, this hypothesis presupposes the subordination of one or more racial stocks to some other, and such subordinations assume and express collective dominance by political means.

According to Dr. Eric Williams, the Creole historian and Premier of Trinidad and Tobago, Caribbean race relations have always been determined by the economic interests and goals of dominant 'racial groups', that is, until his party came to power.[164] Data already cited invalidate such simplistic economic determinism and suggest rather that ' "Gaining the power to rule over the other" is the key to the ethno-political conflicts underlying race antagonisms',[165] and also to racial stratification. Retaining this power of rule and the privileges of rule, restraining the autonomy of others, or at least evading their power to rule — these are complementary concerns of equal relevance that mobilize racial collectivities, demarcate their boundaries and memberships, and impose internal solidarity and external contraposition, thus fixating individual identities in closed segments which, irrespective of physical likeness or difference, assume exclusive ethnic characters and racial status. These Caribbean data illustrate the proposition that 'race prejudice exists basically in a sense of group position'.[166] They also specify the political conditions that determine the relative positions and alignments of racial groups in stratified, segmented, and unstratified societies equally.

H. Hoetink has recently argued that specifically 'racial' factors, such as perceived differences between the 'somatic norm images' or idealized phenotypes of the dominant segment and other racial

162. Leiris (1955), pp. 166-7.
163. Tannenbaum (1946, 1957).
164. Williams (1946, no date, 1957).
165. Rubin (1962), p. 446.
166. Blumer (1961), in Masuoka and Valien (1961), p. 216.

stocks, are the independent and exclusive determinants of 'inter-segmentary mobility' and thus of racial stratification in Caribbean societies.[167] According to Hoetink, 'the only factor which does result in socio-racial change, namely biological-cum-social mingling',[168] characterized by 'social equality' and expressed by 'marriage in the sociological sense',[169] is virtually excluded between whites and Negro or coloured folk in non-Hispanic societies by the rigorous commitments of whites from north-western Europe to maintain the purity of their 'somatic norm image'. Unfortunately for this thesis, data cited above indicate that while whites do marry blacks and coloured folk, in certain contexts they refuse to marry other whites.

Hoetink also asserts that in contrast with these 'private relations', 'public relations' between racial stocks can 'have no direct influence on the social stratification'[170] of racially mixed societies; but again unfortunately for his argument, almost every important development in the racial stratification of Caribbean societies, including the restratifications and destratifications of some populations by revolt or flight, has proceeded through collective action in the public domain and not through 'intimate interracial contacts based on social equality'. Contemporary data suggest that future changes will proceed by similar means.

Evidently this theory of racial determinism, like the alternatives already cited, presupposes the establishment and maintenance of political domination by one race over others. Thus it is meaningless to assert that 'the racial factor in any case remains a decisive determinant of the social position of the dominant segment',[171] since 'the dominant segment' owes its social position and identity to the establishment of its political domination. As Blumer remarks:

The dominant racial group is led to define and re-define the subordinate racial group and the relations between them . . . The process of definition occurs obviously through complex interaction and communication between the members of the dominant group . . . Definitions that are forged in the public arena centre, obviously, about matters that are felt to be of major 'importance . . . It is the events seemingly loaded with great collective significance that are the focal points of the public discussion . . . Definition of these events is chiefly responsible for the development of a racial image and of the sense of group position.[172]

These processes are no less decisive in shaping the interracial accommodations of Caribbean societies today than at any earlier period in their histories.

167. Hoetink (1967), pp. 149-51.
168. ibid., p. 48.
169. ibid., pp. 21-3.
170. ibid., p. 23.
171. ibid., p. 103.
172. Blumer (1961), pp. 223, 225.

13.

To expose the systematic order that underlies the diverse and dynamic interracial accommodations reviewed above, we must show that these are neither accidental nor arbitrary products of historical process, but logically necessary consequences of a finite set of structural alternatives that together prescribe the frameworks for all possible types of society, whether racially and ethnically heterogeneous or not. This exposition requires a brief excursus on the forms and alternative bases of societal incorporation and their implicàtions for the continuities and disjunctions of culture and organization in human societies, following which we can show how the entire series of interracial accommodations reviewed above illustrate the necessary effects of these relations.

There are only three alternative sets of conditions by which societies may incorporate individuals or collectivities as members. All societies must either incorporate their members under one of these alternatives exclusively, or by some coherent combination of them. The three alternative modes of societal incorporation may be characterized as uniform or universalistic, equivalent or segmental, and differential.[173]

Under the first alternative, individuals are incorporated uniformly as citizens of a society by direct enrolment on uniform conditions with formally identical status in its public domain, where the unit's regulative institutions and governmental processes are centred. Thus individuals incorporated under this mode will hold identical legal and political rights, restraints and obligations in the society by virtue of their direct, identical and unmediated incorporation into its public domain. In consequence, they must accordingly share those social, educational and economic institutions which are directly relevant or subject to the public domain; and they will normally also share common institutions of kinship, religion and language. None the less, despite its inclusive design and assimilative effects, societies based on the universalistic or uniform incorporation of their members do not proscribe differences of language, kinship and cult among them. This order merely relegates such institutional forms to the private domain of individually optional and legally equivalent practices which entail no formal civic, legal or political inequalities among the citizens.

---

173. For the essential specifications of these alternative modes of incorporation and their relations to alternative modes of pluralism, see L. Kuper and M.G. Smith (1969), pp. 433, 436, 440-8, and Chapter 6 above, pp. 187-9.

Another recent recognition of the salience of incorporation for the comparative analysis of societies, quite distinct from that presented here, is to be found in Cohen and Middleton (1970), especially pp. 1-24. For my conceptions of corporations, their bases, requisites and implications, see especially the essay on political change and other papers reprinted above.

Thus a regime of universalistic incorporation is equally consistent with cultural homogeneity, heterogeneity or pluralism in those institutions that pertain to the private domain of social action. However, it excludes pluralism at the public or corporate level of social organization.

To determine whether a society that formally proclaims the uniform incorporation of all its members on conditions of civic and political equality fulfils these ideals in practice, we need only examine the historic and contemporary distributions of political and civic rights and burdens within the various categories of its population. If such data reveal systematic legal and political inequalities among the population, then whatever the formal ideology proclaims, actual practice demonstrates institutionalized deviations from these norms. Confronted with such differences of substance and form, analysis must seek to isolate the conditions associated with such structural inconsistency as effects of alternative forms of incorporation that substantially obstruct the uniform enrolment of all citizens in the public domain. In such circumstances we can expect to find that the unequally incorporated collectivities of the society may also be differentiated by culture and social organization, and perhaps by language and race also.

Under the second alternative mode, individuals are incorporated as members of a society by virtue of their prior incorporation in one or other of a series of mutually exclusive segments of formally equivalent status that together constitute the society. As these segments are formally co-ordinate, the status, rights and obligations of their members in the public domain of the wider society will be formally equivalent, though mediated by the prerequisite incorporation of these individuals in the collectivities that constitute the unit. Thus this mode of incorporation constitutes autonomous societies as consociations of mutually exclusive segments which may or may not share common culture and forms of social organization. In consequence, individuals incorporated indirectly in such consociations may differ in their immediate rights, privileges and obligations as an expression of institutional differences in the segments to which they belong; but these segments are jurally and politically equivalent divisions of the inclusive society.

The third alternative mode incorporates individuals differentially into a society by prescribing their prior identifications with one or other of a series of closed collectivities which are ordered unequally as superior and inferior by their differential access to the public domain of the inclusive unit. Normally one of these collectivities dominates the others and thus the society, by denying them access to the public domain and thus prescribing their political and legal subordination. If the subjugated population is also divided into two or more exclusive segments, these may be incorporated as equivalents under common conditions of differential incorporation in the wider society. In that event all the incorporated collectivities will exhibit distinctive cultures and social organizations as conditions and consequences of their differing structural positions. Such systematic institutional differences among the corporate collectivities in a society indicate its pervasive pluralism. In the case under discussion, such pluralism has three modes: differential incorporation of collectivities institutes and sustains their structural pluralism by investing one segment with exclusive control of the legal and political institutions of the society; but the mutually exclusive segments incorporated as equivalents by their common disabilities and exclusion from the public domain display social pluralism in those divergences of social organization and situations that generate and sustain their mutual exclusiveness. Moreover, such differences of internal organization and societal situation will also distinguish the 'dominant collectivity from the two subjugated ones. Thus structural pluralism subsumes social pluralism, although the latter does not entail it. Finally, both these modes of pluralism assume and express institutional divergences of collective culture within the frameworks prescribed by the alternative modes of incorporation under which these collectivities are associated. Thus structural and social pluralism both assume and express cultural pluralism, but in differing forms and with differing intensities.

If two collectivities, *B* and *C*, are incorporated as equivalents in a single society by common subjugation to a third, *A*, and if all members of the latter are incorporated uniformly in the public domain which it monopolizes, then all three modes of incorporation will be found within the society regulating the articulation of these collectivities. Evidently, each of these modes of incorporation may be transformed into either of its alternatives by altering the articulations of these collectivities, or by dissolving or crystallizing their boundaries; but such conversions of collective alignment can only proceed by political action, since this is the basis and character of all relations between incorporated collectivities. However, the conversion of differential incorporation into a universalistic regime by political means cannot immediately eliminate those differences of culture and social organization that formerly characterized these collectivities. The dissolution of such institutional differences within and between collectivities presupposes extensive opportunities for and processes of social and cultural assimilation over a period of at least two or three generations.

Collectivities incorporated under either of the three modes outlined above have the distinctive characteristics of corporations. Moreover, all corporations aggregate in all societies are necessarily incorporated under one or more of these alternatives. As a corporation, each collectivity is presumed to be perpetual and has a unique identity, fixed conditions or modes of recruitment, and thus a determinate membership. Any social unit with these four formal features has the institutional form, closure and perduring qualities of a corporation; but collectivities may be incorporated as categories or as groups. If a collectivity is incorporated solely with the attributes listed above, it is thereby constituted as a corporate category by its lack of the organization necessary to convert it into a group.

Besides the four requisites of corporate status listed above, a corporate group must also have a coextensive organization, appropriate procedures for corporate action, its own exclusive common affairs, and the autonomy it needs to regulate them. These properties endow the corporate group with capacities for positive action as a collectivity which corporate categories do not possess; and as corporate action is always political in basis and character, and since corporate groups have positive political capacities while corporate categories do not, under regimes of differential incorporation, while the dominant collectivity is organized as a corporate group, subjugated collectivities are normally denied the opportunities to organize, and thus constituted as corporate categories. Thus the mode of differential incorporation distinguishes the collectivities it articulates in form as well as legal and political status, the dominant unit reserving to itself the opportunities and advantages of collective organization in order to immobilize the dominated. Thus the way in which these collectivities are incorporated and articulated is explicitly political in basis and corporate in form. As a consequence, collectivities incorporated as equals by common subjugation under structures of differential incorporation must normally be constituted as corporate categories, and they are thus rendered incapable of collective action to redress their grievances.

When their differential incorporation is abolished, these equivalent segments must either dissolve by relaxing the criteria of their mutual exclusions, in which case they will forfeit their corporate closure through processes of social and cultural assimilation by which their members are uniformly incorporated in the public domain of a wider unit; or they must reconstitute themselves as corporate groups by developing the necessary organizational arrangements, in which case they will articulate politically by contraposition or by associational agreements. Only by virtue of their common differential incorporation can equivalent segments remain as corporate categories. Released from differential incorporation, they must either dissolve and amalgamate, or reconstitute themselves as corporate groups. But in either case substantive differences of culture and social organization which formerly characterized these closed equivalent collectivities will persist within and between them for several generations, until their social and cultural assimilation is complete, even though their members may be uniformly incorporated in the public domain of the autonomous society.

These structural alternatives and their transformations are sufficient to explicate all forms of interracial accommodation in human societies, since racial differences can only be institutionalized within societies by constituting racial stocks as corporate collectivities. Thus in racially heterogeneous populations, the only alternative to the incorporation of racial stocks as groups or categories is the incorporation of individuals of differing race directly in the public domain of the wider society on identical conditions that proscribe or effectively discountenance their collective segregation on racial lines. Such an order will generate conditions which are simultaneously favourable to racial amalgamation and to social and cultural assimilation by suppressing racial identifications among the citizens in favour of common identifications with and loyalties to the wider society. Conversely, as such situations indicate, the structural precondition of all interracial accommodations is the incorporation of racial stocks as exclusive corporate units whose articulations or standardized relations express prevailing conditions of corporate organization and distributions of corporate power. The alternative modes of such collective articulation and the essential conditions of their development and change have already been outlined. These alternatives and transformations apply equally to racially homogeneous and to racially mixed societies, being direct logical entailments of the corporate character of societies themselves. Thus in the absence of such gross physical differentiae as racial features, societies must and do select and institutionalize other principles as bases for the differentiation, segmental or universalistic incorporation of their members. These principles include ethnicity, language, cult, locality, occupation, wealth, descent or ancestral status. In so far as these or other differentiae are employed to incorporate collectivities within society, they have direct political implications and corporate expression.

14.

An individual can only be assigned racial status by the observable correspondence of his phenotype with that of some biologically distinct collectivity. Thus differences of race presuppose and refer to biological differences among reproductively closed stocks which are presumptively perpetual, perceptually distinct, and thus conceived as corporate categories. None the less, as a basis for social organization, the only features exclusive and intrinsic to race are those inherent in biology, namely the transmission of collectively distinct phenotypical features by heredity. That such biological characteristics are intrinsically neutral and non-determinative phenomena in relation to social organization is shown by the fact that the conditions and consequences of the three alternative modes of incorporation outlined above govern all possible forms of societal organization in racially homogeneous or heterogeneous societies alike. Thus if racial variables are institutionalized as bases of collective incorporation and articulation in some societies, we must seek the foundations of these social orders in the conditions and consequences of their incorporations. Of these conditions, the simultaneous constitution of racial stocks as collectivities with the corporate characteristics listed above is directly prerequisite and decisive for the forms of interracial accommodations and societal structure alike.

Racial incorporations can only develop in racially heterogeneous societies, and since Caribbean data show that no intrinsically biological facts prevent racial stocks in such societies from amalgamating by miscegenation to produce a homogeneous hybrid group, we must recognize the social and cultural determination of racial incorporations and accommodations. Racial stocks may amalgamate freely or otherwise, as Caribs and Negroes amalgamated in St. Vincent and Dominica, or as Negroes and whites have amalgamated in Petit Martinique and more recently in Saba, or as Chinese indentured workers and Negroes have done in Jamaica. The hybrid offspring of these interracial unions will normally be incorporated in a hybrid collectivity on uniform conditions by virtue of their common racial derivation, status and external distinctness. In consequence they will all share identical rights and obligations that distinguish them as members of their collectivity from others around. If these hybrids are also isolated from other stocks, their collectivity will form a distinct society. The situation and development of black Carib society illustrates this process nicely, as do developments in Saba and Petit Martinique.

If the racially distinct stocks in a society are not incorporated on uniform conditions in its public domain, they must either be incorporated as collectivities of equivalent status, or as superior and inferior, or by some combination of these alternatives. Thus, throughout Caribbean colonialism, whites occupied positions of privilege and dominance. They differentially incorporated Negroes, Indians, Javanese and other stocks successively in the societies they created, ruled and exploited for their own benefit. Such regimes initially institutionalized inequalities of racial stocks on political and legal bases such as conquest, enslavement or indenture, and by specifically political means. To justify and perpetuate these differences, the dominant whites tried to allocate political and legal status on the basis of ascriptive racial criteria; but this attempt was less successful due to inconsistent practices. Though all non-whites were ascriptively subject to differential incorporation, substantial differences were allowed to develop among them, as for example in Saint Dominique and Jamaica during the seventeenth and eighteenth centuries, and between the Creoles and East Indians of Guyana and Trinidad throughout colonialism.

None the less, in Guyana, Surinam and Trinidad, Negroes and East Indians were incorporated as mutually exclusive segments of equivalent status by their common but mutually distinct subordination to the ruling whites. In British Honduras, so were the Negroid Creoles of Belize and the Spanish-mestizo peoples of the interior. At colonial levels, since jural differences between these subject stocks were of little significance, they were differentially incorporated as equivalent. However, being segregated physically, culturally and by differences of social organization, these segments remained bionomically closed and virtually exclusive.

Historically, the successive immigrations by which these racial stocks were introduced to Caribbean societies manifested white political predominance and white institutions of differential incorporation. Evidently white colonists sought also to institutionalize equations of race and political status in these societies, to simplify, consolidate and perpetuate their exclusive political control. However, in this process contrary classifications of the coloured hybrids begotten by white colonists were adopted in Hispanic and non-Hispanic societies. In the former, the coloured were distinguished from Negroes as free, and thus legally assimilated to whites. In non-Hispanic territories, hybrids were initially classified with Negroes in contradistinction to whites, and were then allowed various privileges as a superior Negro stratum, despite their differential incorporation.

The white section of these non-Hispanic societies exhibited another structural inconsistency within its own ranks, since the dominant white elites were sharply distinguished by culture, organization, power and social situation from those 'poor whites' who were descended from indentured workers imported after emancipation as a labour force and reserve militia. Thus, while non-whites were differentially incorporated as non-citizens in these societies, 'poor whites', who lacked political rights, enjoyed the forms but not the substance of legal citizenship. Their communities were thus incorporated on conditions sufficiently similar to those of the emancipated Negroes to demonstrate once more how political alignments and sectional interests have determined the ways in which racial criteria have been institutionalized as bases of collective organization within these societies.

It is equally clear that the institutions by which white colonists incorporated white indentured labourers and other racial stocks differentially through indenture or slavery in the Caribbean societies were merely adaptations and elaborations of the structures of serfdom and helotage familiar in medieval Europe. There, in the absence of obvious racial differentiae, societies had been constituted and perpetuated by political means as ascriptive systems of inequality through the differential incorporation of subject majorities under institutions of serfdom and villeinage. In the racially mixed Caribbean societies created *de novo*, slavery and indenture were employed to subjugate non-whites more rigorously.

Always the dominant whites in these colonial societies organized themselves as a corporate group, to which local 'poor white' enclaves were subordinated. Simultaneously the colonists constituted other racial stocks as subordinate corporate categories under various institutions of differential incorporation — slavery, indenture, and exclusive property franchises — which effectively denied non-whites the opportunities to organize themselves separately. Thus, even when contraposed as segments of parallel status, subordinate racial blocs such as the Negroid Creoles and East Indians lacked the inclusive organization requisite to constitute them as groups capable of collective action to redress their lot. In short, to institute, sustain and extend their political domination, white colonists reserved to themselves opportunities for collective organization in order to incorporate all other stocks differentially. This basic condition governed the form and content of all secondary collective structures by prescribing the basic framework for their operations.

Initially the diverse stocks brought together in these Caribbean societies differed fundamentally in language, religion, values, technology and social organization as well as race. In consequence, the predominant stock had an unchallengeable cultural monopoly of the institutional systems it employed to incorporate and subordinate other stocks, who were also normally subdivided by differences of social and cultural organization among themselves, as, for example, were the African slaves by their tribal cultures and languages, the Hindu and Muslim immigrants from India by religion, and the Portuguese, Chinese, Germans, Jews and others by various criteria. So likewise to a significant degree were the dominant whites divided from 'poor whites' whose ancestors were imported under indenture after Negro emancipation from the metropole, as labourers, settlers and reserve militias. Cultural differences simultaneously segregated local communities of 'poor whites' from the white colonial elites, from the ambiguously situated browns, and from surrounding blacks; but when dispersed and removed from their community matrix, poor whites commonly assimilated to those Creoles whose cultural and social organization most closely resembled their own. Contemporary processes of assimilation in Saba and in Carriacou illustrate the conditions that facilitate dissolution of these racial barriers by symmetrical connubium.

Wherever racial stocks are bound together by structures of differential incorporation, their amalgamation is directly excluded. At best, such structures will only permit asymmetrical forms of miscegenation that express the differential status of the incorporated stocks. Thus if, by exigencies of structural adaptation to local conditions some members of differentially incorporated racial stocks none the less share substantially similar life chances and situations, as do poor whites and Negro peasants around them in various Caribbean societies, symmetrical and asymmetrical miscegenation are both ruled out by the incongruities of their *de facto* equivalence and *de jure* inequivalence.

Conversely, in the absence of such differential incorporation, peoples of diverse race must either amalgamate or maintain their racial boundaries. They will normally do the latter only if they are either physically remote from one another, or separated by severe differences of language and culture, or if they are contraposed as corporate groups in political struggles for dominance or parity. Relations under and since colonialism between Creoles and Asiatics in Surinam, Guyana and Trinidad, and between Creoles and others in British Honduras, illustrate both sets of alternatives. In all other conditions the probability of progressive amalgamation and assimilation by symmetrical miscegenation increases with the cultural and social continuities among the stocks concerned, with their perception of this common culture, and with their indifference to the political inducements of racial exclusions and contrapositions. This particular combination of conditions presently prevails in minuscule Caribbean societies such as Saba and Carriacou. Historically, it also prevailed among racial segments of equally low status in larger societies, which accordingly displayed high rates of amalgamation.

We have seen how differential incorporation perpetuated fundamental cultural and social differences among the racial stocks of Caribbean societies by systematically restricting the opportunities of subordinate stocks for education, intermarriage, political participation, occupational mobility and educational advance, while concentrating these opportunities in the dominant white group. Thus despite the pervasive Creole culture, differentially situated racial stocks continued to exhibit disjunctions of culture, social organization, situation and activities that reinforced their mutual exclusions, even when such segments shared equivalent status by virtue of their common exclusion from the colonial domain monopolized by dominant whites. In this way the structure of differential incorporation preserved the basic social and cultural discontinuities of these societies despite the prevalence and influence of Creole culture among them. The resulting pluralism, intensified by the acutely divergent demographic and political statuses of the dominant whites in non-Hispanic societies, characterized the Creole culture itself as a hotchpotch of distinctive and often contradictory institutions and values, rather than a coherent integrated synthesis of originally diverse traditions. In this context, racial segments that occupied differing physical or economic situations normally exhibited distinctive and formally incompatible systems of culture and social organization, irrespective of their political status. In consequence, following the formal abolition of differential incorporation by decolonization, exclusive racial blocs of equivalent status such as Negroid Creoles, East Indians and Javanese, were readily organized as political units to compete for dominance, power or parity. In effect, then, decolonization converted the structural pluralism institution-

alized by differential incorporation into the social pluralism characterized by institutionally distinct racial blocs contraposed as corporate
groups under political parties. Thus multi-racial Caribbean societies
experienced these developments as direct effects of their decolonization.

In basically bi-racial Creole societies of moderate size, formal
decolonization has not entirely removed the antecedent structures of
differential incorporation. Excluding the peculiar situations of
Martinique, Guadeloupe and Cayenne as overseas departments of
France, universal suffrage and internal autonomy incorporated all
stocks equally in the public domain of other territories, and thus
implicitly transferred political initiatives to the majority race. Whites
accordingly lost their historically exclusive monopoly of political
administration to the mass of the colonized peoples. None the less
there persists today a substantial measure of differential incorporation between the Creole elites, who are mainly coloured, and the
black majority, which operates to the material advantage of local and
foreign whites, without whose support these coloured elites would
soon lose control.

To justify and obscure their present dominance, these hybrid elites
proclaim ideologies of racial equality, national unity, equal opportunities and rewards in the pursuit of economic development. Some
indications of the substantial gaps between these proclamations and
the current social realities have been cited above; but while such
distributions demonstrate that the Negro majority are still substantially subject to differential incorporation in these states, their
differential incorporation is substantive rather than formal, and
coloured elites may argue that it is neither deliberate, official, nor as
extensive as formerly. They argue also that inequality has already
been reduced by recent measures and will continue to be reduced;
but these developments and ideologies alike illustrate the political
bases and character of interracial accommodations and change.

As effects of their recent liberalization, bi-racial Caribbean
societies of moderate size have experienced significantly increased
opportunities for cultural and biological assimilation and social
mobility. Their basically coloured Creole elites have appropriated
positions formerly reserved for whites and, while accepting white
allies, have also recruited appropriately qualified blacks into their
ranks. Thus the ruling personnel in these bi-racial societies of
moderate size now appear to validate the official ideologies of racial
equality and mobility proclaimed by their coloured elites. Data cited
above indicate once more the substantial divergence between reality
and ideology on these questions. The measure of these differences
expresses exactly the degree to which other racial stocks in these
societies remain differentially incorporated in substance, despite
their formal equality.

Correlatively, these differences of social and cultural organization that distinguished the hybrid elites from the Negro majorities of these societies under colonialism, persist in proportion to the prevailing degree of their substantively differential incorporation. In effect, then, decolonization has modified these social structures by formally disestablishing the legal and political conditions under which populations with differing social and cultural systems were incorporated within them, while leaving unchanged other conditions that differentiated these stocks institutionally and culturally. Accordingly, ascriptive influences and inequalities prevail, informally but substantially, in contemporary bi-racial Creole societies to the advantage of their former and the present rulers, and serve to perpetuate the subordination of their black majorities. Even so, the coloured stratum that currently dominates these bi-racial units has materially augmented its strength by alliance with whites and by the recruitment of qualified blacks. Thus, although predominantly hybrid in the racial status of its core, these coloured elites are more accurately defined by cultural and social criteria than in racial terms. None the less, despite its political predominance, the coloured elite ranks in social status and prestige below elite whites and above the Negro mass, as well as the residual 'poor white' enclaves. The latter condition further strengthens the elite ideology that ex-colonial Caribbean societies are now indifferent to race.

Historically, the coloured population have always occupied an intermediate cultural and social position in Creole societies, to their material benefit, and to the advantage of the dominant white minorities, who thereby secured a suitable stratum of subordinates as allies and buffers between themselves and the blacks. Under colonialism, while promoting coloured interests, to restrain the pressures of coloured folk for social assimilation, whites employed two congruent but quite distinct classifications of the Creole colonials. Primarily they distinguished between themselves and non-whites; but among the latter they also distinguished a stratum of coloured hybrids who were culturally interstitial, from the weakly-acculturated Negro majority. Though privileged, this coloured stratum formed part of the Negro majority

During and after slavery, colonial institutions expressed the differential emphases of ruling whites on these congruent but divergent classifications of the Negroid section. Thus whites incorporated non-whites differentially by law, government, and other means; but they also extended educational, economic and symbolic political privileges to bi-cultural hybrids under various arrangements that simultaneously distinguished them from the black majority and intensified their dependence on white patronage. Accordingly the ascriptive racial bases of differential status and advantage in these societies was qualified and situationally obscured by prevailing emphases on cultural criteria in the differentiation of coloured folk. These tendencies and structural inconsistencies first developed under slavery when the free coloured were sharply distinguished by status and culture from coloured slaves.

In biological terms, the coloured category consists of all varieties of Negro-white hybrids; but this biological definition has been obscured and overruled by cultural criteria which distinguish the better-educated and better-endowed hybrids who enjoy distinctive life-chances and life-situations as a social stratum from other members of the biological category, who are thereby classified with Negro folk, despite their hybrid status. Successive census tabulations neatly illustrate these features of the coloured category in Carribean societies and they also reveal how uncertain are the boundaries and membership of the coloured stratum, since indices of cultural and phenotypical qualities vary situationally, and since continuing miscegenation within and beyond the boundaries of this category has prevented its crystallization as a stratum with uniform culture, homogeneous social position, and constant, identifiable phenotype. In short, under and since slavery and colonialism, the coloured stratum has been constituted as an anomalous corporate category of intermediate status with a central core of members who share several distinctive social and cultural institutions, and with situationally fluctuating margins of uncertain membership and size. It is thus equally inevitable and appropriate that coloured Creoles should now exploit these properties of their category to sustain their dominance by assimilating whites and talented blacks to their ranks; and that they should cite such associations as proofs of racial equality and harmony in the societies they now control.

The ambiguous status boundaries of the category of coloured Creoles, coupled with the socio-cultural divisions between elite and poor whites, and between metropolitan whites and other nationals under colonialism, illustrate the ultimate predominance of social and cultural factors in the genesis and institutionalization of racial criteria, boundaries and relations in Caribbean societies. Such social and cultural determinations of racial categories should not surprise us, since the notion of race as a cultural construct is only socially relevant when employed to subdivide and align collectivities within societies. However, besides the generically cultural character of all collective conceptions of race, Caribbean data also show how the specifically social and cultural continuities and disjunctions that characterize these plural societies have distorted racial categories and alignments within them. Coloured Creoles and poor whites provide two obvious examples of such socio-cultural determinations of racial criteria and boundaries; but these are by no means the only cases.

Generated in slavery as a strictly *biological category* of Negro-white hybrids, the coloured Creoles were simultaneously identified by social and cultural criteria as a *social stratum*, intermediate between the white and black populations. By these criteria, those hybrids who lacked the appropriate social and cultural attributes were socially reclassified as black, despite their biological status, while those blacks who possessed these attributes were socially reclassified as coloured. In like fashion, those whites who lacked the social and cultural attributes of the dominant elite were sharply distinguished from them as poor whites, and socially equated with Negro peasants, though socially and racially distinct. Differentiae of culture, institutional practice, status and power thus served to redefine racial categories and their relations, simultaneously dividing the whites into two strata and several national stocks, and the differentially incorporated Negroes into three or four situationally variable categories: those who were biologically and socio-culturally black; those who were biologically black but socio-culturally coloured; those who were biologically coloured but socio-culturally black; and those who were biologically and socio-culturally coloured. Poor whites were those whose status and culture were closest to those of the black. Poor whites accordingly ranked below the socially and culturally coloured elite in status, despite the ascriptive racial scale. Given such concurrent and situationally variable emphases on the biological, social and cultural criteria of racial identification and alignments, complementary, competing and often divergent categorizations of individuals, collectivities and social strata prevailed, so that no simple set of purely biological criteria can accurately describe the racial organization of Caribbean society. Since social, political and cultural factors are always decisive in these relations, they are equally relevant in defining the racial status of individuals. The collective relations and political processes that generated West Indian folk conceptions of racial characteristics and differences and institutionalized them variably in the diverse strata and segments of these societies, ineluctably combined and confused biological traits with differences of culture, status and social situation in formulating racial models of Caribbean social structure. In this way these folk conceptions express the indissoluble though dynamic associations of racial, cultural and structural factors which were forged in frameworks set by the alternative modes and conditions through which diverse racial stocks were successively incorporated in these societies.

15.

To summarize: the diverse and changing forms of interracial accommodation to be found in historic and contemporary Caribbean societies express alternative modes of corporate organization and indicate the political conditions that generate or transform them. For interracial accommodations to develop within a society, its various racial stocks must be categorized and incorporated as mutually exclusive and corporate collectivities, in which case they must either have co-ordinate or differential status. In the former event, and in the absence of external domination, racial segments must either confront one another as contraposed corporate groups that compete for power and parity, or they may collaborate symbiotically in some consociation, while maintaining their closures, or they may relax their connubial exclusion and amalgamate by symmetrical miscegenation, if their cultures and social organizations are sufficiently similar to permit this. Under the various structures of differential incorporation that institutionalize and perpetuate inequality on racial or other bases, only the dominant stock will be organized as a corporate group, while all others will be constituted as categories by that proscription of representative organization on which their subjugation depends. If the dominant and the dominated are racially distinct, this structure prescribes categorical racial inequalities. In such conditions, miscegenation is only possible in asymmetrical forms. Under either equivalent or differential modes of incorporation, mutually exclusive racial stocks will exhibit such divergent forms of institutional practice, culture and social organization that their societies will represent respectively the alternatives of social and structural pluralism. Formally in the multi-racial Caribbean societies, and substantively in bi-racial ones of moderate size, such conditions and structures currently prevail. Only minuscule Caribbean societies, whether racially homogeneous or not, exhibit or experience universalistic incorporation and cultural homogeneity. It is likely, furthermore, that these minuscule units owe their structural and cultural integration to their poverty, uneconomic size, and political insignificance.

Bibliography

Aberle, S.F. et al.	1950	'The functional prerequisites of a society', *Ethics* 60.
Adams, R.N. et al.	1961	*Social Change in Latin America Today: Its Implications for United States Policy*, New York.
Ahiram, E.	1964	'Income distribution in Jamaica', *Social and Economic Studies* 13, no. 3.
	1966	'Distribution of income in Trinidad-Tobago, and comparison with distribution of income in Jamaica', *Social and Economic Studies* 15, no. 2.
Allen, C.K.	1961	*Law in the Making*, 6th ed., Oxford.
Allport, E.A.	1954	'The Mzab', *Journal of the Royal Anthropological Institute* 84.
	1964	'The Ammeln', *Journal of the Royal Anthropological Institute* 94, no. 2.
Almond, G.	1961	Introduction to Almond and Coleman (1961).
Almond, G. and J.S. Coleman (eds.)	1961	*The Politics of the Developing Areas*, Princeton.
Andic, F.M.	1963	'The measurement of inequality in the distribution of taxable incomes in Puerto Rico 1955-8', *Social and Economic Studies* 12, no. 1.
Andic, F.M. and S. Andic	1966*a*	'Economic background of the French Antilles', in Mathews et al. (1966).
	1966*b*	'Economic background of Surinam', in Mathews et al. (1966).
Apthorpe, R. (ed.)	1959	*From Tribal Rule to Modern Government*, Lusaka.
Argyle, J.W.	1966	*The Fon of Dahomey*, Oxford.
Arnett, E.J.	1922	*The Rise of the Sokoto Fulani, Being a Paraphrase and in Some Parts a Translation of the Infaqu'l Maisuri of Sultan Mohammed Bello*, Lagos.
Ayearst, M.	1960	*The British West Indies: The Search for Self-government*, London.
Bacon, E.	1958	*Obok: A Study of Social Structure in Eurasia*, Viking Fund Publications in Anthropology no. 25.
Bailey, F.G.	1960	*Tribe, Caste and Nation*, Manchester.
Balandier, G.	1965	'The colonial situation', in van den Berghe (1965).

Barker, E.	1947	Introduction to Barker (1947a).
	1960	Introduction to Gierke (1960).
Barker, E. (ed.)	1947a	*Social Contract: Essays by Locke, Hume and Rousseau*, London.
Barnes, J.A.	1954	*Politics in a Changing Society*, London.
Barth, F.	1959	*Political Leadership Among Swat Pathans*, Monographs on Social Anthropology, London School of Economics, no. 19.
	1966	*Models of Social Organization*, Royal Anthropological Institute Occasional Paper no. 22, London.
Basham, A.L.	1959	*The Wonder that was India*, New York.
Beals, R.	1953	'Social stratification in Latin America', *American Journal of Sociology* 58.
Beidelman, T.O.	1959	*A Comparative Analysis of the Jajmani System*, New York.
Bell, W.	1964	*Jamaican Leaders: Political Attitudes in a New Nation*, Berkeley and Los Angeles.
Bell, W. (ed.)	1967	*The Democratic Revolution in the West Indies: Studies in Nationalism, Leadership and the Belief in Progress*, Cambridge, Mass.
Bendix, R. and S.M. Lipset (eds.)	1953	*Class, Status and Power: A Reader in Stratification*, New York.
Benedict, B.	1961	*Indians in a Plural Society: A Report on Mauritius*, London.
	1962	'Stratification in plural societies', *American Anthropologist* 64, no. 6.
	1968	'Small societies', in Sills (1968), vol. 14.
Bennett, H.S.	1960	*Life on the English Manor: A Study of Peasant Conditions, 1150-1400*, London.
Benoist, J.	1968	'Types de plantations et groupes sociaux à la Martinique', *Cahiers des Amériques Latines*, no. 2.
Bernal, I.	1963	*Mexico Before Cortez: Art, History and Legend*, translated by Willis Branstone, New York.
Bernardi, B.	1952	'The age-set system of the Nilo-Hamites', *Africa* 22.
Bierstedt, R.	1959	*The Making of Society*, New York.
Birket-Smith, K.	1960	*The Eskimo*, London.
Black, C.V.	1958	*History of Jamaica*, London.
Bloch, M.	1961	*Feudal Society*, translated by L.A. Manyon, London.
Blumer, H.	1955	'Reflections on a theory of race relations', in Lind (1955).
	1959	'Collective behaviour', in Lee (1959).
	1961	'Race prejudice as a sense of group position', in Masuoka and Valien (1961).
	1965	'Industrialization and race relations', in Hunter (1965).
Boas, F.	1940	*Race, Language and Culture*, New York.
Bohannan, L.	1952	'A genealogical charter', *Africa* 22.
Bohannan, L. and P. Bohannan	1953	*The Tiv of Central Nigeria*, Ethnographic Survey of Africa, Western Africa Part 8, International African Institute, London.
Bohannan, P.	1963	*Social Anthropology*, New York.

Bottomore, T.B.	1963	*Sociology: A Guide to Problems and Literature*, London.
Braithwaite, L.	1953	'Social stratification in Trinidad', *Social and Economic Studies* 2, nos. 2 and 3.
	1954	'Cultural integration in Trinidad', *Social and Economic Studies* 3, no. 1.
	1960	'Social stratification and cultural pluralism', in Rubin (1960).
Brion Davis, D.	1966	*The Problem of Slavery in Western Culture*, Ithaca, N.Y.
Brockelmann, C.	1962	*History of the Islamic Peoples*, translated by Joel Carmichael and Moshe Perlmann, New York.
Broom, L.	1954	'The social differentiation of Jamaica', *American Sociological Review* 19, no. 2.
	1960a	'Discussion', in Rubin (1960).
	1960b	'Urbanization and the plural society', in Rubin (1960).
Brown, G.A.	1961	'Economic development and trends in Jamaica (1950-60)', in Cumper (1961).
Brown, P.	1951	'Patterns of authority in West Africa', *Africa* 21.
Buckley, W.	1967	*Sociology and Modern Systems Theory*, Englewood Cliffs, N.J.
Busia, K.A.	1951	*The Position of the Chief in the Modern Political System of Ashanti*, London.
Cardozo, B.N.	1924	*The Growth of the Law*, New Haven.
Caribbean Monthly Bulletin	1967	4, no. 11 (September) and 5, no. 1 (November), Puerto Rico Institute of Caribbean Studies, Rio Piedras.
Cary, M.	1945	*A History of Rome*, London.
Chevalier, F.	1963	*Land and Society in Colonial Mexico*, translated by Alvin Eustis, Berkeley and Los Angeles.
Clarke, C.	1967	'Caste among Hindus in a town in Trinidad: San Fernando', in Schwartz (1967).
Cobb, J.	1940	'Caste and class in Haiti', *American Journal of Sociology* 46.
Cohen, R. and J. Middleton (eds.)	1970	*From Tribe to Nation in Modern Africa: Studies in Incorporation Processes*, Scranton, Pa.
Cohn, N.R.C.	1957	*The Pursuit of the Millennium*, London.
Cole, C.W.	1948	*Land Tenure in Zaria Province*, Kaduna.
Cole, G.D.H. and R. Postgate	1946	*The Common People, 1746-1946*, London.
Coleman, J.S.	1958	*Nigeria: Background to Nationalism*, Berkeley and Los Angeles.
Colson, E.	1962	*The Plateau Tonga of Northern Rhodesia (Zambia): Social and Religious Studies*, Manchester.
Coulborn, R. (ed.)	1956	*Feudalism in History*, Princeton.
Coulton, G.G.	1959	*The Medieval Scene*, London.
Crowder, M.	1962	*Senegal: A Study in French Assimilation Policy*, London.
Crowley, D.J.	1957	'Plural and differential acculturation in

		Trinidad', *American Anthropologist* 59.
	1960	'Cultural assimilation in a multi-racial society', in Rubin (1960).
Cumper, G.	1954	'Labour demand and supply in the Jamaican sugar industry 1830-1950', *Social and Economic Studies* 2, no. 4.
Cumper, G. (ed.)	1961	*Social Needs in a Changing Society: Report of the Conference on Social Development in Jamaica*, July 1961, Kingston.

Davis, A., B.B. Gardner 1941   *Deep South: A Social Anthropological*
and M.R. Gardner   *Study of Caste and Class*, Chicago.

Davis, J.P.	1961	*Corporations*, New York.
Davis, K.	1949	*Human Society*, New York.
	1953	'Reply' to M.M. Tumin, *American Sociological Review* 18.
Davis, K. and	1956	'Some principles of stratification', *American*
W.E. Moore.		*Sociological Review* 10.
Delavignette, R.	1950	*Freedom and Authority in French West Africa*, London.
Despres, L.A.	1963	*New World*, Georgetown, British Guiana.
	1964	'The implications of nationalist policies in British Guiana for the development of cultural theory', *American Anthropologist* 66.
	1967	*Cultural Pluralism and Nationalist Politics in British Guiana*, Chicago.
De Tocqueville, A.	1955	*The Old Regime and the French Revolution*, translated by Stuart Gilbert, Garden City.
Deutscher, I.	1953	*Russia After Stalin: With a Postscript on the Beria Affair*, London.
D'Hertefelt, M.	1960*a*	'Stratification sociale et structure politique au Rwanda', *La Revue nouvelle* 31 (Brussels).
	1960*b*	'Les Élections communales et le consensus politique au Rwanda', *Zaire* 14, nos. 5-6.
	1962*a*	'Le Rwanda', in d'Hertefelt, Troubworst and Scherer (1962).
	1962*b*	'Développements récents', in d'Hertefelt, Troubworst and Scherer (1962).
	1964	'Mythes et idéologies dans le Rwanda ancien et contemporain', in Vansina, Mauny and Thomas (1964).
	1965	'The Rwanda of Rwanda', in Gibbs (1965).
D'Hertefelt, M.,	1962	*Les Anciens Royaumes de la zone inter-*
A. Troubworst and		*lacustrine meridionale: Rwanda, Burundi,*
J. Scherer		*Buha,* International African Institute, London.
Dollard, J.	1957	*Caste and Class in a Southern Town*, New York.
Duke, J.T.	1967	'Egalitarianism and future leaders in Jamaica', in Bell (1967).
Dunn, L.C.	1958	*Race and Biology*, UNESCO, Paris.
Durkheim, E.	1938	*The Rules of Sociological Method*, translated by S.A. Solovay and J.H. Mueller, Glencoe, Ill.
	1947	*The Division of Labour in Society*, trans-

		lated by G. Simpson, Glencoe, Ill.
	1957	*Professional Ethics and Civic Morals*, translated by C. Brookfield, London.
	1959	*Socialism and Saint-Simon*, translated by C. Sattler, London.
Dyson-Hudson, N.	1963	'The Karimojong age system', *Ethnology* 2.
Eastern Caribbean Population Census, 7 April, 1960	1961	Series A, Bulletin no. 1 (1961), Central Statistical Office, Port-of-Spain, Trinidad.
Easton, D.	1957	'An approach to the analysis of political systems', *World Politics* 9, no. 3.
	1965	*A Framework for Political Analysis*, Englewood Cliffs, N.J.
The Economist Intelligence Unit	1959	*A Comparison of the Level of Living in the Bahamas and other Caribbean Islands*, June 1959, London.
Edmonson, M.S.	1958	*Status Terminology and the Social Structure of North American Indians*, Seattle.
Eggan, F.	1950	*Social Organization of the Western Pueblos*, Chicago.
Ehrenberg, V.	1964	*The Greek State*, New York.
Eisenstadt, S.N.	1956	*From Generation to Generation: Age Groups and Social Structure*, Glencoe, Ill.
	1961	'Anthropological studies of complex societies', *Current Anthropology* 2, no. 3.
Elkins, S.M.	1963	*Slavery: A Problem in American Institutional and Intellectual Life*, New York.
Etzioni, A. and E. Etzioni (eds.)	1964	*Social Change: Sources, Patterns and Consequences*, New York.
Evans-Pritchard, E.E.	1940a	*The Nuer: A Description of the Modes of Livelihood and Political Institutions of a Nilotic People*, Oxford.
	1940b	'The political structure of the Nandi-speaking peoples of Kenya', *Africa* 13.
	1948	*The Divine Kingship of the Shilluk of the Nilotic Sudan*, London.
	1951	*Kinship and Marriage among the Nuer*, Oxford.
Evans-Pritchard, E.E. (ed.)	1954	*The Institutions of Primitive Society*, Oxford.
Fallers, L.	1956	*Bantu Bureaucracy*, Cambridge.
Farley, R.	1954	'Rise of a peasantry in British Guiana', *Social and Economic Studies* 2, no. 4.
Forde, D.	1934	*Habitat, Economy and Society*, London.
	1939a	'Kinship in Umor: double unilateral organization in a semi-Bantu society', *American Anthropologist* 41.
	1939b	'Government in Umor', *Africa* 12.
	1950a	'Ward organization among the Yakö', *Africa* 20.
	1950b	'Double descent among the Yakö', in Radcliffe-Brown and Forde (1950).
	1951	*The Yoruba-speaking Peoples of South-western Nigeria*, Ethnographic Survey of

Africa, Western Africa Part 4, International African Institute, London.

	1961	'The governmental role of associations among the Yakö', *Africa* 31.
	1962	'Death and succession', in Gluckman (1962).
	1964	*Yakö Studies*, London.
Forde, D. (ed.)	1954	*African Worlds: Studies in Cosmological Ideas and Social Values of African Peoples*, London.
	1956	*Efik Traders of Old Calabar*, London.
Forde, D. and G.I. Jones	1950	*The Ibo and Ibibio-speaking Peoples of South-eastern Nigeria*, Ethnographic Survey of Africa, Western Africa Part 4, International African Institute, London.
Fortes, M.	1940	'The political system of the Tallensi of the northern territories of the Gold Coast', in Fortes and Evans-Pritchard (1940*b*).
	1945	*The Dynamics of Clanship among the Tallensi*, London.
	1949	*The Web of Kinship among the Tallensi*, London.
	1950	'Kinship and marriage among the Ashanti', in Radcliffe-Brown and Forde (1950).
	1953	'The structure of unilineal descent groups', *American Anthropologist* 55.
	1959	'Descent, filiation and affinity: a rejoinder to Dr. Leach', *Man* 59 (November 1959), pp. 193-7; (December 1959), pp. 206-12.
Fortes, M. and E.E. Evans-Pritchard	1940*a*	Introduction to Fortes and Evans-Pritchard (1940*b*).
Fortes, M. and E.E. Evans-Pritchard (eds.)	(1940*b*)	*African Political Systems*, London.
Fosbrooke, H.A.	1948	'An administrative survey of the Masai social system', *Tanganyika Notes and Records* 26.
Fraenkel, M.	1964	*Tribe and Class in Monrovia*, London.
Francis, O.C.	no date	*The People of Modern Jamaica*, Department of Statistics, Kingston.
Frankenberg, R.	1969	*Communities in Britain: Social Life in Town and Country*, Harmondsworth.
Frazier, E.F.	1940	*The Negro Family in the United States*, Chicago.
	1949	*The Negro in the United States*, New York.
	1962	*Black Bourgeoisie: The Rise of a New Middle Class in the United States*, New York.
Fried, M.H.	1959	*Readings in Anthropology*, New York.
Furnivall, J.S.	1945	'Some problems of tropical economy', in Hinden (1945).
	1948	*Colonial Policy and Practice*, London.
Gamble, D.P.	1957	*The Wolof of Senegambia*, Ethnographic Survey of Africa, Western Africa Part 14 (1), International African Institute, London.
Ganshof, F.L.	1952	*Feudalism*, translated by Philip Grierson, London.
Geertz, C. (ed.)	1963	*Old Societies and New States: The Quest for Modernity in Asia and Africa*, New York.

Gerth, H.H. and C.W. Mills (eds.)	1947	*From Max Weber: Essays in Sociology*, London.
Gibb, H.A.R. and H. Bowen	1950	*Islamic Society and the West*, London.
Gibbs, J.L. (ed.)	1965	*Peoples of Africa*, New York.
Gierke, O.	1900	*Political Theories of the Middle Ages*, translated with an introduction by F.W. Maitland, London.
	1960	*Natural Law and the Theory of Society, 1500-1800*, translated with an introduction by E. Barker, Boston.
Gillin J.	1948	'Mestizo America', in Linton (1948).
	1951	*The Culture of Security in San Carlos*, Middle American Research Institute, publication no. 16, New Orleans.
Gluckman, M.	1940	'The kingdom of the Zulu of South Africa', in Fortes and Evans-Pritchard (1940*b*).
	1948	Introduction to Mitchell and Barnes (1948).
	1950	'Kinship and marriage among the Lozi of Northern Rhodesia and the Zulu of Natal', in Radcliffe-Brown and Forde (1950).
	1954	*Rituals of Rebellion in South-East Africa*, Manchester.
	1955	*Custom and Conflict in Africa*, Oxford.
	1963	*Order and Rebellion in Tribal Africa*, London.
Gluckman, M. (ed.)	1962	*Essays on the Rituals of Social Relations*, Manchester.
Goldman, I.	1970	*Ancient Polynesian Society*, Chicago.
Goody, J.	1957	'Fields of social control among the LoDagaba', *Journal of the Royal Anthropological Institute* 87, part 1.
	1961	'The classification of double descent systems', *Current Anthropology* 2, no. 1.
	1966*a*	Introduction to Goody (1966*b*).
Goody, J. (ed.)	1966*b*	*Succession to High Office*, Cambridge Papers in Social Anthropology no. 4, London.
Gorham Crane, J.	1966	*Concomitants of Selective Emigration on a Caribbean Island*, Columbia University, Ph.D. dissertation in Anthropology, Ann Arbor, Michigan. (University Microfilms, 1967.)
Grousset, R.	1952	*The Rise and Splendour of the Chinese Empire*, translated by Anthony Watson-Gandy and Terence Gordon, London.
Guerra y Sanchez, R.	1964	*Sugar and Society in the Caribbean*, New Haven.
Gulliver, P.H.	1953	'The age-set organization of the Jie tribe', *Journal of the Royal Anthropological Institute* 83.
	1958	'The Turkana age-organization', *American Anthropologist* 60.
Gulliver, P.H. and Pamela Gulliver	1953	*The Central Nilo-Hamites*, London.
Gurvitch, G.	1947	*Sociology of Law*, London.

Hailey, M.   1938   *An African Survey*, London.
Hall, D.   1962   'Slaves and slavery in the British West Indies', *Social and Economic Studies* 11, no. 4.

Hall, J.W.   1962   'Feudalism in Japan: a reassessment', *Comparative Studies in Society and History* 5.

Hammond, S.A.   1945   *The Cost of Education*, Development and Welfare Bulletin no. 5, Bridgetown, Barbados.

Hanbury, H.G.   1944   *English Courts of Law*, London.
Harris, R.   1962   'The political significance of double unilineal descent', *Journal of the Royal Anthropological Institute* 92, part 1.

Hartland, S.   1924   *Primitive Law*, London.
Heard, K.A.   1961   *Political Systems in Multi-racial Societies*, South African Institute of Race Relations, Johannesburg.

Herskovits, M.J.   1938   *Dahomey, an Ancient West African Kingdom*, New York.
                          1941   *The Myth of the Negro Past*, New York.
Hinden, R. (ed.)   1945   *Fabian Colonial Essays*, London.
Hiskett, M.   1960   '*Kitāb al-farq*: a work on the Hausa kingdoms attributed to 'Uthmān dan Fodio', *Bulletin of the School of Oriental and African Studies* (University of London), 23.

Hobbes, T.   1651   *Leviathan*.
Hocart, A.M.   1941   *Kingship*, London.
Hodgkin, T.L.   1961   *African Political Parties*, Harmondsworth.
Hoebel, E.A.   1954   *The Law of Primitive Man*, Cambridge, Mass.
                          1960   *The Cheyennes: Indians of the Great Plains*, New York.
                          1962   'Letter to Editor', *American Anthropologist* 64, no. 4.
Hoernlé, A.W.   1937   'Social organization', in Schapera (1937).
Hoetink, H.   1967   *The Two Variants in Caribbean Race Relations: A Contribution to the Sociology of Segmented Societies*, London.

Hogben, S.J.   1930   *The Muhammadan Emirates of Northern Nigeria*, London.

Holmberg, A.R.   1961   'Changing community attitudes and values in Peru: a case study in guided change', in Adams et al. (1961).

Homans, G.C.   1962   *Sentiments and Activities: Essays in Social Science*, New York.

Horowitz, I.L. (ed.)   1963   *Power, Politics and People: The Collected Essays of C. Wright Mills*, New York.

Horowitz, M.M.   1960   'Metropolitan influences in the Caribbean: the French Antilles', in Rubin (1960).
                          1967   *Morne Paysan: Peasant Village in Martinique*, New York.

Horton, W.H.G.   1954   'The *Ohu* system of slavery in a northern Ibo village group', *Africa* 24, no. 4.

Hunter, G. (ed.)   1965   *Industrialization and Race Relations*, London.
Huntingford, G.W.B.   1953   *The Nandi of Kenya*, London.
                          1955   *The Galla of Ethiopia*, London.

Hutton, J.H.	1946	*Caste in India*, London.
International Institute of Differing Civilizations	1957	*Ethnic and Cultural Pluralism in Inter-Tropical Countries*, Brussels.
Jamaica, Agricultural Census of, 1961-2	no date	Bulletin no. 3, Department of Statistics, Kingston.
Jamaica, Eighth Census of, 1943	1945	Government Printer, Kingston.
Jamaica, Government of	1963	*Five-Year Independence Plan, 1963-8*, Kingston.
Jamaica, Handbook of	1954 1960	Government Printer, Kingston. Government Printer, Kingston.
James, C.L.R.	1963	*The Black Jacobins: Toussaint L'Ouverture and the San Domingo Revolution*, New York.
Jayawardena, C.	1963	*Conflict and Solidarity in a Guianese Plantation*, London.
Johnson, C.S.	1934	*Shadow of the Plantation*, Chicago.
Jones, G.I.	1956	'The political organization of old Calabar', in Forde (1956).
Jowett, B.	1943	Translation of Aristotle's *Politics*, Modern Library edition, New York.
Kaberry, P.M.	1952	*Women of the Grassfields: A Study of the Economic Position of Women in Bamenda, British Cameroons*, Colonial Research Publication no. 14, London.
Kagamé, A.	1957	'Le Pluralisme ethnique et cultural dans le Ruanda', in International Institute of Differing Civilizations (1957).
Kalenda, P.M.	1963	'Toward a model of the Hindu Jajmani system', *Human Organization* 22, no. 1.
Kaminsky, H.	1962	'The free spirit in the Hussite revolution', in Thrupp (1962).
Keur, D.L.	1960	'Metropolitan influence in the Caribbean: the Netherlands Antilles', in Rubin (1960).
Keur, J.Y. and D.L. Keur	1960	*Windward Children: A Study in Human Ecology of the Three Dutch Windward Islands in the Caribbean*, Assen.
Kirchhoff, P.	1959	'The principles of clanship in human society', in Fried (1959), vol. 2.
Klass, M.	1960	'East and West Indian: cultural complexity in Trinidad', in Rubin (1960).
Kluckhohn, F. and F.L. Strodtbeck	1961	*Variations in Value-Orientations*, Evanston, Ill.
Kroeber, A.L. (ed.)	1953	*Anthropology Today*, Chicago.
Kuper, H.	1947	*An African Aristocracy: Rank among the Swazi*, London.
	1950	'Kinship among the Swazi', in Radcliffe-Brown and Forde (1950).
Kuper, H. and L. Kuper (eds.)	1965	*African Law: Development and Adaptation*, Berkeley and Los Angeles.
Kuper, L.	1965	*An African Bourgeoisie: Race, Class and Politics in South Africa*, New Haven.
Kuper, L. and M.G. Smith (eds.)	1969	*Pluralism in Africa*, Berkeley and Los Angeles.

Kushner, G.   1970   'The anthropology of complex societies', in Siegel (1970).

Lambert, H.E.   1956   *Kikuyu Social and Political Institutions*, London.

Lammens, H.   1926   *L'Islam: croyances et institutions*, Beyrouth.

Landtman, G.   1938   *The Origin of the Inequality of Social Classes*, London.

Latortue, G.   1966   'Political status of the French Caribbean', in Mathews et al. (1966).

Leach, E.   1952   'The structural implications of matrilateral cross-cousin marriage', *Journal of the Royal Anthropological Institute* 81.

    1954   *Political Systems of Highland Burma: A Study of Kachin Social Structure*, London.

    1960   *Aspects of Caste in South India, Ceylon and North-west Pakistan*, Cambridge Papers in Social Anthropology no. 2, London.

    1961   'Comments', *Current Anthropology* 2, no. 3.

Lee, A.M. (ed.)   1959   *Principles of Sociology*, New York.

Le Febvre, G.   1955   *The Coming of the French Revolution, 1789*, translated by R.R. Palmer, New York.

Leiris, M.   1955   *Contacts de civilisations en Martinique et en Guadeloupe*, UNESCO, Paris.

LeVine, R.A. and W.H. Sangree   1962   'The diffusion of age-group organization in East Africa: a controlled comparison', *Africa* 32.

Lévi-Strauss, C.   1953   'Social structure', in Kroeber (1953).

Levy, M. Jr.   1952   *The Structure of Society*, Princeton.

Levy, R.   1957   *The Social Structure of Islam*, Cambridge.

Lewis, G.   1962   'The Trinidad and Tobago general election of 1961', *Caribbean Studies* 2, no. 2.

Lewis, I.M. (ed.)   1966   *Islam in Tropical Africa*, London.

Lewis, M.G.   1843   *Journal of a West Indian Proprietor Kept During a Residence on the Island of Jamaica*, London.

Lewis, W.A.   1965   'Beyond African dictatorship: the crisis of the one-party state', *Encounter* 25, no. 2.

Leyburn, J.   1941   *The Haitian People*, New Haven.

Lind, A.W. (ed.)   1955   *Race Relations in World Perspective*, Honolulu.

Linton, R. (ed.)   1948   *Most of the World*, New York.

Little, K.   1949   'The role of the secret society in cultural specialization', *American Anthropologist* 51.

    1951   *The Mende of Sierra Leone*, London.

    1965-6   'The political function of the Poro', *Africa* 35, 36 no. 1.

Lloyd, P.C.   1971*a*   *Classes, Crimes and Coups: Themes in the Sociology of Developing Countries*, London.

    1971*b*   *The Political Development of Yoruba Kingdoms in the Eighteenth and Nineteenth Centuries*, Royal Anthropological Institute Occasional Papers no. 31, London.

Lloyd Warner, W.   1958   *A Black Civilization: A Social Study of an Australian Tribe*, New York.

Lloyd Warner, W. and P.S. Lunt	1941	*The Social Life of a Modern Community*, New Haven.
Lloyd Warner, W., M. Meeker and K. Eells	1949	*Social Class in America: A Manual of Procedure for the Measurement of Social Status*, Chicago.
Lobb, J.	1940	'Caste and class in Haiti', *American Journal of Sociology* 46.
Lowenthal, D.	1957	'The population of Barbados', *Social and Economic Studies* 6, no. 4.
	1960*a*	*The Social Structure of Montserrat, W.1.*, Unpublished.
	1960*b*	'The range and variation of Caribbean societies', in Rubin (1960).
	1967	'Race and colour in the West Indies', *Daedalus*, Spring 1967.
	1972	*West Indian Societies*, London.
Lowie, R.	1926	*The Origin of the State*, London.
	1949	*Primitive Society*, London.
MacGaffey, W.	1961	'Social structure and mobility in Cuba', *Anthropological Quarterly* 34.
MacGaffey, W. and C. Barnet	1965	*Twentieth-Century Cuba: The Background to the Castro Revolution*, New York.
McHenry, J.P.	1962	*A Short History of Mexico*, New York.
MacIver, R.M.	1926	*The Modern State*, Oxford.
Mack, R.W.	1967	'Race, class and power in Barbados', in Bell (1967).
Macmillan, W.M.	1938	*Warning from the West Indies*, Harmondsworth.
MacRae Taylor, D.	1951	*The Black Caribs of British Honduras*, New York.
Maine, H.S.	1875	*Lectures on the Early History of Institutions*, London.
	1905	*Ancient Law*, 5th ed., London.
Mair, L.	1962	*Primitive Government*, Harmondsworth.
Malefijt, A. de W.	1963	*The Javanese of Surinam: Segment of a Plural Society*, Assen.
Malinowski, B.	1944	*A Scientific Theory of Culture and Other Essays*, Chapel Hill, N.C.
	1959	*Crime and Custom in Savage Society*, Paterson, New Jersey.
Manley, D.R.	1963	'Mental ability in Jamaica', *Social and Economic Studies* 12, no. 1.
Maquet, J.J.	1954	'The kingdom of Ruanda', in Forde (1965).
	1961	*The Premise of Inequality in Ruanda*, London.
Marriott, M.	1955	*Village India: Studies in the Little Community*, American Anthropologist Memoir no. 83, vol. 57, no. 3, part 2.
Marshall, L.	1957	'The kin terminology system of the !Kung Bushmen', *Africa* 27.
	1959	'Marriage among the !Kung Bushmen', *Africa* 29.
	1960	'!Kung Bushmen bands', *Africa* 30.
	1961	'Sharing, talking and giving: relief of social tensions among !Kung Bushmen', *Africa* 31.

	1962	'!Kung Bushmen religious beliefs', *Africa* 32.
	1965	'The !Kung Bushmen of the Kalahari desert', in Gibbs (1965).
Marshall, T.H.	1965	*Class, Citizenship and Social Development*, New York.
Marx, K. and F. Engels	1948	*The Communist Manifesto*, London.
Masuoka, J. and P. Valien (eds.)	1961	*Race Relations: Problems and Theory: Essays in Honour of Robert E. Park*, Chapel Hill, N.C.
Mathews, T.G.	1966	'Political picture in Surinam', in Mathews et al. (1966).
Mathews, T.G. et al.	1966	*Politics and Economics in the Caribbean: A Contemporary Analysis of the Dutch, French and British Caribbean*, Institute of Caribbean Studies, Special Study no. 3, Rio Piedras, Puerto Rico.
Mayer, A.	1960	*Caste and Kinship in Central India*, London.
Mayer, K.B.	1955	*Class and Society*, New York.
Mayer, P.	1949	*The Lineage Principle in Gusii Society*, Memorandum no. 24 of the International African Institute, London.
Mercier, P.	1965*a*	'Evolution of Senegalese elites', in van den Berghe (1965).
	1965*b*	'The European community of Dakar', in van den Berghe (1965).
Middleton, J.	1965	*The Lugbara of Uganda*, New York.
Middleton, J. and G. Kershaw	1951	*The Kikuyu and Kamba of Kenya*, Ethnographic Survey of Africa, East Central Africa Part 5, International African Institute, London.
Middleton, J. and D. Tait (eds.)	1958	*Tribes Without Rulers*, London.
Mills, C.W.	1959	*The Sociological Imagination*, New York.
Mintz, S.W.	1959	'Labour and sugar in Puerto Rico and Jamaica, 1800-1850', *Comparative Studies in Society and History* 1, no. 3.
	1964	Foreword to Guerra y Sanchez (1964).
Mitchell, J.C.	1960	*Tribalism and the Plural Society*, London.
Mitchell, J.C. and J.A. Barnes	1948	*The Lamba Village*, Communications of the School of African Studies, no. 24, Cape Town.
Montesquieu, Baron de	1949	*The Spirit of the Laws*, translated by Thomas Nugent, New York.
Moore, S.F.	1954	*Power and Property in Inca Peru*, New York.
Moore, W.E.	1963	*Social Change*, Englewood Cliffs, N.J.
Moreira, A.	1957	'General report, ethnic and cultural pluralism in the inter-tropical societies: legal and political aspects', in *Record of 30th Meeting*, International Institute of Differing Civilizations, Brussels.
Moreno, M.M.	1962	*La Organización Política y Social de los Aztecas*, Instituto Nacional de Antropología, Mexico.
Morgan, L.H.	1851	*League of the Iroquois*, 1962 ed., New York.
	1875	*Ancient Society*, New York.

Moskos, C.J. Jr.	1967	*The Sociology of Independence: A Study of Nationalist Attitudes among West Indian Leaders*, Cambridge, Mass.
Moskos, C.J. Jr. and W. Bell	1964	'Attitudes towards democracy among leaders in four emergent nations', *British Journal of Sociology* 15, no. 4.
Murdock, G.P.	1957	'World ethnographic sample', *American Anthropologist* 59, no. 4.
Myrdal, G.	1944	*An American Dilemma: The Negro Problem and Modern Democracy*, New York.
Nadel, S.F.	1938	'Social symbiosis and tribal organization', *Man* 38.
	1941	*A Black Byzantium: The Kingdom of Nupe in Nigeria*, London.
	1951	*The Foundations of Social Anthropology*, London.
Newman, P.	1964	*British Guiana: Problems of Cohesion in an Immigrant Society*, London.
Nicolaisen, J.	1963	*Ecology and Culture of the Pastoral Tuareg*, Copenhagen.
Niehoff, A. and J. Niehoff	1960	*East Indians in the West Indies*, Milwaukee Museum Publications in Anthropology no. 6.
Nimuendaju, C.	1946	*The Eastern Timbira*, translated and edited by Robert H. Lowie, University of California Publications in American Archaeology and Ethnology, vol. 41, Berkeley.
Olmsted, F.L.	1959	*The Slave States before the Civil War*, New York.
O'Loughlin, C.	1958	'The rice sector in the economy of British Guiana', *Social and Economic Studies* 7, no. 2.
Parry, J.H. and P.M. Sherlock	1956	*A Short History of the West Indies*, London.
Parsons, T.	1940	'An analytical approach to the theory of social stratification', *American Journal of Sociology* 45. Reprinted in Parsons (1949).
	1949	*Essays in Sociological Theory, Pure and Applied*, New York.
	1952	*The Social System*, London.
	1953	'A revised analytical approach to the theory of social stratification', in Bendix and Lipset (1953).
	1964	'A functional theory of change', in A. and E. Etzioni (1964).
	1966	*Societies: Evolutionary and Comparative Perspectives*, Englewood Cliffs, N.J.
Parsons, T. and E. Shils	1951*a*	'Values, motives and systems of action', in Parsons and Shils (1951*b*).
Parson, T. and E. Shils (eds.)	1951*b*	*Towards a General Theory of Action*, Cambridge, Mass.
Pearcy, G.E.	1965	*The West Indian Scene*, Princeton.
Peristiany, J.G.	1939	*The Social Institutions of the Kipsigis*, London.

	1954	'Law', in Evans-Pritchard (1954).
Peters, R.	1956	*Hobbes*, London.
Phillips, U.B.	1963	*Life and Labour in the Old South*, Boston.
Pirenne, H.	1963	*Economic and Social History of Medieval Europe*, New York.
	no date	*Medieval Cities: Their Origins and the Revival of Trade*, New York.
Pitt-Rivers, J.	1967	'Race, colour and class in Central America and the Andes', *Daedalus*, Spring 1967.
Post, K.W.J.	1963	*The Nigerian Federal Election of 1959: Politics and Administration in a Developing Political System*, London.
Postan, M.M., E.E. Rich and E. Miller (eds.)	1963	*Economic Organization and Policies in the Middle Ages, Cambridge Economic History of Europe*, vol. 3, London.
Pound, R.	1913	*Readings on the History and System of the Common Law*, 2nd ed., Boston.
	1959	*Jurisprudence*, St. Paul, Minn.
Powdermaker, H.	1939	*After Freedom: A Cultural Study of the Deep South*, New York.
Prins, A.H.J.	1953	*East African Age-class Systems*, Groningen.
Radcliffe-Brown, A.R.	1930-1	'The social organization of Australian tribes', *Oceania* 1, parts 1-4.
	1940	Preface to Fortes and Evans-Pritchard (1940*b*).
	1941	'The study of kinship systems', *Journal of the Royal Anthropological Institute* 71. Reprinted in Radcliffe-Brown (1952*d*).
	1950	Introduction to Radcliffe-Brown and Forde (1950).
	1952*a*	'Social sanctions', in Radcliffe-Brown (1952*d*).
	1952*b*	'Patrilineal and matrilineal succession', in Radcliffe-Brown (1952*d*).
	1952*c*	'Primitive law', in Radcliffe-Brown (1952*d*).
	1952*d*	*Structure and Function in Primitive Society*, London.
	1957	*A Natural Science of Society*, Glencoe, Ill.
Radcliffe-Brown, A.R. and D. Forde (eds.)	1950	*African Systems of Kinship and Marriage*, London.
Ramos, A.	1939	*The Negro in Brazil*, translated by R. Pattee, Washington.
Ray, V.F. (ed.)	1958	*Systems of Political Control and Bureaucracy in Human Societies*, Seattle.
Redfield, R.	1947	'The folk society', *American Journal of Sociology* 52.
Reischauer, E.O.	1956	'Japan', in Coulborn (1956).
Rheinstein, M. (ed.)	1954	*Max Weber on Law and Economy in Society*, Cambridge, Mass.
Richards, A.I.	1950	'Some types of family structure amongst the Central Bantu', in Radcliffe-Brown and Forde (1950).
Richards, A.I. (ed.)	1960	*East African Chiefs*, London.
Roberts, G.W.	1957	*The Population of Jamaica: An Analysis of its Structure and Growth*, London.

| Roberts, G.W. and N. Abdullah | 1965 | 'Some observations on the educational position of the British Caribbean', *Social and Economic Studies* 14, no. 1. |

Roberts, G.W. and L. Braithwaite — 1963 — 'Mating among East Indian and non-Indian women in Trinidad', *Social and Economic Studies* 11, no. 3.

Robertson Smith, W. — 1885 — *Kinship and Marriage in Early Arabia*, Cambridge.

Royal Anthropological Institute — 1951 — *Notes and Queries on Anthropology*, 6th ed., London.

Rubin, V. — 1962 — 'Culture, politics and race relations', *Social and Economic Studies* 11, no. 4.

Rubin, V. (ed.) — 1957 — *Caribbean Studies: A Symposium*, Kingston Institute of Social and Economic Research, UCWI.

— 1960 — *Social and Cultural Pluralism in the Caribbean*, Annals of the New York Academy of Sciences, vol. 83.

Rudé, G.F.E. — 1964 — *The Crowd in History*, New York.

Runciman, S. — 1961 — *Byzantine Civilization*, New York.

Ryan, S. — 1966 — 'The struggle for Afro-Indian solidarity in Trinidad', *Trinidad and Tobago Index* 4.

Sahlins, M. — 1958 — *Social Stratification in Polynesia*, Seattle.

Salmond, J. — 1947 — *Jurisprudence*, 10th ed., London.

Sansom, G.B. — 1962 — *Japan: A Short Cultural History*, New York.

Schacht, J. — 1950 — *The Origins of Muhammadan Jurisprudence*, Oxford.

Schapera, I. — 1950 — 'Kinship and marriage among the Tswana', in Radcliffe Brown and Forde (1950).

— 1953 — *The Tswana*, International African Institute, London.

— 1956 — *Government and Politics in Tribal Societies*, London.

— 1963 — 'Kinship and politics in Tswana history', *Journal of the Royal Anthropological Institute* 93.

Schapera, I. (ed.) — 1937 — *The Bantu-speaking Tribes of South Africa*, London.

Schneider, D.M. — 1961 — 'Comments', *Current Anthropology* 2, no. 3.

Schumpeter, L. — 1955a — 'Social classes in an ethnically homogeneous environment', in Schumpeter (1955b).

— 1955b — *Imperialism and Social Classes*, New York.

Schwab, W.B. — 1961 — 'Social stratification in Gwelo', in Southall (1961).

Schwartz, B.M. (ed.) — 1967 — *Caste in Overseas Indian Communities*, San Francisco.

Service, E.R. — 1962 — *Primitive Social Organization: An Evolutionary Perspective*, New York.

Sharp, L. — 1958 — 'People without politics', in Ray (1958).

Sheldon, R.C. — 1951 — 'Some observations on theory in the social sciences', in Parsons and Shils (1951b).

Shils, E. — 1962 — *Political Development in the New States*, Gravenhage.

Siegel, B.J. (ed.) — 1970 — *Biennial Review of Anthropology 1969*, Stanford, Calif.

Sills, D.L. (ed.)	1968	*International Encyclopaedia of the Social Sciences*, New York.
Simmons, D.	1956	'An ethnographic sketch of the Efik people', in Forde (1956).
Simpson, G.E.	1941	'Haiti's social structure', *American Sociological Review* 6, no. 5.
	1942	Sexual and familial institutions in Northern Haiti', *American Anthropologist* 44, no. 4.
	1962	'Social stratification in the Caribbean', *Phylon* 24.
Sjoberg, G.	1952	'Folk and feudal societies', *American Journal of Sociology* 58.
Skinner, E.P.	1960	'Group dynamics and social stratification in British Guiana', in Rubin (1960).
Smelser, N.J. and S.M. Lipset	1966a	'Social structure, mobility and development', in Smelser and Lipset (1966b).
Smelser N.J. and S.M. Lipset (eds.)	1966b	*Social Structure and Mobility in Economic Development*, Chicago.
Smith, M.F.	1954	*Baba of Karo: A Woman of the Moslem Hausa*, London.
Smith, M.G.	1952	*The Social Organization and Economy of Kagoro*. Unpublished.
	1953a	'Secondary marriage in Northern Nigeria', *Africa* 23.
	1953b	'Some aspects of social structure in the British Caribbean about 1820', *Social and Economic Studies* 1.
	1954a	Introduction to M.F. Smith (1954).
	1954b	'Slavery and emancipation in two societies', *Social and Economic Studies* 3.
	1955	*The Economy of Hausa Communities of Zaria Province*, Colonial Research Publications no. 16, London.
	1957	'Ethnic and cultural pluralism in the British Caribbean', in *Record of the 30th Meeting*, International Institute of Differing Civilizations, Brussels.
	1959	'The Hausa system of social status', *Africa* 29.
	1960a	*Government in Zazzau, 1881-1950*, London.
	1960b	'Kagoro political development', *Human Organization* 19, no. 3.
	1960c	'Social and cultural pluralism', in Rubin (1960).
	1961	'Kebbi and Hausa stratification', *British Journal of Sociology* 12.
	1962	*Kinship and Community in Carriacou*, New Haven.
	1963	*Dark Puritan*, University of the West Indies, Kingston.
	1964a	Historical and cultural conditions of political corruption among the Hausa', *Comparative Studies in Society and History* 6.
	1964b	'The beginnings of Hausa society', in Vansina et al. (1964).
	1965a	*Stratification in Grenada*, Berkeley and Los

		Angeles.
	1965*b*	'The Hausa of Northern Nigeria', in Gibbs (1965).
	1965*c*	*The Plural Society in the British West Indies*, Berkeley and Los Angeles.
	1966	'The Jihad of Shehu dan Fodio: some problems', in I.M. Lewis (1966).
	1968	'The two variants in Caribbean race relations', *Race* 10, no. 1.
Smith, M.G., R. Augier and R. Nettleford	1960	*The Rastafari Movement in Kingston, Jamaica*, Kingston.
Smith, R.J.	1963	'Aspects of mobility in pre-industrial Japanese cities', *Comparative Studies in Society and History* 5.
Smith, R.T.	1962	*British Guiana*, London.
Soustelle, J.	1962	*Daily Life of the Aztecs*, New York.
Southall, A.	1952	*Lineage Formation among the Luo*, Memorandum 26, International African Institute, London.
	1956	*Alur Society: A Study in Processes of Domination*, Cambridge.
Southall, A. (ed.)	1961	*Social Change in Modern Africa*, London.
Southwold, M.	c. 1960	*Bureaucracy and Chiefship in Buganda*, East African Studies no. 14, East African Institute of Social Research, Kampala.
Spackmann, A.	1967	'The senate of Trinidad and Tobago', *Social and Economic Studies* 16, no. 1.
Speckman, J.D.	1963	'The Indian group in the segmental society of Surinam', *Caribbean Studies* 3, no. 1.
Spencer, H.	1969	*The Principles of Sociology*, edited by Stanislav Andreski, London.
Srinivas, M.N. et al.	1959	'Caste: a trend report and bibliography', *Current Sociology* 8, no. 3.
Stampp, K.M.	1964	*The Peculiar Institution: Slavery in the Ante-Bellum South*, New York.
Stefansson, V.	1962	*My Life with the Eskimo*, New York.
Stenning, D.J.	1959	*Savannah Nomads: A Study of the Wodaabe Pastoral Fulani of Western Bornu Province, Northern Region, Nigeria*, London.
	1965	'The Pastoral Fulani of Northern Nigeria', in Gibbs (1965).
Stevenson, H.N.C.	1954	'Status evaluation in the Hindu caste system', *Journal of the Royal Anthropological Institute* 84.
Steward, J.	1938	*Basin-Plateau Socio-Political Groups*, Bureau of American Ethnology, Bulletin 120, Washington, D.C.
	1955	*Theory of Culture Change*, Illinois.
Tannenbaum, F.	1946	*Slave and Citizen: The Negro in the Americas*, New York.
	1957	'Discussion', in Rubin (1957).
Tawney, R.H.	1961	*Equality*, 4th ed., New York.
Thrupp, S. (ed.)	1962	*Millennial Dreams in Action: Essays in Comparative Study*, The Hague.

Trinidad and Tobago,   1964   *Draft Second Five Year Plan 1964-8*, Port of
   Government of   Spain.
Tumin, M.M.   1952   *Caste in a Peasant Society*, Princeton.
                       1953   'Some principles of stratification: a critical
                                analysis', *American Sociological Review* 18.
Turnbull, C.   1961   *The Forest People*, New York.
                       1965   'The Mbuti Pygmies of the Congo', in Gibbs
                                (1965).
Ullendorf, E.   1965   *The Ethiopians: An Introduction to Country
                                and People*, London.
UNESCO   1969   *Apartheid: Its Effects on Education,
                                Science, Culture and Information*, Paris.

van den Berghe, P.L.   1965   *Africa: Social Problems of Change and
   (ed.)   Conflict*, San Francisco.
                       1967   *South Africa: A Study in Conflict*, San
                                Francisco.
van der Sprenkel, S.   1962   *Legal Institutions in Manchu China*, London.
van Lier, R.A.J.   1950   *The Development and Nature of Society in
                                the West Indies*, Royal Institute for the
                                Indies, Amsterdam.
Vansina, J., R. Mauny 1964   *The Historian in Tropical Africa*, London.
   and L.V. Thomas (eds.)
van Warmelo, N.J.   1931   *Kinship Terminology of the South African
                                Bantu*, Pretoria Department of Native
                                Affairs, Union of South Africa.
Vasiliev, A.A.   1958   *History of the Byzantine Empire*, revised
                                ed., Madison, Wisc.
Vaughan, C.E.   1915   *The Political Writings of Jean-Jacques Rous-
                                seau*, London.
Vinogradoff, P.   1959   *Common Sense in Law*, 3rd ed., revised by
                                H.G. Hanbury, London.
von Grunebaum, G.E.   1953   *Medieval Islam*, 2nd ed., Chicago.

Waddell, D.A.G.   1963   *British Honduras: A Historical and Con-
                                temporary Survey*, London.
Warde Fowler, H.   1952   *The City State of the Greeks and Romans*,
                                London.
Weber, M.   no date *General Economic History*, translated by
                                Frank Knight, New York.
                       1947   *The Theory of Social and Economic Organ-
                                ization*, translated by A.R. Henderson and T.
                                Parsons, London.
                       1954   *Max Weber on Law in Economy and
                                Society*, translated with Introduction by M.
                                Rheinstein, Cambridge, Mass.
                       1960   *The City*, translated and edited by D.
                                Martindale and G. Neuwirth, London.
Wendell-Holmes, O.   1897   *The Path of Law*, cited in J.K. Allen (1961).
West Indian   1950   Government Printer, Kingston.
   Census, 1946
West Indian   1961   'Jamaica's income and its distribution', vol.
Economist   3, no. 11.
West India Royal   1945   *Report*, London.
   Commission
Williams, E.   no date *The Negro in the Caribbean*, Manchester.

	1946	*Capitalism and Slavery*, Chapel Hill, N.C.
	1957	'Race relations in Caribbean society', in Rubin (1957).
Wilson, G. and M.	1948	*The Analysis of Social Change*, London.
Wilwright, A.	1966	'Of colour of skin and St. Vincent', *Flambeau* 3, January 1966.
Winans, E.V.	1962	*Shambala: The Constitution of a Traditional State*, Berkeley and Los Angeles.
Wirth, L.	1938	'Urbanism as a way of life', *American Journal of Sociology* 44.
Wittfogel, K.A. and Feng Chia-Sheng	1949	*History of Chinese Society: Liao (907-1125)*, Transactions of the American Philosophical Society, n.s., 36.
Worsley, P.	1957	*The Trumpet Shall Sound: A Study of 'Cargo' Cults in Melanesia*, London.
	1964	*The Third World*, London.
Zinkin, T.	1960	*Caste Today*, London.

Index

Abbasid caliphate, 246
Aberle, S.F., et al., 135n, 145n, 152n
absolutism, 71, 118, 162
Abu Hanifa, legal school of, 112
accommodation: interracial, 265-8, 272-4, 331-3, 337-47; and miscegenation, 289-97, 323-4
accretion, in lineages, 17, 18, 38, 39, 49, 50
acephalous societies: based on lineages, 18, 35, 82-4; boundaries of, 97-8; compared with centralized societies, 45, 71-2, with stateless societies (q.v.), 80; linked publics in, 208-9; pluralism and, 208-9, 220, 231; political organization and, 81; shared institutions in, 208-9; social conflict in, 97-9, 154
achievement and ascription, in status, 137, 138, 149-51, 154
action: authorized, 27; co-ordinate (common), 44, 99-100, 208; governmental, 26-31, 46-56; in institutions, 206, 208; ultra vires, 29 (see also administrative, collective-, corporate-, political action)
activities, and political authority, 25
'ada, 113
Adams, R.N. et al., 159n
ad hoc agencies, 52-3, 101-2
adjudication, in political systems, 92
administration: and segmentary lineages, 19-56; as mode of action in political systems, 28, 92; bureaucracy and, 21, 28, 29; centralized, 18, 30, 52-5, 117-18, 121-4; law in, 117-8, 121-4; offices in, 52-5; segmentary systems and, 28-30, 47-8; hierarchic form of, 31-5, 51-5; in plural societies, 230-4; super- and subordinate relations in, 27-8, 32; territorial, 19, 47 (see also corporations, government, societies)
administrative action: 26, 27-32, 135; as regulatory action, 85-6; political action and, 28-37, 46-52, 57-8, 67-9
'administrative organs', as offices, 44
adoption, in matrilineages, 74
advantage, see differential distributions
'affairs', in government, 24-5, 27
Africa: colonial societies in, 234-8; emergent nations in, 207, 238; law in, 107-9, 110, 126-31
Africans, in Caribbean, 276, 280-1, 284, 298, 300, 328, 340
age-organization, 141, 145, 201
age-sets: as corporate categories, 100, 201; as segments, 35-7, 54, 59, 74, 78; hierarchies of, 141-2, 145; in complex societies, 252-3, 260-1; in multilineal societies, 260-1
aggregates: biological, 19; in simple societies, 20, 74; publics and, 82; 'systems' and, 204
agnatic descent groups, 41, 61, 68, 110
Ahiram, E., 316n
Ahmad b. Hanbal, legal school of, 112
Akamba, law among, 122
Akan: chiefdoms among, 55; descent groups among, 57
Allah, and law, 110
allocation, in complex societies, 252
Allport, E.A., 250n
Almond, G., 92; and J.S. Coleman (eds.) 255n
Althusius, on federalism, 118
amalgamation: in lineage descent, 32, 49 (see also fusion); of racial segments, 300-1, 338-43
American Negroes, as corporate categories, 101
Amerindians, 274, 280-1, 300, 325; miscegenation among, 276, 288, 290
Amish, 225
analogy, in Muslim law, 111
'analytic structures', 244
Andamanese bands, 30, 52
Andic, F.M., 316n; and S. Andic, 303n, 316n, 321n
Anglo-Saxon law, 122
Anguilla, landholdings in, 302
antecedent corporations, 123
anthropological field study, 73, 75-6, 78, 81
Antigua, 285, 302, 307, 309
apprenticeship, 285
Apthorpe, R., 75n, 79n
Aquinas, on law, 116
Arabs, 110, 264
Arawak, settlers in, 280
'archaic' societies, 73, 246, 249
Argyle, J.W., 266n
Aristotle: on citizenship, 210n; on collective domination, 234n; on law, 115
arms laws, in Caribbean, 298
Arnett, E.J., 233n
articulation: of segments, 259-60; of systems, 184-7, 191-204, 246
associations: dyadic and triadic, 100; hierarchies in, 83-4, 86-7; in lineages, 33, 37, 51, 54; regulatory, 85-7

Assyria, 246
Athens, pluralism in, 230n
Austin, on law, 119
Australian aborigines, 136-7, 247
autarchy: in corporations, 99-100; in law, 117; in lineages, 87; in segmental societies, 245, 264
authority: and force, 30; and government, 27-37; and power, 29-30, 32-3, 104-5, 175, 192-7; and publics, 85-6; 'coercive', 21, 80; 'constituted', 123; decentralized, 105; illegitimate, 195; in corporations, 44, 97; in law, 124; in political systems, 25, 79, 175-6; of leadership, 193-4
autonomy: and co-ordination, 99-100; in complex societies, 237-8, 251, 261, 268-9; in corporations, 73, 85-7, 99-100, 131, 187, 192-4, 196-202, 269; in pluralism, 230; of lineages, 73, 110, 201; of nation-states, 99
Ayearst, M., 326n

Bacon, E., 263n, 265n
Baganda: consociational regime among, 264; law among, 127-8
Bailey, F.G., 155n
Bakongo prophets, 256
Balandier, G., 207n
Ball, John, charismatic leader, 233
bands: Bushmen, 52, 76, 97, 127-8, 188, 247; composite, 258-60; corporate, 97, 177, 180, 188-9; in complex societies, 258
Bantu Kavirondo: fragmentation of function among, 53, 54; status among, 33
Bantu, Southern, sibling status among, 148
Barbados, 235, 265, 285, 292, 300; differential advantage in, 302-9; population of, 278-9, 281
Barbuda: slaves in, 285; stratification in, 302, 306, 308-9
Barker, E., 110, 117n
Barnes, J.A., 78-9
Barth, F., 8n, 96, 158n, 214n, 231, 234n, 250n
Basham, A.L., 155n
bases of incorporation: of groups, 101, 103-4, 180-91, 198-204; of individuals, 181, 192-8, 258-9 (*see also* societal incorporation)
Beals, R., 159n, 160, 254n
Bedouin, 247
Beidelman, T.O., 155n
békés, 294-5, 316
Belize, Creoles in, 287, 339
Bell, W., 329n
Bemba, 16, 33-4, 52, 57, 78
Benedict, B., 160n, 230n, 250n
Bennett, H.S., 156n
Benoist, J., 303n
Bernal, I., 158n
Bernardi, B., 18n, 23, 37n, 78n, 142n
bicameral legislature, in Trinidad, 327
Bierstedt, R., 117n
'bifurcated' stratification, 162
'big men', of Melanesia, 256
bilateral kinship relations, 142-3, 263-5
biological aspects, in segmentation, 19

bi-racial societies, 280, 290-1, 297, 301-5, 317-19, 324-5, 328-9, 342-3
Birket-Smith, K., 102n
birth status, and opportunity, 156-7
'black bourgeoisie', 227, 230
blacks, in Caribbean: differential opportunity of, 303, 306-8, 312-14; distinguished from 'coloureds', 276-7
Black, C.V., 386n
Bloch, M., 156n, 234n, 250n
Blumer, H., 257n, 275n, 280n, 331n, 332n
Bohannan, L., 14, 19, 32, 36n; and P. Bohannan, 188n
Bohannan, P., 137, 145n
'bond slaves', 147
'borough English', 145
Bottomore, T.B., 136n
Brahminical rites, 223
Braithwaite, L., 323n, 328n
Brazil, as heterogeneous society, 213
Brehon law, 122
Brion Davis, D., 282n
Britain: as complex society, 269; as heterogeneous society, 213; as segmental society, 33, 242; medieval, 145; monarchy in, 64
British Administration: in Caribbean, 281, 289, 290-1; in Nigeria, 49; in Zaria, 66
British Colonial Office, 275, 287
British colonists, in Caribbean, 274, 280, 294, 296, 298-9, 301-28
British Guiana, *see* Guyana
British Honduras, 278, 289; census of, 286; immigrants in, 274, 287-8; slavery in, 285, 298-9; stratification in, 289-90, 302, 306-7, 325
British Virgin Islands, 280
Brockelmann, C., 233n
Broom, L., on Jamaica, 160n, 276n, 328n, 329n; on plural societies, 160n, 210, 293n, 328n
Brown, G.A., 315n
Brown, P., 31, 54-5, 78
Buckley, W., 8n
Buddhism, as theocratic regime, 214
Buganda, law in, 127-8
Bulgars, in pluralism, 233
'bull' prophet, 102
Bull Savanna, 288
bureaucracy: and complex societies, 246; and government, 21, 28, 79; and offices, 47; Chinese, 157; Western type, 79
Bushmen: *ad hoc* commissions among, 102; bands among, 52, 76, 97, 128, 247; families among, 144-5; law among, 127-8
Bush Negroes, 290, 325
Busoga, political authority among, 79
butlan, 125n
Bwamba: as acephalous society, 81
Byzantium: as complex society, 246, 262; pluralism in, 233

Caicos Islands, 280, 285, 298
Caliph Omar II, 111
Canella, multiple corporations among, 191
canon law, 116
capacity of systems, 174
Cardozo, B.N., 119-20

cargo cults, 102, 233
Caribbean Monthly Bulletin, 326n
Carib Indians, 280-1, 287, 289, 291-2, 306, 325, 328
Carlyle, Thomas, on slavery, 300
Carolingian Europe, as complex society, 246
Carriacou, 285, 294, 298, 325, 340-1
cartels, 246
Carthage: as complex society, 246; constitution in, 230n
Cary, M., 230n, 232n
'caste endogamy', in Ruanda, 158, 221
caste systems: 'condensation' in, 264; incorporation in, 101, 104; inter-caste relations, 223-4; miscegenation and, 293, 294-5; pluralism and, 215-16, 220-5, stratification and, 137, 155-8, 223-4, 271-345 *passim*
categorial theory, and political change, 167
categorical clans, 101, 187-8
categories: closed, in racial division, 228; contrasted to publics, 82 (*see also* corporate categories)
Cayman Islands, 280, 288, 291, 294, 325, 328
cellular subdivision, 19
censuses: British Honduras, 288; British West Indian, 274, 297, 303, 305, 314; Cuba, 282; Jamaica, 288; Trinidad and West Indian, 275; use of, in stratification study, 297
centralization: dichotomy of, 98-9; of authority, 21, 29, 35, 98; of unilineal societies, 295 (*see also* political centralization, *and under* administration and government)
centralized despotism, 128
centralized societies, 24, 45-9, 55-6, 91, 141-2, 209, 214-15, 255; compared with stateless societies, 71-2; hierarchical, 79; imperfect, 124-5; plural societies and, 220, 231; prerequisites for, 87; social conflict in, 97-9
chamber officials, Zarian, 47
change, forms of, 171-3, 199 (*see also* endogenous-, exogenous-, and political change)
charismatic leadership, 102, 178, 181, 233, 248, 256
chartered companies, in colonies, 262
Chartism, in collective protest, 233
·Chevalier, F., 234n
Cheyenne tribe, 191, 256
chiefships, 33, 48, 52, 53, 55, 78, 112-14, 141, 261
China, as complex society, 233, 246, 249, 262
Chinese, in Caribbean, 274, 275, 300, 303, 338, 340; differential advantages of, 264, 307, 312-13; hybrids, 276, 277, 293; indentured, 286-7, 292, 296
Christianity, as theocratic regime, 214
Christophe, leader, 283, 285
Church, relations with state, 116
Ciboney, 280
civil rights, 188, 237, 276, 290, 298-300, 334, 339 (*see also* differential distributions) 369

civitas, 74
clans, 15, 146; categorical, 101, 187-8; 'conical', 148
Clarke, C., 323n
class: as basis of social systems, 136; in feudalism, 159 (*see* rank, status, stratification)
clientage, 79, 234, 266
closed segments, in pluralism, 209, 224-5, 334
co-activity, in institutions, 208, 211-12
coalitions, 50
Cobb, J., 295n
codes of conduct, in offices, 44
coercion, 21, 24, 30, 80, 120, 125, 132
cognatic systems, 41, 263
Cohen, R., and J. Middleton (eds.), 333n
cohesion, in pluralism, 232
Cohn, N.R.C., 232n, 233n
coincident roles, in colonialism, 243·
Cole, C.W., 113n
Cole, G.D.H., and R. Postgate, 236n
Coleman, J.S., 230n
collateral units, in segmentary societies, 15-16, 19, 35
collective accommodation, 273-4; 289-97, 337-45
collective action, 187, 192-3, 228, 232, 236, 255-6
collective boundaries, in pluralism, 224, 226, 228-30
collective domains, in social organization, 216, 220-39 *passim*
collective domination: in complex societies, 261-2, 266-8; in pluralism, 226-7, 231, 234-7; in stratification, 333, 336, 340
collective emergencies, 192
collective endogamy, 221-2
collective equality, 222
collective incorporation, in stratification, 337-43
collective inequality, 295
collective power, as basis of stratification, 297-301
collective proscriptions, 221, 232, 255, 267
collective protest, 232-3, 235-7
collective regulation, 187, 209, 216-17, 250, 254-62, 268-9
collective responsibility, 82, 259
collective unity, in corporations, 43-4
collectivist society, 249-50
collectivities: closures in, 224-5; in pluralism, 205-11, 214-17, 220-39; in stratification, 253-69, 272-4, 297-301, 331-43
colleges, in corporate groups, 178, 255, 256
colonialism: and situs structure, 162; complexity in, 243-4, 249; government in, 108-10, 179, 207, 215, 220, 290-1
colonial legislatures, 299-300, 327
colonial militia, 298
'coloured' classification, compared to 'black', 276-7
Colson, E., 188n
commissions, 100-2, 178-9, 256-7; *ad hoc*, 52-3, 101-2; distinct from offices, 101-2, 179; ranked series of, 179, 181
common government, in colonialism, 220
common law, 82, 119, 120, 127, 129-30

common value system, 152-3
communities: as corporate groups, 177; political organization and, 23-4
community councils, 201-2
community values, 24, 152-3, 162
comparative analyses: complex societies, 241-70; corporate units, 134-41; governments, 55-6, 77; historical approaches to, 166; law, 121-2; politics, 91-105; racial stratification, 297-8; segmentary lineages, 17, 22; social processes, 134-41
competition: combined with restriction, 156-8; for power, 15-16, 26-7, 67; in law, 117; in political action, 27-8, 47; in stratification, 156-8, 251; inter-caste, 156-8, 290-1; inter-dynastic, 48
complementary filiation, in segmentary lineages, 16, 19, 39, 41, 64
'complexity', 241-6, 256-62, 265-9
complex societies, 241-70; and modern societies, 241; and simple societies, 241-3, 249; characteristics of, 241-2, 248-53, 264-5, 269; continuity of, 251-2; typology of corporate units in, 247-8
'complication', 242
'concrete structures', 133-4, 245-52, 264-5
concubinage, 147-8, 292-3; as institutionalized connubium, 222
'condensation' of societies, 244-7, 264
confederation, and political modernization, 173, 188-9, 196-7
conflict: in law, 127; in pluralism, 232 (see also revolts, revolution, wars, and under race relations)
Confucianism, and stratification, 157
Congress Party, Indian, 232
'conical clans', 148
connubium, 184, 220-2, 292; asymmetrical, 340; symmetrical, 222, 266 (see also miscegenation)
conquest, in complex societies, 263, 265-6
conquest states, 78, 158
consensus, and stratification, 137, 151-9, 161-2; in Muslim law, 111-14
consilium plebis, 232
consociation, interracial, 264-5, 273, 290-1, 334
consociational incorporation, 187-90, 193-7, 333-4
constituted authority, 123
constitution, in Zaria, 48
constitutional law, 110-14, 126-7
'constructivist systems', 244
continuity: concurrent with change, 170; corporateness and, 44, 256, 257-62; in 'composite bands', 259; in pluralism, 230-2
continuous change, in political theory, 172-3
contraposition: in segmentary theory, 15-16, 19, 32, 37-8, 40; of corporations, 227-8, 230
conversion, in pluralism, 233
'coolies', 278
co-ordinate group corporations, 54
co-ordinate relations: autonomy and, 99-100; in complex societies, 191-2,

208, 264, 267; in lineages, 15, 16, 19, 32, 44
corporate action, 43-4, 53, 96, 336-7
corporate bands, 97, 177, 180, 188-9, 258-9
corporate categories, 100-4, 177-8, 182-7, 209, 233, 237, 248, 254-6; collective regulation in, 54, 187, 191-3, 194-9, 228-9, 254-68, 336; proscriptions in, 187, 255, 256
corporate constitution: in pluralism, 205-11; in simple societies, 97-8, 128-31
corporate groups, 17, 39, 43-56, 62-3, 66, 73, 94-7, 143-4; and acephalous societies, 209; as publics, 94; compared with offices, 95-7; lineages and, 42-3, 49, 53-4, 65, 79; political relations and, 49, 176-80; varieties of, 94, 177-8, 196-7
corporateness, characteristics of, 8-10, 44-59, 209
corporate status, 96, 143-4, 208, 254-6, 333-9
corporate units, typology of, 179-80, 247-8
corporations: antecedent, 123; as basis of societies, 124, 254-62, 268-9; autonomy in, 73, 85-7, 99-100, 131, 187, 192-4, 196-202, 269; bases of incorporation, 101, 103-4, 180-91, 198-204, 254-63; differentiation in, 86-7, 97-8, 188, 266, 338-45; hierarchies in, 56, 97, 122-4, 143-4, 179, imperfect, 100-1; in stratification, 189-204, 261-3, 333-9; intercalary, 103-4; law and, 88, 97, 122-4, 128, 131; membership in, 181-2, 187, 199-200, 255, 335-6; modes of incorporation, 183-204, 254-62 (see societal incorporation); occupational, 122; 'perfect', 94, 100-1, 178, quasi-, 100-1, 256 (see commissions); unity in, 43, 94-5; universal characteristics of, 187; varieties of; aggregate and sole, 54-5, 123, 179, groups and categories, 101, 182-3, group and sole, 94-5, 99
corporations aggregate, 123, 189-90, 254-5; and segmentary lineages, 43-4, 52, 54-5; in societal organization, 73, 254-5, 261, 335
corporations sole, 43-56, 59, 94, 179-80, 254; in simple societies, 73, 105, 128 (see also offices)
corporative state, Fascist, 123
Coulton, G.G., 156n
councils, in collective regulation, 201-2, 254-5, 261, 263
Court of Appeal, Dakar, 129
Creoles, 235, 271-345 *passim*; and status structure, 323-4, 341-2; classification of, 276-80, 343-5; corporate contraposition of, 227-8, 230; relations with Indians, 227-8, 322-3, 325-7; social advantages of, 319-24, 327
crime, and stratification, 273
Criollos, *see* Creoles
Crowder, M., 228n
Crow Indians, as origin of state, 75
Crowley, D.J., 228n, 323n
Crown Colony Rule, 275
Cuba, 295; classification in, 275, 277-8, 280, 282; slavery in, 282, 284-6

cult institutions, 218-19, 220; *boyar*, 83; earth cult, 83; 'cargo cults', 102, 233, cult groups, as segments, 35, 37, 259
cultural pluralism, 159-60, 205, 209-10, 228, 340
Curaçao, 285
custom: in law, 110, 114, 120-1, 127, 129-30; in Muslin law, 110, 114; in status, 122
customary law, in Africa, 129-30
cyclical change, 172-3
Cyprus: classification in, 267; complexity in, 250

Dahomey, corporations among, 55
daimyo, 156
Dakar, Court of Appeal, 129
Davis, A. et al., 227n
Davis, J.P., 9, 96, 156n
Davis, K., 138n, 145n; and W.E. Moore, 135n, 138n, 152n, 154n
debt-bondage, 263, 266
decolonization, in Caribbean, 290, 329-31, 341-5
dehumanization, in pluralism, 267-8
Delavignette, R., 129-30
democracies, 28, 50, 71
'democratic reforms' and social pluralism, 230
'demographic condensation' of societies, 264-7
deontology, in Muslim law, 114
deportation, after emancipation, 287-8
descent: agnatic, 61, 68; corporate groups and, 38, 66-7; ideological nature of, 58, 68; in lineage segmentation, 17, 38, 40-1, 64, 143-4, 259-60 (*see also* unilineal descent)
despotism: 'condensation' in, 246; in African law, 128; in stratification, 158
Despres, L.A., 228n, 267n, 286n, 300n, 321n, 322n, 326n
Dessalines, charismatic leader, 233, 283
De Tocqueville, A., 233n
Deutscher, I., 28n
D'Hertefelt, M., 101n, 158n, 214n, 221n, 231n, 234n; et al., 231, 232n
dhimmi, 101, 131, 214
diachronic systems, 174, 275-6
differential distributions: of advantages, opportunities, etc., 133-5, 137-45, 149, 155-8, 226-7, 249, 253, 258-60, 290, 297, 311-22, 341; in education, 226-7, 290, 307-11, 322; in occupational role, 226-7, 290, 311-22; of political rights, 226-7, 290, 296-301, 308, 311; of property, 226-7, 290, 302-5, 319-23
differential incorporation, 187-93, 242-3, 333-6, 338-45
disguised pluralism, 239
dissent: in ruling groups, 232; in secular systems, 160
divine appointment, in imperium, 116
divine kingships, 95, 231
divine law, 110-14, 116-17, 127
divine purpose, in law, 116
'division of labour', in complex societies, 242-7, 253

divorce, among Tallensi, 62
Djuka, Bush Negroes, 290
doglas, 228, 278, 293
domains, in social organization, 216, 220-39 *passim*, 249-56
dominant groups: in Caribbean, 295-6, 337-43; in pluralism, 215, 234-7, 261-2 (*see also* collective domination)
Dominica, 288, 300, 328; amalgamation in, 338; classification in, 274, 277-9, 295; differential advantage in, 302, 307
Dominican Republic (Santo Domingo), 276
dominion, and lineages, 201
dream-prophet, Bantu, 33
Duke, J.T., 330n
Dunn, L.C., 274n
Durkheim, E., 108, 122; *Division of Labour in Society*, 7, 96, 122, 242-3, 244-5, 250n, 258; *Professional Ethics and Civic Morals*, 122, 152, 245, 254n; *Rules of Sociological Method*, 7, 257n
Dutch colonists, 300, 321; and slavery, 281-2
Dutch East Indies, indentured labour, 287
dynamic density, of societies, 244-5
dynamism, in complex societies, 244-6
dynastic wars, 98
dynasties, patrilineal, 48, 56, 64-6
Dyson-Hudson, N., 100, 142n, 192n

East Indians, 270-343 *passim*; corporate contraposition among, 227-8; differential advantages of, 302-3, 308, 311, 321; relations with Creoles, 227-8, 322-3
Easton, D., 8n, 92, 244
ecclesiastical law, 116
ecological factors: in legal systems, 72; in pluralism, 232, 233; in stratification, 287, 289
economic action, 28
economic development, and stratification, 138
economic labour, 242-5
Economist Intelligence Unit, 309n, 316n
economy: in Caribbean, 281-2, 285-7, 299; in pluralism, 206, 232; in simple societies, 76; in Soviet Union and USA, 218
Edmonson, M.S., 150-1
education, in Caribbean, 299, 306-11
Efik, subjugation of, 261, 266
egalitarianism, 136; in simple societies, 181, 192-3; in stratification, 273, 291, 311
Eggan, F., 191n
Egypt: as archaic society, 246, 249; as complex society, 262
Ehrenberg, V., 230n, 234n
Eisenstadt, S.N., 241n, 253n
Ekpe, secret society, 261
elections, 36-7, 315, 326, 329
elites, 107, 108-9, 237, 295-6, 304-5, 308, 316-20, 324-5, 329-30, 342-3
Elkins, S.M., 159n, 227n
emancipation, effects of, 285-7, 299-301, 343-5
'emergent nations', 162, 207, 238, 242, 249
emigration, after emancipation, 287-8
emperors, in Roman law, 115-16

employers' associations, 246
endogamy: and caste, 221-4, 255; in complex societies, 264-5; in racial segments, 287, 289, 292-6, 323
endogenous change, 168, 192-4, 198, 200
Engels, on simple societies, 74
enslavement, *see* slavery
entailments of incorporation, 180-6, 197-201
episodic change, 172-3
equality: formal, 183, 188, 230; 'perfect', 139-40; social, 135-7, 332
equal opportunity, ideology of, 342
equilibrium: in lineage segments, 15; in political action, 24; in systemic articulation, 185, 198-9; stationary, 186-7 (*see also* equilibrium)
equity, in British law, 127
Eskimos: *ad hoc* commissions among, 102; shamans, 256
esprit de corps, in pluralism, 232
Ethiopia, social pluralism in, 238
ethnic categories: and intermarriage, 221; in pluralism, 232; in stratification, 159-60, 271-346 *passim*
ethnocentrism, of law, 110
ethnographic data: for intercalary groups, 103-4; for societal boundaries, 93; in politics, 91; in stratification, 149, 271-346 *passim*
eunuch staff, in Zaria, 47
Europe: federalism in, 118; feudalism in, 234-5; stratification in, 155-6; theocracies and pluralism in, 215, 236
European Common Market, as lineage alliance, 86
Europeanized Africans, 107
European law, influence on African law, 107
Evans-Pritchard, E.E., 62-3, 78n; 'The political structure of the Nandi-speaking peoples of Kenya', 14, 15, 16, 18, 37, 56, 78n; *The Nuer*, 16, 19, 20, 24, 33n, 41-2, 43, 57-9, 63, 67, 69, 78n, 102n, 260n
exegesis, in Muslim law, 111
exogamy, 60-1, 74, 83, 255, 258-9, 264-5
exogenous relations, in systems, 168, 185, 196, 200
expansion, in Ngoni conquest states, 78
'experimental' marriage, 62
extensive change, 171
external articulation, 182-6
Eyre, John, 300

Fallers, L., 79n
familial action, in complex societies, 251
familial domain, in social organization, 216
familial institutions, 220-6, 253
familial structure: and segmentary lineages, 16, 19, 38-9, 83, 171-2; rank, status, and class in, 144-50
famuli, of plebs, 266
Farley, R., 285n
fascist corporative state, 123
federalism, in Europe, 118
federation: and pluralism, 220; West Indian, 327, 330

Fedon, 284
feud, 121; and coercive authority, 21; and co-ordinate lineages, 31, 260; and political action, 24
feudalism, 234; and law, 116-18, 123; and stratification, 156, 159; in complex societies, 246, 249, 250
feudal states, administration in, 28
fictive kinship relations, 143
fiefs, 123
fiqh, 111, 113-14
fission: in lineages, 15, 17, 18, 28, 32, 38, 49-50, 58, 61, 63, 78, 86, 147; internal, in caste, 155-6
Flanders, as complex society, 246
folk societies, 242
folk systems, of classification, 275
Fon of Dahomey, 266
force: and political organization, 20-1, 24, 30, 80, 84, 92; and stratification, 58-9; authorized control of, 30; centralization of, 22-3, 92; coercive, 24, 30; control and regulation of, 20-1; in law, 124; legitimization of, 30
forced immigration, 265-7
Forde, D., 13n, 14n, 24, 37n, 40, 78n, 103n, 191n; and G.I. Jones, 191n
formal egalitarianism, in simple societies, 189
formal equality: in corporations, 183, 188; in social pluralism, 230
formal requisites and entailments, of incorporation, 183-4, 200
forms: in corporations, 180, 183, 191-204; in social relations, 207-8
Forte de France, race riots, 301
Fortes, M., 39n, 95, 188n, 216; *The Dynamics of Clanship among the Tallensi*, 15, 18n, 32n, 62-3; 'The structure of unilineal descent groups', 14-15, 16, 17, 19, 31, 37n, 38n, 40n, 41-4, 144n; typology of societal organization, 247-8; *The Web of Kinship among the Tallensi*, 16, 57-9, 62-3; and E.E. Evans-Pritchard, 16, 21-4, 33n, 77-8
Fosbrooke, H.A., 162n
Fraenkel, M., 238n
France: Caribbean colonialism, 274, 281-4, 288, 294-6; eleventh century states in, 80; incorporation in, 188; pluralism in, 207; Republican government of, 283; stability in, 174
franchise, 226-7, 230, 231, 236, 283, 290-1, 300-1, 308
Francis, O.C., 275n, 314n
Frankenberg, R., 242
Frazier, E.F., 226
free blacks, 276
free coloured, 276, 281-3; *affranchis*, 282-4
French Guiana, 278, 301
Froude, Anthony, on slavery, 300
Fulani, 46-9, 158, 221-2, 233-4 (*see also* Hausa)
Fulani Empire, 26, 46
Fulani *jihad*, 113
function, compared with structure, 149
'functional' analysis of structures, 22
functional differentiation, 14, 27, 54-6,

242-7, 250, 252, 258, 268-70
'functional prerequisites' of social order, 135
Furnivall, J.S., 152, 160n, 206-7
furu, 114
fusion: in lineages, 17, 18, 32, 51, 58; interracial, 300-1 (*see also* amalgamation *and under* race relations)

Gaius, on law, 115
Galla, age sets among, 141, 260
Gamble, D.P., 264n
Gandhi, as charismatic leader, 102, 233
Ganshof, F.L., 234n
gavelkind, 145
Geertz, C. (ed.), 255n
gemeinschaft and *gesellschaft*, 123
genealogical differentiation, in lineages, 259-60
genotypical data, on Grenada elite, 317-20
Georgetown, Guyana, 286, 327
Germans, in Caribbean, 274, 340
Germany: Civil Code in, 123; pluralism and, 207; stability in, 174
Gerth, H.H., and C.W. Mills, 155n, 161n
Gibb, H.A.R., and H. Bowen, 233n
Gierke, O., 9, 73, 96, 118
Gillin, J., 160n
Gluckman, M., 16n, 50n, 79n, 144n, 146n
Goldman, I., 263n
Goody, J., 96, 181n
Gorham Crane, J., 285n, 288n, 291n, 300n
government: administration and, 24, 27-8, 47-9, 57-8; anthropological theory of, 74-6; as process and structure, 25-6; bases of, 24-6, 28, 31, 33-4, 74; centralization of, 52-5, 67-8; collectivities and, 220-1; continuity of, 55, 67; corporations and, 43-56; differentiation in, 30-1, 51, 55-7, 91-2; input and output requisites of, 93; lack of, 16, 74 (*see* acephalous- and stateless societies); local and national, 25; Morgan's 'plans of', 74; political systems and, 21-31, 47-9, 57-8; process in, 25, 28-9, 31; public character of, 93; segmentary lineages and, 16-17, 33, 43-56, 60-1, 63-4, 67-9, 74; structure in, 25-6, 28, 31; substantive and functional approaches to, 92-3 (*see also* administration, societies, state)
governmental action, 26-31, 46-56
governmental order, 99-100
gradualism, Marx and, 237
Grand Cayman, 285
Greece: as complex society, 246, 264; debt bondage in, 263, 266-7; law in, 115; 'seed bed society', 249
Gregory VII, 116
Grenada, 235, 284-328 *passim*; differential advantage in, 302-10, 317-20; genotypical data on elite, 317-20; slavery in, 284, 286; stratification in, 287, 297, 300, 304-5
Grenada Handbook, 304
Grotius, on law, 117-18, 122
group action, 43 (*see also* collective action)
groups: and corporations, 43-4, 49 (*see also* corporate groups); and segmentary line-

ages, 20, 27, 31, 50, 58-70; and stateless societies, 74; based on unilineal descent, 51-2, 68; in simple societies, 71, 76; inter-group relations, 24, 31, 58, 60-1
group unity, 44
Grousset, R., 233n
Guadeloupe, 294, 301; differential advantage in, 302-3, 306, 316; revolt in, 328; slaves in, 284, 286-7, 299
Guatemala, discrimination in, 160
guilds, 104, 122
Gulliver, P.H., 100, 142n, 193n
gurus, 256
Gurvitch, G., 128
Gusii: complexity among, 250, 260; lineages among, 14, 52
Guyana, 277-8, 286, 289-90, 293, 321, 325, 328; independence in, 325-6; stratification in, 228, 230, 267, 306, 307, 322-3
Gwelo, stratification in, 152-3

habituation, in stratification, 156
Hailey, M., 130n
Haiti: American occupation of, 308; conflict in, 233, 325, 328; slaves in, 159, 283-4, 285; stratification in, 160, 233, 278, 295, 309
half-siblingship, 13
Hall, D., 298n
Hall, J.W., 156n
Hammond, S.A., 308n
Hanbury, H.G., 116n
Handbook of Jamacia, 288, 300n
harijans, 93
Harris, R., 144n, 267n
Hartland, S., 121
Hause-Fulani State, 26, 34; government in, 38, 47-9, 68, 176, 233; Muslim Hausa in, 147-8; royal succession in, 34, 64-6, 156; slavery in, 158-9, 234, 266; stratification in, 158-9
Hawaii, promiscuity in, 74
headmanship: in !Kung bands, 142-3; lineage, 45-6
Heard, K.A., 230n
helotage, 215, 235, 269
heredity: in offices, 45, 55, 182; in stratification, 263, 337; in title, 64-6
Herskovits, M.J., 35n, 159n
heterogeneity: in complex societies, 249, 252-3, 263, 265-8; in culture, 109-10, 191-2, 212, 234; in institutions, 212-14, 225, 238; 'modernization' and, 238; heterogeneous societies, 191-2, 213-14, 217, 226-7, 263, 265-8, 272, 280, 337-8
Hidalgo, Miguel, as charismatic leader, 233
Hidatsa, age-sets among, 142
hierarchies: in administrative systems, 28, 31-5, 55-6; in age and sex, 141-2, 145; in allegiance, 79; in authority, 31-5, 86-7; in corporations, 56, 97, 122-4, 143-4, 179; in descent, 143-4; in families, 146-50; in law, 116-17; in political systems, 28, 150; in societal co-ordination, 84, 143-4; in Swazi clans, 146; of associations, 83-4, 86-7; of offices, 33, 44, 47-8, 52-5, 86-7, 235; ranked, in

stratification, 137, 141-2, 222, 267, 273, 292-7; regulatory, 86-7
Hindu caste, 155, 223, 265; 'condensation' in, 246-7
Hindu East Indians, 278, 294, 296, 340
Hinduism: as theocratic regime, 214; socialization to, 221
Hiskett, M., 113n
Hispanic societies, 271, 278-81, 295
'historic empires', 249
Hitler, as charismatic leader, 102
Hobbes, T., 117-18, 122, 139
Hocart, A.M., 231n
Hodgkin, T.L., 230n
Hoebel, E.A., 120n, 124n, 191n
Hoetink, H., 10, 277n, 295-6, 331-2
Holland: as complex society, 213, 269; as colonial power, 281-2, 300, 321
Holmberg, A.R., 234n
Holy Roman Empire, 80, 116-17
holy wars, 111, 113, 130
Homans, G.C., 145n
homogeneity: in complex societies, 251-2; in culture, 109-10, 212, 334; in stratification, 137, 280, 337
Hopi, multiple corporations among, 191
Horowitz, I.L. (ed.), 157n
Horton, W.H.G., 266n
Hugues, Victor, 284, 287
Hunt, James, on slavery, 300
Huntingford, G.W.B., 101n, 142n, 261n
Hussite congregation, 232
Hutterites, prescriptive closures among, 225
Hutton, J.H., 155n, 223
Hutu caste, 101, 128, 158, 221, 234
hybrids, 228, 276-8, 281, 288, 293, 323-4, 339, 342-5
hypergamy, 222, 293

Iberians, miscegenation among, 296
Ibo: collective enslavement among, 266; corporations among, 55, 191; government among, 33, 46, 55; village communities among, 95
Iceland, complexity of, 250
ideologies: in plural regimes, 231-2, 237; of corporateness, 59, 67; of descent, 58, 68; of lineage unity, 59; of racial equality, 342; of stratification, 271
ihtilaf, 112
ijmā, 111-14
ijtihad, 112
illa, 111
illegitimacy, 88, 273
illegitimate authority, 195
illegitimate leadership, 45-6, 195
illiteracy, statistics on, 306-7
imām, 112
immigration: accommodation and, 339-40; in complex societies, 265-7, 269; into Caribbean, 271-340 *passim*; into United States, 219
imperium, and law, 115-16, 118-19, 120, 126-7
impersonal social relations, 249, 264-5, 267-8
implications of societal incorporation, 180-6, 197-201

Inca, collective administration among, 235
income distributions, in Caribbean, 313-19
incorporation, *see* societal incorporation
indentured labour, 266-7, 281, 286-7, 296, 299, 339
independence, in Caribbean colonies, 283, 326
indeterminacy, in authority, 25
India: as complex society, 246, 262; caste in, 104, 155-6, 223-4, 230, 233, 264; indentured labour from, 287; village communities in, 95
Indians: in Caribbean, 290, 293; native, 295, 300
individuals, in complex societies, 243, 249-53, 259-61, 269, 333-4, 338-40
individualist societies, 249
Indonesians (Javanese), 274, 287, 321
infant mortality, and stratification, 273, 289
institutional heterogeneity, 212-14, 225, 238
institutional homogeneity, 206-7, 212-14, 216-17
institutionalization: in Indian caste, 223-4; in social change, 194-8; of connubium, 222; of miscegenation, 296; of racial divisions, 216, 228, 243, 272-3, 336-45; of social relations, 207-8, 233, 261-2
institutional specialization, in complex societies, 243-7, 255-6, 268
institutions: and corporations, 227-30; and government, 21-2; assimilation in, 221, 228-9, 230, 335-6; autonomy of, 217-19; coherence of, 217-19; differentiation in, 205-7, 219, 222, 226, 230, 236-8, 243-9, 255-8, 268, and pluralism, 215-17, 208-13, 220-2, secondary, 206, 213; interconnections of, 211, 217-30; social and cultural aspects of, 212
integrity, in segmental societies, 245
intercalary corporations, 103-4
intercalary lineages, 18
intermarriage: and stratification, 295; and unilineal descent, 184; in bands, 258-9; proscriptions against, 220-2, 231, 292, 295-6 (*see also* connubium, miscegenation)
intermediate corporations, 245-6, 258
intermediate societies, 243, 245-6, 249
internal articulation, 183-6, 190
International Institute of Differing Civilizations, 152n
international law, 122
Iran, as archaic society, 246
Irish, in Caribbean, 274
Iroquois; confederation, 188; war leaders, 256
Islam: and law, 107-8, 110-14, 122, 125n, 126-7; and pluralism, 231-3; as complex society, 246, 249
Israel, 'seed bed society', 249
Italy: as complex society, 246; settlers from, 274; stability in, 174
Ituri Pygmies, kinship among, 142, 144-5

jajmani relations, 223
Jamaica: settlers in, 265, 280-1, 287; slavery

in, 159, 285, 300, 328; stratification in, 275-8, 288, 293, 329-31, 338; differential advantages in, 303-4, 307-16; universal suffrage in, 301
James, C.L.R., 233n
Japan: as complex society, 246; feudalism in, 234, 235; stratification in, 155-6
jati, 155, 233
Javanese: in stratification, 274, 276-7, 287, 325, 338; miscegenation among, 290, 293-4
Jayawardena, C., 321n
Jews, in Caribbean, 274, 276, 277, 312, 313, 328, 340
Jie, age sets among, 141
jihad, 110, 113, 130
jizya, 130
Jones, G.I., 261, 266n
judgment, in Muslim law, 111, 113-14
judicial decision, in British law, 127
judicial institutions, and government, 21
jural autonomy of lineages, 73, 110
jural status, 82, 124, 128, 142, 180, 188
juridical resources, and minority rule, 231
jurisdictions, fragmentation of, 266
jus gentium, in Roman law, 115
Justinian, on law, 116

Kabaka Mutebi, 127-8
Kaberry, P.M., 16n, 35n
Kachins: acephalous polity among, 220; family stratification among, 147; lineage systems among, 62; political systems among, 79, 172
Kadara, age sets among, 142
Kagamé, A., 158n
Kagoro: illustrating corporate constitution, 98; secondary marriage among, 61
Kalenda, P.M., 155n, 233n
Kamakura Japan, and complexity, 250
Kaminsky, H., 232n
Karimojong: age-sets among, 100, 142; categories among, 192
Kekchi tribe, 287
Keur, D.L., 294n
Kikuyu: age sets among, 142; law and, 22; multiple corporations among, 191
kingships: divine, 95, 231, in government, 50, 99; in Zaria, 47-9, 64-6; Ngonde, 95; Shilluk, 95
Kingston, Jamaica, 277; race riots in, 329-30
kinship: as institution, 211-12, 218-19, 220-1; bilateral, 142-3, 263-5; fictive, 143; lineage segmentation and, 16-18, 23, 39, 41, 58-9, 143-4; marriage and, 61-2; social organization and, 59-60, 69-70, 77, 211-12, 216; stratification and, 142-50; unilineal descent and, 37, 49, 262-5
Kipsigi: age-sets among, 141, 260-1; clans among, 101; corporations among, 191
Kirchoff, P., 148n
Klass, M., 323n, 324n
Kluckhohn, F., 151
Koran, and Muslim law, 111-14, 127
Kshatriya caste, 156
!Kung Bushmen, 97, 142-3

Kuper, H., 133n, 146n
Kuper, L., 230n, 268n
Kushner, G., 241n
kwai, maximal lineages, 61
Kwakiutl, multiple corporations among, 191, 247

lability, and complex societies, 246
lagmen, in Swedish law, 122
Lambert, H.E., 142n, 191n
Lammens, H., 111n
land, differential distributions of, 226-7, 302-5
landless free, classification, 284, 299
Landtman, G., 136
Latin America, pluralism in, 159-60, 207
Latortue, G., 301n
law: anthropological theories of, 71-3, 87-8, 120; centralization and, 88, 107, 117-18, 121-4; corporations as framework of, 88, 97, 122-4, 128-31; custom and, 110, 114, 120-2, 127, 129-30; definitions of, 119-22, 124-5; forms of, adjectival, 97, British, 116, 118-19, 127-9, civil, 117, 119, Code Napoléon, 122, 126, 129, common, 82, 119, 120, 127, 129-30, constitutional, 110-14, 126-7, customary, 129-30, divinely revealed, 110-14, 116-17, European, 107, 114-27, 'guaranteed', 125, Islamic, 107-8, 110-14, 122, 125n, 126-7, Muslim, 110-14, 125n, 126-31, natural, 71, 73, 88, 115-18, 120, 'perfect', 124-5, 126, private and public, 122, 126, procedural, 88, 115, 126-7, Roman, 115-18, social contract, 71, 88, 117-18, 123, substantive, 97, 115, 125, 126-7, tribal, 108, 122, 125, 127-8; imperium and, 115-16, 118-19, 120, 126-7; in Africa, 107-9, 126-31; in plural societies, 108-10, 131; in primitive societies, 120-1, 123-5; property and, 88, 113, 119, 128; society and, 72, 81, 87-8, 109-10, 121-6; sociological framework of, 107-31; stratification and, 283, 299-300
Leach, E., 62, 69, 241n; *Aspects of Caste in South India . . .*, 115n, 223n; *Political Systems of Highland Burma*, 79, 147, 172, 220n
leadership: charismatic, 102, 178, 181, 233; collective, 81; illegitimate, 45-6, 195; in lineages, 45-6; in societal change, 193-4; lack of, among !Kung, 97
Lebanese, and stratification, 277, 293-4
Lebanese-Syrians, 275, 287
Leeward Islands, statistics for, 302, 306-7
Le Febvre, G., 233n
legal norms, 22-3
legal status, 38, 42, 122-3, 298-300
legislation: as mode of action in political systems, 92; in British law, 127
Leiris, M., 294n, 299n, 306n
leopard-skin priests, 102
LeVine, R.A., and W.H. Sangree, 142n
Lévi-Strauss, C., 7n
Levy, M.Jr., 7n, 133n, 134n
Levy, R., 111n, 112, 113-14, 127n
Lewis, G., 324n

Lewis, Monk, and slavery, 298
Lewis, N.G., 298n
Lewis, W.A., 230n
lex aeterna, 116
lex talionis, 110
Leyburn, J., 159n, 160n, 233n, 283n, 295n, 308n
Liao, 233
life chances, and stratification, 251, 272-3, 302-16
lineages and lineage systems: accretion in, 17, 18, 38, 39, 49, 50; administrative and political dualism in, 28-37, 46-52, 57-8, 67-9; aristocratic, 52-3, 64-6; as corporate groups, 14, 38, 42, 44, 54, 143-4, 201; growth and development of, 16-17, 32, 37-41, 50-2, 56-70; hierarchical aspect of, 15-16, 32-4, 55, 58-9, 63, 86, 146; co-ordinate, 31-2, 54, 83, 146; differentiation in, 14-16, 38, 40, 51-2, by descent, 14, 32, 39, by rank, 15, 34, 35, 64-5, functional, 53-6, 84, genealogical, 32, 39-40, 50; distinguished from kinship, 16, 17-18, 58-69; equilibrium and, 31, 32-3, 38-40, 59-60; incorporation in, 18, 38-42, 57, 59, 65, 83, 96; interrelations, 31, 53, 61-2, 82-3, 86, 144, 259-61; locality and, 16, 19, 50, 57, 85-6, 88; marriage and, 62, 63, 88; maximal, 14-15, 33, 61; membership in, 65, 104, 144; minimal, 15, 63; offices and, 44-7; political character of, 18, 23, 32-5, 42-3, 59, 61-2; 'principle of contradiction', 67; publics and, 82-3, 86; redefinition of (*see* fission *and* fusion); (*see also* segmentary lineage systems)
linear change, 173
literacy: and complex societies, 246, 249, 250; in Caribbean, 273, 306-7
Little, K., 103n, 261n
Lloyd, P.C., 255n, 264n
Lloyd Warner, W., 142n; and P.S. Lunt, 157n; and M. Meeker, K. Eells, 157n
Lobb, J., 160n
locality, and lineage groups, 38, 40-1, 51, 57
'located labourers', 304
Located Labourers Act (1840), 299
Locke, on law, 118
LoDagaba, corporate constitution among, 97-8
logical *implications* of incorporation, 180-6, 197-201
logically closed systems, 69-70
logical *requisites* and *entailments* of incorporation, 180-6, 197-201
Logoli: *ad hoc* agencies among, 52-3; political structure of, 22, 24
Lollardy, as collective protest, 233
Long, Edward, 300
Lowenthal, D., 10n, 250n, 271n, 276-7, 285n
Lowie, R., 75, 142n
Lozi, lineage organization among, 41
Lugbara, 188

Marshall, L., 97n, 128n, 142n, 143n, 188n, 210n, 236n, 262n
martial law, in Jamaica, 300

Martinique, 265, 284, 299, 301; differential advantages in, 302-3, 306, 316; hybrids in, 293, 294; indentured labour in, 286-7; revolt in, 300
Marx, K., 236n; on economic theory, 218; on materialism, 169
Marxism, 74
Masai: age-sets among, 141, 260-1; prophets, 256
masterless subjects, 237
Mathews, T.G., 290n, 325n
matrilineal descent: and lineages, 13, 39, 74; and status, 143; in village societies, 83-4
maturation ceremony, 253-4
Mauritius, 230
Maya Amerindians, 287, 289
mayam, 147
Mayer, A., 155n
Mayer, K.B., 137n
Mayer, P., 32n, 40n, 260n
mayu, 147
mazālim, 113
mechanical solidarity, 242
membership, and status, 150-1, 156-8 (*see also* under corporations, lineages, offices)
Mende: domination among, 261; Poro (intercalary corporation) 103
Mennonites, 287-8, 289
Mesopotamia, archaic society, 246, 249, 264
mestizos, 159, 235, 277, 278, 287-8, 289-90, 319
metropolitan states, government in, 220
metropolitan whites, 294, 296, 297
Mexico: as heterogeneous society, 213; collective protest in, 233; Spanish in, 235, 280
Middleton, J., 188n; and G. Kershaw, 191n; and D. Tait (eds.), 144n
migration: and stratification, 155, 162; among Nuer, 59; to America, 153 (*see also* immigration)
Mills, C.W., 157n
mines, slaves in, 276, 281
miniscule societies, 280, 297, 341
Mintz, S.W., 282n, 284n
'mixed' classification, 288
miscegenation, 267, 274, 282, 288, 289-97, 323, 338; assymetrical, 292-3, 294-5; patterns of, 289-97; symmetrical, 292, 294, 341
Mitchell, J.C., 230n
mobility: in complex societies, 249, 251-2, 254-5, 259, 263; in stratification, 158-61
modern societies, 73, 120, 123, 134, 173-4, 206, 245-6, 249, 269; basis of 'modernization' in, 120, 173-4, 238
modes of incorporation, 183-206, 254-62 (*see also* societal incorporation)
modes of production, in complex societies, 246
moieties, of lineages, 83
monarchies, absolute, 118
monastic orders, and dominance, 262
Mongols, 233, 265
monocratic centralization, 118
monogamy, in stateless societies, 74

monolineal communities, 260
Montesquieu, Baron de, 7n, 72
Montserrat, 260, 280, 286, 302, 307
Moore, S.F., 234n, 235n
Moore, W.E., 153n
moral density, 242, 258
moral norms, 22-3
Morant Bay, revolt, 300
Moreira, A., 108-9, 126n
Moreno, M.M., 158n
Morgan, L.H., 73-5, 188n
Moskos, C.J. Jr., 326n; and W. Bell, 330n
Mosuor *biis*, 52
Mt. Moritz, 294, 305
Mozabite towns, complexity of, 250
Muhammad, 102, 110-11
mujtahid, 112-14
mulattoes, 276-7, 284, 294, 319
multilineal communities, 259-60, 264-5
multi-party regimes, 238
multiple incorporation, 191-2
multi-racial societies, 280, 289-92, 301, 306-16, 319-28, 341, 344
Murdock, G.P., 262n
Murngin, as acephalous society, 81
Muslims, African, and law, 107-8, 110-14, 125n, 126-31
Muslim Hausa, concubinage among, 147-8
Muslim Paktuns, and pluralism, 214
mustafino, 276
Muteesa I, 127
Myrdal, G., 227n

Nadel, S.F., 134, 136, 157, 158n, 208, 233n
Nandi: age-sets among, 141; clans· among, 101; government among, 33, 56; lineages among, 15, 16
Napoleon, 283-4
Nara Japan, taxation in, 263
nationalism, in British Guiana, 325-6
nation-states, 99; and pluralism, 210-11, 237-8; as corporate groups, 177
naval wars, in Caribbean, 282
Negroes, 275, 281, 291-2, 303, 325-7, 329-30; acculturation of, in USA, 226-7; amalgamation, 338-9; as corporate category, 101; colonial majority, 342-5; hybrids, 276, 297, 323-4; illiteracy among, 306-7; miscegenation, 221; slaves, 227, 284-5, 295, 297; subjugation of, 226-7, 324-5
neighbourhood, in societal microstructure, 257, 258
Netherlands Antilles, 280-1, 301
Nevis, 286, 288, 289-90, 302
Newman, P., 287n
New Scotland, 294
'new states', in complex societies, 242
Ngonde, divine kingships, 95
Niehoff, A. and J., 323n, 324n
Nilo-Hamites, age-sets among, 78
Nimuendaju, C., 191n
nobility, in stratification, 156-7
noblesse oblige, 117
nomadism, 74, 221, 265
normative consensus, and stratification, 137, 151-9, 161-2
norms, moral and legal, 22-3

Nsaw, 16, 33
nucleated settlements, 249, 262-3
Nuer: as acephalous society, 81; lineages among, 16, 43, 58-9, 260; offices among, 33, 52-3, 54, 102, 256; political organization of, 20, 21, 41
nullity, sanction of, 125
Nupe, state organization of, 38, 55

octoroon, 276
oligarchy: and pluralism, 231, 237; and political development, 173-4; Iron Law of, 199
Olmsted, F.L., 227n
O'Loughlin, C., 321n
omulasi, omuseni, ovwali, status, 33
obligation: in corporations, 43-4, 82; individual, 22, 123, 333-4; reciprocal, in bands, 259
offices: and corporate groups, 95-7, 178, 254-5; and corporations sole, 43-56 *passim*, 94; and lineages, 33, 44-7, 67; bureaucracy and, 47; characteristics of, 44-5; differentiation in, 47, 260-1; distinguished from commissions (*q.v.*), 101-2, 179, 256; hereditary, 45, 55, 182; hierarchies of, 33, 44, 47-8, 52-5, 86-7, 235; completed, 52, 54; incomplete, 87; in maximal lineages, 33; internal segmentation of, 45; modes of succession to, 45-6, 181-2; recruitment to, 45, 181-2; rules of action in, 45-6
official cadres, as segments, 35, 37
official orders, in Zaria, 47-9
oikos, 247
opinion, in Muslim law, 111-14
opportunity: differential distribution of, 140, 155-8, 249, 253, ·262, 341; equal, 140, 210
ordered anarchy, 16
'organic solidarity', 242
'organizational aggregates', 204
Ottoman Turks, 233

panchayat, 223
Panama, classification in, 267
Papal law, 116-17
Parry, J.H., and P.M. Sherlock, 159n, 281n, 282n
Parsons, T., 7n, 135n, 157n, 243; and E. Shils, 7, 152, 167, 243
Pathan Swat, collective domination in, 234
patricians, and clientage, 234, 266
patriarchal societies, 73-4
patrilineages, property-holding, 74
patrilineal descent, 13, 64, 83-4
patrilineal dynasties, 48
patrimonial regimes, 182
Pearcy, G.E., 278n
pendular transformations, 172-3
peonage, 162, 235
'perfect' equality, 139-40
Peristiany, J.G., 101n, 142n, 191n, 261n
perpetuity: in group corporations, 43-4, 49; in lineages, 51; in societies, 255
Petit Martinique, 288, 294, 338
phenotypical classifications, 276, 296; and social status, 304-5, 329-30; 'idealized',

331; of Grenada elite, 304-5, 329-30
Phillips, U.B., 227n
'philosophies of history', 166
phratries, of lineages, 83
Pirenne, H., 156n
plaçage, in miscegenation, 295
plantation-based societies, 281-5, 297
plantation slaves, 255, 276, 281-2, 284-5, 298-300
'planter' classification, 317
Plateau Tonga, incorporation in, 188
plebs, and clientage, 234, 266
plebiscitarian democracy, 71
plenipotentiaries, 101-2
plural acculturation, 228
pluralism: alternatives to, 206-13, 215; and corporate groups, 94, 177-8; and law, 108-10, 131; and social heterogeneity, 213-14; and stratification, 155, 162; basic conditions for, 215-17, 220-39; cultural, 108-10, 159-60, 205, 207, 209-10, 228; definitions of, 205; disguised, 239; dissolution of, 232-4; dominance in, 230-9, 267-8; incorporation in, 333-5; institutional and political conditions for, 205-39; minority rule in, 207, 209-11, 214, 215-16, 231, 234-6; social, 108-10, 159-60, 205, 216-17, 224-30, 236, 238, 342; structural, in multi-racialism, 341-2; subjugated majority in, 207, 210, 232-9
plural regimes, stability of, 230-4
plural societies: 'coerced' consensus in, 152; compared with nation-states, 210-11; definitions of, 206-7; law in, 108-10, 131; political structure of, 159-60, 230-4
pochteca, 247
policy, in political action, 26-7, 29, 31
political action: and administrative action, 28-37, 46-52, 57-8, 67-9; and corporations, 43-6, 335; and governmental action, 30-1, 33-5; and public affairs, 84-5; as regulatory action, 85-6; nature of, 20, 23, 24, 25-7, 29, 59-60, 175, 250
political authority, 25, 79, 175-6, 243
political behaviour, and social behaviour, 20-1, 23
political centralization, 92, 197-9; and law, 117-19; and segmentation, 176; incorporation and, 188-90
political change: analytic units for, 175; and corporate centralization, 197-9; and redistribution of power, 192-7; conditions for, 168-9, 170-5, 197-8; endogenous relations in, 168, 192-4; exogenous relations in, 168; historical approach to, 165-6; invariant relations in, 203-4; methods of, 195, 198-203; objects of study in, 167-9; scientific theory of, 166-9; structural approach to, 170-204
political culture, components of, 174-5
political domination, in stratification, 324-5, 328-32 (*see also* pluralism)
political events, defined, 175
political evolution, anthropological schemes of, 71-84
political groups: and bands, 30; and political action, 44

political modernization, 166; and structural change, 173-4
political organization: and force, 30, 84; and law, 81; and stratification, 150, 153; collective in pluralism, 232; corporate units of, 179-80; forms of, 80-2, 84-5, 96; in acephalous societies, 81; in pluralism, 206-39; in segmentary societies, 24, 42 ff., 267; in simple societies, 20-31, 74-9, 91-3; territorial, 16 (*see also* political change, political systems)
political parties, 36-7, 101, 230, 232, 237, 246, 290, 326-7, 329-30
political polarization, Marx on, 237
political power, 109, 175-6, 197, 263; and ruling minorities, 231, 263, 324-5, 328-32
political relations: and segmentary theory, 18, 19 -21, 23-4, 27, 31-2, 49, 59-61; marriage as, 61
political representation, 101; in stratification, 299-301, 326-7
political status, 38, 42, 136, 197-8, 211, 236-7, 275, 295, 333-4
political symbiosis, 221-2, 232-5
political systems: and administration, 24, 25, 28; and government, 21-31, 33-5; and lineage segmentation, 16-17, 23, 31, 34, 42, 47-50, 59; and structural relations, 20-1; boundaries of, 22, 24, 25, 78, 80, 176; centralized, 30, 38, 42, 47-9, 92-3; decentralized, 31, 188-90; differentiation in, 21, 43, 176; ethnographic data in, 91; stability of, 79, 174; typology of, 21, 23-4, 78
political values, 20
polity: African, 77-8; in pluralism, 205-6; modern and simple compared, 92; nature of, 176-9, 191-2
poll tax, 130
polyglot societies, 289
polygynous societies, 39, 145-8, 262
Polynesia, stratification in, 147
'poor whites', 288, 328, 339-40, 343
popular legislature, in pluralism, 231
population: composition, in Caribbean, 277-80, 281-2, 288, 290-1, 302; growth, and lineages, 19; imbalances in sex ratio, 292-3, 296; policy, in pluralism, 232-3; size and complexity of, 250
populus, Roman, 115-16
Poro, secret society, 261
Portugal, pluralism in, 207
Portuguese: in Caribbean, 274, 277, 328; indentured, 286-7, 292-4, 296
positive law, 116
Post, K.W.G., 230n
Postan, M.M. et al., 156n
Pound, R., 97n, 119-20
Powdermaker, H., 226n
power: and authority, 29-30, 32-3, 104-5, 192-7, 256-7; and governmental process, 29-30; and publics, 85-6; centralization of, 29; differential distributions of, 153-4, 229, 296-301; in political action, 175-6; legitimate, 197; monopoly of, in pluralism, 232-3; redistribution of, in political change, 192-9 (*see also* political

power)
praetors, in Roman law, 115
precedent, in law, 127
predictive theory, in political change, 167
prescriptive closures, in pluralism, 225
prestige, as form of status, 136, 263
Prime Minister, office of, 29
primitive societies, law in, 97-8, 121, 123-5
primogeniture: in Britain, 145; in Polynesia, 147
principles of incorporation, 180-6, 191-204
private domain, in social organization, 216, 220-39 *passim*, 249-56
privilege, in collectivities, 229
procedural law, 88, 115, 126-7
promiscuity, in Hawaii, 74
property: and law, 49, 88, 113, 119, 128; transmission of, as basis of government, 74
Property Franchise, Grenada, 300
prophets: Nuer, 33, 102; as commissions, 256
proportional representation, 326
proprietorship, personal, 234-5
proscriptions: collective, 221, 232, 255, 267; in corporate categories, 187, 255, 266; in marriage, 220-2, 292, 295-6
public affairs, 82-3, 84-6, 93, 98-9
public domain, in social organization, 216, 220-39 *passim*, 249-56
publics: and government, 24-5, 82-6, 189; categories in, 93-4, 104-5; in complex societies, 228, 252; 'linked', 104-5
Puerto Rico: classifications in, 277-8, 288; differential advantages in, 309, 316; labour in, 280, 282, 284, 286
punishment, in bands, 128
purpose, in Muslim law, 111
Pygmy bands, 142, 144-5, 188

qāḍī court, 111, 113
qiyās, 111
quadroon, 276
quasi-corporations, 100-1, 256-7

race: native concepts of, 324; sociological definition of, 275
race relations: conflict in, 152-4, 277, 283, 290-1, 300-1, 325-6, 341-2; Creole/Indian, 322-3, 337-47; determinates of, 331-2; interracial accommodation, 265-8, 272-4, 331-3, 337-47; alliances, 283, 299
race and societies: bi-racial, 280, 290-1, 297, 301-5, 317-19, 324-5, 328-9, 342-3; heterogeneous, 226-7, 265-8, 280, 337-8; homogeneous, 280, 337; multiracial, 280, 289-97, 301, 306-16, 319-28, 341, 344; size distinctions, 280, 297, 317, 342
racial classifications: bases of, 215-16, 226-7, 276-8, 288, 305, 337, 345; institutionalization of, 216, 228, 243, 272-3, 278, 336-45; segregation of, 221, 226, 234-5, 280, 290-1, 337 (*see also* censuses, population)
racial discrimination, 160, 224-30, 271-345 *passim* (*see also* differential distri-

butions)
Radcliffe-Brown, A.R., 20-2, 44, 58, 80; *Structure and Function in Primitive Society*, 7n, 37, 88n, 120, 144, 208
radical change, 201
rain-maker, 33
Ramos, A., 159n
rank: and egalitarianism, 137; and lineage segmentation, 15, 64-6; and stratification, 133-4, 138-45, 153-8, 271-4; defined, with status, 136; in Indian caste, 223-4; in stateless societies, 21; of clans, 146; of elites, 304-5, 317-18; of siblings, 144-50; secular, 156; universality of, 271 (*see also* hierarchies, status, stratification)
ra'y, 111-14
Ray, V.F., 142n
rebellions: concentrations of force and, 30; creative, 218; illegitimate leadership and, 46; in centralized societies, 98
reciprocal rights, in composite bands, 259
recruitment: by descent, 156-7; in segmentary lineages, 258-9; restricted, 157-8, 161 (*see also* membership)
Redfield, R., 242
Redondo, 278
reference points in lineages, 14
regulatory action: in corporations, 187-8, 257-62; in political organization, 85-7, 179-80, 256-7, 268
regulatory corporations, in nation-states, 210
regulatory roles, transfer of, 192-6
Reischauer, E.O., 156n
religion: and caste differentiation, 155, 267; and pluralism, 215, 233, 267
religious action, 28
religious authority, 243
repartimiento, collective domination, 234
republican city-states, 246
requisites of corporate organization, 180-6, 191-204
residence: in societal organization, 258-9, 262-3; post-marital, in matrilineages, 74
'residual categories', 241
responsa, 115
restriction, and competition in stratification, 155-60
revolts, 153-4, 328, 329-30; of slaves, 158-9, 284, 287, 300; post-emancipation, 297, 300
revolution, *see* rebellion
revolutionary parties, 36-7
Rheinstein, M. (ed.), 117n, 118n, 125n
Richards, A.I., 16n, 37n, 128n
Rigaud, free coloured leader, 283
rights, 22, 128, 139, 141, 227, 282-3; doctrine of natural, 118; in corporations, 43-4, 82, 128 (*see also* differential distributions)
Rights of Man, 283
riots, race, 243, 300-1
ritual: and political action, 24; and segmentary lineages, 31, 51, 83, 259; in Indian caste, 223
ritual action, 30; prohibitions of, in miscegenation, 293, 296

'rituals of rebellion', 98
ritual status, 155-6, 158-9, 223
Roberts, G.W., 286-7n; and N. Abdullah, 310n; and L. Braithwaite, 323n
Robertson-Smith, W., 110n
role: in complex societies, 242, 245-6; 249, 251-2, 262; in simple societies, 76; in stratification, 135-6, 139-43, 153, 242; multiple, in colonialism, 243, 253; of leaders, 45-9, 193-4; regulatory, 192-6
Roman Catholic Church, 103, 156
Roman Civil Code, 117
Roman law, 115-18
Rome: as complex society, 246, 264, 266; offices in, 49, 73; pluralism in, 230n; statutory commissions in, 178-9
Rousseau, Jean-Jacques, on inequality, 139n
Royal Anthropological Institute, 136n
royal centralization, in Europe, 88
royal competition, in stratification, 156-7
royal law, 116
royal succession, in Zaria, 64-6
royalty: nominal, 65; political or effective, 65
Ruanda: incorporation in, 190; stratification in, 158, 234, 235
Rubin, V., 278n, 298n, 323n, 324n, 327n, 331n
Rudé, G.F.E., 236n
rulers, as corporate groups, 266-8
Runciman, S., 233n
Russia: pluralism in, 207; totalitarianism in, 28
Ryan, S., 324n

Saba, 278, 288, 292; accommodation in, 290-1, 294, 325, 338, 340-1; slaves in, 285, 298-9
sacred differentiation, 223-4
sacred (theocratic) societies, 214-15
Sahlins, M., 136-7, 147, 254n
St. Barthélemy, 285
Saint Dominique, 281; slave revolt in, 282
St. Eustatius, 285, 292
St. Kitts, 285, 302, 307
St. Lucia, 282, 286, 287-8, 328; differential advantages in, 302, 307
St. Maarten, 306, 325; slaves in, 285, 286, 292
St. Vincent: differential advantages in, 302, 307; labour in, 274, 286, 287; miscegenation in, 291-2, 295; racial accommodation in, 328, 338
Salmond, J., 119
sambo, 276
samurai, 156
sanctions: differential distribution of, 134; in offices and lineages, 44; in stratification, 271-3; legal, 120, 122, 124-5; secular, 22
Sansom, G.B., 156n, 234n, 250n, 263n
Santo Domingo, 278, 280, 282, 284
'scale', in complex societies, 250
Scandinavia, as heterogeneous society, 213
scarce values, 152
Schacht, J., 111n
Schapera, I., 75, 80-1, 146n, 176n
Schneider, D.M., 241

scholarships, in Caribbean schools, 308-11
Schumpeter, L., 265n
Schwab, W.B., 152-3
scope, in systems, 174, 198-203
Scotch, in Caribbean, 274
Seaga, E.P.G., 315
secession, 46, 98
secondary communication, in complex societies, 249, 264-5
secularization, in Europe, 215
secular systems, 160
sedition, and concentrations of force, 30
'seed bed' societies, 249
segmentary form, of social systems, 19, 48
segmentary lineage systems: administration and, 28, 31-7, 47-8; as basis of societal organization, 258-60; autarchy and, 100; basis of, 17-19, 27, 37-42; corporate character of, 38-9, 45-7, 52-3, 188; differentiation in, 15, 34, 61; government and, 24, 26-7, 33-5, 43-56; group relations in, 58-70; hierarchic organization in, 31-5, 38-9, 52, 83-4; political organization and, 18, 21, 23-4, 27, 35, 42-3, 47-50, 86-8, 149-50; terminological systems in, 17-18; unilineal descent groups and, 18, 34, 35-52, 143-4, 149-50 (*see also* lineages, segmentation)
segmentary societies, 15, 24, 33, 35, 38, 43-9, 79, 242-53, 258-60; bases, in lineages, 56-70, 258-60; dichotomy with centralized societies, 24, 29, 55-6, 67-9; multi-racial, 325-9, 331-43
segmentation: abstract and formal characters of, 19; and racial stratification, 213, 280, 289-91, 301, 325, 331-4; as structure and process, 18-19, 42, 56-70; contraposition in, 19, 28; contrasted to differentiation, 40; co-ordinate, 31-2, 37-8, 334; in social systems, 242-4, 249, 252-3, 324-5; internal, 19, 38; in territorial organization, 17-19; mechanisms of, 37-43, 50-1; of power and authority, 29
segregation, racial, 221, 226, 234-5, 280, 290-1, 337
Seljuk, 233
Senate, 115-16
seniority principle, in age-sets, 141-2
serfdom, 100-1, 235; contrasted to slavery, 266
Service, E.R., 258n
servitude, collective and personalized, 234-7
sets of incorporative principles, 183, 186
sex: as criteria of allocation, 252-3, 311; grading, in families, 145-9; imbalances in ratio, 292-3, 296; in segmentation, 74
shamanism, 179, 181, 256
sharīa', 112-14, 127
Sharp, L., 142n
Shehu dan Fodio, 102, 233
Sheldon, R.C., 167n
Shilluk, divine kingships, 95
Shils, E., 152
shoen, 247
Shoshonean bands, 188
siblings: in half-siblingship, 13, 16; in lineage segmentation, 38-9, 144-5; in

unilineal descent, 149-50; rank, status and class of, 144-50, 253-4, 282; unity of groups of, 144

Simmons, D., 261n

simple societies: corporate units in, 192 ff.; government in, 74-8, 217; institutional homogeneity in, 206, 216-17; kinship in, 120, 211-12, 217; law in, 77, 125; political systems in, 91-3

Simpson, G.E., 160n, 295n

'situs' systems, and stratification, 137, 142, 151, 161-2

siyāsa, 112-14, 127, 129, 130

size: in complex societies, 250, 264-5; in racial societies, 280, 297, 317, 342

Sjoberg, G., 160n

slave revolts, 158-9, 282, 283-4, 287, 300

slavery, 276-300 *passim*, 328, 343-4; abolition of, 283-4, 285, 299-301; status in, 298

Smelser, N.J., and S.M. Lipset, 133-4, 243

Smith, M.G., 10n, 37n, 61n, 109n, 148n, 154n, 158n, 159n, 222n, 257n, 276n; *Government in Zazzau*, 25n, 49n, 158n; *The Plural Society in the British West Indies*, 212n, 235n, 239n, 278n, 282n, 285n, 286n, 298n, 300n, 308n, 330n; *Stratification in Grenada*, 158n, 222n, 233n, 236n, 305n, 310n, 317n, 324n; and R. Augier, R. Nettleford, 330n

Smith, R.J., 156n

Smith, R.T., 286n, 321n, 326n, 328n

social action, 27, 244

social boundaries, and institutional continuity, 226-30

social class, 136

social differentiation, 138-45, 243-7, 264-5, 269

social environment: and law, 72; and simple societies, 76

social equality, 135-7, 332

social inequality, 137-45, 157, 160, 211, 226-7, 237, 263, 295

social labour, 242-3

social order, prerequisites of, 135

social pluralism, *see under* pluralism

social relations: as institutions, 208; bases of, 207-8; described by status, 73; in complex societies, 251-3; impersonal, 249, 264-5, 267-8; in social change, 192-3

social status, 133-4, 136-45, 160, 295, 304-5

social stratification, and societal incorporation, 136, 189-204, 330-43 (*see also* stratification)

social structure: concepts of, 62, 134-5; units in, 247-8

societal incorporation: 187-94, 254-62, 333-7; consociational, 187-90, 193-7; differential, 187-93, 242-3, 333-6, 338-45; equivalent (segmental), 333-4; universalistic, 187-91, 333-4

societas, 74

societies: anthropological concepts of, 71-89, 135, 269-70; characteristics of, analytic and concrete, 133-4, 'complication', 242, 'complexity', 242-6, 256-62, 265-9, 'condensation', 244-7,

264; continuity, 44, 256, 257-62, institutions common to all, 211-13, stability, 33-4, unity, 98, 103; differentiation of individuals in, 138-45; organizational typology of, 247-8 (*see* acephalous-, centralized-, complex-, modern-, primitive-, simple-, stateless-, undifferentiated societies)

society, state and law, interrelations, 72, 76, 109-10, 121-6

'somatic distance', 296

'somatic norm image', 295-6, 331

Somali, 250

Sotho, 33

Soustelle, J., 158n

South Africa, 269; as racial oligarchy, 173-4; pluralism in, 214, 230

Southall, A., 16n, 32n, 40n, 190n

South St. Elizabeth, 288

Southwold, M., 128n, 264n

sovereign states, 99

sovereignty, 99, 121 (*see also* imperium, kingship)

Soviet Union: as collectivist society, 249; as heterogeneous society, 213; compared with USA, 218

Spackman, A., 327n

Spain: and pluralism, 207; and totalitarianism, 173; source of colonists in Caribbean, 278, 280-2, 284, 295, 298

Sparta: collective domination in, 234-5; complexity in, 269

specialization: in administrative function, 34; in political function, 34; in social organization, 243-4, 261, 268; institutional, 243-7, 255-6, 268

Speckman, J.D., 321n

Spencer, H., 75, 265

Srinivas, M.N., et al., 155n, 223n

stability: and stratification, 154, 160-1, 274; in governmental function, 34; of cycles in structural change, 172-3; of political systems, 154, 174, 230-4 (*see also* equilibrium)

Stampp, K.M., 227n

Staten, 300

stateless societies, 21-2, 26, 55-6, 74; and political centralization, 176; as inclusive corporate categories, 255; compared with acephalous societies (*q.v.*), 80

states: allegiance to, 38; and stateless societies, 26, 45, 55-6; centralized, 45, 47-9; forms of, 21, 44, 49; relations with church, 116-17 (*see also* administration, government, societies)

stationary equilibrium, in corporations, 186-7

status: absolute value of, 154-5; as basis of social structure, 73, 76, 136-7; ascription and achievement of, 137, 138, 149, 150-1, 154; bases of, age and sex, 253-4, birth, 156-7, caste, 155-7, 223, colour, 304-5, 317-19, 323-4, 336-45, custom, 122, economic position, 317, 322-3, prestige and esteem, 138-9, race, 233-4, 271-4, 289, 295-7, 317-19, 336-45, ritual, 155-6, 158-9, 223; collective, 189-202, 229; definitions of, 136-7; in

corporations, 143-4, 197-202, 208, 254-6; in lineages, 47, 143-4; kinship and, 142-4, 262-4; qualifications for higher, 136-7, 199-202; siblings and, 144-50, 253-4, 282 (*see also* hierarchies, rank, stratification)
statutory commissions, 178-9, 181
Stefansson, V., 102n
Stenning, D.J., 222n
Stevenson, H.N.C., 155n
Steward, J., 188n
Stoics, and natural law, 115
stratification: anthropological theory of, 136-7, contrasted to sociological theory, 133-41; as process and state of affairs, 134; as ranking of social units, 133-4, 161, 271; as role differentiation, 135; bases of, consensual normative, 151-8, 161-2, force, 158-60, political, 150-4, 160-1, 189-204, 296-301, 328, 331, racial, 272, 323-4, 327-32, 337; statistics on, 302-17; 'bifurcated', 155, 162; collective power and, 297-301; concrete and analytic, 133-4; corporations and, 189-204, 261-3, 330-43; criteria for, 137, 142, 161; definitions of, 134-7, 152, 271-2, 297; inadequacies of theory of, 150-4; in complex societies, 246, 249, 263-5; in families, 144-50; in modern societies, 134, 226-7; in pre-industrial societies, 133-4, 144-63; institutionalization of, 151, 272; kinship and, 142-50; lack of, 135, 137, 141-50, 325; lineages and, 143-4; restratification and societal change, 199-204; scales for, 133-4, 154-8, 161-2, 317; sociological theory of, 135-6, 138-40, 153; universality of, 145, 149, 162, 271
strikes, of ex-slaves, 300, 326
structural change: bases of, 171-5, 195, 201; distinguished from *extensive*, 171
structural differentiation, 140-1, 243-7, 249, 268
structurally heterogeneous aggregates, 191-2
structural principles, in social processes, 134-41
structural relations: and political systems, 20-1, 171-2, 195; between groups, 20-2, 58
structure: and function, 149; and system, complementary abstractions, 172; concept of, 62, 243-4; static and dynamic, 135
subordination: in conquest, 266-8; in lineages, 32; in stratification, 233, 273, 336; of American Negroes, 226-7
subsistence farming, in Caribbean, 285
substantive equality, in corporations, 183, 188
substantive law, 97, 115, 125, 126-7
substantive requisites and entailments, of incorporation, 183-4
succession: in lineages, 31, 45-6, 64-6; in offices, 45-6, 48, 64-6, 181-2; universal, in corporations, 43-4; wars of, 50
Sudan, pluralism in, 233
Sudras caste, 156
sugar industry, 281, 282, 284-6, 304, 321

Suleibawa dynasty, 65-6
Sunna, and Muslim law, 111-14, 127
superordination, in lineages, 43-4
Surinam, 230, 265, 277-93 *passim*, 301, 325, 338
Swat Paktuns, pluralism among, 214, 264-6
Swazi, hierarchies among, 146
Switzerland, as confederation, 188
symbioses: in pluralism, 221-2, 232, 233-5; in stratification, 273-4, 289-91
synchronic systems, 174, 180
'system', and societies, 269, 70

taboos, in tribal law, 121
Tallensi: law among, 88; marriage among, 62, 83, 88; political structure of, 22, 24, 100; segmentary lineage system of, 16, 38, 42, 52-4, 188; village society of, 83, 86-8
Tannenbaum, F., 277n, 331n
Tawney, R.H., 139n
taxation, 263, 299, 315
technology: in plural societies, 206, 218-19; in stateless societies, 74
tenancy, 226-7, 273, 285, 299
tendaana, Tallensi, 33, 53
Terik, age-sets among, 141
territorial chiefdoms, 78
territorial organization, 17-19, 23-4, 41-2, 52-3, 59
Teutonic corporations, 123
theocracy: in Europe, 118; in Islam, 114, 214; in Roman law, 117
theocratic pragmatism, in Muslim law, 127
theocratic regimes: and plural societies, 214-15; 'condensation' in, 246
Third Estate, 283
'Third World', 242
Thirty Years' War, 118
Thrupp, S. (ed.), 233n
Tiv: complexity among, 250; segmentary lineage system of, 14, 19, 32, 36, 188
tokenism, and corporations, 226, 229-30
'top leaders', in Caribbean, 330-1
totalitarianism, 28, 173, 268
Toussaint L'Ouverture, 233, 283
trade unions, 237, 246, 329
trading associations, 247
transformations, distinguished from change, 172-3
tribal law, 108, 121, 125
'tribal' reserves, 234
tribunals, 97-8, 122, 231
tribunes, in Roman law, 115-16
Trinidad: differential advantages in, 315-16, 322-3; labour in, 285-7; multi-racial society, 227-8; 275-340 *passim*
Trinidad-Tobago, 280, 290; differential advantages in, 302, 307-8, 311
Trobriand Islands, 75, 123
Tswana: class hierarchy among, 146; example of centralized polity, 176
Tuareg, as complex society, 247, 250
Tumin, M.M., 160n, 254n
Tungus, shamans, 256
Turkana: age-sets among, 100, 141; categories among, 192
Turks Islands, 280, 288, 298

Turnbull, C., 142n, 188n
Tutsi, as plural society, 214, 221, 234

ulamā, 111-12
Ullendorf, E., 238n
Ulster, classification in, 267
ultimogeniture, 147
Ummayad, 246
uncentralized societies, 78, 105
undifferentiated societies, 243, 252-3, 258, 262-5
unilineal descent, 13-14, 18, 23, 34-52 *passim*, 56-70, 143-4, 149-50, 182, 184; ideological principle of, 51-2; in complex societies, 258-9, 262-5; logical entailments and implications of, 182-4
unitary state, 196
United States: as complex society, 213, 265; as individualist society, 249; contrasted to Soviet Union, 218; occupation of Haiti, 308; stratification in, 157, 220-1, 224-30, 275
unity: and corporation sole, 45; in composite bands, 259; in corporations, 43, 94-5; in multilineal societies, 260
universal history, and political change, 166
universalistic incorporation, 187-91, 333-4
universal succession, in corporations, 43-4
universal suffrage, 239, 301, 325, 329, 342
'urf, 113-14, 125n, 127, 129, 130

values, in stratification, 152-3, 154-5, 162
van Lier, R.A.J., 160n, 267n
van Warmelo, N.J., 148
vectorial change, 173
Vico, on society, 71, 72
village societies, 83-7, 95, 191-2
Vinogradoff, P., 122n, 125, 129n, 145n
violence, as corporate action, 96
Virgin Islands, 286, 302
'voluntary' associations, 94
von Grunebaum, G.E., 111n, 113
Vugusu: *ad hoc* agencies among, 52-3; as acephalous society, 81

Waddell, D.A.G., 285n, 288n, 298n
wages, in stratification, 275, 311-16, 318
Warde-Fowler, H., 141n, 230n
wards, among Yakö, 17, 83-4
war leaders, as commissions, 33, 256
wars: and 'coercive authority', 21; and political action, 24, 27; dynastic, 98; holy (*jihad*), 111, 113, 130; of succession, 50
wealth: and societal differentiation, 243,

263; and stateless societies, 21
Weber, M., 100, 115n, 125n, 152, 156; *The Theory of Social and Economic Organization*, 9, 43-4, 96, 178, 255n
Wendell Holmes, O., 119-20
West Africa, corporations in, 54-5
West Indian archipelago, 278
West Indian Economist, 315n
West Indian Federation, 327, 331
West Indians, 278, 285
West India Royal Commission, 299n, 300n, 304n
whites: in Caribbean, 274-345 *passim*; advantages of, 302-3, 306-8, 312-14, 338; and miscegenation, 291-2, 294; 'Creole', 274; dominance, 299-300, 324-5, 328, 339-40; expulsion of, 283, 296-7, 325; incorporation of, 338-42; indentured immigrants, 281, 339; 'poor whites', 288, 328, 339-40, 343
Williams, E., 331n
Williams, Dr. Eric, Creole premier, 327, 331
Wilwright, A., 303n
Winans, E.V., 190n
Windward Islands, 294-5, 328; differential distributions in, 302, 306-7, 310
Wirth, L., 242
Wittfogel, K.A., and Feng Chia-Sheng, 233n
Wolof, caste among, 264
women, status of, 110. 146-50
working-class movements, 237
Worsley, P., 102n, 233n, 255n

Yabot, 83-4
Yakamban, 84
Yakö: corporations among, 55, 103; descent among, 13, 14, 17; political organization of, 17, 46, 56; village society of, 83-4, 86-8, 191-2; youth among, 83-4
Yir Yiront, hierarchy among, 142
Yoruba, corporate organization among, 52, 55, 57, 78, 191, 264
Yoruba Ogbani, 94
youth: in lineage assimilation, 260-1; in Yakö society. 83-4
Yucatan, slave revolt, 287

Zaria (Zazzau), 47-9, 64-6
Zinkin, T., 155n
Zulu: differentiation among, 16; dominance of, 264; familial hierarchy among, 146-7; government of, 33-4, 38, 52
zuri'a, 65